Issues in Deaf Education

Edited by

Susan Gregory, Pamela Knight, Wendy McCracken,
Stephen Powers and Linda Watson

David Fulton Publishers

London

David Fulton Publishers Ltd
Ormond House, 26–27 Boswell Street, London WC1N 3JD

First published in Great Britain by David Fulton Publishers 1998

Note: The right of Susan Gregory, Pamela Knight, Wendy McCracken, Stephen Powers and Linda Watson to be identified as the editors of this work has been asserted by them in accordance with the Copyright, Designs and Patents Act 1988.

British Library Cataloguing in Publication Data
A catalogue record for this book is available from the British Library

ISBN 1–85346–512–7

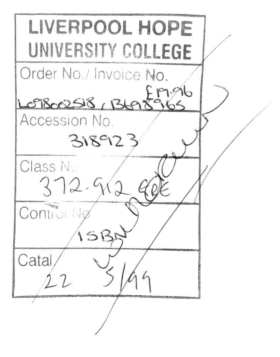
Typeset by FSH Print and Production, London
Printed in Great Britain by The Cromwell Press Ltd, Trowbridge, Wilts.

Contents

Acknowledgement

This book arose as a result of discussions by the group of Course Providers for Programmes for the training of Teachers of the Deaf. We would like to acknowledge the contribution, constructive criticism and support provided by members of this group in the development of the book. We would also wish to thank Lynn Walsh for help with the preparation of the Bibliography.

List of contributors

Waqar Ahmad is a Senior Lecturer and Director at the Ethnicity and Social Policy Research Unit, University of Bradford.

Rob Baker is a linguist with a particular interest in Sign Language. He has worked as a lecturer in the School of Education at Leeds University where he ran a course addressing issues of Total Communication. He currently works in curriculum development in Higher Education.

Lesley Barcham is Distance Education Co-ordinator for the British Institute of Learning Disabilities and formerly a Lecturer in Further Education. Her doctorate was on the policy and development of deaf education in Zimbabwe.

Russell Brett is a Teacher of Hearing Impaired children and an educational audiologist. He is currently Head of the Children's Hearing Services in Wigan, Lancashire and leads a team of peripatetic teachers.

Rampaul Chamba is a Research Fellow at the Ethnicity and Social Policy Research Unit, University of Bradford. He is currently working on a national survey of minority ethnic families caring for a severely disabled child.

Aliya Darr is a Research Fellow in the School of Health Studies, University of Bradford. She has conducted research in the field of ethnicity, deafness and service provision.

Ben Elsendoorn is a Senior Researcher at the Department for Research and Development of the Instituut voor Doven in the Netherlands. He has a PhD in phonetics from the University of Utrecht.

Clare Gallaway is a Lecturer in Education (Language) at the Centre for Audiology, Education of the Deaf and Speech Pathology at the University of Manchester. She has written and lectured widely on the characteristics of interaction with young deaf children.

Susan Gregory is a Senior Lecturer in Education, School of Education, University of Birmingham with responsibility for training Teachers of the Deaf. Her research interests include the development of deaf children and sign bilingual approaches to education.

Sally Hind is a Research Scientist at the MRC Institute of Hearing Research, Nottingham. She has worked on the TARGET project since its inception contributing to the development and standardisation of the Behaviour Assessment Inventory and cognitive assessment.

Lesley Jones is a Senior Research Fellow at the Ethnicity and Social Policy Research Unit, University of Bradford.

Pamela Knight is a Lecturer in the School of Education at Leeds University working in the areas of deaf education and special educational needs. She has wide experience as a Teacher of the Deaf with special interest in preschool support and early years education.

Margaret Kumsang is currently Educational Consultant for the Ewing Foundation and the Post Graduate Diploma in Educational Studies (Hearing Impairment), Oxford Brookes University and formerly the Head of Service for Children with Sensory Impairments in Croydon.

Sue Lewis is an Education Consultant working with the Ewing Foundation. She offers inservice training to teachers and others in relation to the oral education of deaf pupils.

Wendy McCracken is a Lecturer in Education, at the Centre for Audiology, Education of the Deaf and Speech Pathology, School of Education, University of Manchester.

Mairead MacSweeney is a Research Fellow of the Department of Human Communication Science, University College London.

Ted Moore is Head of Service for Children with Sensory Impairment in Oxfordshire and former president of the British Association of Teachers of the Deaf.

Jackie Parsons is Teacher-in-charge of a unit for Hearing-Impaired pupils in Surrey. She has experience of working in integrated units using both oral and Total Communication approaches.

Miranda Pickersgill is Head of the Deaf and Hearing Impaired Support Service in Leeds. Currently she is president of LASER and has been working on developing policies and practices in sign bilingualism.

Stephen Powers is Lecturer in Education, School of Education, University of Birmingham, with a primary responsibility for training Teachers of the Deaf.

Sharon Ridgeway is a research psychologist and is Head of Counselling at the National Centre for Mental Health and Deafness, Manchester. Research interests include identity and psychological distress in deaf people.

Ken Robinson is Director of the Audit and Service Development at the Nottingham programme, which is the largest paediatric cochlear implant programme in the UK. His background is in experimental psychology.

Ruth Swanwick is a Lecturer in Education at Leeds University where she is involved in training Teachers of the Deaf. She is an experienced Teacher of the Deaf with an interest in sign bilingual education and the development of deaf children's English skills.

Tina Wakefield is the Deputy Head of Sheffield Service for Children with Sensory Impairment and Chair of the North Region of the British Association of Teachers of the Deaf.

Peter Watkin is Head of Audiology Services in the London District of Redbridge and Waltham Forest and governor of Hawkswood School for the Deaf, UK.

Linda Watson is a Lecturer in Education at the University of Birmingham, with responsibility for training Teachers of the Deaf. Her research interests include the oral/aural approach to the education of deaf children.

Cara Wheeler is Teacher of the Deaf and Educational Audiologist working for the Stockport Educational Service for Sensory Impaired Children. She specialises in preschool support and language assessment.

Bencie Woll is the Chair of Sign Language Studies in the School of Social and Human Studies at City University. Her interests include development and assessment of sign language in young deaf children.

General introduction

The aim of this book is to explore themes and issues in deaf education within the context of wider and related developments which determine the nature of education for deaf pupils at present. These include radical innovations in education generally and changes in the education of children with special needs, attempts to redefine the notion of disability recognising its social origins, advances in hearing aid technology particularly the increasing use of cochlear implants and major changes in the way in which deafness is understood, including the fact that some Deaf people define themselves as members of a linguistic and cultural minority group.

Most changes that affect the education of deaf children are made in the context of more general education without specific attention to implications for deaf children. Developments in the general educational context rarely take place with deaf pupils in mind. Over the past decade, education in the UK has undergone radical changes with the introduction of a National Curriculum, an increasing emphasis on attainments and assessments, and more recently the focus on the basic skills of literacy and numeracy. Issues relating to the curriculum as it affects deaf children are discussed in Section 3.

The education of pupils with Special Educational Needs (SEN) has undergone significant changes since the Education Act of 1981. Two features of that Act, the removal of classification of pupils by disability and the emphasis on mainstreaming have been influential, the first in restricting the availability of information specifically relating to deaf pupils and the second in furthering the trend towards educating deaf pupils in mainstream schools. More recently, the Government Discussion Paper on the education of pupils with special educational needs, *Excellence for all children* (DfEE 1997a) has called for more inclusive provision, more generic training for those working with pupils with SEN and regional organisation for pupils with low incidence special needs, such as hearing and visual impairment. However, even the topics such as those outlined in the recent Green Paper are concerned with a much wider group, and often the particular needs of deaf children are not reflected. Many of these issues are discussed in Section 5.

Changes in the way in which children with SEN are educated in part reflects changes in society's view of disability in general. The move to seeing the ways in which disability can be socially constructed, together with the pressure for equal opportunities, is influential. However, not all deaf people see themselves as disabled in the same way, and this issue is also discussed in Section 5. The deafness and disability movements have also had an impact on deaf education. The disability movement has stressed how often disablement arises from the way disabled people are treated rather than the disability itself. Such a view stresses the need for society to work to provide equal access to all areas of society including education. Those Deaf people who consider themselves culturally deaf make a similar point although the emphasis is different. They feel they should be considered as a linguistic and cultural minority group with their own language and culture. For them the issue is not so much that society should change to accommodate them, but rather that they should be allowed to be different. This view has specific educational implications.

Deaf children do not, of course, constitute a homogeneous group, and many factors, not simply hearing loss, need to be taken into account in discussing their education. Their cultural and home background, social, personality and cognitive development are all relevant and Section 1 draws particular attention to these. Two major areas of development within deaf education would seem to stress very different concerns. Firstly, there are advances in technology and in particular cochlear implants which seem to promise that more and more children will have useful hearing. These developments and the implications are examined in Section 4. Secondly, the recognition of British Sign Language (BSL) as a full and proper language has implications for education. The number of teachers who can sign and are learning to sign is growing and most courses training teachers of the deaf now address this in their programme. The different approaches are discussed in Section 2.

Traditionally deaf education has been beset by controversy regarding the best way to educate deaf children. Much of this has focused on the language and communication to be used, whether signing should be included, and if so how, or whether a totally oral approach is better. We do not try to take a position on this debate and feel that such a pervasive focus on language and communication rather than teaching and the curriculum has had a detrimental effect on the education of deaf children. The other major debate has concerned the location of education, whether deaf children should be educated in mainstream schools with hearing children or in special schools with other deaf children. While as individuals we have various perspectives on these issues, as a group we do not take any particular position to the exclusion of others. We have tried, by presenting various approaches and options from the perspective of those who support them, to provide a constructive and positive view of such debates. These issues are examined in Sections 2 and 5.

In an area such as deaf education, with its debates and differing viewpoints, terminology can be an issue. Whether or not the population considered by the book is described as 'deaf' or 'hearing impaired', or the lengthier 'deaf or hearing impaired', is one such topic. It is evidenced by the fact that schools and teachers are usually schools for the deaf and teachers of the deaf, whereas services are more often services for the hearing impaired. There is also little consensus on what constitutes the various approaches to the education of deaf children, the oral/aural approach, Total Communication and sign bilingualism. This topic is explicitly addressed in Section 2. It has been mentioned above, that those deaf people who consider themselves culturally deaf often choose to describe themselves as 'Deaf' rather than 'deaf'. Throughout the book, the choice of terminology has been left to individual contributors, to select and use the language that they felt to be most appropriate for them.

The impetus for this book originally came from the group of Course Providers for the training of teachers of the deaf. One concern was the lack of any single text in the UK that covered a wide range of topics in the education of deaf children as information on educational issues is widely dispersed throughout the literature. The other was the need to reflect recent changes such as those mentioned above. These developments have increased the complexity of the demands that are made on teachers of the deaf. Greater knowledge of audiology is required together with an understanding of a range of languages and modes to use in communicating with deaf pupils. A book of this nature allows teachers of the deaf to consider the range of changes within the field of deaf education and the challenges these pose to the profession. The sheer scope of the material covered highlights the importance of accessible research in informing the profession and encouraging positive change in professional practice to meet the needs of all deaf children. While the book takes a UK focus, many of the issues it raises are relevant to deaf education throughout the world.

While it is hoped that this book will meet the needs of teachers of the deaf, particularly those in training, there is of course a much wider audience of professionals as well as other academics who will find the topics discussed of relevance. With growing emphasis on parental choice, the need for up-to-date information on the options available and their implications is important for parents. The Deaf community, too, some of whom will be represented in the group of professionals and parents, have always demonstrated a particular concern with how deaf children are educated. The aim of the book is to explore themes and issues in deaf education. While it covers a range of topical concerns, the scope of the area means that it cannot be totally comprehensive. It is also not prescriptive. However, it does address current issues and draws on recent research relating to the education of deaf children. Each chapter is written by a person or people with a particular interest in, and knowledge of, that area. To this end, we have drawn on the experience and expertise of both academics and practitioners and hope we have achieved a balance between these two perspectives. This means the book includes a range of perspectives and styles.

The first section of the book looks at the developing deaf child and a range of factors that impact on education and educational decisions. The second section focuses on language and communication considering both the acquisition of language and the various language options that are available. The third section focuses on the curriculum, crucial in the current educational climate although an area that, until recently, has been neglected to a major degree in discussions of deaf education. The fourth section looks at audiology and the various advances that have been made in this area, together with their implications for education. The last section examines policy and practice, broadening out the topic to conclude by examining international perspectives.

Susan Gregory, Pamela Knight, Wendy McCracken,
Stephen Powers and Linda Watson
June 1998

THE DEVELOPING DEAF CHILD AND YOUNG PERSON

Introduction

This section takes a number of perspectives on the developing deaf child and young person. The first three chapters focus on different aspects of development; relationships, personality and cognition. These general areas, while not always considered in looking at issues in education, have clear implications for teachers and those involved in making educational decisions. The last two chapters take particular groups of deaf children as their focus; those that have additional special needs and those from minority ethnic groups. While much that is written about deaf children in general also applies to these groups, the education of these pupils raises particular issues which are considered here.

In their chapter, Susan Gregory and Pamela Knight look at the social development of deaf children and young people, both within their families and in their relationships with their peers. They point out that for deaf children and their families there are a number of issues with implications for education. In addition, language and communication choices are often seen as an educational issue, but they have far-reaching consequences for the family and for friendship patterns. While educational decisions about school placement that are made for deaf pupils will often focus on those aspects that are specifically educational such as access to the curriculum, their relationship with peers is also significant for their experience of the educational process. Later as the deaf young person leaves school, their transition to work or college will be affected by social factors as well as educational attainment.

The notion of deaf personality, whether deaf people have particular personality characteristics, has been explored in the literature for many years. Often the notion of a deaf personality has been used to suggest that deaf people are immature or inadequate in some way. Sharon Ridgeway describes this research and looks at some of the implications. She also considers in depth the related notion of Deaf identity. This suggests that Deaf people who are members of the Deaf community and are sign language users, identify with other Deaf people and thus have a Deaf identity. Of course, not all deaf people do identify with the Deaf community, and some may identify with both the hearing and Deaf communities. Ridgeway looks, in particular, at the importance of Deaf identity for those deaf children who grow up to have sign language as their first or preferred language and considers the implications for mental health and development.

A further issue is whether deaf children think and process information differently as, if they do, this has implications for education. Early studies of the relationship between deafness and cognition suggested that deaf people could be considered as without language, a view now discounted. In her chapter Mairead MacSweeeney explores the evidence relating to deaf children's cognition in some detail, looking particularly at IQ and short-term memory. She examines the impact of deafness and use of sign language at both neurological and perceptual levels. She also discusses the evidence relating to the importance of early exposure to language for language development.

A substantial minority of deaf children have additional disabilities, but as Wendy McCracken points out in her chapter, there is lack of understanding of the nature of this group or issues that they pose for education. McCracken considers a range of factors including identification, aetiology, incidence and heterogeneity that are important in considering this population. She also looks at the education of particular groups including those with learning difficulties and those with multi-sensory impairments. In considering how education can best be provided for these pupils, McCracken considers the importance of auditory assessment and decisions about communication. As she argues, in all of these areas, appropriate training of teachers is crucial.

There are particular issues that arise for children and families from minority ethnic communities beyond those that are concerns for all families with deaf children. In their chapter, Rampaul Chamba, Waqar Ahmad, Aliya Darr and Lesley Jones consider Asian deaf children and discuss issues of language, communication and identity and how they impact on education. They consider the complexity of the choices that may face families, particularly with respect to decisions about language and mode of communication. These are set in the wider context of culture, ethnicity and perceptions of deafness. The need for teachers to be more aware of these issues is a theme of this chapter.

Susan Gregory

Chapter 1.1

Social development and family life

Susan Gregory and Pamela Knight

Introduction

In this chapter we look at the social development of deaf children and young people, both within their families and in their relationships with their peers. For deaf children and their families there are a number of issues with implications for education. These include the impact of diagnosis of deafness on the family and the subsequent language and communication choices that are made within the family. Patterns of interaction and family relationships are important, not simply in terms of the immediate family, parents and siblings, but also those relationships with the extended family, including grandparents. While educational decisions about school placement that are made for deaf pupils will often focus on those aspects that are specifically educational such as access to the curriculum, their relationship with peers is also significant for the pupils' experience of the educational process. Later as the deaf young person leaves school for work or college, their transition will be effected by social factors as well as educational attainment.

The impact of deafness on the family

To have a child diagnosed as deaf has far-reaching effects on the family as it becomes a family with a disabled child and the focus of professional advice and attention. Some of those decisions which with hearing children are made relatively easily, e.g. school placement, have to be explicitly thought out by the family with a deaf child and subsequently they may be more dependent on professionals for information about what to expect of their child rather than on friends and relations (for a discussion of these issues see Gregory 1991.)

While these issues may not all be apparent to families at the time of the initial diagnosis, to have a child who is deaf is completely unexpected for most hearing and some deaf parents. Most hearing parents will never have met a deaf person before and have little idea what deafness means. It is not therefore surprising that parental and family reaction to the diagnosis of deafness in their child is strong and variable. Erting (1992) describes two very different reactions from parents. She describes how a mother recalled feeling scared when she and her husband first realised that their daughter (Cathy) was deaf. The father remembers feeling disappointed, more for his daughter than himself. She goes on to say that for others the discovery of deafness is not a tragedy. She describes a father holding his daughter (Mary) and crying for joy. She accounts for these contrasting reactions very simplistically: 'of course, the essential difference between the first set of parents and the second is that Cathy's parents are hearing and Mary's parents are deaf' (p. 29). There can be no automatic assumption, however, that all deaf parents will welcome the news of a deaf child. For Sutherland (1991) who is deaf herself, and therefore in a position to understand what deafness means, admits to being completely taken aback. 'Deep down I knew he was deaf but to be stone deaf was extremely rare ... to say I was a bit upset was an under-statement.' (p. 29) Nevertheless it is generally accepted that deaf parents will respond more positively to the birth of a deaf child than hearing parents (Freeman, Carbin and Boese 1981) particularly if sign language is the language of the home.

Ninety per cent of deaf children are born to hearing families and, in the context of this chapter, concerns surrounding the impact of diagnosis and parental reactions will focus on these hearing families. It is recognised that the initial reactions of hearing parents to the diagnosis of a deaf child are likely to be negative, highly emotional and have a profound effect on the family (Luterman and Ross 1991, Moores 1996). Gregory *et al.* (1995) report that the memory of the moment of diagnosis is often indelibly fixed on parents' minds, such that they can remember verbatim what was said many years later. Some have likened the periods of stress felt by the family to a bereavement (Moores 1996). Mahshie (1995) asserts that the impact is on the family. 'It is the family, not the child, that is in turmoil' (p. 63). As far as the deaf children themselves are concerned 'all is well' (p. 63).

Although there is an accumulated body of knowledge about the impact of deafness on a family, nevertheless for each individual family it is a different process which has to develop in its own unique way. Erting (1992) identifies some common parental needs, at the time of diagnosis:

- emotional support 'through the crisis to a new vision of themselves as parents' (p. 39)
- information on all aspects of deafness
- experience of meeting deaf adults and other children and their families
- guidance through possible education programmes
- establishment of a route to communication with their child.

Moores (1996) comments on the importance of acknowledging that families go through periods of stress throughout the child's development. Often families are described as whether or not they have come to terms with the deafness, but coming to terms may mean different things at different ages. Some parents find the deafness of a baby relatively easy to accept but have great difficulty with a deaf teenager (Gregory *et al.* 1995). Problems within families seem to arise at times of transition. Moores (1996) highlights four significant periods during the families' development. First, the time of diagnosis brings overwhelming feelings of inadequacy and a lack of knowledge. Secondly, there is the entrance of their child into the formal school situation which involves both changes in family relationships and parents in critical choices in relation to educational placement. Thirdly, adolescence brings its own tensions to the family and for the deaf child there may be additional feelings of the lack of a positive identity, both within the family and the wider social community. Finally, there are tensions in the family as the young deaf adult prepares to leave the nuclear family and begin an independent existence.

Language choice and the family

Often the earliest choices made about the form and language to use with the deaf child are made within the family. In families where one or both parents are deaf the choice is often, though not inevitably, sign language. Where parents are hearing, the choice is more complex and the variety of language and modes available means that for parents there is an issue about language and communication. Factors effecting language choice and use can be many and diverse. Some will be related to early advice, as until recently, the positive choice to use sign with deaf infants was rare and unsupported by professional advice. The choice of language is more than a pragmatic one relating to ease of communication, and the relationships with other family members and friends may have to be taken into account. For those children whose hearing loss falls within the mild/moderate categories, the chosen mode of communication by both child and the family is likely to be a spoken one: that of the home. While this may seem initially less problematic for the family, there are issues of language and communication for these families although these receive less attention in the literature. Spoken language may seem the language which potentially provides communication with the largest number of family members but may be difficult for some deaf children to acquire. While the choice to sign may enhance communication, it may also marginalise some family members. Many studies show that even when parents or other members learn to sign they do not necessarily acquire high levels of competency but rather more basic day-to-day communication (Foster 1996). If few hearing family members achieve competence in the use of sign it can mean that the burden of communication can fall on one or two family members and marginalise others. This can have wide-ranging effects for relationships within the family.

Roles within the family

It is often the mother who becomes the most effective communicator with their child which can effect the nature of the relationship. While this may be very satisfying and at one level very helpful, it can also create a burden (Luterman and Ross 1991). In effect, mother may become recipient of all information and experience and regarded as the fount of knowledge and information. This creates pressure both to understand and absorb the information open to her and to transmit it to a wide variety of other people. It places her in the role of interpreter in many situations, where instead of being able to develop her position as a mother, she becomes the child's intermediary (Luterman and Ross 1991). This may not only be in social situations but also in more relaxed home-based settings.

The result of these two factors, the mother as the source of information and as the effective communicator, is that she may be carrying a heavy and disproportionate burden in the context of the whole family. This may be reflected in other members, particularly fathers, becoming both deskilled and unsure of their role, leading to a possible imbalance in family dynamics with resulting areas of stress.

The role of parents in fostering the cognitive and linguist development of their own children is accepted and implicit in the parenting role. Parents with deaf children are often expected to take a more explicit and conscious teaching role (Meadow 1980; Gregory 1991). This can interfere with the fundamental parenting role in that it can affect both the child–parent relationship and the style of interaction and linguistic input. Making behaviour explicit, which is usually implicit, can change the nature of that behaviour. For example, focusing a parent's attention on aspects of their own behaviour and communication can prevent them taking the child's perspective in a way that is characteristic of much early parental interaction with hearing children. Professional support to parents should highlight the fact that teaching is incidental to parenting, 'it should never try to make teachers of parents' (Luterman and Ross 1991, p. 37).

Interactions in the family

The child's early interaction within the family and the importance of them for their social and linguistic development is well documented and the nature and quality of these interactions are explored further in Section 2, Chapter 2.1. However the diagnosis of deafness in a hearing family can disrupt the relationship between parents and children (Bouvet 1990, Gregory and Barlow 1989), brought about by parental feelings about the deafness. While parents are the most appropriate people to foster that early linguistic development in their own children, at the time these skills are needed they may have very substantial emotional needs of their own (Erting 1992).

As the child becomes older, regardless of the means of communication, there are issues relating to the dynamics of communication in the family. While one-to-one communication may be relatively straightforward, group or family communication can be more difficult, whatever the means of communication used. In a study of hearing families with deaf sons or daughters (Gregory *et al.* 1995), many parents reported difficulties in communication, described in terms of a loss of immediacy or difficulty in explaining issues they felt need explaining. Often, the problems arose, not through reluctance to communicate, but because communication within the family could be an effort, and some family members could feel excluded. Sometimes extra attention was given to managing social situations and often the mother assumed significant responsibilities for communication. Sometimes specific plans had to be implemented to allow a deaf son or daughter to join in. Often parents were aware of a responsibility in conveying information and consciously took steps to do so. These difficulties were not a consequence of deafness *per se* but of the nature of communication at the interface between deaf and hearing world.

In this study, deaf young people themselves reported feeling left out of family gatherings or, alternatively, feeling embarrassed by attempts to involve them. An indication of the way in which deaf young people could be left out is the finding that often parents assumed that the deaf person was aware of information that was generally known in the family, even though they were not. The young people were asked whether there were important family matters that they had not known about until a later time and four out of five of those responding said that had happened to them. The events included such major family occurrences as deaths in the family, pregnancy, marital breakdown. This clearly has implications for their relationships within the family and notions of being a family member.

Family relationships and the extended family

Moores argues that the practice of viewing the 'deaf child as a member of a hearing family' is potentially negative (Moores 1996). He suggests that the birth of any child into a family fundamentally changes the nature of that family unit. The family changes into a new stage of adjustment with disruption to the previous family routine. The advent of a deaf child in the family similarly changes the nature of the family. By continuing to view them as a hearing family with a deaf child, the implication is that the child is different and potentially an outsider rather than an integrated member of the family. By definition the family is no longer a hearing family, but a family with both deaf and hearing members.

The family is a system where all parts of the family are interrelated. When a deaf child is born into the family all members of the family are affected, including siblings and grandparents. In general, there have been relatively few studies of sibling relationships and despite their perceived importance, little is known. It is hardly surprising that they are little understood because of their diversity, depending upon family structure, relative position of siblings, gender and age differences. With families with deaf and hearing siblings this can be even more complex.

Luterman (1987) in discussing the issue of deaf and hearing sibling relationships notes that

Siblings form the first social laboratory for the individuals experiments with peer relationships. Within the sibling system, children can learn how to resolve conflicts and support one another. They learn how to negotiate among equals or near equals. (They learn how to deal with authority in their relationships with their parents.) The sibling system teaches them how to make friends and allies, how to save face while losing, and how to achieve recognition for their skills. In the sibling world, children learn how to negotiate, co-operate and compete. The jockeying for position within the family system shapes and moulds children into their adult roles. When children come into contact with the world outside the family, they take with them the knowledge they learned from their siblings to form their peer relationships (p. 73).

Gregory *et al.* (1995) considered sibling relationships, which in general were described by deaf young people in positive terms with nearly half of them describing themselves as getting on very well with their siblings, a further third, quite well, and fewer than 1 in 20 said they did not get on well at all (others differentiated between siblings). One in 5 found their siblings the easiest family member with whom to communicate and of these 16 young people, five had deaf siblings. Even if they were not deaf, siblings were often felt to have a special sort of understanding with the deaf young people. While this study presents a generally positive picture, the literature suggests there are a number of potential causes for concern. Luterman (1987) suggests that a negative impact on sibling relationships can occur when hearing siblings find they have to go outside the family for relationships because they are unable to communicate with their deaf sibling. A further issue is the need for parents to spend more time with the deaf son or daughter, both as a child and as an emerging adult (Morgan-Redshaw *et al.* 1990), which some have reported as a cause of sibling resentment (Gregory *et al.* 1995).

Grandparents' reactions to deafness are usually strong, influential and can be positive or negative. Negativity is usually a reflection of their lack of knowledge and an inherent attitude to deafness and disability. Many of the issues revolve around the mode of communication used by parents and siblings with the child, and grandparents may report feeling deskilled when it is unfamiliar to them, resulting in pressure and stresses within the family. Meadow-Orlans (1990) suggests that the control exerted by grandparents on families with deaf members is often greater than that found in comparable families with no deaf members. This can result in, for example, families not always using the preferred mode of communication with their child in the presence of grandparents (Moores 1996). This in turn leads to poor communication between grandparents and deaf grandchildren, leading to a separation depriving both parties of an ongoing relationship. However the reactions of grandparents can be positive and many families report them to be an important resource for support to the family.

Peer relationships

With the increasing emphasis on preschool education, it is important to consider the social aspects of such education for deaf children. A number of studies by Lederberg and colleagues have looked at preschool deaf children and their behaviours. They showed that stability of friendship patterns and friendship preferences were very similar for deaf and hearing children (Lederberg *et al.* 1987). However, deaf children were more likely to use non-linguistic forms of communication with both deaf and hearing children. Other studies have also shown that despite similarities in play patterns, certain types of play, particularly imaginative play, are more common in those with good language abilities (Schirmer 1989).

However, reviewing the research, Lederberg (1991) concludes that despite that fact that deaf children with good language ability are more likely to play with groups of children, to interact with teachers and to participate in more language interactions than those with less ability, language and social skills are for the most part independent of each other as language is not significantly related to the amount of peer interaction.

There has been very little research which takes as its main focus the peer relationships of school-age deaf children. That which has been carried out is largely in the context of examining the consequences of different educational settings, in particular comparing mainstream and special settings, for friendships and social relationships. Given the move to educate more and more deaf pupils in mainstream school, plus the fact that increasing numbers will also be using sign language, the effect of these factors for a child's social development would seem important to consider. The research is not clear on these issues. While large numbers of studies and accounts see the consequence of education in mainstream school as potentially leading to feelings of isolation for the deaf pupils, others report positive effects, including peer acceptance, which enhance self-esteem (for a review of the research see Holcomb 1996). Changes in educational practice make this an area where further research is necessary.

One problem for many deaf children and young people in interacting with hearing contemporaries is similar to that described in family interactions, communication in groups. Gregory *et al.* (1995) reports that of those young people with hearing friends, over half had great difficulty in the group situation, and just under one third could converse easily. While an important consequence of the problems in following group conversations is the difficulty of participating in social life, a secondary consequence is that much of the informal information transmitted in such interactions, which relates to social conventions and social life, is missed. Foster (1996) notes that 'failure to access the conversations of those around them can result in social as well as professional separation from hearing colleagues' (p. 128).

An interesting question arises as to whether competence in early life in social skills is related to later friendship patterns. Because the research by Gregory *et al.* (1995) involved families that had been involved in an earlier study, when the young people were of pre-school age (Gregory 1976, 1995), it was possible to consider the relationship between early experience and later friendship patterns. The early interviews included questions relating to the sociability of the child. A scale of social skills was devised based on whether or not they made themselves understood easily with other children, whether or not they were able to share toys, the extent to which they understood about taking it in turns and their understanding of games which had a winner. Good skills were classified as a positive response to three or four of the questions, whereas poor skills were indicated by two or fewer positive responses. Considering the relationship between early social competence and the ability as young people to make friends and parental reports of later friendship patterns, the majority of those who made friends easily as young adults had good skills as a child, although those who did not make friends easily now varied in their skills as a child. This was statistically significant. However, the amount that the young people played with other children as a child, whether their parents felt they were left out of games when young, and whether or not they were submissive or bossy with other children did not show statistical relationships with patterns of friendships as an adult, either those reported by the parents or by the young people themselves.

The transition into adulthood

This period of transition from child to adult is generally characterised by developing independence from parents, making decisions about work and training, and establishing an adult social life. It is a critical period both in terms of assuming adult roles and establishing a sense of identity. During this time of transition, the role of the parents is usually eclipsed by that of the peers in constructing and maintaining an adult identity, and one of the tasks of this period for the young person is developing adult social competence and acceptance by peers. As mentioned earlier, it is one of the four major periods of adjustment for families and many parents who have accepted the deafness of their young deaf child now find they have to reflect further as they come to recognise their son or daughter as an adult deaf person. In this respect, language and communication are of paramount importance. Adolescence can be a time of strained relationships and the ability to communicate in order to resolve issues is critical. Morrison and Zetlin (1988) have shown that families with high degrees of cohesiveness have more positive communication patterns.

Deaf young people may be more dependent on their parents than their hearing counterparts (Luterman, 1984; Morgan-Redshaw *et al.* 1990). Parents may have a role in their son or daughter's social life in assisting in contacting friends and making arrangements. Many deaf young people have friends at a distance, and while contact can be maintained through prearranged meetings, parents may mediate or take responsibility for making arrangements through assisting with telephone conversations or passing on messages. Many parents feel they had a greater role in social arrangements than they would have had their son or daughter been hearing, a situation that was not always satisfactory for either party, and in some cases was a cause of concern for the parents (Gregory *et al.* 1995).

Conclusion

This chapter has looked at the social relationships of deaf children and young people and considered the implications for education. This is an important area as changes in attitudes to deafness and in educational practice are likely to have consequences for such development. The chapter has considered the ongoing effects of families' reactions and responses to their deafness. It highlights the crucial issues: namely choice of communication and relationships within the immediate and wider family and the nature and effects of peer relationships particularly in the educational setting. This is an area of continuing concern as changes in attitudes to deafness and educational practice have consequences for the deaf child. An ongoing issue is the effectiveness and sensitivity of interdisciplinary support. Transition into adulthood remains highlighted by growing independence from family influence and pressures.

Further reading

Erting C. (1992) 'Partnership for change: creating possible new worlds for deaf children and their families', in Cebe, J. (ed.) *Bilingual Considerations in the Education of Deaf Children: ASL and English*. Washington, DC: Gallaudet University Press.
This paper introduces the reader to many of the challenges facing the family of a young deaf child. It particularly highlights the importance of establishing a communication pathway for the child and family.

Gregory S., Bishop J., Sheldon L. (1995) *Deaf Young People and Their Families*. Cambridge: Cambridge University Press.
This book, based on interviews with deaf young people and their families, explores many issues relating to social development and family life including communication, family relationships and the friendship patterns of deaf young people.

Chapter 1.2

A deaf personality?

Sharon Ridgeway

Introduction

The notion of a 'deaf personality' has, for many years, been of interest to professionals involved in work with deaf people. It appears that those who think there is a psychology of deafness are those who tend to embrace the medical or clinical model, while those who suggest there is no such psychology favour the cultural and linguistic model of deafness. This chapter contains an exploration of the term 'deaf personality' including a discussion on cultural Deaf identity. Mental health issues are also highlighted.

The use of the term 'Deaf' is based on the premise that deaf children whose deafness means that they do not acquire spoken language through oral means are likely to develop to become culturally Deaf young people. The term 'culturally Deaf' refers to those Deaf people who share similar beliefs, values and norms and who identify with other Deaf people. A number of external factors influence the process of acquisition of Deaf identity but such growth can be re-channelled or diverted. Continuous immersion in culturally hearing environments, lack of access to Deaf awareness, Deaf history, language and lack of contact with culturally Deaf peers and positive role model interaction are all important factors that limit the development of a Deaf identity. External influences which will facilitate the development of Deaf identity cover exposure to Deaf peers including interaction with young Deaf people and adults, knowledge and awareness of Deaf community issues, sign language, culture and history.

Some deaf children, including late deafened children, will not grow into culturally Deaf young people, and function in a meaningful way in the non-deaf world. Many of these pupils will not go on to become members of the Deaf community because they will interact predominantly with non-deaf people, and will function as such, using oral/aural means to communicate, perhaps requiring some technical and human support. This is not to say that these individuals will always function primarily in the non-deaf world. Many may join the Deaf community during school days, teenage years or perhaps later, either as fully immersed active members or on the periphery. The process of identity development is often a lifelong process, with many people 'discovering' their identity much later in life. Sometimes the growth process is deterred by learnt negative attitudes towards deaf people. In addition, society often conveys that one has to be one or the other. This is not necessarily so and in fact more deaf young people today are learning how to successfully balance the two environments and develop a dual identity.

One can appreciate that because a person has the ability to speak a recognised spoken language, this does not always reflect their cultural identity. It does not necessarily reflect a comfortable affiliation and identification with those who express themselves similarly. There are many deaf people who use spoken language well, but this is not in itself an indication that they are culturally hearing. There are also children who will grow to acquire bicultural hearing status identity, Deaf and non-deaf. A number of deaf children will have minority ethnic status and acquire cultural attachment to their ethnic backgrounds as well as to their Deaf heritage. The focus of this chapter will be on those who will naturally develop a culturally Deaf identity given the appropriate external environmental growth factors.

Identification with Deaf community and culture is influenced by external factors; one of the most important seems to be linked to the attitude towards the deafness as in 'attitudinal deafness' (Baker and Cokely 1980). This useful term describes individuals who, *regardless* of audiological status, behave as culturally Deaf people, seeking association with like-minded others, with similar values and attitudes. The term describes a healthy culmination of a process that may be fraught with conflict for the individual struggling with internal and external conflicting dynamics, throughout the history of that individual's identity development, which begins with the immediate family and degree of interaction.

Cross-cultural research has shown that minority group members are likely to suffer from discrimination and oppression throughout childhood, which includes inappropriate environmental circumstances, influences and lack of access to information. More importantly, cross-cultural (transcultural) research awareness developed the idea that dominant cultural beliefs and values are not appropriately applied to minority groups, hence the general enlightened awareness and caution among health and educational professionals working with minority group members.

Deaf children from ethnic, linguistic and racial minority backgrounds have lower levels of achievement, compared to white deaf children. The differences are significant as is seen in a US study of Black and Hispanic deaf children, which includes African-American, Asian, West Indies and Africa (Cohen *et al.* 1990). These often forgotten children present with special issues. The more multicultural assessment teams and service providers are, the more positively this can reinforce the deaf child's self-image, crucial to identify formation, and in particular, towards developing bicultural identity awareness. Having minority role models for minority group children helps to strengthen and enhance self-identity (Sue and Sue 1990). A survey of professionals in deaf education programmes in the USA in 1993 (Andrews and Jordan 1993), found that about 10.4 per cent were of minority group status, and furthermore, only 11.7 per cent of these were deaf.

Identity formation

Identity development and the study of personality structures has been of great interest to educationalists, mental health service providers and researchers. The identification of an emerging Deaf culture and establishing Deaf studies programmes has resulted in an increase in interest in Deaf identity issues. Identity is a complex construct and individuals are not limited to a single identity. Understanding identity constructs can be helpful in understanding identity development in others who experience deafness such as partially deaf (or partially hearing), deafened young people and also may be of use in understanding children of deaf parentage and others who may have varying hearing status. Identity influences rites of passage in life – and identity influences belonging and choices. The process of *how* is important for educational practitioners, who are at the forefront of mental health issues and well-being in deaf children.

A model of identity formation in a deaf person is described shortly, based on similar principles outlined by the interactionist model provided by Cass (1979). The process of acquisition of a Deaf identity depends upon our interactional experiences with others, both Deaf and non-deaf. This interaction experienced with society and ourselves creates development and change in our values and beliefs. Many deaf people refer to themselves as part of a cultural and linguistic minority group. This is an important self-definition statement, resulting in a move away from medical pathology. Although many have dropped the term 'dumb' in self-description, many choose to keep the same sign, in an attempt to challenge stigma or stereotype images. This raises an important aspect of the language Deaf people use (Bahan 1997). The sign is sometimes seen as a way of affirming the Deaf community, the apparent 'deficit' becoming a strength (de Monteflores 1986).

There are six stages in the Cass Model (1979) – which can be seen as a process towards formation of identity beginning with identity confusion, comparison, tolerance, acceptance, pride and finally, synthesis of identity.

Identity confusion refers to the period of time when the deaf individual begins to feel, or starts to acknowledge, there is a difference between them and the rest of society, and that they may feel different from their non-deaf families, perhaps recognising the demands their deafness places on their carers and perhaps experiencing feelings of alienation. Such experiences need not be negative however, and may not always present as a major issue for either the deaf person or the family. Furthermore, the experience of acknowledging differences does not always relate to issues in identity formation, but nevertheless needs to be accepted and recognised, perhaps in order to achieve, or enable, more fuller participation in everyday family life and various aspects of interaction within societal interests.

Moving beyond infancy into development of social behaviour patterns and the deaf child's skills and preferences comes the need to be aware that in families with deaf children, the customs, norms and behaviours expected and learnt in the home environment do not always generalise to behaviour outside the home environment. This means deaf children will have experienced a more restricted range of interpersonal interactions and furthermore might differ from those deaf children from deaf families who will have experienced wider social interactional opportunities (Greenberg and Kusche 1987). These children are more likely to have positive self-image and self-esteem and respond positively to other deaf children. Although this period usually takes place during their childhood years, it can occur much later, depending on educational circumstances and exposure to mainstream society. Young individual deaf children might, on meeting another deaf child, for example, reject the other's similarity. Young deaf children ill-prepared for such an experience may experience disturbing thoughts, feel uncomfortable and may reject the deafness.

Deaf young people might reject deaf teachers for example, preferring to identify in psychodynamic terms, with the perceived 'aggressor' (non-deaf teachers) in the process of affiliating to what is seen as the dominant culture in favour of rejecting the minority or 'weaker' cultural group, thus introjecting mainstream values which are 'picked up' from a very young age. This can be linked to the development of poor self-image and a negative self-concept.

This process can be seen at various stages throughout the child's life, where interaction with others is expected. For many deaf people, more often than not, selecting deaf peers, and later perhaps a partner who is also deaf, can be seen as a positive step towards a fulfilment of being, and of facilitating development of a positive deaf consciousness, rather than be seen as an attempt to actually reject non-deaf people. Sometimes, the selection of hearing peers to the exclusion of accessible deaf peers might be a way of rejecting the deafness. Toleration of identity might follow this stage, whereby deaf individuals start to do 'deaf' things, refer to deaf issues more and might feel a need to 'prove' they are deaf. In this way, the deaf person might begin to feel more 'detached' from the mainstream and more in contact with other deaf people, thus selecting deaf friends and perhaps avoiding contact with hearing people who might cause feelings of discomfort.

There are different directions that a deaf person might move in. They may, perhaps, move on and accept and affirm their own Deaf identity by themselves. Alternatively, some people while acknowledging their deafness and some affiliation to the deafness experience, may not wish for a Deaf identity and so will behave in ways that will give the deafness occasional 'special case' acknowledgement that will make them 'feel better' – such as a compromise, or they might pretend not to be aware of deaf cultural issues. Individuals may identify more with different parts of themselves than others. For example Jon, a culturally Deaf person who is gay and Jewish, at times identifies with other people who are Jewish, rather than a group of the same sexuality, and at other times more with those who share Jewish cultural beliefs and values. This interaction between identities is described by Moorhead (1995). Jon would remain Deaf however, whichever of his identities he feels to be more aware or conscious of at any particular time, although perhaps not overtly culturally Deaf, depending upon which frame of reference he is in contact with. This is not always a conscious process.

Gradually, the deaf individual moving out of this stage develops supportive relationships with their peers and will make links with organisations and centres for deaf people. This stage is probably one of the most vulnerable in terms of future progress as it sensitises to the influence of other deaf people. Whether or not obvious association with other deaf people displaying cultural features and behaviours is made public to the mainstream population is also determined at this stage.

Identity pride, the next stage, is where the individual starts to feel that it is acceptable to be Deaf and begins to show that they are Deaf – not being embarrassed at displaying Deaf behaviours and cultural mannerisms, and being more open about their cultural affiliation. The Deaf individual feels a sense of belonging as a cultural group and develops pride in his affirmed Deaf identity.

Some Deaf people believe that a non-deaf person is more 'clever' and able, and so attribute what they perceive to their own 'shortcomings' to 'Oh, well, it's because they're hearing'. Deaf children do not always understand the meaning of the words 'deaf' and 'hearing', except perhaps from an audiological perceptive. Gregory *et al.* (1995) found about one third of deaf young people had as children thought they would grow up to be hearing. In another study (Gregory *et al.* 1997) deaf children aged 7–11 were asked a series of questions which looked at experiences and attitudes towards school, home and deaf issues. There were a number of responses which reflected positive and non-rejecting attitudes towards their experience of deafness. The aim of the questions was to gain some insight into the deaf children's understanding of the differences between English and British Sign Language (BSL) and as such, have provided some evidence to the contribution of a positive self-identity that a bilingual approach to education brings. A high percentage of deaf people have been found to have a poor self-concept (Brauer 1992) and negative self-esteem, the importance of which cannot be over-emphasised. For some deaf people, internalisation of a degree of oppression results in other defence mechanisms such as rationalisation and reaction formation.

Teachers of deaf children who learn to sign, visit Deaf centres and take part in deaf-related activities help contribute towards the growing congruence and integration of the individual deaf person and their fitting into a diverse society. This process takes place all through life. A whole intra-psychic and interpersonal developmental process is involved which does not stop at any particular stage and will very often extend well beyond teenage and adolescent years. Recognition of the process brings out the issue of deafness as often being stigmatised by society and the stigmatisation of being culturally Deaf.

Mental health issues

The search for a deaf personality probably began when psychologists became interested in the possibilities of learning more about their own personality theories and child psychology through acquiring an understanding of personality formation and issues in deafness. Pintner began such investigations and, at that time, expressed caution that use of non-deaf norms and standards in inventories and assessments of deaf children would be unfair and lead to false conclusions (Pintner *et al.* 1941). His other comments, however, did a disservice to what otherwise would have been a remarkably insightful advancement at that time. Pintner, probably inadvertently, began the thinking that deaf children were emotionally unstable, introverted and immature in reasoning and social skills (Pintner and Paterson 1916). Meyer (1921) had already suggested deaf people were unsocial, morose and suspicious. Heider and Heider (1941) introduced the view that personality tests for non-deaf people were inappropriate for use on a deaf population but the popular interest in deaf people as being psychologically disturbed, by virtue of their deafness, was far too interesting a notion to ignore. One of the key terms often used to describe deaf people's difficulties is *adjustment*. In the field of mental health, the diagnosis of adjustment disorder continues to be applied to deaf individuals who express a range of difficulties including behavioural and emotional.

Past suggestions leading to the creation of a deaf personality have had a powerful influence in the literature and in practice and continue to do so. Lane's examination of the literature on the views and traits that white people (Europeans during the age of colonialism) held of Africans compares almost identically with the many negative traits attributed to deaf people (Lane 1988). This kind of research information provides evidence of the need to consider behaviours and emotions within an appropriate cultural and experiential context but not necessarily as a separate psychological entity. A study (Laurie 1966) of a group of people serving life sentences looked at impulsivity, rigidity and concrete thinking, and found a significant link between these cognitive deficits and deprivation in childhood – referring to limited opportunities for language acquisition.

The Department of Health (1995) produced a fact sheet for its 'Health of the Nation' series, suggesting that about one out of every six or seven people will suffer from mental health problems and that of these mental health difficulties experienced, about 0.4 per cent will experience a more serious illness such as schizophrenia, paranoia or an affective psychosis, which includes short-term psychotic episodes in depression. These are figures for the mainstream population. However, research evidence shows the incidence of mental health difficulties experienced by deaf people is significantly higher than for the non-deaf population. Thirty eight per cent of deaf people indicate psychological difficulties (Ridgeway 1997). Griggs' follow-up of Conrad's (1979) cohort indicates that deaf people experience much greater mental health problems than the hearing population (Griggs, in preparation).

There is a view that a separate psychology for deaf people may be based on the idea that deaf people experience things differently (undoubtedly true) but also to the extent that their particular difficulties and presentation of problems are different. For example, Basilier (1964) suggested the creation of new diagnostic criteria, and coined the term 'surdophrenia', used to describe deaf people whom he diagnosed with emotional and conduct disorders. The term 'surdophrenia' (deaf mind) is not used much now in the UK and is rejected by the European Society for Mental Health and Deafness as a somewhat derogatory term, replaced by the term 'emotional and conduct' disorders (Swanns-Joha *et al.* 1988). Deaf people's presentation of psychotic illness, for example, is not seen to differ from those of non-deaf people (Kitson and Fry 1990 de Feu 1997).

Young deaf people and mental health

A number of research studies have been conducted to look at mental health problems and disorders in the young deaf population. There are variables which need to be considered, such as the degree of deafness, type of school and communication used, both at school and at home. In addition, a larger number of deaf children appear to have disabilities such as learning difficulties of various aetiology when compared to the mainstream. The absence of standardised testing and interview schedules for deaf young people adds further problems to the validity and reliability of research in this field. It was previously believed that deaf children had inferior intelligence and commonly believed that deaf children were about three years behind their hearing peers in tests not involving language, for example, the Pintner Non-Language Mental Test (Myklebust and Bruton 1953). Furth (1966) created a stepping-stone for deaf people, by recognising that some testing may put deaf people at a disadvantage if the tests were laden with spoken language. It was Rosenstein (1961) who insisted that there were no differences between deaf and hearing people's performances in conception, providing one used the matching language level of the deaf person. Although he did not indicate sign language use, this was nevertheless a pointer in a more appropriate direction. Additionally, Rosenstein (1961) challenged the then-held belief that deaf people could not think in abstract terms.

The issue of ego development in deaf children has been of interest in relation to language development. This is linked to interaction in the environment, with others and with cognitive development. On the subject of the ego in personality development theory, it is interesting to observe the thinking that, since the ego is believed to be shaped by speech and hearing, because it is seen as a vocal and auditory mechanism, the ego has often been seen to be weak in deaf children. One of the major concerns facing psychiatry today is the strength of the western influence, and how to accommodate people from different cultural backgrounds. For example, there is some evidence indicating that deaf children are relatively passive and immature emotionally to their hearing peers (e.g. Lederberg 1993; Schlesinger and Meadow 1972) and are reported less likely than hearing children to be aggressive, to have tantrums, be easily distracted and angered and to have poorer self-images (Altshuler 1971; Meadow 1976; Rodda and Grove 1987; Stokoe and Battison 1981). Previous research, particularly psychiatric studies from the mid-twentieth century to date, has tended to apply various characteristics to deaf children. This led to the thinking and belief that deaf children's personality formation was thus characterised by a 'fragile ego'. However, this type of assumption is decreasing with increasing transcultural awareness and knowledge.

Some studies of deaf children show that 40 to 50 per cent of deaf children have emotional or behavioural problems, or sometimes both. This compares with 25 per cent for the general child population (Health Advisory Service 1995). At least 30 per cent of the total US school-age deaf population has multiple disabilities (Schildroth and Motto 1995). In this aspect, aetiology is important as some deaf people have disabilities. Many of the producers of deafness, such as prematurity, meningitis, Rh incompatibility and maternal rubella, are reasons for learning difficulties. The incidence of brain damage in deaf children, as a result of central nervous system disorders, is approximately 9–10 per cent of deaf children (Freeman *et al.* 1975).

Vernon and Andrews (1990) reported that in terms of the frequencies of severe depression and mental retardation, deaf individuals usually have lower rates than the general population. A study by Leigh *et al.* (1989) found, however, that deaf college students were significantly more depressed, as a group, than hearing peers. More than 50 per cent of the deaf students in that study reported being at least mildly depressed (on the Beck Depression Inventory), compared to 33 per cent of the hearing students. Interestingly, both the deaf and hearing students reported greater overprotection and lower maternal care which was associated with a greater incidence of depression. Most of the 40 to 50 per cent identified as having mental health problems (Hindley *et al.* 1994), which include emotional difficulties, behaviour disorders and mental illness, will not need specialist intervention. However, many would probably benefit from involvement from other professionals, in particular those in educational and related disciplines, who might be able to work with or provide advice and guidance to meet the deaf child's mental health needs within the family without compromising communication.

The search for a deaf personality appears to have brought us round, back to the question of the psychological characteristics of deaf people. The answer is to be found in the environment and not within any biological or innate characteristic of the deaf child.

Deaf-centred approaches

Much of the emphasis on the view that there is a psychology of deafness probably stems from a failure to recognise that most of the difficulties that deaf children experience within their non-deaf and deaf families result from a number of external factors, such as lack of guidance and support, lack of access to awareness of deaf issues, deaf community, culture and deaf role-models. Ninety per cent of deaf children are born to non-deaf parents (Reagan 1985; Phoenix 1988) and it appears to be an unusual human experience to have a biologically-related child who may belong to another cultural and linguistic group from that of the parents. Research has shown, however, that non-deaf parents are more often willing to learn about their deaf child's culture and language and thus develop close relationships and positive attachment and bonding with each other (Lederberg and Mobley 1990; Sutherland 1993) than we anticipate. This process is initiated by appropriate contact and interaction with deaf people, both culturally and non-culturally deaf, and access to information and knowledge.

Deaf well-being depends upon the skills and experiences of qualified and trained deaf people, who can provide a range of skills and expertise to help meet the various educational and mental health needs of the deaf population. There is no reason why the field of mental health cannot follow the footsteps of the educational profession, where increased access for deaf people is gradually being made. Deaf people are accessing courses to learn more about providing support in classroom settings which include deaf children, and the number of opportunities for positive involvement of deaf people and deaf teachers are increasing and it is on this positive note that this chapter ends.

Chapter 1.3

Cognition and deafness[1]

Mairead MacSweeney

The idea that deaf people can be studied as a 'without language' group has been rightly dismissed as inaccurate. However, a slightly different misconception took its place. Braden (1994) argues that many researchers still assume 'that language and audition are the only critical factors associated with deafness' (p. 7). This assumption has also been shown to be inaccurate and no longer tenable. We are now more aware of additional factors that distinguish deaf and hearing people, many of which are discussed elsewhere in this book (see Chapters 1.1, 2.1, 2.2). This greater awareness has led to advances in our understanding of deaf children's cognitive processes, while at the same time making the description of those processes an even more complex task than was once thought.

The first part of this chapter explores the impact of deafness and use of sign language at neurological and perceptual levels. Two specific areas of cognitive ability, IQ and short-term memory, are then considered and their relationship to academic achievement of deaf children. Higher level cognitive skills such as reading and numeracy are not dealt with in detail here as they are the focus of later chapters in this book. Finally, studies highlighting the importance of *early* language exposure on cognitive development are discussed.

At the neurological level

In Chapter 4.4 (this volume) Robinson describes the neural reorganisation that occurs as a result of auditory deprivation. This area is not therefore addressed here. Rather, another question that has fascinated researchers since sign language was recognised as a fully-fledged language in the 1960s is explored. That is, are signed and spoken languages processed in the same way by the brain? Although not all deaf children use sign language, a review of this research serves to further highlight the plasticity of the neural system in childhood.

We know that hearing people process language predominantly in the left hemisphere of the brain and visuo-spatial information in the right. Sign language is of particular interest because it is a language that is visually and spatially conveyed and therefore combines both of these functions. One way to determine which parts of the brain are responsible for particular functions is to study patients who have suffered damage to specific areas. Hearing people with damage to areas of the left hemisphere can suffer severe language problems (aphasias). Similarly, Poizner *et al.* (1987) studied three deaf signers with left-hemisphere damage and they too showed severe *sign* language deficits in both production and comprehension. Importantly, these impairments were specifically linguistic, as general motor control and the ability to use gesture remained intact. This indicates similarities at the neurological level between processing of sign language by deaf people and spoken language by hearing people. However, unlike spoken language, which can 'survive' on left hemisphere support alone, sign language appears to need some right-hemisphere input. Deaf signers with right-hemisphere damage studied by Poizner *et al.* showed the general visuo-spatial deficits seen in hearing patients, such as difficulty in picture drawing and spatial disorientation. However, although many aspects of their sentence construction were completely intact, their production and comprehension of space used for the mapping of spatial relations within sign language (topographical space) was impaired. Studies involving non-clinical participants also indicate right-hemisphere involvement in sign language processing (Poizner *et al.* 1979).

Further insights into the cerebral organisation of deaf people have come from studies using modern functional brain imaging techniques. Essentially these indicate which areas of the brain are active when a subject performs a certain task. Using different techniques both Soderfeldt *et al.* (1994a, 1994b) and Neville *et al.* (1997) have shown that for some aspects of visual processing, language background is influential but hearing status is unimportant. Both deaf and hearing people with sign as a first language showed more involvement of structures in the 'visual' part of the brain than did hearing non-signers. They also showed that some brain activity was specific to deaf people only, regardless of sign language knowledge. This indicates that deafness itself and linguistic experience can impact differently on where certain aspects of sign language are processed.

In summary, similarities *and* differences exist between spoken language processing by the hearing and sign language processing by deaf people. For congenitally-deaf signers, syntactic processing of sign language is left-hemisphere-based, as is speech processing in the hearing. However, the special skills of the right-hemisphere in parsing spatial relations (and possibly visual movement) means that it is closely involved in sign language processing. Furthermore, age of language acquisition and age at onset of deafness seem to play different roles in any cerebral reorganisation that occurs during development (Marcotte and Morere 1990). Does this occur to such an extent that the brain is somehow able to 'compensate' for deafness?

Compensation: fact or fiction?

The 'sensory compensation hypothesis' (Blair 1957) is perhaps intuitively attractive. In its strongest form it argues that, without auditory stimulation, the neural pathways responsible for auditory processing will automatically be 'taken over' by the visual cortex. In fact, more is needed for this to happen. A more plausible hypothesis is that with sufficient appropriate visual stimulation a certain degree of neural compensation will occur. In support of this Neville and Lawson (1987) found that, when processing peripheral visual stimuli, deaf subjects showed greater neural activity than hearing subjects. Furthermore, there were slight differences between groups as to which areas of the brain were active.

Many studies have shown behavioural evidence of this enhanced neural activity in deaf people in the form of superior performance on a variety of visuo-spatial tasks (see Bellugi *et al.* 1994). There are two possible explanations for this. In line with the compensation idea, deaf infants may simply give more attention to visual stimuli in their environment, resulting in superior visual processing abilities. Alternatively the use of a sign language, a visuo-spatial language, may enhance visuo-spatial skills.

Emmorey (in press) discusses this latter possibility and claims that there is strong evidence that early sign language experience 'enhances *specific* cognitive processes'. For example Emmorey *et al.* (1993) found that native signers, both deaf and hearing, were better at generating complex images and detecting mirror reversals than hearing non-signers. However, these enhanced abilities appear to be language-specific, as no differences were found between signers and non-signers on skills they argue are not involved in sign language processing, such as memory for images or ability to rotate images. Similarly, Bettger *et al.* (1997) found that deaf and hearing native signers were better able to discriminate faces than hearing non-signers. However, there were group differences in the discrimination of *inverted* faces. Bettger *et al.* argue this is because 'sign language affects only mechanisms specific to face processing' (p. 229) which are not used when processing inverted faces.

These studies involved deaf native signers. Another way to distinguish between the impact of sign language use and deafness itself on spatial cognition is to consider the performance of deaf non-signers. Chamberlain and Mayberry (1995) and Parasnis *et al.* (1996) both showed that on tests of visuo-spatial ability there were no differences in performance between congenitally deaf non-signers and hearing non-signers. Both researchers argue that enhanced visuo-spatial abilities are likely to be due to sign language knowledge rather than deafness itself. However, in the Parasnis *et al.* study three of the five visuo-spatial tasks administered had not been previously tested with deaf signing children or adults. Therefore we do not know whether signing children would show enhanced performance on these tasks and so conclusions drawn from this study may be premature.

Despite this, it is clear from Emmorey's work that there are some aspects of visuo-spatial processing at which deaf signers can excel. It is also clear that 'spatial cognition' should not be thought of as a single form of processing that is either better or worse in different populations. Rather, different skills are involved. Prising apart the skills affected by cerebral changes resulting from lack of auditory stimulation from those affected by experience of a visuo-spatial language is an area for future research. The important question from an educational perspective is do such skills have an impact on aspects of cognitive ability?

Deafness and IQ

Performance by hearing children on tests of IQ is reliably related to academic achievement. This section considers how deaf children perform on tests of IQ and also whether such tests are useful predictors of their academic abilities.

Whether IQ differences are found between deaf and hearing children depends on which aspect of IQ is tested – verbal or non-verbal IQ (NVIQ). Not surprisingly, tests of verbal IQ measure different aspects of verbal ability. NVIQ can be tested in two ways: performance tests and motor-free tests. Performance tests, such as the matrices from the British Ability Scales (BAS), involve the manipulation of objects or patterns. The BAS involves showing the child a grid. Within all but one of the squares there is an abstract figure. The child's task is to draw a figure in the empty square that logically follows on from the figures along the rows and columns of the grid. Motor-free tests, such as Ravens Progressive Matrices, are similar but they do not involve any 'hands-on' manipulation. Rather the subject must choose the correct 'missing' figure from several possibilities.

In a review of this area Braden (1994) compiles data from 208 studies which have reported the IQ of deaf populations in a form that can be converted into a standardised score. This allows direct comparison between these findings and hearing norms, where the mean score is 100 with a standard deviation of 15. Verbal IQ scores of deaf groups (mean = 85.54) were significantly lower than their hearing peers. When NVIQ is tested there is a discrepancy between the two types of tests available. There is no difference in performance IQ between hearing and deaf groups (mean = 99.95). However, on motor-free tests the performance of deaf groups (mean = 94.57) is significantly lower than that of hearing peers.

Braden proposes a number of possible explanations for this discrepancy in NVIQ scores. Firstly, it is easy to *show* what is required in performance tests, whereas in motor-free tests more explanation is required. Secondly, he proposes that experience of sign language may lead to better manual dexterity and that this influences performance IQ. The third possibility is that success on motor-free tests of NVIQ may require verbal mediation, whereas performance tests do not. Distinguishing between these explanations is not possible, although all three may contribute independently.

IQ and parental hearing status

The findings outlined above represent the pattern from a cross-section of the deaf population, the vast majority of whom are deaf children of hearing parents (HPs) with hearing siblings. When this group is broken down further Braden found that the performance IQ of deaf children of deaf parents (DPs) and deaf children of hearing parents but with deaf siblings (HP/DS) was significantly *higher* than that of hearing peers. The motor-free IQ of these children was equivalent to that of the hearing population. This differential pattern could be interpreted as indicating a genetic link between hereditary deafness and NVIQ or alternatively indicating the importance of the child's environment. Evidence against the genetic view comes from Conrad (1979) who found performance IQ of DPs was significantly higher than that of HPs whose deafness was identified as hereditary. This highlights a child's environment not their genetic make-up as the influential factor. Many researchers have simply attributed this finding to early sign language exposure. However, it is not necessarily true to assume that sign language is used in all deaf households. In addition factors such as greater emotional support and parental expectation are likely to differ between deaf and hearing parents of deaf children (for further discussion see Marschark 1993). That said, with regard to the issue at question here 'why is the performance IQ of DPs *higher* than that of hearing children of hearing parents?' the sign language answer does appear to be the most logical. Deafness itself cannot explain this finding, or all deaf children would show enhanced performance IQ. Deafness aside, if we assume that DPs and hearing children of hearing parents receive the same amount of language input, support and so on, then the major factor that differentiates these two groups is that the *majority* of DPs are likely to be native signers. This would seem to indicate that visuo-spatial benefits from exposure to sign language can transfer to cognitive skills such as NVIQ. However, early and extensive exposure seems necessary for this to happen.

The relationship between IQ and academic achievement

We have seen that with the appropriate tests deaf and hearing children can show similar levels of non-verbal IQ. However, unless performance on IQ tests relate to an external criterion, such as academic ability, then their validity is questionable. Braden's analysis confirms that we can have some faith in such tests. He found that both verbal and non-verbal IQ are good predictors of deaf children's academic performance. Of the two, verbal IQ is the best predictor. This is not surprising as measures of academic achievement usually also test some form of verbal skill. This highlights the fact that we need to interpret IQ scores with caution. A deaf and hearing child may have the same NVIQ score. However, the hearing child is likely to have a higher verbal IQ and therefore a higher level of academic ability.

Short-term memory

Another cognitive skill thought to relate to academic performance is short-term memory ability. The term short-term memory (STM) is used to refer to the storage of information over a very short period of time (for discussion see Baddeley 1990). This means seconds rather than minutes. The classic everyday example is that of remembering a new phone number. Most hearing people would represent this within STM using a verbal code or 'inner voice'. Rehearsal is then used to refresh this representation, without which it would decay after about two seconds. In addition to everyday situations STM also appears to be involved in educational activities, such as learning to read, reading comprehension and numeracy (Gathercole and Baddeley 1993). This makes STM abilities in deaf children an important area of research.

Do deaf children use a speech-based code in STM?

Numerous studies testing STM for *order* report that deaf subjects recall fewer items than hearing subjects (e.g. Campbell and Wright 1990; Hanson 1982b). Perhaps surprisingly the same pattern is found in deaf and hearing signers' recall of sign stimuli (Logan *et al.* 1996; Krakow and Hanson 1985). Logan *et al.* propose that this may be due to hearing signers using a verbal code to remember the signs. This argument supports the widely held notion that a speech-based code is particularly suited to recalling items in order (e.g. Hanson 1982b).

Early researchers in this area assumed that deaf people could not establish a speech-based code. However, research over the past twenty years shows that this is not the case. Dodd and Hermelin (1977) believe that deaf children derive information from lip-reading which can form the basis of a speech-based code. Campbell and Wright (1990) argue that if this is the case then such a code is likely to be qualitatively different from the speech-based code used by hearing people. Furthermore, it is useful to think of a speech-based code as developing in stages, as opposed to something a child either does or does not have. For example, one child may have a gross phonological representation of a word only at the syllabic level, whereas another child may have a fully specified phonological representation of the word with knowledge of rhyming properties, and so on.

The heterogeneity of the deaf population leads to great variability as to what level of speech-based code a deaf child will successfully develop. Influential factors include degree of hearing loss, reading ability and speech intelligibility (for discussion see Campbell 1992). Furthermore, different tasks require different levels of phonological awareness. For example, if a verbal response is required a deaf subject is more likely to use a speech-based code than if a non-verbal response is required (Campbell and Wright 1990). Despite our awareness of the factors influencing the use of a speech-based code we are still a long way from determining why some deaf children are more able to use such a code than others (Dodd and Murphy 1992).

Alternative codes used in STM

The preceding discussion indicates that alternative STM codes must also be available if only a minority of deaf people use a speech-based code and only in some situations. A possible alternative for deaf signers appears to be a STM code based on the properties of sign language (for a review see Wilson and Emmorey 1997). Bellugi et al. (1975) have even proposed that it may account for the apparent difference in memory span between deaf and hearing groups. They argue that because signs take longer to produce than speech they take up more memory capacity than speech-based representations, therefore leading to an apparently lower span. One line of evidence that supports the existence of such a code comes from an analogy of the 'phonological similarity effect' seen in hearing people. Here recall of similar sounding items e.g. 'B, T, V' is poorer than recall of dissimilar items e.g. 'N, R, L' (Conrad and Hull 1964). This is explained in terms of similar memory traces that become confused in storage. Similarly, deaf people's recall of signs that are structurally similar is often worse than recall of dissimilar signs (Klima and Bellugi 1979; Shand 1982). An example of this in BSL would be recalling 'CHOCOLATE'[2] for 'SISTER' where the handshape, orientation and movement of the sign are the same and only location differs. Once again task demands influence whether an effect is seen. When written rather than signed stimuli are used sign similarity effect is less evident (Hansen 1990).

What of visual or spatial codes? A visual code appears to be a rich resource for deaf children long after it has been dropped by hearing children (MacSweeney et al. 1996).

However, many visual items can still be verbally labelled and therefore deaf subjects often recall fewer items than hearing subjects. Devising stimuli that cannot be verbally labelled is extremely difficult. However, in tasks that have attempted to do this no difference in recall has been found between deaf and hearing subjects (Poizner and Tallal 1987; Emmorey *et al.* 1993). Similarly, deaf and hearing subjects do not differ on recall of spatial locations, perhaps because these are difficult to label verbally (Logan *et al.* 1996).

Summary – Short-term memory

When non-linguistic stimuli are used deaf and hearing children's recall abilities appear to be roughly equivalent. Despite the apparent 'flexibility' in STM codes available to them, deaf children still seem to recall less than their hearing peers when stimuli can be labelled linguistically. Perhaps this is due to the poor use of a speech-based code which may be particularly suited to STM tasks (Hanson 1982a). Or, as suggested by Bellugi *et al.* (1975), the use of a STM code based on sign language may result in fewer items being recalled.

Others have suggested that deaf children may have more general problems in using STM strategies such as rehearsal (Bebko and Metcalfe-Haggert 1997). Marschark and Everhart (1997) extend this to more general problem solving strategies. They found that in a game of twenty questions, deaf and hearing children with previous experience of the game did not differ in performance. However, for children unfamiliar with the game, hearing children were more successful than deaf children. Development of research in this area may have great implications for the education of deaf children.

What news then for the teacher of the deaf?

The evidence presented in this chapter shows that if the cognitive abilities of deaf children are tested using non-linguistic stimuli they can perform at a level comparable to hearing peers. However, with stimuli that can be labelled verbally their performance tends to fall in comparison. What are the educational implications of this?

First of all, in one sense it is reassuring to know that deaf children have the same 'cognitive potential' as their hearing peers, at least as measured by performance IQ. However, this is a very specific test of intelligence and although predictive of academic achievement, it is not as important a predictor as verbal IQ. At present there are no widely accepted tests of BSL ability (however see Woll, this volume). Therefore we cannot say whether sign language competence would be as good a predictor of academic achievement as verbal IQ. However, we do know that deaf children of deaf parents are often held up as examples of what deaf children can potentially achieve. The possible reasons for this advantage have already been discussed and it is likely that a combination of many factors are responsible. However, one of the primary reasons appears to be a rich language background, whether in sign or speech.

An early concern regarding deaf children's early exposure to sign language was that this would limit their spoken language development and therefore subsequent literacy development. This is not the case. A recent study has shown the importance of language ability, irrespective of modality, in relation to reading ability. Strong and Prinz (1997) assessed 160 deaf children and found that better American Sign Language (ASL) skills were related to better literacy. Interestingly, they also found that deaf children equally skilled in ASL had equivalent literacy abilities, regardless of whether their parents were deaf or hearing. They obviously do not claim that this is the only way for a deaf child to achieve literacy. The point is rather that language skill, regardless of modality, is the important factor.

This point has been emphasised by Mayberry (1993) who compared congenitally deaf adults who learnt ASL as a first language in either early or late childhood with deaf adults who became deaf in late childhood and learnt ASL as a second language. The results showed that subjects who learnt ASL as a second language were better at ASL processing and a STM task than those who learnt ASL at the *same age* but as a first language. Furthermore, in those that learnt ASL as a first language, as age of acquisition increased processing skill declined.

An obvious conclusion from this discussion, and one that is by no means novel, is that giving a deaf child *early* and extensive exposure to good language models, regardless of modality, is crucial. Deaf children's performance on non-verbal IQ tests indicate that they should have the same 'cognitive potential' as hearing children. Fostering robust language skills early on in deaf children will be the key that enables them to fulfill this potential.

Further reading

Braden, J. P. (1994) *Deafness, Deprivation and IQ*. New York: Plenum Press.
This gives a meta-analysis of studies that have reported IQ data from deaf subjects. It also provides an excellent review of the factors that contribute to individual differences between deaf children on tests of IQ. These points are also relevant to all aspects of cognition.

Marschark, M. (1993) *Psychological Development of Deaf Children*. New York: Oxford University Press.
Although this book includes chapters on all round psychological development of deaf children, a large proportion is devoted to cognitive issues. There are individual chapters on intelligence and cognitive development; short-term memory; long-term memory; creativity and literacy. All of these chapters contain comprehensive literature reviews of the area.

Notes

1. I would like to thank Abe Sterne, Ruth Campbell and Sue Gregory for comments on an earlier draft of this chapter.
2. Regional variation means that this sign can be produced with either a tapping movement, as in sister, or a downward movement from the chin.

Chapter 1.4

Deaf children with disabilities

Wendy McCracken

Introduction

This chapter considers the challenge posed to professionals by a group of children who have a range of disabilities and are also deaf. While this group have been recognised as a significant minority amongst the population of children with permanent childhood deafness, our understanding of the nature of this group is anything but complete. Issues concerning this group include clear identification of the children involved, an under-standing of the diversity of specific needs presented and the wide range of professionals who attempt to meet the learning needs of these children and their families. The numbers alone demand that services have a proactive approach to these children but there are challenges which threaten such an approach. These include lack of agreement over the nature of such groups, difficulty with the ranking of hearing loss within a range of special learning needs, lack of specialised training opportunities and pressures on services to have clearly identifiable outcome measures related to positive intervention. The further challenges of working within a multidisciplinary team are considered together with the wider issues regarding training and advocacy.

Identification of the group

The field of the education of deaf children has been beset by a range of terminology which, rather than clarifying the issues has clouded the situation, leading to misunderstandings and some confusion. When considering children who are deaf and who have additional learning needs the terminology is not standardised either within the UK or internationally. The challenge of finding terms which are precise and which positively add to the quality of provision for these children has yet to be met. Definitions within this field are particularly difficult because of the many variables involved. Lack of standardisation of terms also makes it difficult to compare studies relating to incidence and prevalence rates. This represents a major problem in trying to establish a stable research base from which lessons can be drawn and programmes developed. Shroyer (1982 p. 3) points out that 'Definitions typically reflect the current sociocultural standards of a given society, and those are subject to constant change'. Professionals bring their own training and specialism to bear and may choose to emphasise a particular aspect of a child, while failing to perceive the interactive nature of coexisting conditions. As a result data relating to this population tends to use generic definitions which, while giving a broad overview, fail to explore the complex relationships that may exist between different conditions. Failure to take into account these relationships at the point of service delivery can have potentially catastrophic results for children who have a range of disabilities. The search for appropriate terminology has to consider whether terms reflect a medical view of deafness or take into account a cultural/linguistic perspective. This is a complex area as traditionally children who, for example, have a severe learning disability are, in the author's experience, unlikely to be viewed as culturally deaf. In addition, effective service delivery is difficult, not only because the range of disabilities is vast but also because assessing the summative effects is often all but impossible.

Aetiology

Fortnum *et al.* (1996) reporting on a comprehensive study of aetiology and referral patterns of hearing impaired children within the Trent Health Authority in the UK, group together children under the classification of 'Clinical or Developmental Disability in addition to Hearing Impairment'.

This broad category is subdivided into seven areas:

- visual problems
- neuro-motor problems
- cerebral dysfunction
- cognitive deficit
- cranio-facial abnormality
- other systematic disorder, including conditions such as asthma, hepatic dysfunction and eczema
- named syndrome.

The study draws attention to the difficulty of assessing the exact nature and degree of disability experienced by any individual child. All conditions were deemed to result in visits to a range of therapists which would in themselves result in increased pressure on the family system. This classification is a medical one which fails to take into account the range of learning disabilities. It offers little to educational services in respect of the nature of individual needs.

The Office of Demographic Studies at Gallaudet College has carried out an annual survey looking at the incidence of children with hearing impairment within the school population across the US. The Annual Survey data includes a range of demographic information including 'educationally relevant disabilities' (Schildroth 1994 cited in Moores 1996, p. 117). Survey categories are as follows:

Health

- legal blindness
- uncorrected visual impairment
- brain damage/injury
- epilepsy
- orthopaedic problems
- cerebral disorder
- heart disorder
- other health impairment.

Educational

- mental retardation
- emotional/behavioural disability
- specific learning disorder
- attention deficit
- other.

Future demographic studies are likely to include more categories as a result of increased awareness and acceptance of the many subtle factors that affect the learning process. Brown (1994) notes that the more complex the society the greater the likelihood of disabilities being recognised and the greater the likelihood of new disabilities emerging.

As new categories emerge teachers of the deaf are likely to come under increasing pressure to offer a differentiated service to children who are recognised as having special auditory needs which fall outside the traditional bounds of service delivery, for example an individual may be recognised as having central auditory processing disorder in addition to a visual impairment.

Surveys are likely to be an underestimate of the incidence of disability, as specialist facilities for children with severe and profound learning disability are excluded from the data. Those children identified as having permanent childhood deafness are included. For those children who have a range of disabilities hearing status may be unclear and may vary over time, making definitive numbers difficult to establish. A number of problems are associated with classifications. While giving a broad perspective of the incidence of disability amongst deaf children both the Trent and Gallaudet surveys mask the nature of these difficulties. The category of visual impairment gives no information about the nature of the difficulty. It could refer to any number of conditions including coloboma, retinitis pigmentosa, heminopia, inability to track or fixate, or colour blindness. The diversity of conditions associated within any of the categories reduce the practical value of these surveys to those planning individualised service delivery. Medical models of deafness may well be effective in planning medical services but the relevance of such models in predicting educational needs is unclear.

Incidence

Studies of incidence do provide ample evidence of the need for services to consider a wide range of needs that will typically be presented by children who are hearing impaired. Studies vary in definitions and methods of data collection but produce very similar estimates of the challenge facing services.

Table 1.4:1 Summary of recent studies of hearing impaired children with educationally relevant disabilities

Karchmer (1985)	Overall incidence 31 per cent
Schildroth and Motto (1994)	Overall incidence 34 per cent
Stredler-Brown and Yoshiago-Itano (1994)	Overall incidence 41 per cent
Fortnum *et al.* (1996)	Overall incidence 39 per cent

This group represent a considerable proportion of these children who have permanent childhood deafness. In reviewing the literature pertaining to this group the range of terms is considerable. Do these labels positively affect service provision, service delivery or outcomes for the individual child? Do these terms help in the process of identifying the nature of complex relationships that may exist between different conditions? Labels may inform but can also confuse and blur important factors which hinder a child's development.

In the UK an example of difference in terminology is both regional and international. 'Mental impairment' was the accepted term in England in 1983, contrasting with the term 'mental handicap' used in Scotland. Increasing awareness of the implications of descriptive labels led to the Department of Health Guidelines (1991) recommending that the appropriate term for this group is 'individuals with learning disability'. Whereas such a change in label may be helpful within the context of the UK it presents other problems internationally. The term 'learning disability' in the US is defined by the Individuals with Disabilities Act of 1990 (PL101-476) as referring to 'children with specific learning disabilities' and includes 'such conditions as minimal brain dysfunction, dyslexia and developmental aphasia'. In contrast to the UK term 'learning disability' the term 'mental retardation' is accepted within the US. Terminology is culture-specific and one accepted as a defining term within one cultural setting may be deemed to be offensive and degrading in another. Clearly studies comparing incidence, service delivery or individual habilitation programmes for children with hearing impairment and additional disability from different countries are likely to be compromised if such differences in terminology are not recognised.

Specific groups

The major additional disabilities identified within studies of this population are learning disability (Department of Health Guidelines' definition), visual impairment, specific learning disability (dyslexia), cerebral palsy and emotional/behaviour problems. Armitage *et al.* (1995) report that 35 per cent of severely and profoundly deaf children have a visual impairment. If the accent on identification is placed within a specialism other than deafness similarly high reports of hearing impairment are to be found. Gillham (1986) reported the incidence of hearing impairment in children with cerebral palsy as 20 per cent. Amongst individuals who have profound and multiple learning disability the incidence of hearing impairment is high, reported as 37 per cent (Yeates 1995). Children who are deaf and have learning disabilities are characterised by their heterogeneity, representing a wide range of social, emotional, physical, cognitive, intellectual and educational needs. While labels may not be helpful in some respects they do allow consideration of some of the major groups of children and should lead to a more sensitive approach in ensuring quality of provision and support.

Down's Syndrome

Children with Down's Syndrome constitute the largest and most well documented single group of children with learning disability (Von Tetzchner and Martinsen 1992). The incidence of hearing loss amongst this group has also been the focus of research. Despite an information base being available this has not been applied to produce a nationally agreed programme of intervention. Classically there is agreement that chronic conductive hearing loss is the rule rather than the exception (Cunningham and McArthur 1981). Buchanan (1990) reported a high incidence of sensori-neural hearing loss that is thought to occur as a result of premature ageing in this population. This is reported as being common within the first decade. Additionally Balkany (1980) reported that individuals with Down's Syndrome have shortened auditory meati. Failure to take this into account when fitting hearing aids is likely to result in appropriate amplification. There is no evidence that this information is being taken into account when hearing aids are being fitted; as a result many children will be 'over'-amplified. Hearing aid rejection is likely to result from specialists failing to apply current knowledge and technology. Teachers of the deaf may attribute a range of challenges in providing service to this specific population to the label of Down's Syndrome and fail to take into account the repercussions of chronic middle ear conditions and compromised audiological management.

Multi-sensory impairment

Services for children with dual and multi-sensory impairment have seen considerable development over the last decade. The more traditional area of deafblind education has been further developed to cater for children who, in addition to dual sensory impairment, have profound or multiple learning disabilities. Even within the group of children who are deafblind there are major differences between those who are congenitally deafblind and those who, as a result of Usher's Syndrome or other trauma, become adventitiously deafblind. The known incidence of profoundly deaf children who have Usher's Syndrome together with the profound implications that this condition has for the individual and family are well established. The lack of routine ophthalmalogical testing of deaf children and of training available to teachers of the deaf in recognising what may be early symptoms of this condition suggest an unwarranted complacency.

Perception of needs

The many needs of children who have learning disabilities in addition to hearing loss can only be met effectively if there is sensitive multidisciplinary working. Teachers of the deaf need to recognise their areas of expertise and to ensure that the subtle effects of hearing loss are not missed or trivialised. The role of a teacher of the deaf extends to all children who have a hearing loss. Thus a child who is deaf and has learning disabilities may be perceived as a legitimate client for service delivery from a teacher of the deaf. In contrast, a child who has cerebral palsy and learning disability with a mild hearing loss is at risk if professionals view deafness *per se* as a minor part of the individual's overall needs. Educationalists, therapists and parents may be less effective in meeting such an individual's needs as a result of this. It may be hard to justify the involvement of a teacher of the deaf. Changes in educational practice and funding mechanisms demand that services can demonstrate measures of value added following service intervention. Within the field of deaf education such measures are complex and must take into account long-term measures of language competency, curricula access and performance across a range of tests. Economic and social independence are frequently cited as appropriate goals. For children who have a range of disabilities, measuring the value of intervention from a teacher of the deaf is problematic, particularly when these disabilities are severe. The repercussions of failing to recognise and specifically intervene when a child has a mild to moderate loss, whether conductive or sensori-neural, can be considerable. Emotional and behavioural difficulties can be compounded by mishearing information or misunderstanding instructions. Attempts to modify behaviour which fail to take account of sensory loss are unlikely to be effective. For a child with restricted motor abilities the difficulties of moving nearer to a quiet sound source may give the appearance that a child is withdrawn or excessively passive. A label of learning disability may reduce parents' and professionals' expectations and result in the positive involvement of a teacher of the deaf being given low priority in meeting what are perceived to be the child's most important needs.

Service delivery

Whatever label may be used, all children should, as a right, have access to fast efficient and appropriate assessment of auditory status. While technological innovation continues to offer the hope of a definitive, non-invasive and accurate way of measuring auditory status, at present audiological services are not able to ensure that children with a range of special needs have such an assessment. In a recent pilot survey of parents of children who had profound and multiple learning difficulties fourteen parents from six health authorities responded to a questionnaire considering levels of satisfaction with the assessment of their child's hearing.

Ninety three per cent of this group had little or no satisfaction with the way in which the test was carried out. While 66 per cent of the group had some level of confidence that hearing levels had been established 71 per cent were unhappy about the way the test results were explained to them and 93 per cent felt that the testers were not very effective or were totally ineffective at taking their child's special learning needs into account (McCracken 1997).

Assessment is only useful if it then informs practice and ensures quality provision of appropriate services. Auditory assessment is only useful if it ensures that appropriate hearing aids are fitted, the fitting is verified and the quality of the listening environment is ensured. Such tasks are difficult with a paediatric population and are particularly challenging if an infant has a range of learning disabilities. Establishing meaningful measurements of benefit accrued from the use of amplification is problematic. The nature and scope of additional disability will vary enormously. For a child with cerebral palsy the main challenge may be ensuring that ergonomic considerations are fully taken into account. It is inappropriate to suggest that amplification is irrelevant for any child who has a degree of hearing loss. The challenge to professionals lies in identifying an appropriate tool for measuring improved quality of life within this context. A developmental framework suggested by Coninx (1995) is a useful reference point. Amplification is seen as being one of the ways of enabling a multiply-handicapped child to become more aware from a basic awareness level of enabling a child to reducing the level of isolation and to providing a bridge to the immediate environment, reducing stress by providing the opportunity for anticipation of events following an auditory clue and reducing negative behaviour such as excessive self-stimulation. Goals at this basic level of functioning need to be clearly identified and agreed if parents and other professionals are to ensure that auditory needs are addressed.

Teachers of the deaf have a wealth of specialist knowledge that can be applied to any setting. In the experience of the author, teachers of the deaf frequently feel deskilled when presented with children who have learning disabilities. Within the fields of communication and audiology teachers of the deaf need to apply their skills. Children with a range of disabilities are reliant on others to advocate on their behalf. The emphasis should be on ensuring quality of experience in both accessing a means of communication and in the listening environment.

Communication

In any area of the education of deaf children the issue of effective communication is central. For children who have a hearing loss and learning disability the situation is complex. A detailed consideration of the individual child's special learning needs, their developmental level and an assessment of communication skills is essential to inform any approach. Sensitive language assessment can be difficult when an individual is developmentally within the pre-verbal stage. For those children who are most challenged developmentally, video allows the fine detail of pre-verbal behaviour to be viewed and assessed, in relation to both the child's behaviour and the communication behaviour of the other communicator.

Research has shown the value of sign in developing communication skills in children who are autistic and in children who have learning disabilities (Konstantares *et al.* 1977).

In addition to oral or sign language, there are a wide range of alternative and augmentative communication systems available. The individuality within this group demands a creative rather than a dogmatic approach. The range of factors which will impact on the suitability of any communication system is considerable. Such factors include gross and fine motor skills, vision, cognitive ability, ease of use, adaptability, access to training, a user community and motivation. A comprehensive overview of alternative and augmentative communication systems, including the use of signs, is provided by Von Tetzchner and Martinsen 1992.

The motivation of a family to give time and effort to a specific communication approach must be viewed within the parents' hierarchy of perceived needs. The health and care routines of some children with profound and multiple learning disabilities will put very considerable demands on families. Communication approaches should take this into account. A functional approach to communication which enhances the quality of experience is most likely to be successful.

Training

Gallaudet University in the US has a long-established specialist training course for teachers who work with multiply-handicapped deaf children (Moores 1996). In a survey of 119 specialist services for deaf children with learning disabilities conducted by Jones and Johnson (1985) no consistent pattern was established relating to curricular design and delivery, in the training of staff or in the training programmes that were utilised with these children. The availability of training to work with additional disability is established in the UK for those working with deafblind children and is becoming established for learners who have profound or multiple learning disability and sensory impairment. A unique approach to meeting the need for training has been developed by a training initiative involving Manchester University, MENCAP and Royal Schools for the Deaf (Manchester). This course is unusual in that, rather than seeking to train teachers alone it seeks to train all those who may care for or work with this very special group. Training is provided for carers and professionals to allow an advocacy base to be established. This can help ensure pressure is brought to bear which in itself may improve and ensure quality of provision and services for individuals with profound learning disabilities.

Across all areas of disability, time and lack of expertise make it impossible to meet the needs of such a diverse population within initial training courses. Although failure to engage with this area would represent failure to engage with an important area of deaf education, representing as many as 40 per cent of those with permanent hearing loss, wider issues also warrant attention. Interdisciplinary working is held to be central to providing effective services to deaf children and their families and essential where children have a range of disabilities. Such thinking is not new (Myklebust and Bruton 1953). While changes in statutes support this concept there is little evidence that professionals are receiving specific training in developing the skills necessary to put this approach into practice. Matkin (1994) clearly identifies six major constraints that limit effective teamwork:

1. the trend towards speciality rather than interdisciplinary training amongst all the professional groups that may be involved with a particular child;
2. a lack of common terminology;
3. lack of specific training in inter-agency working;
4. the existence of a professional pecking order which enforces a tier rather than a peer model of service delivery;
5. the high cost of interdisciplinary working which may preclude a service from being able to implement appropriate programmes;
6. personality differences which can limit interdisciplinary working.

Each individual involved within the assessment and delivery of services to these children has a hierarchy of needs which act as a constraint. A parent may for social, cultural or economic reasons not place value on a programme which fails to take these into account. Any professional will have a perspective reflecting their training, their specialism, the caseload carried, perceptions of relevance to an overall programme and personal experiences of trying to effectively achieve interdisciplinary working. The training implications are not simply an issue for teachers of the deaf but for all professionals who are likely to be partners in providing a service for this population.

Without a major reconsideration of training across a range of disciplines that includes the development of skills in promoting effective communication and sensitivity to other professionals and to families, the outlook is pessimistic. Some teams are approaching this area very practically and positively; such an approach needs to permeate all services which hope to offer effective intervention, focusing beyond the immediate to long-term outcomes.

Inclusion

'A key concept of inclusion is that children are not excluded from mainstream education' (Thomas 1997, p. 103). Inclusion is a fashionable term which supports the idea that challenges in accessing education within a school setting 'may arise from a multiplicity of factors related to disability, language, family income, cultural background, gender or ethnic origin and it is, therefore, inappropriate to differentiate these factors' (Thomas 1997, p. 103). While such factors may appear to stigmatise and to militate against equal opportunity, failure to take such factors into account when implementing an intervention programme dooms it to failure. An ecological approach, which views an individual within the framework of their individual real-life experiences and needs, is essential for sensitive and effective service delivery (Brofenbrenner 1979). The importance of sharing professional information and having families as central to, rather than peripheral from, intervention programmes is well documented. While the need for additional training in the short-term may be met by inservice training the availability of recognised additional training which is part of an ongoing accreditation for teachers of the deaf is central to improving the quality of service provision. Teachers of the deaf have a professional responsibility that extends to all children who have a degree of hearing loss.

Conclusion

At a time when labelling children is viewed as limiting children, it is also time to move beyond the traditional medical categories. However, it should be recognised that changes in societal habits can result in higher incidence of children who have a range of complex learning needs, for instance drug and solvent abuse and the rise of HIV infection are all reported as causative agents of multiple handicap (Condon 1991).

A positive approach to recognising the scale of this area of work and its complexity is essential. It ensures the possibility of high quality provision for all children with a degree of hearing loss and a range of disabilities. It is time this issue is no longer approached as merely an add-on but is seen as more central within the field of education of deaf children.

The education of Asian deaf children

Rampaul Chamba, Waqar I. U. Ahmad, Aliya Darr and Lesley Jones

Introduction

Any discussion of education needs to be set in the broader social context. In discussing education of Asian deaf children, the socio-economic position of Asian communities, and debates and developments in multicultural and anti-racist education provide important background. We briefly summarise these before considering the education of deaf Asian children. In Britain, Asians (predominantly of Indian, Pakistani and Bangladeshi origin) now constitute the largest minority ethnic population, numbering 1.48 million people (CSO 1996). Of this, 840,000 are of Indian, 477,000 of Pakistani and 163,000 of Bangladeshi origin. The population is heavily skewed with relatively few people in the retirement age and a high proportion in the under-16 age group. This is reflected in the child dependency ratio (ratio of children to the working age population) of 72 for the Pakistani/Bangladeshi and 37 for Indian, compared to 33 for the white population (cited in CSO 1996). The skewed age distribution translates directly to disproportionate need for schooling.

On the whole, the socio-economic profile of the Bangladeshi and Pakistani groups is poorer than that of the white population, while that of the Indian population is close to that of the white population. The Indian population appears to be more 'integrated' within Britain than the Pakistani or Bangladeshi groups, as evidenced by a number of characteristics: areas of residence, family size, age distribution or wearing of western clothes (CSO 1996; Peach 1996).

This diversity is also represented in experiences of health, illness and disability (Ahmad 1993), with the Bangladeshi and Pakistani populations experiencing poorer health and greater problems in access to services. The Indian population occupies a position between these groups and the white population. There is some evidence that the Pakistani and Bangladeshi populations have raised prevalence of deafness compared to the Indian and white groups (Vanniasegaram *et al.* 1993; Naeem and Newton 1996).

In what follows, we provide a rapid overview of some key debates in education and ethnicity before concentrating on education of Asian deaf children. As we will see, issues of cultural identity are central to these debates.

Education of Asian children

Asian communities hold education in high regard. Indeed from personal experience we know people who regard the education system as the major, or perhaps the only, gift of being in Britain. Accompanying this high regard for education is a strong belief in meritocracy; education, it is held, allows the best chance of personal and family betterment (Cashmore and Troyna 1988). Although rising out of poverty and low socio-economic status is possible through education, education has not been a major vehicle for class mobility. Marxist critics have regarded the education system as a major tool for social control and the perpetuation of gender, class and 'racial' oppression. Ideologies and oppressive relationships work at their best when they appear 'natural', when we are not even aware that what we think or experience has an ideological basis (Ahmad and Husband 1993). Evidence on the relatively poor educational achievements of minority ethnic children is vast and arguments well rehearsed (for an introduction see Gill *et al.* 1992; Rattansi 1992). Here we briefly introduce some of these debates.

Early years of large-scale migration of people from the Indo-Pak subcontinent (1960s) were followed by concerns about their children's schooling. The dominant policy approach of the time, one of facilitating assimilation, led to dispersal of Asian (and other 'black') children by 'bussing' them to different schools, constituting the first main controversy in this area. The dominant educational approach of the time undermined Asian languages and cultures, discouraging the use of mother tongue at home; debates about cultural sensitivity were very much things of the future. The Swann Report of 1985, with all its flaws (and its critics and criticisms are many – see Gill *et al.* 1992), was instrumental in placing 'multiculturalism' on the official education agenda. For the first time, issues of cultural and religious identity and sensibilities became important and education authorities, with different levels of commitment and success, started addressing issues of cultural plurality and 'tolerance' (see Husband 1991 for a wider discussion of multi-culturalism). Unfortunately some banal interpretations of multiculturalism reduced minority cultures into artefacts – the rightly ridiculed 'saris, samosas and steelbands' approach to minority cultures.

Anti-racism, the more radical offspring of multiculturalism, criticised the fetishism of reducing minority cultures into exotica. It emphasised the historical and contemporary power relations, racism in the wider society and the education system, biases in curricula, and racism in the classroom and the playground. As an approach, it was critical of the attempts to promote a dominant white national identity at the cost of undermining minority ethnic group achievements and contribution to British life. To anti-racists it was not in the least surprising that the British schools failed minority ethnic children. Schools reflect and reproduce societal racism through racist science, negative images of non-white cultures in geography and history, and through paying little or no attention to non-European literature (see Gill *et al.* 1992; Rattansi 1992). Contemporary media images of 'black' countries emphasise famine, war and their subservient status in relation to western nations as the salient characteristics of these countries. The racist treatment of non-white people by wider social institutions, ranging from the immigration service to police and welfare agencies, is consistent with this overall negative picture of non-white people. Throughout the period of debates around multicultural and anti-racist education, alongside improving the educational experience of minority ethnic children, the issue of ethnic and cultural identity has been central. Indeed, partly in response to the failure of formal schooling to cultivate positive minority ethnic identities, places such as Bradford have developed an extensive and extremely well attended network of after-school classes for religious education and mother-tongue teaching. As we will see, issues of ethnic identity and access to home language are equally vital to debates around the teaching of deaf Asian children.

That minority ethnic children fare less well educationally, compared to white children, is well established although explanations for this remain contested (Gill *et al.* 1992). For Asian children, the picture is made more complex with a divergence in performance between the impressive performance of Indian and the relatively poor performance of Bangladeshi and Pakistani children. To an extent this is consistent with the better socio-economic position and the earlier arrival of the Indian population compared to Pakistanis and Bangladeshis. As noted earlier, Pakistani and Bangladeshi children also experience higher prevalence rates for deafness compared to other Asian, or white children. Both the relatively poorer background and higher prevalence of deafness among Pakistani and Bangladeshi children have implications for their education.

Language, communication and identity

Language and communication is a central feature of social and linguistic development and is particularly important for deaf people as it mediates access to information and resources as well as being an important signifier of identity and community membership. The importance of language and culture has been politicised within the deaf world over the last 30 years. Many Deaf people see themselves as a linguistic minority with their own culture and language. Being part of a linguistic minority oppressed by a dominant spoken language is symbolic of Deaf people's attempts to raise the profile of sign language (Woodward 1976; Kyle and Woll 1985; Lane *et al.* 1996). For these reasons, language has assumed a central role in the communication and educational needs of deaf children for parents and teachers of the deaf.

Clearly, children vary in degree of hearing loss which will influence language choice and strength of affiliation, if any, with Deaf culture and identity whether they are Asian or non-Asian. Parents of deaf children make decisions about language choice which are influenced by a number of factors including the child's level of hearing loss, dominant trends in deaf education and services as well as parental preferences. The sometimes overwhelming sense of invasion by professional advice is commented on by Lane (1992). Our ongoing work (Chamba *et al.*) shows that parents are able to exercise more discretion about language choice where the child uses some speech, alongside sign supported language. In these cases, parents' views about how they should communicate with their deaf child were informed by the degree of the child's deafness, personal preferences of parents, previous experiences, perceptions of disability and deafness, available support, professional advice and concerns about education and integration in deaf/hearing/ethnic communities. Some parents showed personal prejudice against BSL, or felt that their views were influenced by wider societal prejudices. All the parents showed support for spoken language development. On the whole, parents we interviewed valued professional advice which came mainly from teachers of deaf children and varied between teachers. Reflecting the variety of influences on parental choice, most parents used a variety of languages while others concentrated on English or on first language alone. This diversity is also reported by Speedy (1987) who found that 47 different spoken languages were used by families of deaf children in the UK.

Language and communication, however, raise additional issues for children and young people from minority ethnic groups, particularly where the child can use spoken languages alongside BSL. For many Asian parents and their families, 'Deaf culture' and its major signifier, BSL, is seen as an extension of white culture and the English language. Previous policies of dissuading minority ethnic parents from using home language with their deaf children have led to a number of deaf Asian young people with little access to their home language, limited communication with members of family, and poorly developed ethnic, religious and community affiliations. These emerge as significant concerns for deaf people and their families in our own work (Darr *et al.* in press; Chamba *et al.*, ongoing work). Furthermore, Asian parents often have to make decisions about language choice on the basis of inadequate information; Darr *et al.* (in press) note that parents of deaf children relied on professionals for much information support, and families of Asian deaf children often had insufficient information to make informed choices about language and communication.

Parents of deaf children have written about their experience of choosing a language amid uncertainty and lack of knowledge (Spradley and Spradley 1971; Fletcher 1987; Robinson 1991). Parents who use spoken languages other than English are placed in an ambivalent position with regard to which spoken language to use and how to accommodate the needs of other family members as well as adopting a language which allows easy access to religious and cultural socialisation (see Darr *et al.* in press, for discussion). If everyone in the family speaks Punjabi, Urdu or Hindi and the only English spoken is with the deaf child, this sets up an additional barrier. Isolation from knowledge of mother tongue may exclude the deaf child from full family life and hinders the development of a positive ethnic and religious identity (Darr *et al.* in press). This may compromise the relationship between mothers and deaf children more than fathers, with mothers likely to be the main caregivers and more likely not to speak English. Ahmad *et al.* (forthcoming) note that many parents felt schools for deaf children and the white deaf culture did not do enough to promote a positive ethnic or religious identity (see also a personal account by Abedi 1988). Consistent with both deaf people's and their families' perspectives, some parents felt that unquestioning acceptance of professional advice to only use English with deaf children undermined children's cultural identity and compromised communication with the wider family. Ahmad *et al.* (in press) noted considerable resentment on the part of both deaf young people and their families about the loss of home language and, indirectly, fuller cultural socialisation (see also Gregory *et al.* 1995).

Darr *et al.* (in press) and ongoing work by Chamba *et al.*, however, show that families of deaf children felt there had been a welcome change in advice given to parents on language development. Our ongoing work shows that the importance of a positive ethnic and religious identity for deaf children is now more readily, though not universally, accepted by teachers. However, accounts by teachers indicate a disjunction between their adherence to a total communication philosophy in principle, and what a number of them do in practice. There was also inconsistency between the views of teachers, even when they worked in the same institution. The different positions identified in our interviews with teachers is on one level not surprising, given that differences in philosophy, policy and practice continue to pervade academic and professional discourse on language and communication for deaf children (cf., Gregory and Pickersgill 1997; Young 1995/6).

In our ongoing research, three positions were identified about BSL and its relationship to spoken languages. First, the denial of access to mother tongue to the previous generation of deaf Asian children was regarded by some teachers as 'racism of the finest kind', something which had damaged the relationship between deaf children and their families, and left them resentful of services – sentiments close to those described by Ahmad *et al.* (in press). Secondly, those who favoured only spoken English, in addition to BSL, felt that simultaneous or sequential acquisition of more than one spoken language leads to confusion for the deaf child and limits their language development. Reliance on English would make the child's life easier and was perceived to be consistent with the child's language of education as there was concern about deaf children who entered school with little or no English, with the children's residence in an English speaking country, and becoming 'useful citizens'. Thirdly, those who supported multilingualism, emphasised the importance of the deaf child having a full family and social life, and developing a positive cultural identity. Significantly for parents, teachers of deaf children also expressed different views about the relationship between spoken languages such as Punjabi and Urdu with BSL and the relative ease with which parents could acquire BSL.

The varied and often conflicting positions expressed by teachers have implications for the support given to parents, deaf children and the role of teachers in working with deaf Asian children. Specifically, it suggests the need for local, regional and national reviews on bilingual and trilingual communication policies so that there is greater clarity and consistency in philosophy, policy and practice. Some endeavours are being made in this regard (cf., Gregory and Pickersgill 1997).

Culture, ethnicity and perceptions of deafness

Language is vital for the transmission of cultural values and cultural retention is an area of concern for minority ethnic communities; ethnic/cultural/religious identity has occupied a key place in debates around education of minority ethnic children (see Anwar 1979;

Modood 1994; Ahmad 1996). As Darr *et al.* (in press, chapter 3) argue, it may have particular salience for parents of deaf children and their development of ethnic and Deaf identities. A major concern for parents revolved around the need to reproduce appropriate cultural and religious values in their deaf children. This relates to the role of home language which is both a resource for learning and as a signifier of religious and group identity. Thus, Darr *et al.* note that a wide range of activity led by minority ethnic Deaf people and their families was based around religious and cultural identity, aspects of life which Deaf people and their families felt were ignored by the Deaf young people's immersion in the 'white' Deaf culture or specialist education.

Professionals, including teachers of deaf children, are a significant medium through which cultural meanings about deafness are conveyed to deaf children and young people. The relative lack of emphasis on culture, religion and languages has worried parents of deaf Asian children; however, Darr *et al.* note positive developments in some schools through both deaf and hearing paid and voluntary staff. Many Asian deaf children suffer considerable frustration and confusion related to their identity leading to problems which are only beginning to be acknowledged by teachers working in multicultural educational settings. At school it is apparent that deaf children from Asian as well as other minority ethnic backgrounds are provided with limited opportunities to learn about their own cultural and religious backgrounds (Darr *et al.* in press). The limited presence of minority ethnic professionals in deaf education also features as an important issue for growing deaf Asian children in helping to cultivate both ethnic and deaf identities.

Numerous studies have highlighted how effective communication channels are needed within the home to ensure that Asian deaf children are able to participate in normal family life (Meherali 1994; Badat and Whall-Roberts 1994; Sharma and Love 1991). It is often the case that many Asian deaf children do not have full access to what is happening or being discussed within the home which leads to the build-up of feelings of resentment and increasing alienation from the rest of the family (Gregory *et al.* 1995). Although many other family dynamics are involved, under these circumstances Asian deaf children may be more likely to choose the company of their Deaf peers against their hearing siblings and associate more with Deaf culture rather than suffer feelings of loneliness and rejection within their own homes.

Hearing Asian parents with limited signing skills have experienced considerable difficulties in attempting to instil their deaf offspring with values, behaviour and knowledge essential to a positive ethnic identity (Darr *et al.* in press). Similarly, using English as the only spoken language, which was a common approach about a decade ago, has meant that Asian deaf children have had little communication with other family members who speak mother tongue and remain isolated – as described by one mother, they are often 'strangers' within their own families and communities. This is a cause for concern for many Asian parents who are anxious that their children do not grow up to become totally immersed in Deaf culture without any understanding of their own ethnic heritage and history. It is also reflected in the growth of sign language classes which have been set up by some education authorities in response to a need amongst non-English-speaking Asian parents to improve communication and develop stronger relationships with their deaf children (Darr *et al.* in press; Lynas and Turner 1995).

Cultural meanings of deafness are cross-cut by other axes of identity and difference. Minority ethnic groups are not a homogenous category and many Deaf people (as a 'linguistic minority') oppose amalgamation into the disability movement while recognising benefits of an alliance. Darr *et al.* note criticism of the white Deaf community by minority ethnic Deaf people for undermining ethnic identity and not regarding them as equal members. Young deaf Asian people are contesting, reconstituting and celebrating cultural meanings of Deafness in relation to their own perceived ethnic and religious identities, their families and the wider socio-political environment of the deaf world. Notions of a dominant and essentialist Deaf identity are being contested: self-organisation of Asian Deaf young people reflects their multiple and situational identities where 'race', ethnicity, religion and gender become important sites of identity claims and political mobilisation.

Conclusion

Research and speculative literature on Asian deaf children remains limited. However, as we have argued, a consideration of their education must encompass debates around the education of deaf as well as minority ethnic children. Central to debates in both these areas have been questions of language, identity and equality of treatment. Criticisms in both areas have focused on the marginalisation of cultural heritage and show little respect for difference. Schools too often have reflected societal prejudices against minority ethnic groups and deaf people.

The relationship between identity claims and translating them into educational policy and practice is not straightforward. However, the need for greater clarity and consistency in policy and practice on language and communication support to Asian deaf children must be recognised. The child's ethnic identity and involvement in family life needs to be facilitated, a task increasingly being recognised by teachers and schools for deaf children.

We have acknowledged the importance of recognising differences among Asian deaf children, not all of whom may identify equally with the use of BSL, Deaf identity and culture. At the same time, there are those who do and we have outlined the many parental and professional influences which may inform the cultivation of multiple identities. The potential for empowering education which equips Asian deaf children not just with instrumental skills in literacy and numeracy but with pride in themselves, their communities and positive self identity remains to be realised.

Further reading

Chamba, R., Ahmad, W. I. U., Jones, L. (forthcoming) *Improving Health Care for Asian Deaf Children*. Bradford, Ethnicity and Social Policy Research Unit, University of Bradford.

This report is based on research funded by the Department of Health. It describes Asian parents' experiences of caring for a deaf child and access to health, education and social care services. It also describes providers' and commissioners' perspectives on the nature of service delivery and how to improve services for Asian deaf children.

Darr, A., Jones, L., Ahmad, W .I. U., Nisar, G. (in press) *Ethnicity and Deafness: Projects and Initiatives*. Bristol: Policy Press.
This book is based on research funded by the Joseph Rowntree Foundation and describes the emergence and development of projects, initiatives and services within the statutory and independent sector around ethnicity, gender, religion and language in the context of debates around politics of identity, recognition and difference.

Gill, D., Mayor, B., Blair, M. (1992) *Racism and Education: Structures and Strategies*. London: Sage Publications.
This edited book brings together a number of chapters which explore the dynamics of ethnicity in informing educational policy and practice. It provides a general but critical introduction to key debates related to multicultural and antiracist education policies addressing issues such as the effectiveness of legislation and local antiracist initiatives, and the operation of racism within schools at individual, social and institutional levels.

Sharma, A. and Love, D. (1991) *A Change in Approach: A Report on the Experience of Deaf People from Black and Ethnic Minority Communities*. London: Royal Association in Aid of Deaf People.
This book highlights the problems experienced by deaf people from minority ethnic groups and their experiences of accessing a wide range of public services. The report calls for a change in attitudes and improved services for deaf people by local and central government and increased user participation in the organisation and delivery of services for deaf people from minority ethnic groups.

LANGUAGE AND COMMUNICATION

Introduction

Issues concerned with the development of language and the related methodology, as reflected in policies and practice, are strongly interlinked. This section addresses both of these issues, firstly considering aspects of language development and secondly modes of communication as used in current practice. A complete consideration of all issues related to language development is beyond the scope of this section.

In the first two chapters discussion focuses on two fundamental areas, namely the role of early interaction and the subsequent need for assessment of developing language both signed and spoken. Marschark (1993) comments upon the importance of early linguistic stimulation for the child, in any mode of communication, and the requirement for regular input and feedback during the first two to three years of life. Gallaway and Woll (1994) suggest that successful early interaction is now regarded as a prerequisite for language acquisition and Clare Gallaway's chapter here enlarges on this by considering fully the issues and current research related to early interaction for both hearing and deaf children.

An understanding of developing language and the issues of assessment are of importance to all teachers working with deaf children. Bencie Woll describes current research on signed and spoken language development and the implications for the language acquisition of developing bilingual deaf children. She then addresses the issues related to the assessment of language, identifying the difficulties and constraints of using English-based assessments with deaf children. The underlying principles of assessing deaf children's developing language are outlined together with discussion of recently developed tools for the assessment of sign language.

The following three chapters on oralism, Total Communication (TC) and sign bilingualism consider communication modes and methodologies in terms of philosophy, policy and practice. The chapters reflect a contrasting style, which may in itself be a reflection of current thinking, in relation to the modes of communication to be found in practice in schools and services in the UK. Oralism has a long-established role within the education of deaf children and continues to develop teaching strategies and methodologies, particularly in response to current considerations about the development of spoken language in hearing children and to rapid advances in technology. TC is a relatively recent (1970s) response both to pressures from some educationalists and linguists and to relevant research findings, particularly a seminal study by Conrad (1979), to include the use of sign in some form in the language development and educational provision for deaf children. A bilingual approach has developed in an attempt to formalise the growing use of spoken, signed and manually coded languages with deaf children and to identify appropriate language use by situation and in response to the needs of individual deaf children.

In the third chapter Linda Watson gives a clear rationale for the oral/aural approach to deaf education, and outlines the thinking that has led to the change in the use of terminology. There is a full description of current teaching approaches and strategies. She highlights challenges of the oral/aural approach for teachers of the deaf, particularly those currently posed by the diagnosis of deafness in very young babies.

The chapter on Total Communication is largely based upon a recent research project which aimed to identify the current definition of TC as reflected in policy and practice in the UK in 1997. The authors, Rob Baker and Pamela Knight, having first explored the history and derivation of the term TC then consider how the term is defined currently by schools and services working within this policy. The project then proceeds to enquire how teachers implement this policy in the reality of the classroom setting.

In the final chapter Miranda Pickersgill considers bilingualism in terms of the rationale for a bilingual approach to the education of deaf children and aspects of philosophy, policy and practice which need to be in place before an education programme can be considered to be bilingual. Bilingualism is seen as a developing area, and current research and developing teaching strategies are explored as well as the main issues local education authorities would need to consider when implementing a bilingual policy for deaf pupils in their schools.

Pamela Knight

Early interaction

Clare Gallaway

Early communication and its linguistic context

The situation of deaf infants

Children learn the language they hear – or see – around them. That much is indisputable; however, the relationship between a child's linguistic environment and the way the child acquires that language is far from obvious. The manner in which this is achieved is more complex than it first appears, and in spite of three decades of research, is still not well understood. However, a consensus on the general conditions relevant to the acquisition of a first language is less difficult to come by. First, from birth, babies are exposed to language which occurs in conversational settings and which is provided by those close to them: parents, other caregivers and various members of the family. Secondly, a first language is acquired by infants through communicative interaction with competent users of that language. Thirdly, the language addressed to the child displays some characteristics which make it especially helpful for the young language learner who is an immature conversational partner. These characteristics include not only the structural and semantic features of the language but particular communicative behaviours, such as the management of the child's attention by the adult who is trying to communicate with the child.

Given these three conditions, which are almost always present in the early lives of normally developing infants in all cultures, receiving enough, and good enough, language input for successful language development is rarely a problem for them. The process has been described variously as 'well-buffered' (Snow 1994) or as having an 'input cushion' (Nelson *et al.* 1993). In other words, for normally developing children, language acquisition is a robust process which fails only in cases of extreme deprivation, as there is normally far more relevant and useful language input than is needed to trigger the processes of language acquisition. However, for infants with a severe to profound prelingual hearing loss, this is usually not the case, and ensuring that they experience enough language to activate their natural language acquisition processes can be a problem.

Deaf children of deaf parents who are born into signing families find themselves in a less problematic situation with respect to the natural processes of language acquisition than those where there is a mismatch of hearing status (Meadow-Orlans 1997). The conditions outlined above are in place, and a first language may be acquired in a relatively trouble-free way. If there is a mismatch of hearing status, however, as there is for the great majority of deaf infants, then the baseline requirements for input are often not met for the acquisition of either a signed or a spoken language. For a deaf child born into a hearing family, sign language will not be present in the child's home environment in the conditions set out above – that is, used copiously by close family members, who are competent users, and with special modifications. However, with respect to spoken language, the presence of a hearing loss means that the child's intake of spoken language may not reach the minimum level required for the child to acquire the spoken language comfortably.

To sum up, then, the circumstances in which deaf children acquire their first and perhaps their second and third languages are often less than optimal. It may be the case that neither spoken nor signed language is accessible to the deaf infant in sufficient quantity/quality to allow easy acquisition of a first language (for a much more detailed discussion of this issue, see Nelson *et al.* 1993, pp. 129–134). However, the picture painted above is not as depressing as it may appear for two reasons. First, human beings have an overwhelmingly strong drive to communicate and are capable of adapting to unusual circumstances. Secondly, it should be possible for adults to tinker with and re-arrange the learning environment in ways which facilitate language acquisition for young deaf children (for example, by adopting particular attention management strategies, or by introducing signing adults into a child's environment).

The main aim in intervention must be that language exchanges between infants and their carers should be structured so that (a) interaction works and (b) the child receives the maximum quantity of useful linguistic input. In order to achieve this, it is necessary for professionals to arrive at a thorough understanding of the crucial defining characteristics of early interaction, and in particular, what aspects may be facilitative to early language acquisition. However, this kind of guidance has not been available from the research until quite recently. The main source of knowledge about the underpinnings of early communicative interaction has been from observations and analysis of hearing mother–child dyads, generally within mainstream psycholinguistic research (see Sachs 1997, for a summary and Messer 1994, for a detailed survey). Recently, significant progress has been made in understanding how deaf mothers interact successfully with their deaf infants (see, for example, Harris and Mohay 1997). However, neither deaf–deaf nor hearing–hearing mother–child dyads provide an immediate model for hearing–deaf situations, and the current task facing professionals and parents is to work out what insights may be helpful. The rest of this chapter describes some current findings and their implications.

Establishing early interaction 0–18 months

Neonates are already equipped with a range of abilities. They are sociable beings, programmed to take special interest in human faces and human voices, and to imitate and then assimilate the behaviour of the adults around them. They have sophisticated perceptual abilities and cognitive capacities such as problem-solving and rule-learning which underlie the future development of a linguistic system. However, all these skills have to be activated and put to use in the context of the day-to-day communicative situation. The following sections describe different aspects of early communicative behaviour.

Turn-taking behaviour

It has long been believed that early caregiver–child interaction is structured in a way that forms the basis for later conversations, with mothers responding to their infants' early vocalizations as though they were conversational 'turns'. Mothers may be less likely to respond to their children if their vocalisations are not very speech-like (Cheskin 1982; Mogford and Gregory 1982), and less likely to chat normally to their babies if they feel that little can be heard, and this has been cited as a possible disruption in the early communicative development of deaf babies with hearing mothers.

Differences in visual behaviour

Gaze, or looking behaviour, plays an important role with respect to the context and the progress of early language development. Hearing children experience the world through sound and vision which are available simultaneously. This fact has an important role in how infants come to understand what language is about, and also determines ways in which the child's attention is managed. When mother and child are using a signed language, the visuo-spatial nature of sign languages, and the lack or fragmentary nature of the auditory channel, causes interactions to be structured differently. Deaf parents may be more likely to be sensitive to such differences (Gallaway and Woll 1994), even if they are not using sign language (Marschark 1993) but this does not mean that hearing parents cannot also respond appropriately to the communicative needs of their deaf infants (Erting *et al.* 1990). In addition, there is also individual variation in the communicative behaviour of mothers of deaf infants (Harris *et al.* 1989; Swisher 1992; Robinshaw and Evans 1995; Harris and Mohay 1997). Ultimately, the concern is not to draw a distinction between deaf and hearing mothers, but rather to find out what strategies work to foster successful communication.

Joint attention, the emergence of reference and vocabulary learning

Infants are not born with the knowledge that words symbolise things, i.e. that certain sound clusters refer to objects in the environment. What helps them discover this fact is the predominantly context-bound nature of maternal language to infants. When mothers talk about objects in the immediate environment, and when infants experience the object and the word for it simultaneously, they eventually realise that the two are connected (see Sachs 1997). This realisation, called the 'naming insight', emerges at around one year and is a necessary prerequisite to language development. Evidence for the importance of this stage and an indication of how caregivers contribute to it is given by Adamson *et al.* (1990). Their work is concerned with 'documenting the normative developmental relationship between conventionalized communicative acts and infants' attention to people and to objects' (p. 34) and with ascertaining 'what, if any, special role sophisticated partners might play in supporting the attentional context for an infant's first use of words and objects'. They categorised infants' states of engagement in three ways – with person, with object, and with both object and person. The last state had most significance for vocabulary development. Infants were more likely to produce their first words and gestures while they were attending to both object and person, and were also more likely to have larger vocabularies at a later point. The creation of joint attention to objects and language referring to them is, therefore, an important issue in early development.

Hearing children do not need to look at their mothers for communication to take place; they may look at an object which is being named and are therefore not looking at their mothers (Harris and Mohay 1997). However, for deaf infants, the situation is different: if words are signed, then they have to look at the sign and object in sequence, and if spoken, then lip-reading is needed, so they will be looking at mother's face rather than at the object. An early insight from Wood (1982) was that, since deaf infants have to experience the object and the language to go with it sequentially rather than simultaneously, the emergence of reference may be delayed.

Attention management strategies

Attention management strategies used by mothers of deaf children have been investigated extensively. Deaf mothers were able to draw their children's attention to a referent more successfully than hearing mothers (Kyle 1990) and were able to maintain and sustain communication (Gregory and Barlow 1989; both this and Kyle's study are described in Gallaway and Woll 1994). However, four deaf signing mothers with infants at 7, 10, 16 and 20 months were studied (Harris *et al.* 1989; Harris 1992) chiefly to investigate whether mothers presented signs which were tied to the context. Mothers produced a high proportion of signs within the child's visual field and manipulated their children's attention, but there was some variation between mothers, and Harris concluded that creating the right attentional and context conditions may be tricky even in deaf–deaf dyads. In a study by Baker and van den Bogaerde (1996) concerned with language input given by deaf mothers (with Sign Language of the Netherlands as their first language) to their deaf and hearing children, hearing status alone did not predict the development of attentional behaviour in children; a variety of socio-linguistic factors must also be taken into account.

The language addressed to children ('motherese')

The term 'motherese' is frequently used to indicate modifications in speech addressed to young children. It is not a particularly appropriate term, since not only mothers adapt their speech thus, and it should not be taken to mean that one distinct type of language can be defined. More accurately, adults and older children speaking to, or signing to, young children tailor their conversational style and the substance of what they are saying in ways which foster success in the communicative exchange. We have already discussed how the context-bound nature (the 'here and now') of much adult speech to infants is a factor in helping them to 'crack the code'. There are many other features of the language addressed to young children which appear to be supportive of their language learning processes. These are by now well-known. For example, compared to speech addressed to adults, child-directed speech tends to be simpler, with shorter sentences and less complex grammatical structures, more repetitive, and may have more exaggerated prosodic features. There may be more questions and imperatives. There will not be overt corrections of the child's grammatical errors, but there will be various ways in which the adult picks up what the child has said and expands or adds to it.

Discussions of the general features of 'motherese' and their likely significance can be found in all major language acquisition textbooks and in Gallaway and Richards (1994) and Snow (1995). It has proved problematic to ascertain which of these features are necessary and sufficient for language acquisition (see, e.g. discussions in Pine 1994; Gleason 1997; Hoff-Ginsberg 1997; Nelson *et al.* 1993). One reason for this difficulty is that modifications are not identical across all cultures (Lieven 1994), and therefore it is proving more useful to investigate the apparent reasons for these modifications rather than simply their manifestations (Richards and Gallaway 1994). In the next two sections, two central issues are dealt with. First, under 'Child-adapted signing' the sort of modifications that occur in signing to young children are described. Secondly, some modifications in spoken language are described and it is considered whether they should be essentially the same for deaf children as for hearing children.

Child-adapted signing

It can be predicted that signing mothers use language to their infants which differs from adult-to-adult sign language and that these modifications are likely to take different forms from those used in spoken language. And so this has proved to be, although extensive evidence is not yet available. Many differences centre round attention, as previously discussed. Deaf mothers and other adults are persistent in gaining their children's attention and tend to use physical strategies more than hearing mothers. For instance, they may tap the infant or wave their hand in front of the child (Waxman and Spencer 1997; Harris *et al.* 1989; Smith 1996). (In spoken language, exaggerated intonation, high pitch and vocatives are thought to achieve similar functions.)

Strategies used by deaf mothers to ensure the visibility and clarity of signs being presented to the infant were first observed by Maestas y Moores (1980) and subsequently other researchers. These strategies include signing in the child's space, signing on a child's body (Maestas y Moores 1980; Harris *et al.* 1989), and signing slowly (Maestas y Moores 1980). Signs might be exaggerated in size and shape (Harris *et al.* 1989; Erting *et al.* 1990) and may be reduplicated (Gallaway and Woll, 1994). More single signs are used (Kyle and Woll 1985; Erting *et al.* 1990) and fewer signs altogether than words in spoken language (Harris *et al.* 1989).

This last fact demonstrates a problem encountered in comparisons of findings from input studies of spoken language acquisition. One well-attested fact is that quantity of language addressed to the hearing child correlates positively with future language development (Ellis and Wells 1980). However in studies of deaf mothers and their children, sheer quantity of input does not seem to be an issue – rather, the issue is to provide input in the best possible circumstances. Deaf mothers do not sign to their children unless they are watching, and more effort is devoted to the attention factor, ensuring that signs are seen and comprehended by the child. Spencer (1993) found that in a group of infants with hearing loss at the ages of 12 and 18 months, the quantity of language offered by signing mothers was relatively low, but their early sign acquisition was still age-appropriate, indicating that a low amount of input is not detrimental to language development in signing children.

Adapting one's language appropriately to address young children requires native mastery of the language in question. Signing children in signing families will experience some or all of the modifications described above, which will support their language learning. However, if parents are hearing and new to signing, then it is unlikely that they will be able to provide appropriate sign language input (for further references and discussion of this, see Marschark 1993, pp. 119–120.) This speaks strongly for the necessity to bring fluent native signing adults into the young deaf child's environment to facilitate the acquisition of sign language.

Prosody

The often observed (but not universal) exaggerated intonation and high pitch occurring in spoken motherese has been interpreted as having an attention-getting function. However, a recent theory has suggested an additional function: that the correlation between intonation and syntax helps the child learn grammatical chunks and word-boundaries (Morgan and Demuth 1996; Hoff-Ginsberg 1997). Among teachers of deaf children, there has long been a general belief that good (perhaps meaning 'clear') intonation is important in the language addressed to children; perhaps these two strands of research are at last providing empirical support for this belief.

Directiveness and questions

As early as the 1970s, control and directiveness in maternal conversation were declared to be a problem in speech addressed to deaf children by their mothers. The general view was that hearing mothers of deaf children were too controlling and not responsive enough, and that this was detrimental to language acquisition. This notion was based on studies of normally-developing children's language acquisition in which linguistic advance in children correlated with a less controlling maternal conversational style. This aspect has now been investigated with respect to deaf infants and deaf children of school age and through a variety of methodologies.

The issue of what constitutes directiveness and control, and how various researchers have defined and investigated these dimensions, is complex and beyond the scope of this chapter (but see Musselman and Churchill 1993: Gallaway and Woll 1994). However, with respect to practice, it is a crucial area in which advice is often sought and given to parents. Drawing practical implications from research findings is never straightforward, and in this case it has been too easy to fall into oversimplification and even mis-interpretation of the findings.

First, many of the studies associating maternal control with low language levels in children were not concerned with development over time. That is, they did not show that controlling language from mothers resulted in slow development; rather, they were cross-sectional and simply showed that mothers used more controlling language to children with lower levels, i.e. the maternal style was a response to, rather than a cause of, the child's language level. There is only sparse evidence of any developmental effect in infants (Musselman and Churchill 1993). Secondly, what might class as 'controlling' or even 'intrusive' is tricky. Syntactic imperatives ('eat your peas'), are the most overtly directive form, but language to young hearing children does include many of these, which later give way to questions with the same function ('aren't you going to eat your peas?') as the child advances linguistically (Bellinger 1979). Simple language like this which puts little demand on the child may function as 'scaffolding', i.e. it supports the child's language comprehension and production processes. It has been widely observed that mothers sometimes comment on their infants' actions using the imperative format: 'That's right. Put the little man on the horse', and that this form does not have a directive function (McConkey 1986; Caissie and Cole 1993; Gallaway and Lewis 1993). Musselman and Churchill's (1993) study supports the suggestion that effects of maternal conversational control are stage-related – that is, that conversations structured like this are helpful to children with lower levels of communicative competence, but not so when children are more advanced.

The role of question forms in speech addressed to children has been the subject of some confusion with respect to research on children with hearing losses. This topic has been discussed widely with relation to school-aged children. Wood and his colleagues (1982), following insights from the now classical research of Barnes *et al.* (1969), looked at the role of 'closed' and 'open' questions in teachers' language to children. Closed questions (those which can only be answered with 'yes' or 'no') do not stimulate children's conversational participation in the classroom. They are, however, frequently – and legitimately – used in educational contexts to direct children through a progression of logical steps in thinking. However, hearing children in the classroom are not generally still in need of language input which may facilitate their core language acquisition processes, whereas deaf children acquiring spoken language often are. Language well-suited to educational purposes may not be very facilitative to language acquisition. Another confusing factor is that, in the research on speech to hearing infants, a high proportion of question forms in maternal speech has been related to later language gain (see e.g. Richards 1994). Questions are, of course, a normal and necessary component of conversation, and there should be a fair number in speech addressed to children for several reasons: they present particular structures, they involve the child in the discourse, and so on. The idea that using closed questions to young children is detrimental to their language development should never have gained currency as a general principle; language input to all children should include a wide variety of linguistic structures. Bodner-Johnson (1991) studied family conversations with deaf children and found (unsurprisingly in this writer's view) that parental questions fostered the most participation by their deaf children.

Corrections

Explicit corrections of grammatical errors occur rarely in adults' speech to infants (Brown and Hanlon 1970) nor are they generally heeded when they do (McNeill 1966). However, this does not mean that children get no feedback about their incorrect utterances. Conversation is, of course, a two-way activity, and listeners have a duty to respond to and acknowledge what speakers say. As they do this, they may indicate to the speaker that the utterance was not clear or incorrect, perhaps by repetition with a questioning intonation:

> Child: I eated it.
> Adult: You ate it, did you?

Many believe such indirect feedback plays a role in language acquisition processes (Sokolov and Snow 1994; Saxton 1997). The most useful type of feedback is probably the category of recast – where an adult takes a child's incorrect utterance and corrects and adds to it (Nelson *et al.* 1993).

Although overt correction (such as saying 'not eated – ate') does not normally play a role in language acquisition, one cannot extrapolate that such correction is always wrong or detrimental – but the role of any type of correction must be subordinate to the primary aim of the exchange, which is to communicate. There has been little investigation of corrective feedback in spoken language addressed to young deaf children (and none about sign language). In a small study (Gallaway and Johnston 1996) some evidence of similar conversational patterns was found. A recent study of young deaf children speaking English and Sylheti carried out in a conversational analysis framework shows significant variation in the way parents provide such feedback (Mahon 1997). Clearly, much more research is needed.

Implications

The strongest implication for understanding interaction and language acquisition in young deaf children must surely come in terms of a caveat: that it is essential not to draw out over-simplified rules of thumb from a mass of complex research. Studies of hearing children cannot give answers; they can only give indications of what aspects of interaction need to be investigated in the context of a hearing loss. Some features of 'motherese' observed with hearing children may not be important for deaf children (such as quantity) but other features may be (such as the importance of managing attention). There have been other confusions in the research. For instance, negative effects of imperatives and/or questions used in conversation have been too widely assumed; it has sometimes been overlooked that findings relate to particular stages of language acquisition and are not necessarily valid for other stages or situations.

A positive recommendation is simply that young deaf children should experience a wide variety of language input and that all interlocutors should aim primarily at ensuring successful communication in the chosen language.

Further reading

Bodner-Johnson, B. (1991) 'Family conversation style: its effect on the deaf child's participation', *Exceptional Children* 57 (6), 502–509.
Conversational study including practical recommendations.

Gallaway, C. and Woll, B. (1994) 'Interaction and childhood deafness', in Gallaway, C. and Richards, B. J. (eds) *Input and Interaction in Language Acquisition.* Cambridge: Cambridge University Press.
A survey of the research.

Marschark, M. (1993) *Psychological Development of Deaf Children.* New York: Oxford University Press.
Section: Parental Input and Language Acquisition. From p. 118 – end of chapter. Deals with language addressed to deaf children.

Nelson, K. E., Loncke, F., Camarata, S. (1993) 'Implications of research on deaf and hearing children's language learning', in Marschark, M. and Clark, M. D. (eds) *Psychological Perspectives on Deafness.* New Jersey: Lawrence Erlbaum Associates.
A unique attempt to formulate conditions which could support deaf children's language acquisition.

Sachs, J. (1997) 'Communication development in infancy', in Gleason, J. B. (ed.) *The Development of Language.* Needham Heights, NJ: Allyn and Bacon.
A description of prelinguistic development in hearing children.

Chapter 2.2

Development of signed and spoken languages

Bencie Woll

Introduction

The development of language is a crucial factor in a deaf child's cognitive and social development, and central to the work of deaf educators since the first schools for the deaf were established in the eighteenth century. However, how normal development can be best achieved, and which language or languages should be learnt, is a continuing source of controversy.

Those most concerned with spoken language development have focused on the factors which may promote or hinder acquisition and on the extent to which language delay results in language deviance and difficulties. Educational interest in sign language acquisition is relatively recent. Following their recognition in the 1970s as complete languages with their own grammars and lexicons, neither primitive gestural systems nor derivatives of spoken languages, sign languages have been seen as worthy of study, not only in their own right, but as a means to develop understanding of general aspects of human language, both spoken and signed. Much research on sign language and its acquisition has been designed to address the question of whether sign language and spoken language are localised to the same brain areas, as well as issues of neural plasticity, critical periods for language development, and the long term outcomes of late first language acquisition.

In this chapter, current research on spoken and signed language development will be described, beginning with early pre-linguistic communication (babbling and gesture) and proceeding through the stages of lexical and grammatical development to later acquired discourse skills. Consideration will be given to implications for language acquisition of the developing bilingualism of most deaf children exposed to signed and spoken language. A timetable for the normal acquisition of BSL will be presented.

A major part of the chapter will be devoted to a presentation of issues relating to the assessment of language. While there is an enormous body of assessment material for English, the administration of English measures to deaf children is itself problematic, raising questions of age norms, language of testing, etc. In contrast to the large number of English assessments, there are limited tools available for assessing sign language. Underlying principles of assessing sign will be outlined and assessment tools currently under development for BSL will be discussed.

Pre-linguistic communication

Infants are born with the potential to learn any human language. Which language or languages they actually learn depends on which languages they have access to. The term 'access' is preferred here, since for deaf children, there needs to be careful and separate consideration of parental language output and child language uptake.

From birth to around 8 months in all infants, vocal babbling progresses from vocalic sounds to syllabic combinations. These later syllabic combinations are influenced by the phonology of the spoken language heard by the baby. When well-formed syllabic combinations begin to appear, parents perceive these as intentional communication on the part of the infant, and respond accordingly. This in turn leads to changes in patterns of adult–child vocal interaction.

Deaf babies exhibit early vocal babbling which is similar to that of hearing babies (interestingly, deaf mothers also vocalise, even to deaf infants, though neither can hear the sound (Woll and Kyle 1989)), but after the first few months, the vocal babbling of deaf babies decreases, in contrast to the steady increase in quantity and syllabic variability in hearing babies. The absence of the normal babbling pattern may lead to changes in interaction patterns with hearing parents, and the usual vocal interactive turn-taking may not proceed normally. This impairment of interaction has implications for later social and cognitive development as well as for language development.

Recent research has indicated that 'manual babbling' can be observed in infants exposed to sign languages. All infants move their hands and arms, and those infants exposed to sign languages imitate hand and arm movements. Just as hearing/speaking parents respond with changes in their interaction patterns to syllabic vocal babbling, signing parents respond to manual babbling as if it were intentional communication on the part of the infant. Manual babbling thus provides a motivation for both infant and parent to engage in conversations in the same way as vocal babbling does (Petitto and Marentette 1991).

Early research on child language tended to ignore the role of gesture in the development of language. It is now recognised that gestures are particularly important in early social interaction with adults, and that all children gesture to communicate their wants and interests. There is a well-structured pattern of gesture development, and gestures continue to be used in conjunction with language throughout life. Gestures develop from early expressions of deixis (pointing or otherwise indicating objects or people) to referential gestures (labelling or naming of objects and actions). All children also progress to two-gesture combinations such as *THERE DOLLY*, however, only children exposed to sign language appear to develop combinations of referential gestures (*DOLLY BIG*) (Volterra 1983).

First words and signs

Because of the difference in modality between gestures and words, the transition from pre-linguistic to linguistic communication appears more clearly in the development of spoken language (although the very first words are better interpreted as vocalic gestures or 'proto-words' rather than as true linguistic structures) (Volterra and Caselli 1985). For a child learning sign language, the transition is obscured by the identity of modality between gesture and sign. This led some researchers in the 1980s to claim that sign language is acquired much earlier than spoken language (Prinz and Prinz 1979).

However, research on the development of pointing behaviour in children exposed to sign language provides evidence of discontinuity between gestures and signs, even when they have the same surface forms (Abrahamsen *et al.* 1985). Gestural pointing appears at about 9 months of age and is used independently and as an accompaniment to speech throughout life. Children exposed to sign language initially use pointing to indicate people, objects and locations, as do all children. From about 12 to 18 months of age, however, signing children do not use pointing to refer to people, although they continue to use pointing to refer to objects and locations. Pointing to people returns at around 18 months, but is assimilated to the linguistic requirements of personal pronouns in sign language, and thus has been recategorised as a linguistic, and not gestural, form.

Some studies have reported that children learning to sign have larger vocabularies during the first two years than children learning spoken languages (Ackerman *et al.* 1990). Any such difference is only transitory. Hearing children generally have a lexicon of about ten words at 15 months and 50 words at 20 months; studies of ASL report that children learning to sign have similar-sized lexicons.

It has been suggested that iconicity in sign language might make it easier to acquire signs. As we saw earlier, gestures and signs may appear identical in form and thus difficult to differentiate. Research on ASL has demonstrated however, that children of normal abilities find visually-motivated signs no easier to learn than arbitrary signs. It is also important to remember that signs which appear iconic to an adult may not be iconic to a child: the visual motivation of the sign MILK, which is historically derived from the action of hand-milking a cow, is likely to be opaque to a child growing up in the UK.

Acquisition of grammar

Signs and words also begin to be combined at similar ages. Children acquiring a given language usually go through similar stages of development, with most of the syntax and morphology acquired before starting school, although development of the full use of discourse structures is not completed until the end of the primary school years, and there is evidence that the acquisition of some syntactic structures is also extended through the first ten years of life.

Deaf children acquiring English generally do not follow the normal developmental pattern of acquisition, especially if language acquisition is delayed. Apart from deviant phonology, which can be ascribed to difficulties in hearing sound contrasts, other linguistic areas may also show deviance from normal development. Productive vocabulary often reflects the different language experience of the deaf child: parents may have explicitly taught colour terms, for example (Ackerman *et al.* 1990). The vocabulary is also likely to reflect the child's chronological, rather than linguistic, age, and so may not be comparable to that of a much younger hearing child with the same level of language development. It is beyond the scope of this chapter to discuss in detail the numerous studies of English language development in deaf children. It is important however, to note that any language delay is likely to be associated with some degree of deviance from the normal developmental pattern (Geers *et al.* 1984; Geers and Schick 1988).

Sign language development

There have been a number of studies of normal BSL development from birth to 13 years, which have allowed us to begin to describe milestones in the same way as has been done for English (Harris *et al.* 1989; Kyle *et al.* 1987; Morgan 1996). It should be noted that these studies are based on research with children of deaf parents, who are exposed to BSL from infancy, and that children of parents not fluent in BSL may not be expected to follow exactly the same pattern. However, preliminary evidence from children in hearing families where there are alternative models of sign language from an early age (enrolment in bilingual early intervention programmes with fluent signers in the environment) is that their language development appears identical to that of deaf children of deaf parents. Research on ASL fluency has found no difference between children exposed to ASL from infancy and those exposed from 2 years of age (Mayberry and Eichen 1991).

The aim of the section below is to illuminate for the reader the complexity of BSL structure. Selected linguistic features whose development is characteristic of developmental age bands are described. The terminology used in sign language linguistics is essentially identical to that used in spoken language linguistics, for example, verb inflection, classifiers, pro-forms, etc. In earlier studies of sign languages, sign language specific terms such as 'cherology' ('hand-study') were used, but contemporary sign linguistics has reverted to using standard terminology. For example, 'phonology' ('sound-study') is used to refer to the contrastive elements in signs (handshape, location, etc.) to emphasise that in both spoken and sign languages, linguistic terms refer to underlying structures and not surface forms. The only sign-language-specific terminology is found in descriptions of verbs, where three main classes have been identified: plain verbs (those which do not inflect); agreement verbs (those which inflect for grammatical roles); and spatial verbs (those which inflect for location of objects, and in which classifier handshapes are found). Full explanations of the linguistic terminology used here may be found in Sutton-Spence and Woll (in press).

Stages of BSL acquisition

0–9 months
Babbling and gestures
- As discussed above, within the first 9 months sign babbling and the first copying of sign-related gross motor gestures of parents occur.
- Independent gestures (including those which are sometimes described as the first signs) occur at the end of this period.

9 months – 1;0
Pointing
- Non-linguistic pointing to self, other people and objects appears.

1;0 – 1;5
Pronominal reference, vocabulary
- Pointing to people drops out in this period, although pointing to objects is maintained.
- The first true signs appear at this stage. There is often over-generalisation (e.g. CAR used to refer to cars and buses).

1;6 – 1;11
Pronominal reference
- Linguistic pointing to other people appears.

Morphology
- Verbs appear in the lexicon, but there is no productive verb morphology, with only citation forms of verbs used (i.e. no subject or object agreement in agreement verbs, no use of pro-forms in spatial verbs).
- There is no use of derivational morphology and consequently no morphological distinction between nouns and verbs.

Syntax
- The first two-sign utterances appear.
- In contrast to adult signing, where verb inflection, for example, is used to mark subject and object on agreement verbs, sign order is used to mark semantic relations.

2;0 – 2;5
Phonology
- Phonology differs greatly from that of adult signers, with regular patterns of reductions of contrast and omissions of phonological features. There appears to be a universal pattern of handshape development, with maximally visually contrasting handshapes (e.g. fist, pointing hand, flat hand) appearing first. There has been less

research on location and movement, but it appears that children substitute simple for more complex movements, and often exhibit perseveration in movement. Some research from ASL suggests that sign location within the centre of the child's visual field (e.g. signs made on the face or body) is mastered earlier than signs in the periphery (e.g. signs located on the top of the head).

Pronominal reference
- Pointing to addressee (YOU) appears at about 2 years. Some children show evidence of self/addressee reversal errors (e.g. YOU PICK meaning I PICK).
- Pointing to third person begins slightly later, and by 2;5 first, second and third person are correctly distinguished.

Morphology
- Verbs requiring agreement begin to be used, but are most often produced in citation form, with agreement omitted, or as unanalysed rote forms.
- There is often over-generalisation of the verb inflection rule, with plain verbs inflected, where this is not grammatical in adult BSL.
- The first morphological distinctions between nouns and verbs occur, but the contrast is made incorrectly.

2;6 – 2;11
Morphology
- First appearance of classifiers used in spatial verbs. However these appear to be unanalysed wholes, with no evidence of productive use. These early classifiers often use unmarked or incorrect handshapes.
- Verbs do not yet show morphological marking of manner (either through facial expression or altered movement).
- The first productive use of verb agreement occurs at the beginning of this period.
- Noun/verb pairs are distinguished but this is frequently in non-adult ways, for example, by marking one of the pair with a distinctive facial expression, body posture, or speed of movement.

3;0 – 3;5
Morphology
- Inflection of spatial verbs for movement or manner occurs, but children do not yet combine these. Thus if movement exhibits inflection, manner is signalled separately from the verb.
- The first correct use of classifiers occurs at this stage.
- Verb agreement is mastered in sentences where reference is made to objects present in the environment. However, omission of verb agreement with abstract spatial loci continues until well after 3;0.
- The first correct use of some number and aspect morphemes is found with spatial and agreement verbs.

3;6 – 3;11
Phonology
- Lexical compounds are used, but these are articulated without the characteristic phonological pattern (i.e., both parts of the compound are stressed).

Morphology
- Spatial and agreement verbs now have both movement and manner, but these are produced sequentially rather than simultaneously; towards the end of this period, there is the beginning of co-ordinated usage of both.
- Verb agreement begins to be found with abstract loci, but this occurs without coordinated establishment of referents at those loci.

4;0 – 4;11
Phonology
- Innovative compounds appear, although they are not adult-like either in phonology or in meaning.

Morphology
- Overt establishment of loci associated with referents is still absent in the first part of this stage. A moderate degree of control of the use of abstract loci, including their establishment, use and maintenance, is achieved by 4;11.
- Children still make occasional over-generalisations of verb inflection rules, although agreement with single subject is usually correctly marked.
- The noun-verb distinction is clear, but innovative forms are still seen in addition to correct forms.

5;0 – 5;11
Morphology
- The mastery of most morphology is completed and used with reasonable skill, though the most complex polymorphemic forms still cause difficulty.

Between 6 and 10 years, there is ongoing development of the requirements of narrative. While acquisition of most structures has been completed at the sentence level, the application of grammatical structures to the requirements of narrative, including cohesion, use of narrative role, etc., is still developing during this period.

8;0 – 8;11
Morphology
- The use of classifiers and spatial verbs is largely mastered, although some errors on complex forms are still noted.

9;0 – 9;11
Morphology
- Mastery of the productive use of classifiers and spatial verbs is completed.

The findings described above have not yet been developed into formal assessments and provisions of norms for BSL acquisition. As a result, this section should be regarded as an orientation to the topic, rather than as a checklist for use by teachers, psychologists or speech and language therapists.

Age of acquisition effects

It is often argued that sign language can be learned by deaf children at any age. Although there are no measurable differences in fluency between children exposed to sign language from birth and those exposed to sign language from 2 years onwards, research on ASL has demonstrated that later exposure results in incomplete mastery of grammar. Children who have not acquired fluency in a first language by the age of 5 do not subsequently catch up, either in a signed or spoken language (Mayberry and Eichen 1991; Loncke *et al.* 1990).

Language assessment

The availability of information about normal patterns of BSL development will allow the creation of language assessment tools, closer monitoring of children's progress in learning BSL, and the possibility of identifying children with general language disorders affecting the development of both signed and spoken language.

The recognition that the goal of fluent monolingualism in a spoken language is unattainable for many deaf children has been accompanied by a shift to the ideal of bilingualism in spoken and signed language, and increasingly there have been moves towards bilingual and bicultural education in the UK and other countries. It is clearly important to have some way of monitoring the success of such programmes, and in particular the progress made by children in each of their languages. However, there are as yet no standardised measures which can be used by professionals working with deaf children to assess their developing competence in sign language. This has resulted in either no assessment of sign language or *ad hoc* approaches to assessment.

A survey in 1995 of existing assessment practice in the UK revealed that signing was assessed through a variety of approaches: observations of conversation, adaptations of existing English language tests or adaptations of sign language assessments designed for hearing learners of BSL (Herman, in press). The content of assessment also varies enormously: although there are attempts to code information about vocabulary, grammar or discourse, these are not based on information about developmental progression in the acquisition of these structures.

In general, there is little overlap between what is assessed in different schools and units. Some of this variation arises from different perspectives about sign language and its assessment. In those programmes which describe themselves as bilingual there is a more explicitly recognised need to have norm-referenced tests of BSL based on Deaf language and culture; in those programmes which describe themselves as total communication, there is a greater tendency to perceive assessment of signing as equivalent to assessment of English via a different modality.

It should be recognised that assessment of a deaf child's abilities in English raises other problems. Tests of English are often administered in spoken English accompanied by gestures or signs. On the one hand it is known that administration of test instructions to hearing children in gesture results in poorer scores, and reliance on gesture by deaf children may depress results, even on tests of non-verbal abilities. In contrast, use of accompanying signs or gestures may create falsely high scores (Crittenden *et al.* 1986). In one study test items from the British Picture Vocabulary Scales were translated into BSL and administered to hearing children who knew no sign language (Kirk *et al.* 1990). Of 97 items taken from the BPVS, 19 per cent were correctly guessed by over 80 per cent of the hearing children. Only 24 per cent of items were correctly guessed at chance or less than chance level (25 per cent chance of correctly selecting one picture out of four). In other words only 24 per cent of items could actually be used to test children's knowledge of sign vocabulary.

The unsuitability of translation of test material is due to a number of factors: many vocabulary test items are names of body parts. Signing these requires pointing to or touching the body part. In a test situation, a child would only need to match the indicated body part with the picture: knowledge of BSL would not be assessed. The same is true for many visually-motivated signs, where, for example a gesture to the head might suffice to help the child to correctly select the word 'hat' from the other pictures displayed. The opposite situation can also arise: a single word in English may not be expressed by a single sign in BSL. What may appear to be a simple concept when signed in BSL (e.g. PARALLEL) may be much more complex in English.

An assessment is currently being developed which will provide norms for receptive and productive BSL grammar for children aged 3–11 (Herman *et al.*, in preparation). The assessment is the first to use the findings of BSL acquisition studies as a basis. As with studies of sign language acquisition, by using norms for deaf children of signing deaf parents, the effect of the non-optimal language environments often experienced by deaf children in hearing families can be explored.

There are a number of important additional considerations in the assessment of BSL, which are discussed briefly below.

Bilingualism

The British Deaf community must be regarded as a bilingual community, with individual members exhibiting varying degrees of fluency in BSL, written and spoken English. As in all examples of childhood bilingualism, a variety of factors may affect the course of acquisition and the final levels of fluency. Deaf children's bilingual balance will depend in part on the age of onset and degree of hearing loss. Other factors, such as parental fluencies (signing by hearing parents, speech by deaf parents) and type of educational setting, will also be important.

Because it is possible to produce at least some elements from a sign language and spoken language simultaneously, any analysis needs to include use of either or both languages. It is not known, for example, whether deaf children's early vocabulary consists of pairs of signs and words, or whether children are more likely to have either a sign or a word for a concept, but not both.

There is evidence that bilingual children begin to be able to 'code-switch' (choose one or other language or variety for social reasons) from around 3 years of age. As well as code switching, 'code mixing' or 'interlanguage' is often found. This mixing has been described in early descriptions of signing as occurring along a continuum between BSL and English. This description is no longer considered appropriate, as it is clear that relative fluency in each of the two languages underpins the mix available to any individual signer, and that, for example, the 'sign supported English' (SSE) of a person with a high degree of fluency in BSL and limited skills in English will be different from that of a person with a high degree of fluency in English and limited skills in BSL, although the term SSE is used to describe both (Woll 1994).

Variation

There is substantial lexical variation in BSL, affecting some semantic fields more than others. This poses some potential problems for the design of assessments, but lexical variation has been well described and can be designed into assessments. There is no evidence of systematic regional variation in BSL grammar.

Other issues

One of the main issues in assessing child BSL is the lack of appropriate assessors. Even within bilingual programmes, there is often no individual with bilingual skills: hearing staff may have limited knowledge of BSL and deaf staff may have limited knowledge of English, and neither of these groups may have had any training either in the linguistics of BSL or in the acquisition of BSL. On occasion, language assessments are undertaken by professionals who do not know BSL or who have limited experience of deaf children. Sometimes interpreters are used, which is always unsatisfactory. The variability in language experience of deaf children in both spoken and signed language may also make it difficult to interpret the results of assessments, and in the absence of norms, to distinguish delayed from deviant language.

Summary

Much work remains to be done on language acquisition in deaf children, particularly on the pattern of language development in the context of BSL–English bilingualism, and on the effects of delayed first language acquisition on subsequent linguistic, cognitive and educational achievement. Of equal importance is ensuring the successful communication of the results of such research to educators and others concerned with deaf children's development.

Further reading

Sutton-Spence, R. L. and Woll, B. (in press) *The Linguistics of British Sign Language: An introduction.* Cambridge: Cambridge University Press.
A description of BSL linguistics for the general reader. Although the book does not discuss sign language acquisition, it provides an essential underpinning for those concerned with describing BSL and how it is learned by deaf children.

Volterra, V. and Erting, C. J. (1994) *From Gesture to Language in Hearing and Deaf Children.* Washington, DC: Gallaudet University Press.
An excellent collection of papers originally published in 1990. Following an introductory section on early gesture and language development in hearing children, there are four sections on: deaf children with sign language input; deaf children without sign language input; hearing children with spoken and sign language input, and a final section comparing hearing and deaf children.

Oralism – current policy and practice

Linda Watson

Introduction

The majority of deaf and hearing-impaired children are born to hearing parents. The aim of an oral approach is to teach these children to speak so that they can communicate with their family and the rest of the hearing community into which they have been born. The promotion of intelligible spoken language and the ability to understand spoken language are therefore seen as primary goals of an oral approach, with the assumption that they will then be able to use their development of spoken language both as a language for thought and as a basis for developing literacy skills and achieving access to other curriculum areas.

This concentration on the development of spoken language is seen as broadening deaf children's opportunities by enabling them not only to communicate freely with hearing children and adults but to compete with them on their own terms. It is also seen as offering deaf children a choice later in life. Once having established a sound grasp of spoken language, then they are free to choose whether to communicate exclusively by means of spoken language or whether to learn the language of the deaf community, British Sign Language (BSL). The argument is therefore that they can move freely between the hearing community and the deaf community (i.e. deaf people whose preferred mode of communication is by sign language) and decide where to spend their time. While it could be argued that this aim can be achieved just as easily if deaf children are taught to use sign language as their first language and then learn to talk once the use of sign language has been established, oralists would contend that the best way to promote spoken language is through the use of residual hearing and this must be exploited as soon as possible after birth. Support for this view is drawn from recent work on neural plasticity (Gibson 1997). Similar arguments to those which obtain for the necessity to perform cochlear implants at an early age are used by oralists for the promotion of the early use of residual hearing.

Terminology and definitions

The term 'oralism' can be used to encompass several different teaching approaches. The maternal reflective approach (van Uden 1977) is one oral approach which has been adopted by some schools in the UK, notably St John's, Boston Spa. This approach is based upon conversational interaction between the deaf child and a more mature language user. The initial conversation is used as a 'deposit' for discussion and analysis of grammatical structure. A central role is given within the approach to the use of the written form of language to support the development of spoken language. A second oral approach is what can be described as 'structured oralism'. This is not a clearly defined approach, but can be used as an umbrella term to cover both attempts to teach language structure directly and attempts to control the language structures to which a young deaf child in the process of language acquisition is exposed, for example the Guidelines scheme (Ingall 1980).

In addition to the examples outlined above, there have been many other approaches which have been developed. In fact, many teachers of the deaf, lacking a precise methodology to follow, have developed their own strategies, often using elements of other approaches. Examples of this would be the use of written material to support the learning of spoken language borrowed from the maternal reflective approach, but lacking the precision of implementation which comes from training in the approach, or attempts to teach structure which are not based on developmental principles.

The emergence of such idiosyncratic teaching practices makes it impossible to speak in terms of an established oral approach, or approaches. Nevertheless, a new and distinctive oral approach has evolved which, while sharing the aim of more established approaches, namely the promotion of spoken language as the deaf child's primary means of communication, differs from them in several ways. This new approach draws on advances in hearing aid technology and in understanding of the process of language acquisition in young hearing children.

In the early 1980s, a group of oralist teachers of the deaf met because they seemed to be using similar strategies, although these had not been recognised as an approach. These teachers formed the National Aural Group (NAG). They described the method they were using initially as 'natural oralism' (Harrison 1980), then gradually changed to 'natural auralism'. The word 'aural' indicated the emphasis given to the use of residual hearing, while 'natural' was seen as describing the approach to language development. Drawing on the work of writers such as Brown (1973), Wells (1986a and b) and others who have described the process of language acquisition in hearing children, the aim is to replicate for deaf children those conditions which have been identified as being facilitative in encouraging language development in young hearing children. Parents are encouraged to engage their child in meaningful conversational exchanges; to use features of motherese; to refrain from any attempt to force the child to talk or imitate while responding positively to every attempt at vocalisation made by the child (Lewis and Richards 1988).

As with any educational approach, it is interpreted and applied differently by different practitioners. The term 'natural aural' has been widely adopted and used to describe all oral approaches, whether they uphold the basic tenets of natural auralism as originally conceived or not. The use of the term 'natural' has come to be regarded by some proponents of this approach as unhelpful since it is open to misinterpretation, and so the terms oral/aural or auditory/oral have come to be used as alternatives. The National Aural Group has also changed its name to Deaf Education Through Listening and Talking

(DELTA), in order to put across the approach in a less ambiguous way.

The emphasis on the use of residual hearing has been assisted by advances in audiology and technology which have led to improvements in early detection and accurate diagnosis of hearing loss, and major advances in hearing aid design and performance (Smith 1997). The applicability of the approach is not considered to be restricted to those children with easily identifiable residual hearing. No child is precluded from the approach on the grounds of being too deaf. Lip-reading is not denied, which gives the opportunity for those children who are unable to comprehend using hearing alone to gain additional information from lip-reading and natural gesture. No emphasis, however, is placed on lip-reading and there is always concern that as far as possible audition should take precedence over vision for the child (Clark 1989).

Recent developments in hearing aid technology have meant that the residual hearing of even profoundly deaf children can be made accessible, demonstrated by improved levels of aided thresholds. Output limitation measures on hearing aids and more accurate assessments both of loudness discomfort levels and tolerance problems in children yield the possibility of exploiting residual hearing to the full while decreasing the likelihood of rejection of the hearing aids on the grounds of discomfort (Smith 1997). The increasing use of cochlear implants with very young profoundly deaf children and the impressive aided threshold levels of many of these children, post implantation, makes the approach viable for children from the whole range of degree of hearing loss.

Natural auralism in practice

This oral/aural or natural aural approach should be seen as quite distinct from traditional forms of oralism. There is no place within the approach for some language teaching practices which were widely used within traditional oralism, for example enforced repetition of either words or sentences, or the inculcation of language structure rules. Within an oral/aural approach, the emphasis is placed on the exchange of meaning, and the rules and structures of language are assumed to be gradually learnt by the child through experiment in use, in much the same way that a young hearing child gradually learns the rules of language (Wells 1986b). Meta-linguistic awareness is seen as a helpful way of analysing language that has already been acquired in the spoken form and encouraging reflection thereon. This is in keeping with recent initiatives in the UK aimed at raising standards of achievement, for example the National Literacy Project (DfEE 1997c), but is different from the 'reflection' advocated by van Uden (1977). Andrews (1988) gives a clear account of the similarities and differences between the maternal reflective approach and natural auralism.

Other tenets of traditional oral approaches such as the structured teaching of speech sounds are also precluded. Careful attention is paid to maintaining hearing aids in peak working order and ensuring that they are worn consistently throughout the day, and every attempt is made to provide favourable listening conditions. Having taken these measures, it is assumed that deaf children can utilise their hearing via hearing aids in order to develop the sounds of speech. Correction of speech sounds while the child is learning to talk is restricted to encouragement to listen carefully. At a much later stage, once language is well established, it may prove desirable to work with the pupil on improving their sound system, but only in a minority of cases. The emphasis would always be, in the first instance, on providing the most appropriate amplification and expecting the child to use this in order to develop intelligible spoken language, assisted by the use of lip-reading (or face-reading as it is sometimes called) as necessary. Since the emphasis is on the use of hearing, adults working within this approach, while they would ensure that they had gained the child's attention prior to speaking (that is to say they would ensure that the child could hear them), would not see it as essential to gain the child's visual attention, but would leave the child to watch as necessary. The reliance on lip-reading varies from child to child, and this would be appreciated and taken into account by the adults working with that child, as would the child's level of development of attending skills (Reynell 1977). The emphasis on the provision of appropriate hearing aids and favourable listening conditions is coupled with the promotion of active listening skills, encouraging the child to develop strategies for using their residual hearing to support their learning.

A further tenet of the approach is the promotion of an attitude towards communication in which the child is encouraged to be an active participant in attempting to receive and express meaning, using clues from context and their wider knowledge of the world to assist in the process. This active involvement of the child in the communication process should translate into an active approach towards general learning in educational contexts.

Issues and implications

Early diagnosis is seen as highly desirable, followed as quickly as possible by the fitting of hearing aids and support for the family from a teacher of the deaf in order to promote the development of spoken language (Carr 1997). The introduction of universal neonatal screening raises the possibility of widespread fitting of hearing aids to very young deaf babies, within weeks of birth (Watkin 1997). This prospect is seen as both exciting and challenging. It demands that teachers of the deaf who work with these babies and their families should have an understanding both of the nature of early interaction between hearing babies and their parents which leads to the development of spoken language and also of how to promote this early interaction between hearing parents and their deaf babies.

As the average age of diagnosis of deafness in young children has decreased over the years, so teachers of the deaf have become accustomed to working with younger and younger children. However, it is a very different matter to be faced with a very young baby (Watkin (1997) reported a median age of referral to the educational support services of children with severe or profound losses of 11 weeks) from working with an older preschool child or even a baby approaching one year of age, which has been the norm. For a hearing baby in the early stages of developing spoken language, the whole context of an action conveys the meaning. Thus, the total routine of bath time, for example, with its attendant sensations, smells and verbal comments becomes assimilated and gradually the child begins to understand and then use the associated language. The importance of the interactional context for the promotion of language development in young deaf children (described by Wood *et al.* (1986)) and the necessity of providing 'highly processible input' (Nelson *et al.* 1993) have come to be recognised by teachers of the deaf working with young deaf children, and the advice and support offered to parents reflects this understanding.

The situation for a very young deaf baby is not so readily apparent. The role of audition in the development of communication prior to the emergence of spoken language in hearing babies, and thus the advice that should be given to parents of very young deaf babies who are seeking to promote the development of spoken language through the use of residual hearing, is new territory. The implications of the nature of very early communication between hearing babies and their caregivers needs to be explored. It is clear, for example, that hearing babies gesture before they speak and this fact needs to be borne in mind when working with deaf babies. Paul and Quigley (1994), after stating that 'it is extremely difficult to interpret the language performance of children, especially in the early stages of development' (p. 99), give a concise summary of some of the research in this area. In addition, Gallaway (this volume) considers the nature of early interaction. There is an issue here for those working with deaf babies and their families. While spoken language is the ultimate aim, it must always be borne in mind that the purpose is communication and for young babies there are many aspects to a communicative act. Paul and Quigley (1994, p. 105) discuss some major aspects of the pre-linguistic period and highlight not only the lengthy period of very sensitive listening which precedes the development of spoken language but also the development of mutual eye gazing. The importance of focusing on the transfer of meaning has been emphasised in work with older preschool deaf children. The means of fostering communication which will lead to spoken language in very young deaf babies are uncharted waters. It is an area in which teachers of the deaf who are working within an oral/aural philosophy will require in-service training. The opportunity afforded by very early diagnosis of stimulating residual hearing in very young deaf babies must be maximised, but there is a pitfall to be avoided. Too narrow a focus on the exploitation of hearing without placing it in the wider context of communication could disrupt the normal pattern of interaction between any new-born baby and their parents which leads to the development of early communication and ultimately of spoken language.

The increasingly early diagnosis of deafness in babies, with the opportunity for teachers of the deaf to work with babies and their families from a very young age, comes at a time in the UK when the budget for specialist teaching and support services has been cut. In some areas of the country this has resulted in a reduction in, or complete withdrawal of, services for preschool deaf children and their families, particularly under the age of 2 years, which is currently non-statutory provision.

Audiological support

The stress on the importance of the provision of appropriate hearing aids which are maintained in good working order at all times, which is a fundamental principle of a modern oral/aural approach, poses a particular challenge for supporting the large numbers of pupils who are being educated in mainstream schools, without a specialist facility for the hearing-impaired. In the school context there is other amplifying equipment in addition to personal hearing aids, for example radio hearing aids, which require maintenance. For these pupils, who rely so heavily on their hearing aids and other amplifying equipment in order to access the curriculum, it is essential that a reliable system for managing and maintaining equipment is implemented (Lewis and Lyon 1997). The issue of ensuring that all equipment is working optimally becomes a challenge for all those involved with these pupils.

Language and curriculum issues

Following the diagnosis of deafness and initial fitting of hearing aids there may be several months of listening and assimilating prior to the production of the child's first words. Modern oral/aural approaches allow for this, recognising the child's need to acclimatise to wearing hearing aids and then to learn to listen. Once the child makes a start at language development, it is anticipated that progress will speed up. The result of this relatively slow start may mean that the deaf child enters school with a level of spoken language development that is considerably delayed by comparison with hearing peers. The challenge is to enable the deaf child to access the curriculum and ensure that concepts are grasped. This will mean presenting concepts and ideas in language which is easily understood by the child while ensuring that the concepts themselves have not been simplified. The curriculum given to deaf children must be cognitively challenging. This balance between ensuring comprehension without compromising ideas can be difficult to strike.

Dilemmas

It is widely, although not universally, recognised among professionals working within an oral/aural approach that there is a minority of deaf children for whom this approach is not the most appropriate. The reasons for this are not always readily apparent and may be complex. The degree of hearing loss, which may seem the obvious cause, while relevant, is not often the determining factor in the applicability of the approach. As mentioned above, improvements in hearing aid technology in recent years have increased the viability of the oral/aural approach, although it does require a commitment on the part of all those involved with the child to ensuring that hearing aids are in good working order and used effectively.

While professionals would not want a child to continue with an oral/aural approach if the approach was not going to succeed, neither will they want to be too quick to abandon an approach within which it is recognised that progress may be slow in the initial stages, if it appears that the child will acquire both intelligible spoken language and the ability to use language as a tool for thought and access to the curriculum given sufficient time and opportunity. There is therefore a dilemma, which can lead to tension, between the desire to ensure that no child is left without a language for communication and thought and which will enable access to the curriculum, and the reluctance to relinquish too readily an approach which will allow the child easy communication with the hearing world. Professionals who favour the use of an oral/aural approach frequently feel under pressure to achieve a high degree of proficiency in spoken language in the deaf child prior to entry to school, although this may not be realistic. The onus lies with the teachers of the deaf working with young deaf pupils to monitor progress carefully, particularly in relation to the development of comprehension and expression of spoken language. Since it takes time for young deaf children to learn to respond, they need to be allowed an adequate period of time following the provision and fitting of appropriate hearing aids, consistently worn within a stimulating language environment, to show whether they are going to respond to the approach. Initially, especially if the diagnosis has been made relatively late, they may be more dependent on vision than hearing but gradually the emphasis will shift, in much the same way as Tait (1994) has documented, for children following cochlear implants. It is not therefore considered desirable to decide on the most appropriate communication approach for young deaf children by observing their preference for audition or vision until they have had adequate opportunity to develop the use of their residual hearing.

Use of sign

The rise in recent years in the use of sign language, in the form of both Manually Coded English (MCE) and British Sign Language (BSL) in the education of deaf children and the increased interest in the use of sign in the population at large and in the media, has led to greater awareness of sign language and signing issues. This has proved relevant to professionals working within an oral/aural approach in several ways. Pressure is often brought to bear, by other professionals, to introduce the use of some form of signing system where progress in spoken language development is deemed to be slow in the early stages, even if the parents have expressed a strong desire that the child should be educated orally.

In the current climate, the decision regarding the communication approach to use with a young deaf child should be made by the parents, with advice and support offered by professionals, both in making and implementing that decision. This means that it is no longer acceptable for a local service for the hearing-impaired to adopt a 'blanket' communication policy or to advise parents in such a way that they feel that they have no option but to follow that advice. Parents are now much more likely to question advice offered by any professional on any subject than was previously the case.

A small minority of parents who have chosen an oral/aural approach to communication for their child, have themselves introduced some basic signs alongside the oral/aural approach to ease communication at home in the early years. While the use of natural gesture has been encouraged by those using an oral/aural approach, particularly in the early stages of language development, the use of any formal sign system has no place within natural auralism.

A flexible approach to oral language communication, which includes a high degree of responsiveness to the child's contribution and a relaxed attitude to communication with the use of gesture as necessary, has been found to be facilitative in encouraging the development of spoken language in deaf children (Montanini-Manfredi 1993). However, there is concern that the use of sign language will encourage the deaf child to begin to rely more on vision than on audition, thus making the implementation of an oral/aural approach more difficult. In the early stages it is acknowledged that it is no mean task to encourage young profoundly deaf children to learn to listen and use their aided hearing, but the goal is a long-term one and the eventual result of being able to converse readily within the hearing world using intelligible speech and language is seen as worth striving for.

Conclusion

This is an exciting time for those working within the oral/aural approach to deaf education. The advances in hearing aid technology, the increasingly early diagnosis of many deaf babies and the possibilities extended by the more widespread use of cochlear implants, especially with very young deaf children, together with the benefits of greater understanding of the way in which children learn to speak, mean that there exists for the first time a real opportunity to enable deaf children to develop spoken language.

The major issue facing professionals who wish to promote the new form of oralism is to demonstrate that the new oral/aural approach is fundamentally different from traditional oral approaches which served many pupils well but left others without any form of functional language. While being ready to identify those children for whom it is not proving to be a viable way forward, there needs to be a demonstration, supported by rigorous research, that an oral/aural approach can mean the possibility of deaf children developing not only intelligible speech and language, which will facilitate easy communication within the hearing world, but also a level of language development which will serve as a language for thought and will enable access to all areas of the curriculum.

Chapter 2.4

'Total Communication' – current policy and practice

Rob Baker and Pamela Knight

Introduction

This chapter outlines the origins of the term 'Total Communication' and its ambiguous interpretation in the educational context. Problems of implementation are discussed and a number of surveys of communication policies and practices in the UK are summarised. Finally a recent survey by the authors is described investigating current interpretations of the term 'Total Communication' in schools and units in the UK.

Origins

The term 'Total Communication', as used in the education of deaf children, originated in the USA in the late 1960s, although the term appears to have been borrowed from the anthropologist, Margaret Mead (1964). In the anthropological context it referred to the whole gamut of linguistic and paralinguistic behaviours and cultural rules that hold a society together across generations.

The most famous formulation of Total Communication in relation to communication with deaf children comes from Denton (1976), Superintendent of the Maryland School for the Deaf. In Denton's paper, moreover, we find an early instance of ambiguity in the use of the term. Denton's first and best known description reads: 'Total Communication includes the full spectrum of language modes, child-devised gestures, the language of signs, speech, speech reading, finger spelling, reading and writing' (Denton 1976, p. 4).

However two pages on we read: 'In regard to the day to day practical aspects of Total Communication, the concept simply means that, in so far as possible, those persons within the child's immediate environment should talk and sign simultaneously' (Denton 1976, p. 6). There is a shift here from a liberal philosophical stance to a recommendation for a method, which itself recalls a much earlier concept of speaking and signing together, the 'combined system', a term used by Edward Miner Gallaudet, the first President of Gallaudet College (Lane 1984). The 'combined system' itself has its precursor in the systematised method of simultaneous signing and speaking promoted by the Abbé de l'Epée in eighteenth century France (Lane 1984).

Implementation

The identification of Total Communication (henceforth TC) with the combined system proliferated in the 1970s (e.g. Klopping 1972; White and Stevenson 1975) as well as the notion of 'systematising' sign language for educational use, for example 'The manual component of total communication should be a standardized and systematized version of the sign language already in use by deaf adults' (Verney 1976, cited in Evans 1982, p. 19). The notion of TC as a method rather than a philosophy continued into the 1980s, both in the US (Caccamise and Newell 1984) and the UK. Moore, a head teacher of a school for the deaf, speaking at a British Deaf Association (BDA) residential seminar on TC in 1983, asked: 'How can we ensure that staff are competent to understand and carry out such a teaching method ?' (British Deaf Association 1983, p. 2).

Meanwhile a few voices consistently called for acknowledgement of the role of sign language *per se* as a component of the full spectrum of language modes within a TC philosophy:

> If total communication is to be what it claims to be, then it must include in its total more than just American English and all the many ways of coding it in visual symbols. Total Communication as a force in the education of the deaf must include the knowledge and use of sign (Stokoe 1972, cited in Evans 1982, p. 14).

Evans, then a head teacher at a school for the deaf, speaking at the aforementioned BDA seminar, called for an 'authoritative study of the terminology of Total Communication' (BDA 1983), an enterprise to which he had already made a substantial contribution (Evans 1982). Ambiguity over the term persisted, especially in Scotland: 'Today ... schools use Total Communication, the method which employs a synthesis of oral and manual skills' (Montgomery 1986, p. 27).

Evans (1982) indicates that there are external factors that have favoured the narrow interpretation of TC. First, hearing adults, whether teachers or parents, are likely to 'have difficulty with sign language structure and will adapt signs to English structure' (Evans 1982, p. 73). Evans nevertheless states clearly that the philosophical outlook originally intended by TC will require that 'if the total communication philosophy advocates an eventual choice for deaf people (to use sign language, Signed-English (SE) or both), then its methodology must provide scope for an option' (Evans 1982, p. 107). Secondly, in recommending the use of a natural language as early as possible in the development of the deaf child and implying that natural sign language may best fulfil this role, Evans nevertheless recognises this as a potential barrier to the predominantly hearing parents of deaf children: 'It is one thing to advocate early exposure to signing; it is quite another proposition to expect all parents of young deaf children to sign fluently' (Evans 1982, p. 116). This seems like an impasse.

Criticism

A breakthrough of sorts occurred in the 1980s when researchers began to question the communicative and educational efficacy of TC as a method. In the early stages of implementation in schools in the 1970s simultaneous signing and speaking had occasioned a general sense of relief amongst educators that, after decades of dogmatic oralism, communication was at last taking place. It was no longer a choice between oral and manual methods, which earlier in this century had caused a historic rift between educational and social services for deaf people; instead we now seemingly had a perfect compromise which suited parents, teachers, social workers and, on the face of it, deaf people. Evidence for the relative success of the new compromise was not hard to find. Morris (1986), for example, cited his own research of 1979–80 which found significantly enhanced expressive and receptive communication skills, coupled with improved social–emotional adjustment in children in a school with a TC approach, compared with an orally taught group in the same school a year earlier. The children were matched for age, hearing loss, non-verbal IQ and socio-economic status.

During the 1970s a plethora of systems had been developed, especially in the USA, in attempts to optimise the combination of sign and speech (Quigley and Paul 1984). The main factor distinguishing, for example, Seeing Essential English (SEE1) from Signing Exact English (SEE2) or Linguistics of Visual English (LOVE) appears to be the extent to which each method seeks to provide manual represention for English inflectional and derivational morphology. However, none of these systems seemed to be delivering the promised benefits in terms of academic attainment (Maxwell 1992). A seminal paper by Johnson *et al.* (1989) drew together much of the research and presents a ruthless indictment of 'Sign Supported Speech' (as they now termed it) as 'crypto-oralism'. Criticisms were framed in terms of the mismatch between the signed and spoken messages, with the signed message frequently being incomplete or even contradictory to the spoken message, and the spoken message itself delivered at an unnatural speech rate. In addition it had been found that teachers using what was now coming to be known as SimCom spoke in an unidiomatic fashion and avoided saying things that they did not know how to sign, resulting in arbitrary constraints on the delivery of the curriculum (Newton 1985). Such findings, together with the difficulties hearing people are said to experience in acquiring fluent sign language skills, suggest that the 'Total' of Total Communication means 'the best we can do in the circumstances'.

There are two main responses to these criticisms. The first is to seek ways of improving the practice of simultaneous communication, with the most interesting contributions coming from deaf and hearing-impaired expert users of this method, e.g. Newell *et al.* (1990). Their recommendations primarily focus on optimising the visual natural-sign-language-based aspects of simultaneous communication (SC):

This data would indicate that *effective* [authors' italics] SC is primarily sign driven: that is an effective SC communicator must have thorough knowledge of and automatic recall for the 'appropriate' sign(s) as well as have command of grammatical/ inflectional devices of ASL (Newell *et al.* 1990, p. 409).

A radical alternative would be to abandon the attempt to reconcile two divergent languages in a hybrid form and work towards a bilingual approach where sign language and English each has a role but they are separated (Bouvet 1990, and Chapter 2.5 this volume). Either of these courses of action will have considerable implications for staff development and both are likely to require an increased involvement of deaf adults in education.

Total Communication in the UK

An investigation of actual practice in the education of deaf children may help to identify trends in either of these two directions, i.e. whether towards enhancing SimCom as a method or towards including bilingual approaches in the context of a TC philosphy. In 1980 Jordan conducted a survey of Scottish and English classes in schools for the deaf and partially hearing units (Jordan 1986). At this time 58 per cent of primary classes in schools for the deaf reported using oral methods alone and 40 per cent reported using TC. Sixty-five per cent of secondary classes in schools for the deaf used oral methods and 35 per cent used TC. Jordan found a striking difference between Scottish and English secondary classes such that the majority (55 per cent) of Scottish secondary classes were using TC, compared with 30 per cent in England. It appears that the TC 'revolution' (at least in its narrow sense) took place earlier and with greater fervour in Scotland. Another major difference in the study was between schools and units, with only 9 per cent of primary unit classes and 7 per cent of secondary unit classes using TC.

Jordan's study also revealed an interesting trend. All schools and units were asked whether they had recently implemented changes in communication policy. Of the 39 changes reported 36 were from oral methods to TC. The continuation of this trend, at least in schools for the deaf, is confirmed in data from the RNID, collected in 1983 (RNID 1984) By this time 57 per cent of schools for the deaf in Britain claimed to be using TC, as against 9 per cent of units.

In 1989 Child (1991) surveyed all the remaining schools for the deaf in the UK (reduced from 75 in 1980 to 56 in 1983 and 40 in 1989). Of the schools in Child's study 21 (53 per cent) were using TC only, 11 (28 per cent) were using both TC and oral methods, and eight (20 per cent) were using oral methods only. A more direct comparison with Jordan's data (assuming relatively uniform class sizes across schools) was made by calculating the proportion of pupils using oral methods or TC. Now we see that the pupils using TC in primary classes in special schools has risen from 40 per cent (Jordan's data) to 69 per cent, and in secondary classes from 35 per cent to 54 per cent. Child considered that the trend towards TC had been maintained.

The survey

The current NDCS Directory (National Deaf Children's Society 1996a), used for the study described below, lists all special schools and units in the UK providing education for deaf and hearing-impaired children. 'Unit' is a general term used by NDCS to cover a range of degrees of integration of hearing and deaf/hearing-impaired children. All schools and units were asked to specify their communication policies. Of the surviving 31 schools, 15 (48 per cent) specified TC, seven (23 per cent) specified oral only, four (13 per cent) specified bilingual, and five (16 per cent) declined to specify. Of the 468 units, 104 (22 per cent) specified TC, 129 (28 per cent) specified oral only, 15 (3 per cent) specified bilingual (to which should perhaps be added four of the TC units which specified bilingual in addition), and 220 (48 per cent) declined to specify. We see here the continuing shrinking of the special school sector, balanced by an increase in units, but with use of TC increasing steadily in both sectors, thus enabling us to reject purely demographic factors (i.e. the shift of children from schools to units) in the trend towards TC in provision for deaf pupils. We also see a number of institutions stating a bilingual policy. The study reported below sets out to examine further the situation in the late 1990s.

Method

All 15 schools and 104 units specifying a TC policy in the 1996 NDCS Directory were circulated with a short questionnaire (Appendix 1). The questionnaire is in two parts, the first asking respondents to select from three definitions of Total Communication. The first of these is Denton's 1976 definition, chosen for its wide currency over many years, the second a simplistic description of simultaneous communication, and the third was taken from a statement on communication policy from Leeds LEA's Deaf and Hearing Impaired Support Service (Leeds Local Education Authority 1995). This last definition specifically refers to a 'philosophy' and explicitly bases the choice of methods on the needs of individual children and identifies specific language use.

The second part of the questionnaire asks schools and units to quantify impressionistically the extent of their use of four different communication options with deaf and hearing-impaired children: Spoken English without sign, British Sign Language without voice (BSL), Sign-Supported English (SSE), and Signed English (SE). Further definition of these terms was not provided on the assumption that they would be familiar to the respondents. This part of the questionnaire was intended as a follow-up to Baker and Child's (1993) in-depth study of communication methods in a small sample of British schools for the deaf, and also to furnish a cross-reference with the institutions' preferred definitions of TC.

Results

In total 88 questionnaires were returned, of which three were incompletely filled in and accordingly omitted from the analysis, leaving a percentage return rate of 71 per cent. Thirteen out of the 15 schools for the deaf responded (87 per cent), and 72 of the 104 units (69 per cent). Table 2.4:1 shows the institutions' chosen definitions of TC.

Table 2.4:1 Schools' and units' preferred definitions of Total Communication

	Denton's definition	Speaking and signing at the same time	Leeds LEA's definition	Alternative definition
Schools (n = 13)	1	–	10	1
Units (n = 72)	16	–	55	1
Total	17	–	65	2

Overall 20 per cent (8 per cent of schools and 22 per cent of units) selected Denton's definition. No respondent selected the simplistic definition, an encouraging result in itself. The majority of both schools and units (78 per cent and 76 per cent respectively) preferred the Leeds definition, a clear preference for an approach based on individual needs. In addition two schools commented that they now rarely or never use the term TC and have moved over to a bilingual policy (adding to the four schools and 19 units already specifying bilingual policy in the NDCS Directory). One school and one unit showed no preference for any of the given definitions and provided an alternative (alternative definitions in Appendix 2). Three schools (including one that did not select a definition) and one unit supplied documentation clarifying their policies.

The results for the four communication options are shown in Table 2.54:2.

Table 2.4:2 Stated extent of use (%) of four communication options in schools and units

		Never	Occasionally	Regularly	Always
Spoken English without sign	Schools	30.8	53.8	15.4	–
	Units	9.7	33.3	47.2	9.7
BSL without voice	Schools	15.4	15.4	69.2	–
	Units	29.2	38.9	29.2	2.8
Sign Supported English (SSE)	Schools	7.7	–	76.9	15.4
	Units	6.9	6.9	63.9	22.2
Signed English (SE)	Schools	15.4	23.1	46.2	15.4
	Units	37.5	34.7	23.6	4.2

Schools for the deaf are less likely to be using Spoken English without sign regularly and more likely to be using BSL without voice regularly, with units presenting a mirror image, most probably reflecting the demographic trends that are influencing placement in schools for the deaf and in units. The dominance of SSE is evident both in schools and in units. The demise of Signed English is more evident in units than in schools.

It is important to add that a significant proportion of the respondents modified the wording of the second part of the questionnaire in order to emphasise that choice of communication method is influenced both by individual children's needs (amended by two schools and 12 units) and by the demands of the communication situation (amended by two schools and 25 units). Assuming that these are not mere policy slogans, this reflects an increasingly sophisticated and differentiated approach to TC.

Table 2.4:2 can be compared, albeit as a rather rough measure, with Table 2.4:3, adapted from Baker and Child's 1993 study of nine schools for the deaf professing a TC policy and their use of each communication option in 15 selected communication situations, covering a range of more and less formal academic and social settings.

Table 2.4:3 Overall use (%) of four communication options found by Baker and Child (1993) in a sample of schools for the deaf

	Spoken English alone	BSL	SSE	SE
Overall percentage use in 15 school situations	18	43	66	22

Tables 2.4:2 and 2.4:3 provide evidence of the continuing dominance of SSE. There is also evidence in the present study of increased awareness and use of BSL with over 70 per cent of total respondents (85 per cent of schools and 68 per cent of units) using it occasionally or regularly. Use of Spoken English without sign also appears to show an increase from the earlier study to the present one, perhaps indicating a growing awareness that spoken and signed methods of communication each have a place in an overarching philosophy of TC.

Cross-tabulation of the two preferred definitions of TC with the four communication options reveals the following tendencies:

1. Preferred TC definition in relation to use of Spoken English without sign

Respondents selecting the Denton definition are more likely to use Spoken English without sign either occasionally or regularly (94 per cent in total) than those selecting the Leeds definition (77 per cent). Respondents selecting the Leeds definition are more likely to never use Spoken English without sign (15 per cent) than those selecting the Denton definition (0 per cent).

2. Preferred TC definition in relation to use of BSL without voice

Respondents selecting the Denton definition are more likely to never use BSL without voice (67 per cent) than those selecting the Leeds definition (17 per cent). Respondents selecting the Leeds definition are more likely to use BSL without voice occasionally or regularly (80 per cent in total) than those selecting the Denton definition (33 per cent in total).

3. Preferred TC definition in relation to use of SSE
Respondents selecting the Leeds definition are more likely to use SSE regularly or always (93 per cent in total) than those selecting the Denton definition (73 per cent in total).

4. Preferred TC definition in relation to use of SE
Respondents selecting the Denton definition are more likely to use SE regularly or always (53 per cent) than those selecting the Leeds definition (29 per cent). This is particularly the case with units (57 per cent of units selecting the Denton definition use SE regularly or always, compared to 21 per cent of Units selecting the Leeds definition). There are no other notable differences between schools and units in these tendencies.

Overall, greater use of both BSL and SSE and lesser use of Spoken English and SE is associated with the Leeds definition, indicating a connection between policy and practice in terms of a move towards more child-centred approaches and reduced emphasis on English-based communication methods.

Cross-tabulations within the four communication options also provide some hints about the mix of options. For example:

1. Only 48 per cent of those who never use BSL without voice, regularly use SSE, compared to 80 per cent of those who regularly use BSL without voice.
2. Fifty-four per cent of those who never use Spoken English without sign, regularly use BSL without voice, compared to only 39 per cent of those who regularly use Spoken English without sign.
3. Eighty per cent of those who occasionally use SSE, regularly use Spoken English without sign, compared to only 45 per cent of those who regularly use SSE.

These results are consistent with the results of the cross-tabulations of communication options with selected definitions of TC. Overall, the increased use of SSE is associated with increased use of BSL and decreased use of Spoken English.

Conclusions and discussion

The trend towards TC as a policy (as identified in the latest NDCS Directory) has continued over three decades in spite of major shifts in the educational placement of deaf and hearing-impaired children. The preference expressed by our questionnaire respondents for the more philosophical and explicitly child-centred definition of the three choices offered may be taken to indicate an increasingly sophisticated understanding of the term TC. If this is so, then the results of the cross-tabulations above suggest a growing trend towards more sign-based (SSE and BSL) and less English-based (SE and Spoken English) approaches, and a small but steady trend towards claiming a bilingual approach.

The fact that many institutions supplied more detailed information on their policy and practice than our simplistic questionnaire allowed reflects a growing awareness of the need to develop policy and evaluate it in practice. It also helps point out the direction for further research. Possible research questions are:

1. What are the factors in individual children and in actual communication settings that influence the choice of a particular communication method?
2. Are teachers actually able to meet the needs of all children in all situations, and if not, what are the training needs and staffing implications?

Results of the present study build on the work begun by Baker and Child (1993) and set the context for further investigations.

Further reading

Baker, R. and Child, D (1993) 'Communication approaches used in schools for the deaf in the UK: a follow-up study', *Journal of the British Association of Teachers of the Deaf* 17 (2) 36–47.
This article summarises previous research on the use of TC in schools for the deaf. The current chapter built upon this initial research.

Evans, L. (1982) *Total Communication: Structure and Strategy.* Washington, DC: Gallaudet College Press.
This book gives a thorough overview of the emergence of the term TC in both the USA and UK and subsequent definitions and practice.

Lynas, W. (1994) *Communication Options in the Education of Deaf Children.* London: Whurr Publishers.
This book aims to offer an overview of the 'communication debate'. Chapter 3 considers the case for, and an evaluation of, TC.

Appendix 1

The Questionnaire: What is Total Communication?

Below are three statements that have been used when discussing the term 'Total Communication'.

Please tick which of the statements best reflects your school's/unit's understanding of the term 'Total Communication'. If you feel that none of them truly reflects your School's/Unit's view, please feel free to supply an alternative definition in the space provided.

1. Total Communication comprises the full spectrum of language modes, child-devised gesture, the language of signs, speech reading, finger spelling, reading and writing, and the development of residual hearing for the enhancement of speech and speech reading skills

2. Total Communication is the simultaneous use of speech and signing

3. Total Communication is a philosophy in which the methods of communication used with the child are based on the needs of the child as appropriately assessed. The methods can include those based on English, e.g. speech, lip-reading, reading, writing, amplification of residual hearing and sign support systems such as Signed English and Sign Supported English. Other methods used are based on British Sign Language as a language for classroom instruction and for linguistic and cognitive development as well as for social interaction

Space for an alternative definition, if desired:

In the table below a range of communication options are presented. Please indicate the extent of their use by specialist teachers of the deaf with deaf children at your school/unit.

	Always	Regularly	Occasionally	Never
Spoken English without sign				
BSL without voice				
Sign-Supported English (SSE)				
Signed English (SE)				

Any other comments (continue overleaf if required)

Thank you for your co-operation.
Please return the completed questionnaire in the stamped addressed envelope supplied.

Appendix 2

Alternative definitions of Total Communication offered by two institutions

1. 'Total Communication is a philosophy which allows deaf and hearing people to communicate with each other by whatever means is available. It is not a methodology! It is the philosophical interface between two disparate linguistic groups.'

2. 'Total communication is a philosophy in which the methods of communication used with the child are based on the needs of the child as appropriately assessed. TC comprises the full spectrum of language modes, child-devised gesture, the language of signs, speech reading, finger spelling, reading and writing, and the development of residual hearing for the enhancement of speech and speech reading skills' (i.e. a combination of Denton's and the Leeds' definitions).

Bilingualism – current policy and practice

Miranda Pickersgill

Introduction

The sign bilingual approach to meeting the communicative and educational needs of deaf children is a developing area in educational thinking and practice. Our increasing understanding of the nature of sign bilingualism has implications for developing policy and practice in both inclusive (or integrated) and segregated settings. This chapter will explore a current definition of sign bilingualism and the subsequent challenges it presents to educators. Consideration will be given to existing bilingual and education programmes. Ongoing developments and current research will be described and indications given as to future practice.

What is sign bilingualism?

Sign bilingualism is an approach to the education of deaf children, which uses both the sign language of the Deaf Community and the spoken and written language of the hearing community. In the UK, this is British Sign Language (BSL), English and, for some families, other spoken languages.

The development of sign bilingual policies and practices has been supported by significant research findings:

- concerns about the under-achievement of deaf children in leaving school from largely oral programmes (Conrad 1979);
- the relative academic success of deaf children of deaf parents (for further discussion see Marschark 1997);
- the recognition of sign languages as languages in their own right (Brennan 1984 and Stokoe 1978);
- concerns about the use of manually-coded spoken language systems in teaching (Maxwell 1992).

The case continues to be supported by the following:

- evidence for high levels of reading and overall achievement in sign bilingual programmes in Scandinavia (for further discussion see Mahshie 1995);
- evidence from bilingual programmes for hearing minority language users (Baker 1993).

The definition

The term 'sign bilingualism' describes the use of two languages in different modalities, i.e. a signed and a spoken language, as distinct from the use of two spoken languages. (The term 'sign multilingualism' can also be used to describe the situation where the home language is neither English nor BSL.)

Models of bilingual education for hearing children need to be adapted and modified to suit the circumstances of deaf children. There are many parallels between the linguistic and cultural situations of bilingual deaf and hearing children. However, there are also significant differences (for further discussion see Baker 1996).

To further clarify the term 'sign bilingualism' as an approach, there is a need to distinguish between philosophy, policy and practice.

Philosophy

The philosophy underpinning sign bilingualism is based on a linguistic and cultural minority model of deafness and a social model of disability. Deaf people are respected as members of a minority group defined on the basis of language (Sign Language) and culture (Deaf Culture). The goals of sign bilingualism are to enable deaf children to become bilingual and bi-cultural, and participate fully in both the hearing society and the 'Deaf World'. Deafness is not regarded as a barrier to linguistic development, educational achievement or social integration. Society should value the inherent richness of linguistic and cultural pluralism. This philosophy underpins the policies and practices of schools and services.

Policy and practice

Policy and practice are inextricably linked. The principles enshrined in policy should be reflected in all aspects of educational practice.

A sign bilingual policy places emphasis on the role of Sign Language and Deaf adults in the linguistic and educational development of deaf children. An effective bilingual education should reflect a range of criteria beyond those purely related to academic achievement. For example, deaf awareness in hearing children and adults and the development of a deaf identity in the deaf child (Gregory *et al.* 1997) should be priorities.

The practice of sign bilingualism has developed principally around the use of Sign Language with those children for whom it is identified as the preferred language. There is also a need to develop sign bilingual programmes for deaf children with preferred spoken languages to enhance their educational and social opportunities. This suggests a continuum of language use which involves the planned and systematic use of both Sign Language and English. The balance of languages varies according to individual need

(Gregory and Pickersgill 1997). Children are likely to be at different points on the continuum depending upon their own linguistic development and preferences and the demands of the curriculum.

The following components of the policies are defined. Implications for classroom practice are shown in italics.

1. Language and communication

The term 'preferred language', as used in this section, is defined as the language which the child most readily acquires and prefers to use as well as being the basis for cognitive and emotional development.

- Sign Language is recognised as a language of education. Sign Language and English should be accorded equal status.
  References are made to the status and role of Sign Language in policy documents.
- Exposure to Sign Language as a full and natural language, should begin as early as possible.
  Young deaf children and their families have access to support from Deaf adults who are native users of Sign Language. The child's developmental response to early two language exposure is the basis for decision-making about linguistic support and educational placement.
- Sign Language and English should be used throughout the child's schooling with high levels of competence and proficiency expected in both.
  For children who have Sign Language as their preferred language, this is the primary language of instruction and the basis for development of the second language.
- The interdependence of Sign Language and English, and the transfer of skills between them, should be encouraged. Priority is given to the development of literacy skills.
  Teaching strategies to promote the child's understanding and use of Sign Language in the development of English skills are used. These interdependent skills are used to access the curriculum appropriately.
- Sign Language and English (spoken and written) should be kept separate for teaching purposes.
  The languages can be separated by person, time, topic and place. Boundaries are established to avoid the majority language (English) displacing the minority language (Sign Language).
- The place of Manually Coded English (MCE), which includes Sign Supported English (SSE) and Signed English (SE), should be defined.
  MCE may be used to facilitate the development of English and, to a limited extent, in curriculum delivery.

2. Curriculum and assessment

The learning needs of deaf children are recognised as different from those of hearing children. Decisions about linguistic support, access to the curriculum and relevant assessments should be based on strengths and not perceived weaknesses of the children.

- Both Sign Language and English should be languages of instruction and subjects of study.
  For children with Sign Language as the preferred language, this is used more than English to deliver and give access to the curriculum and to written English. Curricula are available for Sign Language and English. Specific assessments of Sign Language and English are used. Some are based on these curricula.
- The curriculum should respond to the linguistic and cultural pluralism of society.
  There is a Deaf Studies curriculum containing strands of language, culture and history. Account is taken of other languages, including heritage languages.
- The development of curriculum-based signs should be done by, and in consultation with, Deaf people.
  Discussion takes place between Deaf and hearing staff regarding the most appropriate signs and register to be used when conveying curriculum content.
- Both Sign Language and English should be used according to the child's preference, when conducting curriculum assessments.
  There are agreed presentations of assessment tasks and tests for Sign Language users.

3. Staffing

All staff should be bilingual, including senior managers, and reflect the range of linguistic as well as educational needs of the pupils.
- Deaf staff with native Sign Language skills should be employed.
  Deaf staff have job descriptions which reflect their position and status as language and role models, teachers, etc. The interpreting needs of Deaf staff are addressed.
- Hearing staff with native English skills should be employed.
  Bilingual hearing staff work in teaching, communication support or interpreting roles.
- In-service training should be provided to enable all staff to work collaboratively within a sign bilingual setting.
  Specific training and relevant qualifications are expected of and provided for staff.

4. Links with the community

The linguistic and cultural resources of the Deaf Community have an important role in the development of sign bilingualism.
- Links with the Deaf Community and ethnic minority communities should be promoted.
  Recruitment of staff or Governors from the Deaf Community and access to Deaf Youth Clubs, is promoted. Parents have contact with Deaf adults, through home visits and workshops, and have opportunities to develop Sign Language skills.
- The child should have access to a community of deaf Sign Language users (peers and adults).
  The child is part of a peer group of deaf Sign Language users in school and also has access to users of English.

These are the ingredients of a model sign bilingual programme. In developing and implementing such a programme, there are a number of implications for practitioners.

Implications for current practice

It is accepted that practice can only be developed from a foundation of sound philosophy and policy. In reality there are always implications for practice from the educational contexts in which implementation takes place. The following are some of the issues to be addressed when establishing a sign bilingual programme.

1. The range of children to be considered

A sign bilingual approach is seen as benefiting a range of children, not only those who were initially identified as having a preference for Sign Language and for whom a bilingual education was considered to be essential. In Scandinavia, where separate provision is made for deaf and hard of hearing children, the latter group are increasingly included in sign bilingual education (Mahshie 1995). In the UK such a pragmatic response can be seen in services such as Leeds where a wider range of children (in terms of hearing loss, language profile and disability) is being included in the bilingual preschool and nursery provision. This has major implications for services which previously identified children for an auditory–oral programme, a bilingual programme or a bimodal/sign-supported programme.

It is still common practice for some services to provide auditory–oral support at preschool. When this is shown to have been unsuccessful, the child is transferred to a 'total communication' programme and/or a sign bilingual programme. Such late and failure-based transfers are not appropriate. The advantage of a sign bilingual programme at preschool is that the most suitable placement and support for children can be identified on the basis of positive features of the child's linguistic development.

The question remains 'Is there a case for sign bilingualism for all deaf children?' Some would argue for this on moral grounds. The concept of a sign bilingual continuum with a range of language preference and dominance has many advantages.

2. Educational settings

Current provision for deaf children is organised within a range of mainstream and special schools. Within the mixed economy, of placements that currently exist, the conditions for sign bilingualism can only be met in specific educational settings. Both inclusive and segregated settings can be considered to have constraints and opportunities.

There are a number of conditions required for sign bilingualism to be effective. These include sufficient numbers of children and an adequate level of resources with appropriate staffing arrangements. In mainstream schools there are implications and responsibilities arising from the investment and commitment of the host schools themselves, as well as support services.

3. When and how to introduce English

Deaf children's achievements in English are the main yardstick against which the success of sign bilingual education will be measured. With the wishes of Deaf people themselves and the dominance of English in society, this contributes to attention being focused particularly on the development of these skills. For many of the children, the approach taken to their development of English will be as a second or foreign language. Fundamental to this is the foundation provided by Sign Language as a first language both in terms of linguistic development and in approaches to teaching. While there are arguments for delaying the introduction of English until Sign Language is well established, there are aspects of English in the life of the child which cannot be ignored. Reference to English can be made early on in the child's education through the prevalence of print, the production of early writing and the spoken language of hearing peers and adults.

4. Language separation, roles of deaf and hearing staff

The issue of separation in the use of Sign Language and spoken language, arises from knowledge and experience of spoken language bilingualism. The use of Sign Language and English (spoken or written) can be separated by topic, time, person or place. Each language may be used for different subjects, at particular times of the day, by a specific member of staff and in specific linguistic environments. More flexible approaches to language separation in which both languages are used concurrently, are being developed. These strategies are described by Jacobson (1995).

This concurrent use of two languages requires more flexible staffing. Bilingual staff who can use both languages flexibly, rather than members of the team using their dominant or preferred language, are needed. If children are clear about the use of languages through explicit teaching and staff are confident in these new roles, the concurrent approach can work well. This approach takes as its starting point the learning needs of the child and the most appropriate language to use at each stage of the learning task or situation.

5. Signs across the curriculum

The use of Sign Language within teaching on a planned bilingual basis is a recent innovation. The language does not yet have the range of vocabulary required for complex curricular and technical content. There is a current debate around how complex concepts can best be conveyed (Brennan 1997; Gregory 1996). Should a standard set of curriculum signs be developed or should the richness of BSL as used by skilled Deaf teachers, be exploited? This is an area of much debate both for those who are teaching and those who are in an interpreting or communication support role. At the heart of the issue are teamwork and mutual respect for colleagues' contributions to the children's learning (Erting and Stone 1992; Collins 1988).

6. The use of Manually Coded English (MCE) systems

The debate about the use of sign support systems within a sign bilingual approach is ongoing. According to the rules of language separation, MCE, in which signs from Sign Language are presented but in the order and structure of English, does not have a place. However one is familiar with the use within deaf–hearing interactions, of pidgin varieties of Sign Language and English. Indeed one is likely to promote these strategies for communicating with hearing people and in the development of literacy (Mayer and Wells 1996). Nonetheless, one should be cautious about using MCE as a teaching medium, particularly for children with Sign Language as their preferred language. Assumptions are made about our ability to present children with clear, comprehensive information and a model of spoken English simultaneously. We also assume children's ability to 'read' this as English while fully comprehending the information contained therein. While this may be possible for children who have English as their preferred language, it is less effective for those for whom Sign Language is preferred (Maxwell 1992 and Mahshie 1995).

Pidgin Sign English (PSE) or MCE may be used with mixed groups of deaf and hearing children in order to provide both groups with some, if not full, access to the content of the communication. Hearing parents are often advised to use PSE or MCE as an initial interactive mode. Some consider PSE or MCE as used in hearing families as the 'bridge' to communication between the deaf and hearing communities (Bouvet 1990).

Since there remain reservations about providing visual support to spoken language through sign, e.g. MCE, a logical development is the use of an alternative cueing system using handshapes related to finger spelling, together with clues to articulation. This builds on knowledge of the written form and gives access to a visual phonological system.

7. Cultural issues

Sign bilingualism cannot be considered separately from bi-culturalism. There is a need for the curriculum to have a multicultural basis and to accommodate Deaf Studies as a subject. There is also a place for including 'hearing culture' since there are aspects of the lives of hearing people of which deaf children should be made aware. Despite placement in mainstream schools and living within a hearing family, deaf children do not automatically grasp the subtleties of, for example, spoken discourse or hearing humour.

While there is likely to be an imbalance in numbers between hearing and deaf children in a mainstream school, Deaf cultural identity should be acknowledged and regarded as of value by the school, enriching the lives of hearing children, parents and staff.

Current research and development

Much of the current literature explores a wide spectrum of research and developing practice. In the context of new initiatives, it is inevitable that development and research go hand in hand. While research into sign bilingualism is as yet limited, the following areas are amongst the most relevant.

1. The application of models of hearing bilingual education for deaf children

Baker (1996) has drawn parallels and made distinctions between deaf and hearing bilinguals, particularly in the context of an enrichment model of bilingual education. His work provides a good background knowledge of the hearing bilingual field (Baker 1993; Garcia and Baker 1995) and its implications for sign bilingualism. It also points to the need for reflection on the differences between hearing and deaf bilinguals and the modification of policies and practices in response to this.

2. Teaching English to children who have BSL as preferred language: approaches to literacy and oracy development

Teaching strategies are being developed to 'bridge the gap' between Sign Language and written or spoken English. The issue of 'bridges' (Mayer and Wells 1996) is linked to the notion of a transfer of skills between languages. The transfer between BSL and written English is complicated by the fact that Sign Languages have no written form and that competence in the spoken form of English may not precede the development of the written form. However, transfer is more than just at the level of reading and writing. Other forms of literacy and transfer are described in Marschark (1997).

The following themes are addressed in the research into deaf children in sign bilingual programmes:

- reading achievement in Scandinavian deaf children and the content of programmes which support this (Mahshie 1995; Svartholm 1994);
- the learning strategies for English as a second language, used by British deaf children (Swanwick 1996);
- the strategies which are used by Deaf adults in developing children's reading (Heineman 1997);
- the positive influence of sign language development on deaf children's writing (Wells 1994).

3. The role of Deaf adults in a sign bilingual setting

- The work of Deaf professionals in a range of educational settings has been fully described and used to inform those who are responsible for training and employment (Collins 1988 and Hughes *et al.* 1997).
- The effect of the presence of Deaf adults on the play and interaction of deaf children both in mainstream and BSL nursery settings is described in Knight (1996).

4. Assessment of Sign Language

- The development of appropriate test materials for assessing deaf children's Sign Language development is currently being provided (Holmes 1997).

In conclusion, the primary focus of the research outlined above is the nature of bilingualism, language use, teaching and learning strategies and assessment. More research is needed to inform ongoing developments such as assessment techniques and the use of alternative curricula.

The way forward

1. National policy?

This chapter has described current sign bilingual policy and practice. However, as it is an area in which there is ongoing debate, discussion and research, there are inevitably a number of exciting developments likely for the future. The issues identified in the research and development section, form part of the way forward. An important next step is a nationally agreed policy on sign bilingualism which is crucial to its continued development.

2. Ownership

Sign bilingualism is not just an educational matter but also an issue for other agencies working in the field of deafness, such as social workers with Deaf people, and Sign Language interpreting services. In many Deaf organisations such as the BDA, the LAnguage of Sign as an Education Resource (LASER) and the Alliance of Deaf Service Users and Providers (ADSUP), the use of Sign Language is accepted and promoted. Deaf education is no longer the preserve of teachers of the deaf. There are many other stake-holders including parents and the Deaf Community. The ownership of deaf education is shifting towards a shared relationship between providers, consumers and clients.

3. The challenge

Sign bilingualism is a significant challenge to professionals and parents and to attitudes to deafness and Deaf people. It challenges the structure and policies of educational institutions and the classroom practices that reflect them. Part of the challenge is the scale of change needed to develop sign bilingualism. Services or schools need to respond to this. A number of schools are working towards being sign bilingual, yet lack the support for the structural and procedural practices which such an approach requires. In order to address this situation the features of a sign bilingual model to guide those who wish to implement it in their school or service are being identified (Pickersgill 1997).

Sign bilingualism is not a fashionable whim. It is here to stay, to be nurtured, refined and valued as a central theme in the education of deaf children and young people.

Further reading

1. Bilingual education – general

Baker C. (1993) *Foundations of Bilingual Education and Bilingualism.* Clevedon: Multilingual Matters.
Section A addresses fundamantal issues related to hearing bilingualism. Section B focuses on bilingual policies and practices in education.

Garcia O. and Baker C. (eds) (1995) *Policy and Practice in Bilingual Education: Extending the Foundations.* Clevedon: Multilingual Matters.
Section 2 gives examples of bilingual policies affecting the structure of schools. Section 3 focuses on classroom practice. Section 4 addresses issues to do with parents.

2. Bilingual education – deaf

Rudser S. F. (1988) 'Sign language instruction and its implications for the deaf', and Strong M. (1988) 'A bilingual approach to the education of young deaf children: ASL and English', both in Strong M. (ed.) *Language, Learning and Deafness.* Cambridge: Cambridge University Press.
Rudser's chapter focuses on the sign language needs of teachers, parents and interpreters in

education. Strong's chapter gives background to and describes an experimental curriculum from the USA.

Paul P. V. and Quigley S. P. (1994) *Language and Deafness* (2nd edn.). San Diego, CA: Singular Publishing Group.

Chapter 6 (Bilingualism and Second Language Learning) is useful and has been updated in response to recent developments in this second edition.

Bouvet D. (1990) *The Path to Language*. Clevedon: Multilingual Matters.

An account of, and rationale for the development of, a sign bilingual programme in a French kindergarten.

Mahshie S. M. (1995) *Educating Deaf Children Bilingually*. Washington, DC: Gallaudet University Press.

This book contains reflections – including research findings – on the sign bilingual programmes developed in Scandinavia. It is a comprehensive description of theory and practice, successes and pitfalls.

SECTION 3
TEACHING AND LEARNING

Introduction

The practice of teaching and learning in the education of deaf pupils has changed considerably in recent years. Some changes in practice have resulted from insights gained from research and advances in technology, while others have resulted from changes in policy. This section draws together many of the research findings described in other sections of the book and applies them to the classroom setting. Increased understanding of deaf pupils' development of their first language, be that spoken or signed, impinges on the way that literacy and mathematics are taught, while advances in audiology challenge teachers of the deaf to utilise the new technology to assist deaf pupils in the use of their residual hearing in the classroom, and the increased use of information technology is relevant to many aspects of teaching and learning.

Literacy has long been seen as of vital importance to deaf pupils, but for many it seemed to be an elusive goal, a fact highlighted by Conrad's research (1979). New approaches to communication with deaf pupils have, however, brought with them new ideas on teaching literacy to these pupils. Sue Lewis, in her chapter on reading and writing within an oral/aural approach, cites research which demonstrates much higher levels of attainment in reading among some pupils using this approach (Lewis 1996) and considers how strategies used to teach literacy to hearing pupils can be used to good effect with deaf pupils.

Ruth Swanwick, writing from the very different perspective of developing literacy within a sign bilingual approach, advocates some very different strategies. She draws on insights from research into literacy development in children who are bilingual in two spoken languages and shows how deaf pupils can learn to read and write English using their knowledge of British Sign Language (BSL) to assist them but without continuously making direct translations between the two languages.

Susan Gregory considers the question of mathematics. She summarises some of the research in the area and challenges teachers to reflect on how they are teaching mathematics to deaf pupils. There are implications concerning the language of mathematics which are relevant to teaching all deaf pupils. There are additional considerations to bear in mind for those deaf pupils who use spoken language but may think in spatial terms, and further points to consider when teaching pupils using sign.

The next two chapters raise issues related to deaf pupils' access to the curriculum. Tina

Wakefield addresses the question of deaf pupils' rights to access to a broad and balanced curriculum. She considers the legislation and assessment procedures and deals with ways of ensuring access. Linda Watson and Jackie Parsons consider the way in which increasing integration of deaf pupils in mainstream settings has led to the necessity to plan their support with care. The practical issues involved in ensuring that deaf pupils in mainstream settings are supported appropriately, and the difficulties which might arise, are discussed.

The final chapter in this section concerns the use of information technology with deaf pupils. This complements the previous two chapters since information technology can be extremely useful in helping deaf pupils achieve access to the curriculum but, owing to the difficulties which can be encountered, it is often under-used. Ben Elsendoorn writes from his perspective of designing interactive learning packages for use with deaf pupils of both the advantages and the challenges.

Linda Watson

Reading and writing within an oral/aural approach

Sue Lewis

The presence in a child of a severe sensori-neural hearing loss has been described by some as a 'promissory' for reading failure (Brooks 1978). Varied research evidence from Pintner and Paterson in 1916 to Conrad in 1979, confirms what for many teachers of hearing-impaired children is the reality of the classroom, i.e. that large numbers of hearing-impaired children have left school without achieving functional literacy. More recent researchers in the UK (Lewis 1996) and the USA (Geers and Moog 1989) have, however, reported higher levels of attainment among pupils educated within an oral/aural approach. All three groups of researchers report mean reading levels of approximately 13 years for deaf school leavers within such approaches, with one third of Geers and Moog's sample and a quarter of Lewis's sample reading at or above chronological age.

So why might the products of today's auditory/oral approaches read better than many such pupils in the past? This chapter is concerned not so much to revisit old arguments as to the efficacy of auditory/oral versus other approaches, but to explore factors and practices that do appear to contribute to higher literacy attainment in reading with deaf children within auditory/oral approaches.

Literacy has always been seen as potentially playing a key role in the education of deaf children. Whereas for the hearing child reading might be seen as a 'window into knowledge' (Webster 1986) the written word has also been seen as providing access to primary *linguistic* knowledge and understandings for many deaf children. In line with such views, deaf children have often been 'taught' to read and write from as soon as they enter their nursery school, predominantly by word recognition and decoding methods. If many deaf school leavers, however, have still not achieved functional literacy, then the notion of such reading levels being a primary means of access to linguistic understanding would appear to be fundamentally flawed. It also begs the question as to whether literacy can support language acquisition in this way, i.e. does literacy development in deaf children build on existing language skills itself or can it be a primary vehicle for developing them?

For the hearing child reading and writing are parasitic on language – they build on a developed auditory-based language and pre-existing understanding about language. The auditory/oral approach described below (a natural aural approach) assumes a similar relationship between language and literacy for deaf children as for hearing children. Thus the written word is 'not seen as a medium through which language is learnt. As with all children, establishment of a hearing-impaired child's spoken language should precede the use of its written form' (Harrison 1980, p. 11).

It follows then that if literacy development is to proceed smoothly it must be promoted within the context of the deaf child's existing linguistic understanding, knowledge and competence.

To understand the emphases within a natural aural approach to literacy it is important to explore the emphases within the approach to language acquisition and learning in general and to take account of current models of the reading process. The chapter by Watson (this volume) defines the essence of natural auralism. Fundamental to the approach to literacy is the child's active participation in the creation and exchange of meaning, not the decoding of individual words in isolation.

Laying the foundations

Many broader spoken language skills lay the foundations for subsequent reading and writing behaviour and success. Research with hearing children has demonstrated the importance of the quantity and quality of the preschool child's conversational, story, rhyme and play experiences and their link to later language and literacy levels (Wells 1986a and b). Beginner readers use their knowledge of language and the world to help them to anticipate and understand messages in print. Feelings of acceptance, competence and self-worth learnt in social interaction, conversation, story book reading and play with interested, listening adults, all impact on children's verbal fluency and the way in which they think about the language directed to them, and are directly linked to later literacy attainments (Wells 1985, 1986a and b; Beard 1987).

Previous researchers have, however, demonstrated differences in both picture-book reading between young deaf children and their mothers (Gregory and Mogford 1981) and in the conversational experiences of deaf children generally at home and at school (Wood *et al.* 1986 and Huntington and Watton 1981). A natural aural approach seeks to provide the quality and intimacy of such play experiences, conversation and styles of book sharing for deaf children that have been found to contribute to high levels of literacy attainment for hearing children. The extent and quality of the deaf child's conversational experiences in general and around books in particular are carefully monitored to ensure that they contain the facilitative features of child-directed speech that are known to support high linguistic attainment in hearing children (Gallaway and Richards 1994).

Approaches to literacy

Currently three major models of reading are identifiable, each of which has implications for teachers concerned with the teaching of reading to hearing-impaired children. Generally the models differ according to their emphasis on text level, or 'bottom–up' features (such as word recognition, letter identification), or on 'top–down' features brought to the text by the reader (such as previous experience, knowledge of language, and so on).

Bottom–up models present learning to read as a sort of 'code cracking' activity in which meaning is derived from print in a step-by-step linear fashion. Wray and Medwell (1991) point out that such a model, while apparently fitting some aspects of reading behaviour, particularly when the reader is faced with an unfamiliar word or meaning, does not readily explain the behaviour of fluent readers who are able to read a sentence such as 'If yUo aer a fluet reOdur yUo wll hve oN prblme reOdng ths sNtnce' (Wray and Medwell 1991, p. 98), nor does it explain how when we read the letters 'bow', we interpret them as either what we do when we meet the queen, what we tie in our hair, part of a ship ... and so on.

In *top–down models* reading development does not so much involve great precision in text recognition and identification, but rather is concerned with what the reader knows and brings to the task. The reader is seen as active, purposeful and selective; their ability to use the semantic and syntactic cues in the text, to anticipate and predict meanings is intricately interlinked with, and dependent on, prior experience and understandings of language, reading and the world.

Interactive models of reading recognise that the reader's previous experience, the reading context and the distinctive features of the text itself, all interact in the creation of meaning. How much reliance is placed on bottom–up or top–down strategies at any one time will depend on the familiarity of the ideas in the text, the complexity of the language in which it is encoded and the individual's linguistic and real world knowledge (Beard 1987; Wray and Medwell 1991).

Beginner readers, whether deaf or hearing, rely heavily on their top–down strategies. Skilled readers have a range of bottom–up and top–down skills which they can bring into play to make sense of print. Less skilled readers, or those experiencing difficulties in learning to read, may become 'hung up' on a single strategy, for example the use of picture clues, initial letter clues or word shape (Beard 1987; Wray and Medwell 1991), when another strategy might be more productive.

Two clear messages emerge from an interactive approach to reading then – that children draw on their competence as speakers when they are learning to read (Weber 1984; Beard 1987) and that reading is an active process, one which involves trying to identify the author's intended meaning but from a starting point of one's own experiences, knowledge and values. Deaf children of course will not only bring reduced language and listening skills to the reading task – a delay which may interfere in the smooth acquisition of bottom–up skills such as decoding – they may also have reduced real-world and language experience to bring to bear, i.e. their top–down skills may not be so developed either.

Supporting reading and writing: practical implications

What does a natural aural approach to reading and writing look like in the home and the classroom? How does it translate into practice? For the purposes of this chapter we will deal separately with the approach to reading and writing. This is an artificial distinction as within the approach deaf children's writing is often their reading as teachers scribe for the child and ask them to read it back.

A natural aural approach to reading is interactive – recognising the importance of bottom–up and top–down skills and strategies, while acknowledging the interactive nature of learning and the need for such skills and strategies to be developed within reading contexts that retain meaningfulness and purpose for the child. If deaf children's reading development is to proceed smoothly within an interactive approach however then a number of conditions must be fulfilled.

1. A basic level of linguistic understanding must be established before formal reading programmes are introduced.

Although picture-book reading, shared reading and conversations around books can take place whatever the child's linguistic functioning level, some fundamental linguistic understandings must be established in deaf children before more formal reading can proceed. Children must understand that we express meaning through language; they should be used to exchanging meanings with others and they must themselves be using a simple grammar.

2. The integrity of reading as a receptive process must be preserved.

Wood *et al.* (1986) cite examples of contexts where the meaningfulness of the reading activity is violated by teachers with deaf children for whom reading may become not a reflective activity but a performance activity for teacher.

3. The language and ideas that are used to promote deaf children's earliest reading insights must be accessible to them.

It must not be too far in advance of their own linguistic expression and should concern meanings and concepts that they already know. Once a deaf child has a certain level of reading competence then it will be possible, as with hearing children, to use that reading to learn and to extend the child's language. It is for this reason that heavier and more extended use is made of home made materials with deaf children (see below).

The early school years

If preschool experiences lay the foundation for later reading and writing success then the emphasis within the deaf child's early years environment is on those features of the language, reading, social and play environment that are known to be supportive for hearing children. Finger rhymes, nursery rhymes, traditional and family stories all play their part as parents and teachers help extend the child's linguistic understandings, and ability to anticipate and predict meanings and to join in much loved stories and routines. The importance of such activities is recognised within the National Curriculum Programmes of Study. As research evidence (Wood *et al.* 1986) points to deaf children having reduced exposure to such activities preschool, teachers of the deaf may well have to provide age-relevant experiences within these areas throughout the primary years.

Starting more formal reading programmes

On entering school many deaf children have much smaller vocabularies, more restricted world knowledge and experiences and more limited inferencing skills than their hearing peers. This, plus delayed linguistic skills, might mean that a later start to formal reading than for their hearing peers is often recommended.

Early book-type reading materials

Early reading materials should not contain language or vocabulary too far in advance of deaf children's own linguistic competence, nor meanings too far outside their experience. It is for this reason that home-made books or re-scripted books are used extensively in the 'learning to read' stage. Often the child's own version of a story will be used (Example 1). Such language is not 'corrected' in the writing up, since it is grammatically correct from the developmental point of view. The adult will however 'recast ' the utterance orally to the child (Gallaway and Richards 1994) and if children themselves spontaneously amend the utterance in response to such techniques it may well be recorded in its more mature form.

Example 1: Tom's reading book: Peace at Last

Old bear. Can't do it old bear. Can't go sleep.
Downstairs. Ow Ow Ow. Can't do it again.
Downstairs in the kitchen. Can't do it again.
In the garden. Go to sleep. Miaou, miaou.
Can't do it the cat.
Oh no. Old Bear in the car; can't go sleep.
Can't do it – the birds.
Upstairs, brr brr brr. Old bear wake up now.
Got the paper. Have a drink.

If a published reading scheme book is used the teacher may 'share' the story with the child, putting no pressure on the child to read words not yet within their own linguistic grasp: thus the child might read 'Biff wants to play on the go-kart' as 'Biff want play go-kart'.

The adult will then read the text using a recast or expansion technique similar to that used in conversations. Alternatively the child may tell the story in their own words and the re-tell will be used to replace the text in the 'reader'.

Banks, Gray and Fyfe (1990) suggest the focus of teaching of reading to deaf children may lie in providing them with strategies for comprehension rather than concentrating on decoding skills, vocabulary and grammar. This is certainly the main thrust of a natural aural approach, with the emphasis on comprehension rather than word-by-word reading.

Ewoldt (1985) provides evidence that supports the emphasis within natural auralism on careful selection of early reading materials including the following:

1. reading for meaning methods in the early stages foster a greater depth of understanding at syntactic and semantic levels;

2. the whole story v. the sentence approach is more productive; reading materials that have a clear story line and which the child is encouraged to read as a story rather than page-by-page are important;

3. as deaf children's reading progresses, providing them with more context than an isolated sentence or paragraph gives the opportunity to construct meaning regardless of difficult syntax or unfamiliar words.

As the child starts to read to learn then the practice of over-controlling reading experiences through constant reduction of text to the child's linguistic level is seen as non-productive. Cumming *et al.* (1985) provide evidence of deaf students scoring better when passages or short stories are used. Webster (1986) and Ewoldt (1985) found that deaf children understood sentences with more information content more easily than sentences with only limited elements of meaning. If deaf children are not exposed to difficult structures in text nor to inference or figurative language then it is not surprising if they do not develop the skills for dealing with it.

Phonics work

It makes little sense to try to teach phoneme/grapheme relationships through a sound which as yet is not part of the deaf child's phonological system. In all early phonics work the first sounds explored will be ones already in use by the child. Once the basic principle of phoneme/grapheme correspondence has been grasped then other less stable 'phonic' elements can be explored. The advisory role of the teacher of the deaf in ensuring that the more formal reading tasks which deaf children are set, e.g. within the literacy hour, are potentially as meaningful and decodable to them as for other early readers is critical.

Later reading and reading to learn

As children's reading competence and confidence moves on, text is modified through expansion and discussion, rather than simplified. Recognition of humour in print, of puns, inference, metaphor, reading between the lines are all essential skills for real access to Key Stage 3 curriculum. Foundations for these understandings are laid in numerous verbal reasoning games, auditory memory and prediction/hypothesis testing games.

Discussion of reading remains particularly important for deaf children, whatever their age and level of reading ability. Such talk serves to both exemplify ways of thinking about the text and provide linguistic models which will also aid their understanding of spoken language. Pre- rather than post-tutoring – familiarising children with the ideas that they are likely to meet in the text – significantly aids their ability to access text for themselves, even text which at first sight may appear to be outside their current reading and linguistic level.

A natural aural approach looks towards establishing independence in reading – children are expected to have views about what they have read and to increasingly take on responsibility for monitoring their own understanding. Attempts to apply useful strategies, e.g. reading on, rereading, use of picture clue, checking against prior reading and sounding out, are all reinforced. Reading is after all both a receptive process and a personal experience. It is the children who acquire the skills; although extensive interpretation of the text by the teacher may be necessary for other reasons, continual use of such a practice takes the responsibility for reading for meaning away from the child and locates it inappropriately with the teacher.

The importance of narrative and discourse

Particular care is taken to ensure children's understanding of narrative and discourse. Stories are told orally and shared from books. Although individual words and phrases may be drawn out in the telling, the primary emphasis is on being able to perceive relationships, sequence together key events and identify characterisation. The type of 'reading lesson' that Wood *et al.* (1986) describe, where children are repeatedly asked to demonstrate their understandings of individual words and phrases, has no place within the approach. Where children have been exposed to it they often fail to progress beyond the word/phrase identification level (often termed word-stabbing). Research with hearing children demonstrates a similar phenomenon – beginner readers are not helped by constant stops and questioning – this fragments rather than supports understanding.

Since children's understanding of narrative, discourse, ability to bring what they know to their reading and their willingness to reflect on what they have read have all been linked to later reading attainment, such skills are catered for proactively. Extensive use is made of Directed Activities Related to Text (DARTs) to support children's study skills and their more general ability to access text (for a description of the principles and practice of DARTs see Lunzer and Gardner 1984). Pupils work in pairs or small groups in DARTs activities; the sharing of skills and discussions allows the completion of a task that might defeat them singly.

Story re-tell programmes

If pupils are demonstrating difficulties in remembering or reflecting on what they have read then a story re-tell programme may be appropriate to assist their verbal recall, sequencing, independent learning behaviour and self-confidence in writing. In such programmes pupils are first told or read a story at their current level of verbal recall and understanding of narrative. The child is then asked to re-tell the story, but with no prompts from the teacher. The first of these re-tells and a number of subsequent ones are filmed. The videotapes are transcribed with the child and analysed by the teacher in relation to pupils' targets. Example 2 represents the work of a 7-year-old deaf child whose confidence, initiative and involvement in written work and in mainstream contexts was giving rise for concern.

Example 2
First re-tell
(Bold – child's writing; text – child's re-tell)
   man dig potato. Eat. Yum yum

After three weeks – twice per week
   Three bear. **daddy mummy bear, baby,** love porridge.
   Too hot
   Out walk Goldilocks **come** ...
   Mummy bear, daddy bear, baby bear home
   Oh no!
   Baby bear cry – look my porridge
   Look my chair
   Poor baby
   Upstairs bedroom. **Who my bed?**
   Goldilocks ... Agh Run away
   Shout mum

Fifth video re-tell (one term later)
(Bold – pupil's own writing; words in brackets – pupil's correction on viewing video)

   Long time ago, Jack live small house.
   Mummy (got) no money.
   Jack no daddy. Jack very sad. Jack very hungry ...
   Then (Jack) think 'Oh dear, what (will) mummy will say?'
   Mummy see no cow. Think hurrah we eat dinner tonight.
   Lovely dinner perhaps ice cream'
   Mummy very cross and (she) throw away the beans. 'Magic beans rubbish. You go to bed ...
   and so the story continues for two more pages!

After the initial filmed re-tell the child and teacher watch the video and transcribe it together verbatim. No pressure is put on the child to write, although they quickly start to transcribe for themselves, stopping and starting the video and increasingly self-correcting.

Some pupils for a range of reasons display a lack of confidence in writing, particularly where they (may) have experienced their writing being corrected to an adult model beyond their current linguistic understanding or where they are led to believe that the game is to write what the teacher expects rather than what they want to express. The story re-tell programme can help children regain confidence in writing as a means of self-expression.

Approaches to writing

Most readers will be familiar with developmental approaches to writing – sometimes termed 'emergent writing' (Nicholls *et al.* 1989). Such approaches sit happily within a natural aural framework; they recognise that children's early attempts at writing should be considered within their developmental context and in the context of the child's current linguistic functioning. Although there is a point when the accuracy of the writing form, organisation and grammar become significant, it is the child's communicative attempts that are responded to and reinforced. Deaf children's writing is compared with developmental writing schedules (see Nicholls *et al.* (1989) for an example) and also with their current linguistic levels and targets. This means that deaf children who are at the two to three element stage in terms of syntax, for example, should not be expected to write sentences that are in advance of this – a two to three word written utterance such as that in Example 3 is correct grammatically, i.e. it is developmentally appropriate. Any demand to raise the grammar of such written language to a more adult-like form is inappropriate; it will confuse the child by expecting him/her to use structures currently too far in advance of linguistic functioning.

Example 3

yesterday I shop. Mummy gave drink; My have orange; John fell over, hurt leg. Mummy 'Oh Dear, never mind.' Put plaster on knee.

Deaf children's confidence in writing and their understandings of the purpose of writing, its various forms and audiences must be encouraged from the earliest stages. Copying sentences, cloze procedure, formatted sentences may be good handwriting practice but have limited usefulness for promoting written language development. They constrain pupil initiative and self-confidence in writing.

Some of the 'reading' experiences described above clearly also lay the foundations for the child's emergent writing skills and understandings. When approaching writing within a natural aural approach the fundamental principles underpinning it are the same as those for a hearing child. The focus initially is on writing as a means of self-expression either for an audience or for self. Priority is given to children seeing the relevance of the writing process for them and to writing for a range of purposes from the very beginning. Thus in homes parents are encouraged to write in front of their children and to share the activity with them writing postcards, filling in forms, making lists, writing birthday cards and letters, and games are played where messages are left and clues given! As they write parents are encouraged to verbalise so that children begin to understand the connection between what they say and what is written. Children's own marks on paper are responded to as meaningful and interesting. The foundations of writing, its purposes and audience, are laid in nursery and preschool years in everyday contexts with meaningful tasks. At school the role of the adult is crucial – as 'observers, facilitators, modellers, readers and supporters. Through these roles the teacher intervenes in the child's learning, most often by a careful structuring of the contexts for writing' (Department of Educational Services 1990).

Each child's programme will be firmly based on detailed analysis of their spoken language as well as their written language level. It would be wrong to say that grammar or expression are never corrected. From the beginning children are encouraged to 'read back' their own writing, to evaluate and self-correct. Adult spoken feedback extends the writing and if the child is felt to be writing at a stage below their capabilities the adult will ask them to focus on a specific aspect of grammar, meaning, style or vocabulary.

The expectations within the approach are that children should at each stage be exposed to the same range of different writing activities as their hearing peers. Some aspects of their writing – their ideas, organisation etc. – will be judged from a similar basis while acknowledging that other aspects may be immature. Extended writing opportunities, scripting plays and videos, writing new endings/middles or beginnings for old stories, writing to pen pals, drafting advertisements, shopping lists, jokes – all will support written expression – as will the range of activities suggested for writing for different purposes within National Curriculum Programmes of Study for English at all key stages.

The importance of assessment and monitoring

The assessment of the child's current linguistic, reading and writing level is critical if effectively targeted support is to be provided at every stage of the child's educational career. Such assessment is integral to the approach – developmental schedules and assessments such as the Edinburgh Reading Test are used diagnostically and alongside national tests to ascertain levels, identify strengths and weaknesses, establish targets and inform planning. A natural aural approach to promoting reading and written language expression with deaf children then *does* intervene, it is both proactive in trying to lay effective linguistic foundations and learning attitudes for writing, and reactive in that if skills and strategies are not emerging it will actively plan to develop these.

Although there is no room for complacency, the evidence cited at the beginning of the chapter indicates that such focused support for language, learning and literacy does result in higher literacy attainments in deaf children than previous researchers have suggested. Since a certain level of language and literacy skills is essential if mainstream curriculum is to be effectively accessed, continued exploration of the practices that promote literacy in deaf children is vital.

Chapter 3.2

The teaching and learning of literacy within a sign bilingual approach

Ruth Swanwick

Much has been written about deaf children's difficulties with reading and writing, showing how their performance in literacy tasks falls well below levels achieved by their hearing peers. Most of this research concentrates on deaf children who are being educated in settings where the development of spoken and written English skills is the primary goal and where sign language is used essentially as a means of supporting access to spoken English. This chapter will explore some of the theoretical and practical issues of the teaching and learning of literacy within a sign bilingual approach focusing on deaf children's different learning styles and particular strengths as bilingual language learners.

A *sign bilingual approach* recognises that BSL (British Sign Language) is the preferred or primary language of some deaf children and where this is the case that BSL should be used for instruction across all areas of the curriculum including the teaching of spoken and written English. A clear distinction is made in this chapter between the different *sign languages*, which are naturally evolved languages, and the various *sign systems* which have been developed to encode and to be used alongside spoken language. It is essential to make this distinction if we are to challenge the assumption that using signs borrowed from BSL to support the spoken form of English will automatically improve the children's English, as this approach has not proved to be successful (Maxwell 1992). This system blurs the boundaries between the two languages which must be definite if we are to use sign language to successfully teach written English to sign bilingual deaf children.

Literacy for a bilingual deaf person is fundamental to enabling equal participation in a hearing society. Achieving this goal presents a significant challenge because of the unique features of sign bilingualism. In this language learning situation there are not only two languages but also two modes present (bimodalism) in that spoken and signed languages are produced and perceived differently. The implications of the presence of these two language modes for the acquisition of literacy skills becomes more apparent as we examine the following theoretical perspective.

Professionals working with bilingual deaf children have adopted a 'best fit' model of literacy instruction based on research into the bilingual language development of hearing children. The current theoretical model draws on the developmental interdependence theory (Cummins 1991, 1994) and proposes that the most appropriate route to bilingualism for deaf children involves using the learner's well developed skills in sign language as a basis for developing literacy skills in the second language. It is suggested that in this way literacy skills in the second language can be achieved without exposure to the spoken form (Johnson *et al.* 1989). Adopting this theory wholesale is problematic because it rests on several key assumptions which cannot be applied to sign bilingualism.

The first assumption intrinsic to the interdependence theory is that the learner brings age-appropriate receptive and expressive first language skills to the learning context and that literacy instruction will therefore be based on their established skills as communicators and language users. While we know that sign language can be acquired as a first language for deaf children who grow up in a sign language environment with one or more deaf parents, most deaf children are born into hearing families who do not know a natural sign language. We cannot make assumptions therefore about the level of deaf children's sign language skills when they enter school, and certainly not all bilingual deaf children will have age-appropriate sign language skills when they first begin to learn English as second language.

It is also assumed in the theory proposed by Cummins that aspects of literate proficiency will be transferred from the first language to the second language. In their critique of this theory Mayer and Wells (1996) point out that bilingual deaf children have not had the opportunity to acquire literacy skills in their primary language because sign language has no orthography. There are some parallels with other learners whose first language (L1) does not have a written form but these learners are still able to benefit from the support of the spoken form of the second language (L2) when learning the use the written form of the L2. Mayer and Wells (1996) examine this problem of applying the theory of transfer between L1 and L2 in some depth by exploring the role of inner speech in the writing process and how this relates to deaf children. They suggest that, even for children who have successfully acquired sign language as a primary language, the transfer of skills from one language to another is still problematic. For these children there is evidence to suggest that their inner speech might be a visual-gestural code (Klima and Bellugi 1979), but we cannot assume that meaning which has been constructed in internal visual-gestural speech can be transferred to linear written language. Sign language can not be written down, not least because there is no reliable one-to-one correspondence between words and signs, but also because certain other meaning-carrying features, such as the use of non-manual signs, spatial location and directional movement, cannot be encoded in written English.

As this critique by Mayer and Wells demonstrates, we cannot simply lift a second-language learning model from research into hearing bilingualism and apply the same principles to sign bilingualism. The model we must work from needs to be tailored to match the second-language learning situation of bilingual deaf children. The real advances in our knowledge in this area are coming from 'grassroots' work where teaching approaches and learning strategies are being explored. It is ultimately from these initiatives that a more fitting model of sign bilingual literacy is evolving. For the linguistic interdependence theory to be applicable it requires that all the appropriate conditions for the successful learning of a second language are present, such as accessible exposure to the second language, opportunities to use the second language for real purposes in communicative contexts and clear separation of the two languages. Although these conditions can be difficult to achieve in a sign bilingual classroom there are other ways of developing literacy skills within a sign bilingual approach which take account of deaf children's strengths as bilingual learners and capitalise on the role of sign language in the teaching and learning process.

There are two key principles which deserve much greater emphasis in a model of second-language literacy development for bilingual deaf children. The first is the role of sign language instruction. This crucial principle is all too often lost in general statements about sign language providing the foundation for the development of second language skills. The nature of this foundation needs to be made more explicit. It is a significant strength of sign bilingual approaches that deaf children's high levels of sign language skills can enable them to benefit from literacy instruction in their preferred language. Sign language can be used in literacy instruction by deaf and hearing adults for presentation, discussion, analysis and explanation of tasks in a way that can bring reading and writing alive for deaf children. The importance of establishing these sign language skills should therefore be emphasised

This leads to the second pillar of the emerging model which is meta-linguistic understanding. This is a route to second-language literacy for deaf children which is often overlooked. If anything can be transferred across two languages and two modes surely meta-linguistic concepts can, as they are by definition 'language-free'. Meta-linguistic awareness requires a more abstract knowledge and understanding of language which involves the ability to think and talk about language, to recognise characteristics of a language and to see how language is structured (Bialystok 1991). For sign bilingual deaf children with limited access to the spoken form of the language they are learning, the development of meta-linguistic understanding provides an alternative means of constructing the second language. Meta-linguistic skills can only be part of a literacy teaching programme if sign language is used as the language of instruction, but the combination of these two principles results in a very powerful teaching and learning model. Professionals working in bilingual programmes are now starting to explore literacy teaching approaches which successfully combine these two principles, as the following examples illustrate.

Features of current practice

This section of the chapter will explore ways in which the teaching of literacy skills is being tackled within bilingual approaches in Sweden, Denmark, the USA and the UK. Much of this section draws on material from conferences and workshops where the most recent and exciting developments are being discussed.

In the USA the educational goal for the majority of deaf children is still monolingual (English). Many are still educated using pure auditory–oral methods but the larger proportion are educated using what is referred to as simultaneous communication (sim-com) which is spoken English accompanied by signs borrowed from American Sign

Language (ASL). Because of growing concern over the use of sim-com (Maxwell 1992) and the increased recognition of ASL as a naturally evolved language, more innovative approaches to teaching English literacy as a second language have been explored over the last ten years.

Schneiderman (1986) describes an approach which involves videoing ASL descriptions and then asking the students to analyse how the information is conveyed in ASL. The students then jot down key English words and discuss as a group how to create the equivalent description using written English. This is a translation task which involves meta-linguistic skills in the analysis of both languages.

A study carried out by Neilson and Armour (1983) found that students who carried out linguistic analysis of ASL and translation work as part of their English literature teaching programme benefited in both language areas from being made aware of their 'tacit linguistic knowledge'. The benefits they describe include improved sign language skills, improved comprehension of English through sim-com and improved reading and writing skills. Akamatsu and Armour (1987) followed up this study by examining the effect on high school students of a programme focused on raising students' language awareness of both ASL and written English in terms of rules, comparisons and contrasting features. They used a teaching programme which combined specific instruction in ASL, trans-literation and translation skills and editing written English texts. When they looked at the gains of this intervention over a ten-week period the outcomes they identified included improved awareness of rule systems, ASL and written language and improved writing at grammatical level. They note that the practicalities of such an intervention demand that the hearing adult must be proficient in ASL or work alongside a deaf adult and both adults need a working knowledge of how both languages are structured. The onus on the teachers to provide appropriate language models and opportunities for language learning is emphasised by Erting and Pfau (1994) in their work on meta-linguistic awareness with preschool children.

Neuroth-Gimbrone and Logiodice (1990) discuss another example of an English literacy teaching approach which emphasises the development of meta-linguistic skills. In this approach the students analysed stories told in ASL by deaf adults looking at some of the rules of ASL and particularly at how non-manual features were used to convey meaning. Following this the students wrote an English gloss of the ASL story (a transliteration of the ASL into the nearest equivalent English words) and then developed this into a full written translation of the ASL. In the early stages an interim task was provided where students were given several alternative written English translations of the ASL stories and were asked to select which one best captured the full intended meaning of the ASL. This actively involved the students in thinking about appropriate translation from one language to another without having to generate their own written English.

In Sweden and Denmark bilingual education for deaf children is widely accepted and in both countries respectively Swedish (SSL) and Danish Sign language (DSL) are used as the language of instruction and are also taught as curriculum subjects. Bilingual approaches to teaching literacy in Sweden and Denmark share certain key principles.

Emphasis is placed on the learner's continued development of knowledge and skills in SSL and DSL from preschool level. Learners are expected to be able to analyse sign language and to use it to discuss features of the second language and to be able to compare and contrast sign language with the written language. Mahshie (1995) reports in her comprehensive review of bilingual education in Denmark and Sweden that deaf students in bilingual classes demonstrate reading levels comparable to those of their hearing peers. Mahshie describes a teaching approach from Sweden which incorporates the use of a specially designed set of texts and parallel SSL video tapes which centre on a deaf child and his family. Emphasis is placed on discussion and contrastive analysis of the grammar of the two languages rather than on word-for-word reading of the written Swedish. In this way children are allowed to discover for themselves the contrasting and similar ways in which meaning can be communicated in both languages. The use of sim-com is avoided as teachers say that it is easier to talk about two languages when they are kept clearly separate (Davies 1994).

In Denmark, approaches to literacy teaching also include contrastive analysis and translation work but spoken Danish is seen as being as integral to the development of literacy skills. The use of manually-coded Danish for word-for-word reading aloud is accepted as a transitional phase in learning to read. Hansen (1990) illustrates this in her description of the approach at Copenhagen School for the Deaf. The children work in groups to translate the DSL story into a written Danish version and then practise reading the written version aloud without sign support, following the teacher's indications of rhythm and phrasing.

Currently in the UK more and more schools and services are describing their approach as bilingual. There is a growing concern that although many education authorities do include the use of some sign language in their teaching, their overall approach could by no means be defined as bilingual. Gregory and Pickersgill (1997) stress the need for consistency in the use of these terms and some nationally accepted descriptors for a sign bilingual approach.

In the sign bilingual educational model outlined by Gregory and Pickersgill (1997) the prerequisites for the teaching of literacy share the principles outlined in the Swedish and Danish models. BSL and spoken and written English are both taught as curriculum subjects. A basis of skills in BSL is recognised as central to the successful learning of English literacy. BSL is used as the language of instruction in the teaching of English and the children's language awareness skills established in BSL are expected to be transferable to their English literacy learning. Manually-coded English (MCE) is not expected to be used as a language of instruction indiscriminately, but for clearly defined teaching purposes such as supporting the learner's exposure to the spoken form of English.

Sign bilingual children work towards the same National Curriculum literacy goals as their hearing peers although English literacy is likely to be taught within a Modern Foreign Language (MFL) framework where the skills focus, the teaching approaches and the materials are more appropriate for their needs as second language literacy learners (Swanwick 1994). Across the small number of schools and services working in this way there are some common approaches and teaching materials which are currently being developed.

The use of DARTs (Directed Activities Related to Text) has been found to be a successful teaching strategy in sign bilingual approaches. DARTs is an activity-based approach aimed at enabling children with limited reading skills to read for meaning. DARTs help pupils to access information from text by giving them structured analysis and reconstruction tasks to do which actively involve them in the text and encourage them to see reading as a means of learning across the curriculum and not as a discrete activity (Lunzer and Gardner 1984). DARTs has been popular with teachers working with sign bilingual children because they can be designed for individuals, they encourage group work and discussion and they give deaf children useful strategies to approach text (Swanwick 1993).

Dialogue journals are also a common feature of sign bilingual approaches (Baker 1990). A dialogue journal is a shared journal in which adult and learner communicate in writing on any topic. The communication is natural, purposeful and individualised and therefore the pupils are motivated to contribute and keep this contact going. The adult responds but does not correct the pupil's English. This makes the communication a bit special and encourages the pupils to attempt writing things in English that they would not otherwise risk. The adult does have the opportunity to model the correct written English for the pupil in his/her response and so can extend their reading and writing skills in this way. The children are highly motivated to keep a journal, especially with a deaf adult, and so they provide an ideal opportunity to give deaf children the experience of real communication through the written form of English.

The use of video analysis is not as developed as we have seen it is in Scandinavian countries but is gradually becoming a more prominent feature of sign bilingual approaches in the UK. Partridge (1996) describes the different methods with which he has experimented to create a video bilingual version of the children's reading scheme. One of the key benefits that he highlights is the opportunities that this resource presents for raising the children's language awareness (meta-linguistic) skills through encouraging them to compare and contrast the two languages.

Professionals involved in teaching literacy to sign bilingual deaf children have drawn teaching ideas and curriculum materials from the fields of foreign and second language teaching. One of the particular principles of MFL teaching which has been adopted is the importance of making children aware of patterns in language and making the grammar rules of language more accessible to them so that they are able to be creative in their own use of written or spoken English (Passman 1994). In accordance with good MFL practice this formal grammar work is built into language topics and so it is learnt and practised by the learners within a meaningful context.

Alongside a more formal approach to grammar teaching some of the more communicative aspects of foreign and second language teaching have been adapted for sign bilingual settings. These include the importance of learning language in authentic communicative situations; the emphasis on top–down skills, such as the ability to use contextual cues and prior experiences to interpret text and infer meaning, and the importance of meta-linguistic skills, such as the ability to talk about, compare and contrast languages. The team of teachers in Leeds have developed an adapted MFL curriculum for sign bilingual deaf children which is used primarily for planning and targeting English learning objectives, recording progress and reporting to parents (DAHISS 1996).

Implications for advancing practice

By looking at some of these practical examples of how literacy is being taught within various bilingual contexts we can see that a more appropriate model of sign bilingual literacy instruction is evolving based on the following principles.

Sign language is the language in which literacy tasks are explained by the adults and responded to by the pupils. Sign language also plays a central role in the development of the pupil's meta-linguistic awareness. The translation tasks described in the examples involve a high level of discussion about language in sign language and require the pupils to reflect on how both written language and sign language are structured. These tasks develop the pupil's understanding and use of meta-linguistic terms and equip them with the crucial transferable skills involved in analysing and discussing language.

In the model that is evolving, the role of spoken language in literacy instruction is seen as supporting the literacy process but not as a prerequisite for the development of literacy skills. Wherever possible learners are taught to draw on their spoken language skills to support the development of their literacy skills. It is also accepted that for some sign bilingual children the spoken language cannot provide a bridge to the written form, hence the emphasis on exposure to the diversity of written forms of the language and on the development of more analytical language learning strategies. Recent research suggests that limited auditory experience does not necessarily prohibit the development of a phonological code such as an awareness of rhyme, syllable and word length (Sterne 1996). A bilingual approach to literacy instruction, which emphasises the importance of knowledge about language, provides the ideal context for direct training in these phonologial awareness skills which will support reading development.

An essential feature of this model is that the distinction between the two languages is made perfectly clear to the learners. Developing the learner's language awareness and analytical skills relies on a clear separation of the two languages. This does not mean that there is no place for manually coded English in literacy instruction but that its role should be carefully defined and made explicit to the learners. The children's need to read word-for-word using signs from BSL is accepted as an important stage in the process, although the use of contextually correct signs and the recognition of whole units of meaning in written English is emphasised.

Finally, it is the perspective of this model which makes the difference. Instead of considering these pupils' literacy achievements in the context of their hearing peers we are recognising that they are a unique group of bilingual learners. Rather than focusing on what they cannot do we are exploring what different strategies they have as second language literacy learners and this leads us to consider what teaching approaches from the field of second and foreign language learning we can usefully adopt.

The main implication of this evolving model of literacy instruction for sign bilingual children centres on the skills required by deaf and hearing adults involved. The onus is on these adults to provide the right combination of exposure to the written form of the second language alongside formal literacy instruction in sign language. The exposure must be plentiful and varied and the formal teaching must draw on the children's understanding of how their own language works.

> To be able to teach a subject as abstract and intellectual as a written language to someone that has no access to the spoken form requires more than good communication skills. That teacher needs to know a lot about the grammar of the language he teaches as well as the language he is teaching in (Ahlgren 1990, p. 93).

It is therefore imperative that deaf and hearing adults involved in teaching literacy in sign bilingual approaches have an insight into the structure of both languages so that they are able to provide appropriate comparisons between the languages and anticipate possible areas of difficulty. This dynamic and exciting way of working certainly brightens up the hitherto gloomy domain of literacy instruction for sign bilingual deaf children but in order that these goals are realised, training in this area for deaf and hearing professionals must be a priority.

Further reading

Bialystok, E. (1991) (ed.) *Language Processing in Bilingual Children.* Cambridge: Cambridge University Press.
This edited book of research-based papers thoroughly examines ways in which bilingual children cope with two language systems. It includes chapters which explore the interdependence theory (chapter 4) and the development of meta-linguistic skills and awareness (chapters 5, 6 and 7).

Mahshie, S. N. (1995) *Educating Deaf Children Bilingually.* Washington, DC: Gallaudet University Press.
Chapter 1 describes practical approaches to developing deaf children's literacy skills in Sweden and Denmark and explores the relevance of current research into bilingualism and second language development.

Snider, B. D. (ed.) (1994) *Post Milan, ASL and English Literacy: Issues, Trends and Research.* Washington, DC: Gallaudet University Press.
This publication of conference proceedings includes many interesting reports of innovative projects aimed at developing deaf students' literacy skills through ASL.

Chapter 3.3

Mathematics and deaf children

Susan Gregory

Introduction

Most studies of the attainments of deaf children have focused on language and literacy as these are the areas of most apparent concern. However, there have been some studies which have looked at mathematical development. This is important for a number of reasons. In particular, understanding mathematical development of deaf children can inform our teaching practices. There are, however, more general implications that can be drawn relating to the relationship between language and mathematical thinking.

There has been a change in emphasis in studies of mathematics and deaf pupils. Earlier studies tended to focus on attainments of deaf children and describe how their abilities compared with those of hearing children. Patterns of attainments of different groups of deaf children were also explored. Later research looked at how deaf children solved mathematical problems and the nature of the difficulties they experienced. This also allowed a discussion of what can be learnt about deaf children's thinking from considering their attainments in mathematics. More recent developments in the teaching of mathematics using sign language have raised research questions about the relationship of language to the structure of mathematics teaching.

Studies of attainment

Studies of the mathematical attainments of deaf pupils have largely focused on computational skills. Some would argue rightly that this is a very limited view of mathematical thinking and achievement. It is not necessarily the case that performance on attainment tasks indicates anything about a person's ability to solve mathematical problems. Nevertheless, as this is the data that is available, this will be considered first, before going on to more general issues.

An early study carried out by the National Council of Teachers of the Deaf used the Schonell Arithmetic Test. They tested 246 children in four schools in England and obtained scores giving an average difference between deaf and hearing children of 2.5 years (National Council of Teachers of the Deaf 1957). A later study by Wollman (1965) yielded similar results. He assessed one third of the pupils from 13 schools for the deaf in the UK and compared them with 162 pupils from secondary modern (non-selective) schools. Again, deaf pupils were found to lag behind their hearing counterparts, by around one standard deviation.

The most comprehensive study is probably that of Wood and his colleagues carried out in the 1980s. (Wood *et al.* 1983, 1986). They looked at 414 deaf school leavers and compared them with 465 comprehensive school pupils of the same age, using the Vernon and Miller Graded Mathematics Test. They found that the mathematics age of hearing school leavers was about 15.5 years, compared with a mathematical age of deaf pupils of 12.3 years, a difference which is statistically significant.

It is worth noting that while deaf pupils lagged behind their hearing peers, the delay was not as great as that for reading, where the median reading age for hearing school leavers was 9.0 years (Conrad 1979). Thus, even although deaf pupils were behind with mathematics age, they were not as far behind as they were in their literacy levels. Also 15 per cent had mathematics ages at or above their chronological ages, compared with a negligible proportion for reading age.

Factors influencing attainment

In order to understand more about the factors that can affect attainment we need to know more about patterns of attainment scores and a number of studies have attempted to look at the effect of different factors on attainment. The degree of hearing loss, gender and school placement are among those that have been considered.

Wood *et al.* (1986) considered hearing loss by correlating the degree of loss in the better ear with mathematics age. This showed a small but significant negative correlation, suggesting that a greater degree of hearing loss is marginally correlated with decreasing mathematical ability. However, it did not seem to be a major factor.

This study also considered gender and found that, while hearing boys and girls differed significantly in their mathematical age (boys mean mathematics age 15.7, girls mean mathematics age 15.2) the difference between deaf boys and girls was not significant although boys achieved a higher mean score (deaf boys 12.5 years, deaf girls 12.1 years). The correlation of hearing loss and mathematics age was considered separately for boys and girls. The relationship was statistically significant for girls but not for boys. Thus while deafer girls do less well in tests of mathematical attainment, hearing loss is not shown to be a factor in the performance of boys.

Rather than considering this in terms of why there is no statistically significant difference between deaf boys and girls it may be more useful to reflect on why hearing boys do better than hearing girls. It has been suggested that this relates to the problems posed by mathematics which involve thinking spatially and mechanically, an area in which boys often excel. Could this account for why deaf boys and deaf girls are similar in their mathematics attainments, as their ability to think spatially is very important and it may therefore be the same for both?

In considering school placement, Wood *et al.* (1983, 1986) found no difference in those educated in special schools and those educated in Units, despite the difference in hearing loss of the two populations (Units, average loss 68 dB, Special Schools, 92 dB). They suggest this 'lack of significant difference underlines the weak relationship between hearing loss and mathematical attainment within the hearing impaired sample'(1983, p. 70)

A study by Zweibel and Allen (1988) in Israel compared profoundly deaf pupils of about ten years of age, in segregated classes (special provision), class integrated (a number of deaf pupils in a mainstream class) and individually integrated pupils. As with other studies they found that hearing-impaired pupils were behind their hearing contemporaries in mathematical achievement. A major criticism of work that considers the attainments of pupils in different settings is that children are selected for the various settings for reasons that relate to attainment and thus any differences may relate to individual differences between the groups. Zweibel and Allen tried to take account of this by controlling for communication skill and intellectual potential in comparing the groups, although intellectual potential was only assessed on a three point scale. Even when these factors were controlled for, results showed that the ratings of mathematical potential in the pupils were lower for those in segregated classrooms. However, Zweibel and Allen do not suggest a causal factor, as they recognise that other factors, home background, teacher and parent expectations, may play a part.

Kluwin and Moores (1989) investigated further the effect of placement on attainment in mathematics, giving serious consideration to the problems of previous research which relate to how the children are initially selected for such placements. They studied 215 students with an average age of 16.7 years and compared those in self-contained (specialist) setting with those in mainstream. They suggest that because the selection process means that the students in the two settings are different, student background factors are primary predictors of achievement and that these accounted for more of the difference between the two groups than did school placement. They conclude 'placement contributes very little to accounting for the overall variance' (p. 334). However, they found that the quality of instruction received by the child is the main factor in achievement. Effects they identified here were supportive teachers, regular and extensive reviews of the material, devoting time to direct instruction, positive encouragement and high demands on students.

The results from both Wood *et al.* and Kluwin and Moores suggest that attainment is not simply a result of school placement, and Wood *et al.* suggests that neither is it due to gender or degree of hearing loss. In fact Wood *et al.* concluded that the major determinant of mathematical ability in hearing-impaired children were factors beyond those (gender, hearing loss, placement) that they considered.

Mathematical thinking

There have been very few studies that have attempted to consider mathematical thinking in deaf children although Furth in the 1960s carried out a number of studies to explore Piagetian stages of development in deaf children, his goal being to understand the relationship between thought and language by looking at deaf children whom he considered as without language. He believed that deaf children 'do not acquire functional language competence, even after undergoing many years of intensive training' (1966, p. 13). While that simple proposition is untenable, nevertheless the studies themselves yield some interesting results.

Furth found a delay in deaf children's ability in a number of these tasks including conservation. In a conservation task the appearance of a liquid or solid is changed without varying the amount, for example water is poured from a short fat flask into a tall thin one and pupils have to say whether or not the amount remains the same. For both liquids and solids deaf pupils showed delay compared to hearing pupils in understanding that the amount remained the same. Furth attributed this to what he described as the language deficits of deaf children. Other studies have explored these concepts paying more attention to language use, both sign (Rittenhouse and Spiro 1979) and oral language (Lister *et al.* 1988), and obtained similar evidence of delay.

The nature of the difficulty

Why should mathematics and mathematical thinking be more difficult for deaf pupils? Why are they not doing as well as hearing pupils? This section explores some other factors that could contribute to the delay.

The language of mathematics

Clearly if pupils lack the language necessary to understand and solve mathematical questions, there will be problems. Some of the words which are critical for developing mathematical understanding are the words with which deaf children have the most difficulties, logical connectives such as 'if' and 'because'. The way in which language is used in mathematical problems, where it often has very specific meaning, could also create problems. There is also a set of specialist vocabulary for mathematics, e.g. hypotenuse, denominator, isosceles. This means that particular terms have to be learnt and meanings established for problems to be solved.

An even more difficult issue may be that there are everyday words in general use in the English language which, when used in mathematics, have very particular meanings: they are used in particular ways different from the general sense. These words have a more exact use when used mathematically than when used in general conversation, e.g. similar, difference, divide. A high number does not mean a number which is printed high, (i.e. towards the top of the page), but one which is large in magnitude.

A further reason why mathematics may be difficult for deaf children is the use of symbols, alone or in mathematical sentences, e.g.

$$\Sigma, \times \pi,$$
$$x + y = a + b,$$
$$f = m \times a$$

Literacy and mathematics

Pau (1995) showed a relationship between reading competence and the ability to solve mathematical problems in 8- to 12-year-old profoundly deaf children, who were all of average intelligence or above. He also showed the nature of the problems had an effect. Among the easiest problems to solve were:

Mary has three marbles. John has four marbles more than Mary. How many marbles does John have?

While a difficult problem would be:

Mary has five marbles. John has eight marbles. How many marbles does John have more than Mary?

Pau suggests that the problems are easier if the data, the unknown factor and the order are presented in the order in which the operation is to be carried out. He also found that pupils tended to ignore comparative linguistic forms when reading the text and the words 'more' 'some' and 'together' presented problems. For example in the problem 'together John and Mary have X marbles' some pupils understood it to mean that they each had X marbles.

Kidd (1991) provides an analysis of a number of mathematical problems, based on a text book in use with deaf students at the time of the study. She suggests that while syntactically the problems are similar to normal written language there are some significant differences. Firstly, there are many more prepositions, which are known to be difficult for deaf children. Secondly, there are many phrases dealing with time. Nominalisation, the use of verbs as nouns, is said to be difficult for deaf children (Quigley et al. 1978, cited by Kidd) yet a high proportion of the mathematical problems investigated contained these. Lastly, she pointed out the high number of propositions to be considered within problems as a complicating factor. This would seem to imply that it is not simply the process of reading that is the issue but understanding the meaning through understanding the context.

Access to mathematical conversation

However, there is a more general issue, that of access to conversation about number and mathematical ideas. Hearing children hear mathematical talk almost from birth, 'wait a minute', 'that's too small for you now', 'it's miles away'. Most hearing children are also involved in mathematical talk themselves from early on, of which counting is a prime example. Durkin et al. (1986) in their review of the literature suggest that hearing children can produce a numbers word sequence at two years of age and by three years of age have some ability to discriminate acceptable and unacceptable counting by others. They studied ten children and their mothers from when the children were 9 months of age until they were 30 months. They filmed the mothers and children in interaction, in a situation not specifically focused on number words. They found that mothers used many number words the most frequent being the first four numbers. There were six main categories of number use, nursery rhymes, fixed counting sequences, e.g. 'one two three, go', reciting numbers, counting specific elements, mother and child alternating in counting, incidental use (e.g.

house numbers). Most children encountered numbers in most of these categories, illustrating a range of use of the same terms in interaction. Numbers were used with children from at least 9 months of age, so prior to speech. Numbers were also sometimes used in ways that were potentially confusing, adding to the possibility of misunderstanding, e.g. '"How many cameras is there?" "Four ... One there, one there, then there's one over there and one up there"'.

Counting has been shown to develop more slowly in deaf than in hearing children regardless of whether they speak or sign (Secada 1984). Oral counting seems difficult and Nunes and Moreno (1997a) report confusions, particularly between words that have phonological similarity, and children would jump from 18 to 81 as if it were 80, 81. Lip-reading numbers that have similar lip patterns can be a source of problems. There are particular difficulties in the development of counting using signs which are discussed in the section on issues in using sign language. However, a study by Nunes and Moreno (1997a) suggests that knowledge of the counting string is a significant predictor of performance on some numerical problems and they suggest that a 'greater stress in teaching young hearing impaired children to count in school is likely to have a positive impact on their numerical knowledge' (p. 25).

Counting is relevant to the preschool age, but conversations relating to mathematical ideas continue throughout the school years. The extent of the difficulty can be appreciated, if we consider the incidental information that hearing children pick up throughout their school lives, which will be more difficult for many deaf children to access, whether they use sign or speech. The speed of cars, the size of clothes, the times of television programmes, the size of pay claims, family finances, are a few of the many ideas that are likely to be background information for most hearing children growing up. Gregory *et al.* (1995) suggest that lack of access to incidental information is as important as language and communication in a consideration of factors affecting deaf children growing up.

Special issues in the use of sign language in teaching mathematics

The development of a sign bilingual approach to the education of deaf children has focused attention on the use of sign language in the teaching of different curriculum areas. Intuitively it would seem that sign language, being a visually-spatially-organised language, could have much to offer the teaching of mathematics. Because the language conveys more information about size, location and spatial relationships than spoken language, it could be a rich language for exploring and explaining mathematical concepts.

An indication of the richness of sign language in conveying mathematical concepts is hinted at by the Reference Notes to the National Curriculum Assessment (1993) where it states 'Although sign can be used to present and respond to the mathematics standard assessment tasks, care should be taken that the signs used in presentation do not give clues to the answer, nor cause confusion' (p. 4).

There is some research that seems to indicate strengths that deaf children who use sign language may have which are relevant to mathematics. A study by Braden (1994) collected together all the studies of intelligence and deaf children. He compared non-verbal intelligence and verbal intelligence. Verbal intelligence relates to problem solving where there is a verbal/linguistic component, it has a linguistic basis while non-verbal intelligence involves solving problems which do not have an apparent language component. Braden reviewed 208 studies, which included 171,517 deaf subjects from 234 independent samples, involving 324 reports of IQ. He found that the mean IQ from all studies (324 reports) was 97, the mean verbal IQ (32 studies) was 86, and the mean non-verbal IQ (195 reports) was 100, establishing that deaf people had the same non-verbal intelligence as hearing people. However, he then went on to consider those deaf people who had deaf parents and found that the average non-verbal IQ of those with deaf parents was 108, a score which differs significantly from that of hearing people.

This is an important finding when we think about teaching mathematics. It may be that if deaf children use sign language they develop a particular area of intelligence to a higher level – the organisation of space and memory for spatial concepts. Studies have shown that the ability to think spatially is related to mathematical ability (Bishop 1980).

There are a few studies which endorse this finding (reported in Bellugi *et al.* 1994). A Chinese study found that if deaf children of deaf parents were presented with a light that moved around to make a Chinese symbol (the whole symbol was never there at one time, the symbol disappears as it is being created) deaf children of deaf parents could then draw that symbol but hearing children could not. In an American study of facial discrimination, children were given a picture of a face. Then they were given six faces of different orientation: side view, three quarters view, and so on. They had to say which of the pictures were of the same faces. Deaf children of deaf parents were much better at this. If we start to think about teaching deaf children not in terms of their weaknesses but of their strengths then we have to start considering this as a strength.

There has been very little research on the use of signing in the teaching of mathematics. However, Nunes and Moreno (1997b) have looked at counting and suggested that care has to be taken to avoid counting and signing being in conflict. At a basic level, deaf children who wish to count by pointing to one object at a time will find their fingers are taken up with the counting process. If they try and count while pointing they may become confused and the two processes need to be separated.

There is a further potential for confusion, for counting on the fingers and the signs for number could be confusing. Many hearing children, in performing simple arithmetic operations, will use their fingers to count up or down depending on the problem. However, signs for numbers above five do not directly represent the number of objects, e.g. the sign for six is likely to be one finger raised, depending on the counting signs in use. In their study, Nunes and Moreno (1997a) observed six profoundly deaf primary-aged school children who used sign-supported English at school. They found children had more difficulty solving problems when counting through signs than when counting actual objects. However, some pupils had developed a more complex solution to this. They found that pupils using sign could develop an algorithm where they made the sign for two different numbers, each on a different hand. They could then transfer the numbers by counting up or down from one hand to the other. This process used effectively could solve the problem.

In the development of mathematics teaching through sign language a further difficulty arises. Because of its suppression in education, sign language has not been developed in the area of mathematics in the past and signs for many mathematical concepts do not currently exist. If we are thinking of developing signs for mathematical words, how should these be developed, who should develop them and should signs be related to the processes they represent? This is an important issue as mathematical and scientific words are arbitrary, yet when people try to evolve signs they often try to make them relate in some way to the concept they represent. A workshop in Leeds that sought to address these issues considered in some detail the sign that had been developed in the sign bilingual programme in Leeds. Even taking such concepts as addition which seem superficially simple, the task was complex. A number of different signs were required, depending on the process of addition being discussed, adding one amount to another, bringing two things together, or using the conventional symbol for addition.

Conclusion

This chapter has considered the mathematical attainments of deaf pupils and some of the factors that could contribute to the delay demonstrated in the research. It has also looked at the use of sign language both in terms of the abilities of deaf children of deaf parents and the special issues arising when sign is used as the medium of instruction. It suggests that a consideration of pupils' strengths as well as their areas of difficulty is important in developing the teaching of mathematics.

Further reading

Nunes, T. and Moreno, C. (1998) 'The signed algorithm and its bugs', *Educational Studies in Mathematics* 5, 85–92.
This paper looks at the role of sign in mathematical thinking for deaf children, and in particular at the use of a signed algorithm. Other papers by these authors are likely to be published over the next few years and warrant attention by those interested in this topic.

Wood D., Wood H., Griffiths A., Howarth I. (1986) *Teaching and Talking with Deaf Children*. Chichester: John Wiley.
Chapter 9 reviews the research on mathematical attainments of deaf children up to the time of its publication, and explores some of the factors that could contribute to their lower attainments.

Achieving access to a broad and balanced curriculum

Tina Wakefield

The British Association of Teachers of the Deaf (BATOD) produced a document in 1996 entitled 'Towards a national policy in the education of deaf children and young people', which included among the educational entitlements considered essential 'the entitlement to a broad, balanced and relevant curriculum. The entitlement to appropriate forms of assessment and accreditation'.

The manner of provision of these entitlements – which may at first glance seem to be of almost simplistic educational validity, applicable to all children whether exhibiting Special Educational Needs (SEN) or not – has been the subject of considerable debate, consultation and heart searching amongst teachers of the deaf, educationalists, civil servants and government mandarins. The conclusions drawn from these consultations are often neither clear-cut nor permanent, with the result that many newly established rights and entitlements are written on the shifting sand of political expediency with no actual legislative power or permanence. It is to be hoped that this may change after the implementation of some of the suggestions put forward in the governmental Green Paper discussion document 'Excellence for All Children – Meeting Special Educational Needs' (DfEE 1997a).

The introduction of a National Curriculum into schools for the first time in this country was a landmark in the education of all children and had significant implications for those with a hearing impairment. It was looked forward to with eager anticipation and hopes of equal access, although there was a realisation that there was a fundamental need for sufficient resources to facilitate access rather than disapplication and for fair assessment rather than merely a measure of disability (Elphick 1989).

Unfortunately the National Curriculum in its initial form produced specific difficulties for the education of deaf children and was also criticised in general by mainstream teachers. For the majority of children with special educational needs (SEN) there were problems with the amount of content that had to be covered. The additional help needed by deaf children outside the strict definition of the curriculum, e.g. language work, listening activities, communication therapy, meant that while engaged in these activities they would miss other, legally determined, areas of the curriculum.

The more flexible curriculum introduced by Sir Ron Dearing in 1993 was a welcome innovation, reducing the huge content and allowing for a period of time each week to be available for non-National Curriculum activities; although a recent survey of 200 teachers of the deaf on curriculum issues showed that only 58 per cent were aware of this 'freed-up' time, and only 31 per cent of teachers actually used this time for non-National Curriculum activities (Wakefield 1998).

One of the major issues brought about by the introduction of a structured curriculum, is that in many mainstream schools there is continued difficulty for the teacher of the deaf to negotiate the time for, and to achieve acceptance of the crucial importance of, the various educational areas in which work is necessary for the specific educational development of the deaf child.

These areas include:

- communication skills in all their variations from lip-reading through to a truly bilingual approach;
- the reinforcement of basic core skills of reading, writing and numeracy;
- deaf awareness issues ranging from access and knowledge of the local and national Deaf community to Deaf issues and peer awareness.

The time available for these special elements of educational provision has to be balanced, as in the recent past, by the teacher of the deaf against the value of the work done, versus its intrusion into the broad mainstream curriculum. This allowance of time has now also to be argued for with the host school Special Educational Needs Co-ordinator (SENCO) or head teacher, who may view any withdrawal from the mainstream curriculum as necessarily detrimental for all pupils. Issues specific to deafness, even those easily seen as educationally valid, such as linguistic delay, may not be understood or valued by the host school and need constant explanation and emphasis, never mind the more esoteric elements of access to, and knowledge of, Deaf culture.

The imposition of the National Curriculum has led to other constraints on what is taught – in both content and teaching styles. For example the teacher might want the children to be investigative but have to exercise a more didactic method of teaching in order to get through the content in the required period of time.

The Education Act of 1981 specified that 'wherever possible' children with SEN should be educated in mainstream schools; this, alongside the worldwide increasing enthusiasm for inclusive education, has meant that in recent years there has been a movement towards, not only the oral deaf, but also profoundly deaf signing pupils, being integrated into mainstream lessons in both primary and secondary schools. The lessons attended are designed for hearing pupils but can give deaf pupils opportunity for access to the curriculum if effective support is offered to the teacher and to both the hearing and the deaf participants.

In some local education authorities, such as Leeds, since the closure of schools for the deaf a bilingual approach for some children is achieved using 'ordinary schools' with the wide use of deaf adults as support, and a high profile given to BSL, links with the local Deaf community and some specific lessons such as sex education and 'deaf drama' being taught separately (Powers 1996c). This type of facility is centrally funded with generous staffing, but, as noted by Powers, would be difficult to maintain in the case of delegated budgets.

The Non-Maintained and Independent Special Schools for Hearing Impaired Children have addressed the criticism that they may not deliver an appropriate curriculum, by trying to establish a role that complements that of the maintained sector by educating children with very specific needs or creating 'centres of excellence' based on high quality specific resources, with a distinctive ethos and staff with particular areas of expertise (Bown 1993).

The disapplication of statemented children from areas of the curriculum such as modern foreign languages (MFL) may have the advantage of freeing up more time for special curricular needs. There has been recent support for BSL to be included as an official MFL. This would give a variety of access to deaf children ranging from the bilingual pupil gaining a qualification in their 'mother tongue' through to purely oral pupils enhancing their access to the Deaf community.

The issue of how assessment can influence and even control teaching has attracted the interest of government not just in Britain but around the world; especially the areas of accountability and what is seen as the maintaining of 'traditional academic' standards through the use of externally set tests. The personal needs of the small number of special needs children has tended to be generally overlooked in the stampede for national information, on the basis of which the quality of teachers, schools and even the education system as a whole can be judged.

Broadfoot (1996) noted that the ideology and associated practice of formal assessment is now so firmly embedded in any national curriculum that the two areas seem to be inseparable, and any attempt to release education from the constraints of assessment procedures would be likely to result in the collapse of the system itself.

The government policy initiative that led, through many different government bodies – from the Assessment of Performance Unit, to the setting up of the School's Curriculum and Assessment Authority (SCAA), which later merged with the National Council for Vocational Qualifications to form the Qualifications and Curriculum Authority (QCA) – can be seen not only as an attempt by central authority to gain formal control within the system of assessment but also as an attempt to influence the criteria teachers adopt as a basis of their own, self-imposed, professional accountability (Broadfoot 1996).

The results of these assessments are required to be published and have often been interpreted uncritically and out of context. The desire to publish 'raw scores' rather than the more contextualised 'value added scores' may change in the future, as QCA has stated that it will work on 'establishing a national system of value added measures, based on the results of national tests and public examinations', and that it has a long-term aim of working with the inspectorate in the Office for Standards in Education (OFSTED) and the government's Department for Education and Employment (DfEE) to provide more detailed analyses, using school-level and pupil-level variables to assist schools in establishing more individual benchmarks for their own performance and setting targets for improvement (SCAA/QCA 1997a).

The importance of a more ipsative, value added approach for deaf children cannot be emphasised too greatly. Even with all the modifications and special arrangements available in the assessment process throughout their school life, the end result of each assessment period is the deaf child being compared with national norms, and levels of attainment which inevitably lead to the individual and the family feeling failure and disappointment. Although the child's results will still be compared to national norms their own ipsative scores, from baseline onward, should be available and their own progress tracked and hopefully praised by staff and school to help boost the self-esteem that assessment procedures can so easily destroy.

In France the mass testing at entry to each stage of schooling is confidential to the school and the individual pupil's parents, and there is at present no intention of using this information for public inter-school comparisons, although generalised data is used to inform regional and national educational policies.

In comparison, the introduction in England and Wales of performance tables using the national test results in both the primary and secondary sector, has many implications for the education of deaf children, not least in the host school's response to any 'lowering' effect of having an integrated resource or unit for the deaf attached to the school and therefore included in the school's results.

For many schools their place in the performance or 'league' table can have a marked effect on their popularity with parents and present very real problems in a time of falling rolls. Even the most sympathetic school will be forced to think twice about the establishment of a unit if it may in the long term threaten the jobs of their mainstream staff. Proposals to present the scores of statemented pupils separately from those of their peers in the mainstream may reduce school pressure on the hearing-impaired student, but are difficult to reconcile with a truly inclusive philosophy.

Many schools now coach their children for the national tests, with practice papers, homework in the style of the assessment and even full-scale 'mock' examinations undertaken formally in the school hall. This coaching encroaches on teaching time, but more importantly raises the importance of the assessment in the minds of the deaf pupils, often setting them up for inevitable failure.

It is to be hoped that the proposed target setting and benchmarking procedures to be introduced into all schools from September 1998 will be 'realistic and yet challenging' (DfEE 1997c) and not just another way for schools to be compared, and therefore perhaps become even less willing to take on roll deaf pupils who may lower their results.

Teachers of the deaf have been consulted from the earliest days of the instigation of a National Curriculum, and are still involved in the formation of new areas of curriculum and assessment procedures as in the recent development of baseline assessment. The Draft Proposals supplied to BATOD by SCAA (1996b) were sent out via the National Curriculum Sub-committee to approximately 20 practising teachers of the deaf with infant experience in various educational settings and various communication modes.

These teachers were asked to comment on the proposals and their responses were then assembled into a formal reply which was sent to SCAA and was included in their later document 'SCAA Consultation on Baseline Assessment' (SCAA 1997c). Several practical difficulties were noted in the draft proposals, such as when a child was expected to 'recognise the letters' shape and sound', 'hear the sounds in words and write the corresponding letters in a sequence', and such performance criteria as, 'listen attentively and talk about his or her experiences', 'listen and respond to direct questions', 'speaking audibly', etc.

The pilot study for baseline assessment took place in 1997, and all schools will be required to take up an accredited scheme by September 1998. Teachers of the deaf should be used in the trialling of all such assessment developments but despite regular communication with SCAA/QCA, this is only sporadically offered and often at a very late stage in the development when major changes of style or content are impossible.

Baseline assessment links with the more detailed assessment of children with SEN required under the Code of Practice (DoE 1994a), but most national assessments such as baseline schemes will not provide sufficiently detailed assessment on their own to place a child on the school's register of children with SEN or lead through to a statement. Head teachers are allowed to 'exempt' children who already have a statement in place or are being considered for one, but this can be seen as counter-productive in that it may prevent a comparable baseline value being set for the deaf child that will be one of the basic measurements in any value added measure attempted in the future.

Teacher of the deaf involvement in the Standard Assessment Tasks (SATs) which are now taken by all children at the ages of seven, eleven and fourteen, goes back to the first pilot studies in 1990. At this very early stage Wilson and Wakefield (1990) noted that the linguistic and developmental difficulties experienced by the deaf cannot be solved merely by individual modification of the tests carried out in the classroom, but that the specific needs of the hearing impaired must be considered at all stages of development of the SATs and that a generic approach to the assessment of children with SEN is not sufficient to ensure genuine access for deaf children. For example some of the SAT activities involved simultaneously listening and writing answers, which is extremely difficult for those children who need to lip-read to follow speech.

In the general principles for special arrangements issued by SCAA it is stated that the tests are designed to be accessible for the vast majority of pupils, and that advice has been taken from a variety of experts as to the suitability of draft questions, including representatives from the British Association of Teachers of the Deaf.

SCAA publishes recommendations for special arrangements and involves teachers of the deaf in the modification at source of most of the national tests at the end of the first three Key Stages: Key Stage 1 – covering children from 5 to 7 years, Key Stage 2 – 8 to 11 years and Key Stage 3 – 12 to 14 years. SCAA does, however, always keep the power to reject or accept these recommendations without explanation. Many teachers involved in the paper setting report how detailed modifications are sent to SCAA, and yet when the papers are sent to the schools only some of the modifications have been included. This would be more acceptable to the contributors if a detailed explanation was provided of why particular aspects had been allowed and others not.

As a contributor to the Teacher Writer Group involved in the development of the English tests I have experienced the academic rigour and genuine desire to allow access to the paper for children with SEN that is the underlying rationale of the teachers and researchers involved in the test development, and have on many occasions been impressed by their willingness to try to understand the needs of the deaf pupil. There is, however, a large gap both in time, often two years, and in the personnel involved in the final development before the papers are sent out to schools, during which many changes are made.

In recent discussions with SCAA over testing, an important aspect of underlying ideology became clear. Although the administrators of the assessments do have a real desire to allow fair access, special needs children are only a very small percentage of the vast numbers being dealt with, and as such are considered as individuals whose different special arrangements can be dealt with to a large extent by their specific teacher not by national edict. SCAA has a need not to be seen to allow special needs to become the 'tail that wags the dog'.

This is understandable in the more practical aspects of special arrangements such as arranging optimum acoustics of the test room, seating position and allowing time for lip-reading during dictation exercises, but leads to uncertainty and confusion when applied to modifying written papers or signing the questions, especially at the higher Key Stages.

Communicators may be used in mathematics and science but not in English except for the general instructions. Pupils are allowed to sign their response in these subjects and the teacher can record the pupil's answers. In the advice for special arrangements it is specified that, 'Care should be taken that signs used by the adult signer do not indicate the answer required' (SCAA 1997b). The insoluble difficulty of signing such mathematical concepts as 'rectangle' without giving essential information as to its shape have led to lengthy and ongoing correspondence with the examiners and great heart-searching among the teachers of the deaf who have to communicate these tests.

The specific needs of the low incidence, geographically widespread, deaf child population are not always acknowledged by those administrating the assessment procedures. For example in largely rural areas such as Cornwall the physical distances between deaf pupils supported by the peripatetic teachers of the deaf mean that the early opening of papers in order to make special arrangements five days before the tests are to be taken, is logistically impossible, especially at Key Stage 1, the youngest stage, as schools are allowed to take the tests at any date during a particular month. Therefore, five days before the papers are taken in the west of the county, may not be the same date as in the east of the county, or even the neighbouring school, which means that any systematic modification of papers at a central location becomes an impossibility.

Arrangements for the twelve- to fourteen-year-olds, at Key Stage 3, are generally thought of, however, as individually flexible in comparison with the General Certificate of Secondary Education (GCSE) taken at 16 years, which has a very tightly controlled system. Historically teachers of the deaf have managed to develop excellent links with the GCSE Examining Boards, obtaining specific special arrangements and papers for deaf students. The crucial difference between the GCSE examinations being seen primarily to have strong individual and vocational purpose, and the National Curriculum assessments which are embedded in the ideological and political rationale of the National Curriculum, has made specific arrangements for deaf children in this area easier to arrange on a formal and centralised basis.

The eligibility for a child to qualify for special arrangements is not necessarily linked to a statement. Previously the candidate had to be severely pre-lingually hearing impaired but this is now decided upon by evidence of need submitted by the teacher of the deaf and the school. The special arrangements available are in many ways similar to those used in the national tests: extra time, alternative accommodation, means of access to questions (signing, flashcards), support with coursework and means of response. The major difference is that the signing of responses is not permitted: responses must be written or spoken in oral examinations.

In the 1980s a sub-committee was set up by BATOD to liaise and negotiate with the examination boards, with a representative sitting on the Joint Forum of Examining Boards and other members organising modifications and running workshops to help train teachers to be able to modify examination papers.

In order to establish high standards for modifications and to ensure that the boards are receiving a consistent approach, all those involved have to complete a trial paper which is assessed. Some boards produce papers with modified language on request, but others are becoming aware that the modified language improves access to the paper for all candidates and are inviting a teacher of the deaf to be involved in the initial writing of the paper, and these 'modified at source' papers are sent out to all candidates.

This echoes the views of teachers of the deaf over the years that many of the techniques used in curriculum delivery and assessment, that help the deaf pupil, do in fact help all pupils and are pedagogically to be preferred for all children. The use of clear short sentences and increased ease of readability as described by Mobley (1987) and later made more specific by BATOD (1995) can be of paramount importance for allowing true access to the curriculum through worksheets, textbooks and school examinations. Indeed, a national rejection of the complicated diglossia used in official forms and instructions would improve access to daily life not just for the adult deaf but for all.

Development of links with General National Vocational Qualification (GNVQ) and vocational training, 'A' levels and examinations in higher education continue, and now that intervention on behalf of the deaf student has a precedent future involvement seems assured. But those involved in these areas must not risk complacency, as there always looms the spectre of the belief that by making special arrangements we are somehow making things easier for deaf children and thereby threatening the standards of the whole system.

The National Foundation for Educational Research (NFER) carried out research, involving teachers of the deaf, into assessing and recording the achievements of pupils who make small steps of progress and how to accredit their achievements by the age of 16 at the end of Key Stage 4. SCAA reported (1996a) that although a variety of specific assessments can be used as a way of recognising and valuing all progress however small in all aspects of the curriculum and be used to inform future teaching and target setting, these assessment procedures must still have authority within a wider public context. It also concluded that these records must be informative for a range of audiences, specifically at Key Stage 4 when the pupil is leaving school and entering adult life.

It is important that any accreditation systems at Key Stage 4 should have national recognition and acceptability. It may be that, with the plethora of systems now being developed to meet this need, clarity of what is being accredited is not yet being achieved. In the recent questionnaire on curriculum issues (Wakefield 1998) over fourteen different systems were reported as presently being used by deaf children, ranging through those specific to the deaf – such as Council for the Advancement of Communication with Deaf People (CACDP) qualifications; those specific to one local education authority – such as the Sheffield Units of Accreditation; those relating to GCSE boards – such as the Associated Examining Board Basic Tests; and those linked to GNVQ – such as Award Scheme Development and Accreditation Network (ASDAN). Both Wales and Scotland also have excellent schemes.

Development of accreditation which recognises this wide range of achievement is to be applauded; especially the flexibility of content and approach and the encouragement of all achievement, however limited. But there is still a real danger that the schemes will not be understood by further education and employers unless some unification and clarification of standards is developed.

In the development and revision of the curriculum in the next millennium it is of vital importance that teachers of the deaf continue to be a vocal and consistent pressure group for the rights of all hearing-impaired children and an advocate for true equality of access.

Chapter 3.5

Supporting deaf pupils in mainstream settings

Linda Watson and Jackie Parsons

In recent years a silent but revolutionary change has occurred in the education of deaf children in the UK. Based on data collected by the British Association of Teachers of the Deaf (BATOD), Lynas *et al.* (1997) estimate that 85 per cent of deaf pupils are being taught in mainstream schools, and that three fifths of teachers of the deaf now work in such schools, either in units for hearing-impaired pupils or as peripatetic teachers. This change has passed largely unnoticed by writers and researchers alike.

In addition to the trend to educate deaf pupils in mainstream settings, there has been a parallel trend towards offering in-class support rather than withdrawal from class which was previously the norm. Writing in 1989, Ward does not even list offering in-class support in his description of the role of the teacher of the deaf, but in 1990, Powers suggested that secondary-aged pupils were already receiving slightly more in-class support than withdrawal and this practice has become more prevalent. While some have welcomed this move, others have actively opposed the idea. Harrison (1993), for example, concludes that in-class support can be not only an uneconomic use of the specialist teacher's time but may actually be detrimental to the pupil's progress, since the mainstream teacher may tend to work through the specialist teacher of the deaf rather than interacting with the pupil directly. Taking a more positive attitude towards the practice of offering in-class support, it is possible to see the teacher of the deaf fulfilling a valuable role in this area. However, the view of writers such as Harrison (1993) serves to highlight the need for planning and collaboration in order to ensure that the teacher of the deaf's role is clearly defined and beneficial to the pupil concerned. Joint planning of lessons, with team teaching, is one possibility. For pupils in Key Stages 1 and 2 this should mean playing to each teacher's strengths and should prove beneficial to the class as a whole. For older pupils successful team teaching relies on the teacher of the deaf being able to offer subject specialisms in addition to having specialist knowledge of teaching deaf pupils. In a secondary school which is resourced for meeting the needs of deaf pupils, it is desirable to ensure as far as possible that the subject specialisms of the teachers of the deaf are not only complementary but also that they cover the whole range of subjects.

The practice of offering support within the context of the mainstream classroom fits within an inclusive policy in which each pupil and member of staff is fully integrated into the school. While the discussion on inclusion and its implementation for deaf pupils (Powers 1996a and 1996b, 1996c) is beyond the scope of this chapter, the issues which it raises for support are highly pertinent. These issues are overtly concerned with the support required to ensure the pupils' access to the curriculum and to assist them in reaching their educational potential, but extend beyond purely educational considerations to ensuring that deaf pupils' mental health and cultural needs are both addressed, in short to ensuring that the needs of the pupil as a whole person are being met. Powers suggests an approach 'that seeks to maximise opportunity, independence and participation for all pupils according to individual needs and wishes but that recognises that these different aims are not always mutually compatible' (1996b, p. 68).

A truly inclusive policy should mean that pupils are naturally placed in their neighbourhood school, a pattern which is advocated for deaf pupils by some writers (Simpson *et al.* (1989) and Deaf Education Through Listening and Talking (DELTA 1997)). Other writers favour a model in which deaf pupils are segregated for their education as a means of preparation for subsequent integration into society (Shaw (1989) and British Deaf Association (1996)). The starting point for the chapter is that where pupils are integrated for all or part of their education into mainstream classes, searching questions must be asked about the nature and amount of specialist support which is required to allow these pupils to access the curriculum, while bearing in mind their broader educational and social needs. If a school is operating an inclusive policy then deaf pupils will be valued for the contribution that they can make to the school community. Their presence within the school will not only be accepted but welcomed. In the early days of integration policy some deaf pupils were viewed as a burden on mainstream staff and as a consequence teachers of the deaf in a supporting role felt obliged to make themselves as unobtrusive as possible and to attempt to minimise the demands made on mainstream staff. Working within a collaborative approach and an inclusive policy, however, gives the teacher of the deaf a positive role.

Patterns of support

There are different patterns of support which may be employed. The applicability of one pattern over another may vary depending on many factors, including age of the pupil; teaching style adopted by the mainstream teacher(s); physical environment of the school; and the communication mode in which the support is being offered. Decisions concerning the support should be a subject of negotiation between the mainstream staff, the teacher of the deaf, the pupils themselves and their parents. Under the Code of Practice (DfE 1994a), an Individual Education Plan (IEP) will be drawn up for any pupil with SEN and should include detail of the type and amount of support being offered to the pupil. Some general questions need to be considered for all pupils, then specific questions will arise according to individual circumstances. The concern must be to ensure that individual deaf pupils are offered the pattern of support which will best meet their particular needs: this could involve decisions concerning the level of integration and the amount of support offered. If the decision for any pupil is that some support should be offered by withdrawal from the mainstream class then the purpose and nature of the support must be specified and the reasons why it should take place in a withdrawal setting should be given.

The advent of the National Curriculum and the recognition that all pupils should have access to the whole curriculum, with relatively few disapplications, gives added incentive for deaf pupils, like other pupils with SEN, to be educated in the mainstream. This move has been given further impetus by the recent Green Paper (DfEE 1997a) on educating pupils with SEN. Whereas it was often the case that deaf pupils were offered a restricted curriculum, their right to access to a broad and balanced curriculum, including the National Curriculum, is now established. There is, however, still scope for pupils to be offered extra subjects, an opportunity which Wakefield (this volume) suggests is not always seized.

Support within an oral approach

Since there are different considerations to bear in mind according to the educational setting and the nature of the support being offered, it may be helpful to discuss them under separate headings. Deaf pupils who are integrated into a mainstream class and who communicate orally may still need a considerable amount of support in order to ensure full access to the curriculum, even those pupils whose level of spoken language development is high and who are able to make maximum use of amplification to support their residual hearing. In order to decide the appropriate type and level of support, questions need to be asked concerning the pupils' ability to access the lesson. Some pupils will be able to participate fully in the lesson provided that their amplification needs are met, but may still need note-taking support. Other pupils may require considerable additional explanation of the subject matter, but then be able to perform quite competently in class.

It is often the case that such pupils will gain more benefit if the additional information is given before the lesson as pre-tutoring, but for others the offer of additional explanation during the lesson will suffice. Other pupils, who are experiencing a greater degree of difficulty, may require a considerable amount of follow-up work in order to grasp the subject matter. For such pupils, the question then arises of when and where this support should be offered. It may also be the case that these pupils require differentiated materials, which may be provided by the mainstream teacher or the teacher of the deaf.

Having considered some of these fundamental questions concerning the pupils' requirements for support in order to access the curriculum, in particular the National Curriculum, further issues may arise. As mentioned above, a decision needs to be made regarding the actual location of the support offered. While withdrawal from the mainstream class may be regarded as undesirable either on pedagogic grounds or on the grounds of possible stigmatisation for the pupils themselves, this does not always hold for deaf pupils. Some pupils feel less stigmatised by being offered support outside the mainstream classroom, where they feel more free to admit to their lack of comprehension and seek clarification. Other pupils find the fact that the acoustic conditions in a withdrawal setting may be so superior to those that obtain in the typical mainstream classroom that they request support to be offered outside the mainstream class (Watson 1996).

The question frequently arises as to who should offer in-class support, a teacher of the deaf or a learning support assistant. Such assistants have been used to support the work of teachers and pupils in the education of deaf pupils for many years, and increasingly they are being employed to work in the mainstream classroom. If the requirement is for a note-taker, then a learning support assistant sitting at the back of the class with a lap-top taking pupil-friendly notes which the pupil can then print off after the lesson may provide the best solution. Alternatively, the assistant and pupil might have linked lap-tops so that as the assistant types the notes they appear on the pupil's screen. An assistant who is seated close to the pupil has the advantage of being able to offer quick on-the-spot explanations of new vocabulary which the pupil has not understood and will be able to report back to the mainstream teacher or teacher of the deaf on any difficulties the pupil encountered in the lesson. If the support is in essence teaching, then clearly it should be offered by a teacher of the deaf. There are funding implications which can be relevant, but which should not be allowed to guide decision making. It is important for teachers to be able to argue clearly and with practical evidence for the level of support which is required for any pupil and to specify whether this needs to be offered by a teacher of the deaf. DES Circular 11/90 (DES 1990), for example, suggests that the same staff : pupil ratio should apply in units as in special schools. This ignores the fact that pupils in units may be one per year group, all requiring support at the same time, or in secondary schools may be following different GCSE options.

Whoever supplies the support, it needs to be given sensitively, with the development of the whole pupil in mind. It is possible for the support teacher or assistant to impede the social integration and development of independence. Deaf pupils in mainstream schools sometimes have problems relating to hearing pupils as friends (Cross and Prowse (1988); Markides (1989); Owers (1996); Fraser (1996)) and various imaginative schemes have been tried (Close (1995) and Sugden (1997)). While recognising that it is impossible to legislate for friendships, there will be opportunity, both inside and outside the classroom, to foster contact between deaf and hearing pupils. The value of any support which gets in the way of the deaf pupil developing friendships, either with hearing pupils or with other deaf pupils, must be called into question.

There are some practical issues which need to be faced in integrated settings. Deaf pupils who are being educated orally without any sign support will be highly dependent on amplification, both in the form of personal hearing aids and other equipment, for example radio systems. It is essential that all such amplification is both maintained in excellent working order and used effectively. As they mature pupils should be able to assume responsibility for the management of such equipment themselves, supported by the teacher of the deaf. Correct use of the radio system can make a great deal of difference to a pupil's ability to access the lesson and there will be a need for mainstream staff to be offered in-service training in this area.

There are, however, issues surrounding the use of the radio system which require sensitive handling and may demand that teachers of the deaf involved in supporting pupils and staff are called upon to exercise considerable skill to ensure that the system is utilised correctly and the maximum benefit gained from it. Supplying advice and information on this subject may occupy a considerable amount of the teacher of the deaf's time. The practical issues concerning correct and appropriate use of radio systems may not prove quite as straightforward as one might imagine. There are clear guidelines concerning the optimal positioning of the microphone of the transmitter and the practice of switching the transmitter on or off, depending on whether the teacher is addressing the whole class, a group containing the deaf pupil, or a group which does not contain the deaf pupil. These points can be demonstrated and explained and often become automatic. However, there are circumstances in which radio aids are not beneficial or some other system, for instance a conference microphone, may be more appropriate and these situations also need to be discussed. The question of background noise in mainstream classes is an important issue for pupils who are reliant either on personal hearing aids or on hearing aids used in conjunction with radio systems. The use of a radio system will go some way towards re-establishing a favourable signal : noise ratio, although this cannot be taken for granted (Smythe and Bamford 1997).

More difficult to deal with is the attitude of the deaf pupils themselves towards using a radio system. While wearing hearing aids may be an issue for some deaf pupils, those who use purely oral means of communication will usually accept them as essential, indeed, some wear them 24 hours a day, even sleeping in them. However, the radio system can be the cause of difficulty for some pupils. While it is to be hoped that the adoption of an inclusive policy in which each pupil is valued will serve to alleviate the stigma of feeling different which many pupils can experience for a variety of reasons, the radio system can mark deaf pupils out and be the source of embarrassment to some. The situation requires diplomacy and discussion and a compromise may be needed. While nobody would want deaf pupils to feel uncomfortable, abandoning the use of the radio system is likely to have a detrimental effect on deaf pupils who are being expected to depend on the use of their residual hearing. It has been found to be the case that for some deaf pupils the radio system serves to focus the attention for all those involved with that pupil on the necessity for them to face questions of their own identity. The emotional needs of deaf pupils who communicate freely with the hearing world can sometimes be overlooked or underestimated.

Support within a Total Communication approach

Those deaf pupils in mainstream settings who are using some form of sign support (Total Communication, Sign-Supported English, Manually Coded English) will make different demands on the support teacher or assistant. Some pupils may be able to access the majority of the lesson orally, as outlined above, with the support of a note-taker where appropriate, but may additionally require some sign support. A pupil such as this should be able to attend to the mainstream teacher the majority of the time, then look towards the support teacher or assistant when unfamiliar vocabulary is introduced or the pupil requires some additional explanation. The support teacher might then sign or finger-spell the key word or brief explanation, after which the pupil will look back to the teacher.

However, for pupils who require a considerable amount of sign support, careful planning is essential. Such issues as how to manage the pupils' attention and whether it is appropriate for the pupils to have an amplified signal must be addressed. Unless such situations are managed appropriately, the situation may arise in which a pupil receives the amplified signal from the mainstream teacher, via the radio system, while the support teacher or assistant is offering sign support and mouthing without using their voice. This 'worst case' scenario means that the pupil is hearing one signal through their ears without the aid of lip-reading since they are not attending to the mainstream teacher who is speaking, then they are receiving a different set of signals through their eyes in the form of a mouthed message which is not synchronous with the spoken message coming via the radio system, plus the signing of key words. The unsatisfactory nature of such support for the pupil must surely be apparent.

There may be problems with signing curriculum content vocabulary. Now that the National Curriculum is established, a body of essential vocabulary items appears to be emerging. Some local authorities, for example Bromley and Wolverhampton, have begun to produce sign language dictionaries for specific curriculum areas (London Borough of Bromley 1994, 1997 and Wolverhampton Metropolitan Borough Council 1996). However, in the context of a lesson the support teacher or assistant cannot wait for a dictionary to appear, nor contact a local deaf consultant. A short-term solution can be to discuss with the pupil the meaning of the word and how best to encapsulate this in a sign, and then replace this with the agreed sign should one be published.

The question concerning the best position in the classroom for the support teacher or assistant in these circumstances requires planning. While Dowe (1995) suggests a position at the front of the class, next to the class teacher, a position which permits the pupil to switch attention easily between the signer and the teacher, it may be that a different position would be more helpful, particularly if there is likely to be some interaction between the support teacher or assistant and the pupil while the teacher is talking, a possibility mentioned above.

Support in BSL

The situation for pupils whose preferred language is BSL and who are being supported in that mode, raises different issues. These pupils will probably choose to attend solely to the support teacher or assistant while the mainstream teacher is addressing the whole class. It will probably be concluded that the use of any amplification system additional to the pupil's personal hearing aids is not appropriate. However, the role of the support teacher or assistant merits consideration. Is the support required simply interpretation of the lesson, or does the pupil also require further explanation in order to grasp the concepts or subject matter? It could be argued that in the former case an interpreter is required, and thus the major concern will be that they should have a high level of signing skill, while in the latter case it would be more appropriate for a teacher to be both interpreting and giving additional teacher support.

The role of deaf colleagues in working with deaf pupils in mainstream settings demands clarification. In recent years it has been seen that deaf adults can play a very significant role in working alongside other professionals supporting deaf pupils, particularly those whose preferred mode of communication is BSL. The ability of deaf adults to convey concepts to deaf pupils in an unambiguous manner has been recognised. However, this raises the question as to whether deaf adults are being asked to teach language, and if they are being asked to teach, then there are possible implications both for training and remuneration.

Where there is a team of different professionals working together, some deaf pupils may be supported by more than one person at the same time, for example a deaf adult and a hearing teacher of the deaf. In addition to the need to clarify roles, this raises the question of the experience for the pupil. It is not difficult to imagine why some deaf adults, for example Ladd (1991), argue against integration for deaf pupils. The need to examine the nature of the whole educational experience for deaf pupils, and to make decisions which consider individual needs rather than slavishly follow a policy, is readily apparent.

Peripatetic support teachers

Teachers of the deaf are employed in different capacities and follow different working practices. Where there are several deaf pupils in one school then frequently the teacher of the deaf will be based at the school. This affords the opportunity for the teacher of the deaf to be fully involved in the life of the school and to be seen as a member of the school staff. Other deaf pupils are supported by peripatetic teachers, who may be known by various titles, for example visiting teachers, advisory teachers or teacher advisors. The situation for these support teachers raises different issues. Communication between the teacher of the deaf and mainstream staff, vital to the progress of the deaf pupil, can present difficulties and requires commitment on both sides. A visiting teacher of the deaf is unlikely to have a great deal of flexibility in their timetable and, because of other constraints on their time, may find it extremely difficult to find a convenient time for consulting with mainstream staff. It can be difficult for teachers of the deaf to keep fully abreast of changes in all the local schools with which they are involved.

Where a teacher of the deaf is employed in a peripatetic capacity, probably supporting pupils in several different schools, there is the same need to ensure that the nature and extent of the support being offered is negotiated as was discussed with reference to teachers of the deaf working exclusively in one school. For ease, many services for the hearing impaired have drawn up service agreements which result from negotiation between the mainstream school and teacher of the deaf. This means that both parties are clear what each has undertaken to contribute. Thus the teacher of the deaf might agree to support individual pupils at certain specified times, take responsibility for specialist equipment and provide an agreed amount of in-service training. The mainstream school might agree that staff will furnish the teacher of the deaf with lesson plans, use the specialist equipment as recommended, attend in-service training, etc. A pro forma can make the whole process easier. In the current climate of accountability and value for money, the advantages of such an agreement are obvious.

The teacher of the deaf as consultant and agent of change

It will be clear from the discussion in this chapter that the role of the support teacher of the deaf is very different from the more traditional teaching roles of class teacher or subject specialist, demanding different skills. Teachers of the deaf working in a support capacity will be acting as consultants to other staff, giving advice and information. They will therefore be expected to be knowledgeable about all aspects of education of the deaf and to be able to tailor their advice to fit the needs of individual pupils.

This role of consultant can enable the teacher of the deaf to act as an agent of change, challenging entrenched views about hearing loss or deaf people, in short being an advocate for the needs of all deaf pupils, different though those needs may be.

Chapter 3.6

Information technology and deaf pupils

Ben Elsendoorn

Introduction

The use of information technology (IT) in deaf education is slowly beginning to emerge, showing its enormous potential for supporting the development of communication and language skills, as well as for teaching subjects such as geography, mathematics and biology. Whereas the former type of IT application aims at improving receptive (and occasionally, expressive) communication skills such as speech reading and understanding signed or written language, the latter type of application is particularly useful to support the transfer of information. In these cases sign language or spoken/written language is used as a vehicle to reach this goal.

Within the framework of this chapter, we will primarily focus on IT that supports training in communication and language proficiency, as many of the issues presented in this respect will relate to both types of applications.

Until recently, IT for training communication and language skills took the shape of dedicated hardware, which was usually very expensive and nearly impossible to produce in large numbers. Working prototypes would be available at schools for the deaf or at university institutes, but in general, industry was not interested (and in fact, still is not) in adopting these prototypes for large-series productions. This was due to high development costs because of the special hardware and the fact that the market is relatively small – especially in Europe when viewed per nation, each having its own language. As a result, the wheel kept on being re-invented time and again at different places with eventually only a small number of people benefiting.

In the past few years a number of IT applications have been developed in the form of software programs, which are easier and less costly to reproduce, thus becoming available to an extensive deaf audience.

Defining IT applications; advantages and disadvantages

In order to confine the field of systems that would be acceptable as IT systems, they should be defined as having the possibility of random, yet exact, access. Also, they should use some form of electronics (which makes us get rid of books and videotapes, and leaves us with special dedicated hardware, computers or any carrier that can be played by a computer or a special playback machine). The most widely used technology for storing software and database materials includes CD-ROM, laser-video disks, CD-i (compact disc interactive), and in the near future the digital video disc (DVD).

Each of these systems has its (dis)advantages. The advantage of special, dedicated hardware is that it usually provides the optimal system: the application works fast and smoothly. The disadvantage is the fact that these systems can be (and usually *are*) very expensive, and, of course, that they cannot be used for anything else. An example of such a system on special hardware is the German SFT equipment.[1] It is used as a support system to improve deaf students' pronunciation by presenting the amplitude envelope of a speech signal as a function of time, filled with varying colours that depend on the spectral composition of the speech. It is claimed that using this system will help to improve the learner's pronunciation of isolated words (Nolte *et al.* 1993).

Since many of the recent IT applications are being developed on computer systems, we find a growing market of IT applications realised as software which needs a computer for playback. Computers need not necessarily be less expensive than the dedicated hardware, yet they have the advantage that they can be used for other applications as well. Examples of these include the IBM Speech Viewer® (Destombes 1993) and the Visual Speech Apparatus (VSA), which was designed by the Instituut voor Doven/IvD (Arends 1993). The computers necessary to run these applications can also be used to play back other programs.

Many programs are now being distributed on CD-ROM. They can be played directly from CD-ROM, or can be downloaded onto the hard disk for improved (i.e. faster) performance. CD-ROM is also ideal for presenting large databases. A disadvantage of storing an application on CD-ROM is the fact that it will not always play back on any type of computer system. System requirements must be carefully defined, which includes the mentioning of additional sound and image processing boards if necessary. Especially the latter type of boards can result in playback problems as image coding and decoding techniques are still developing very quickly, resulting in one 'standard' being replaced by the next.

Contrary to CD-ROM, CD-i does not experience these kind of problems. It has excellent sound and video playback, and the special CD players can be connected to any type of television set and will work. Unfortunately, CD-i did not receive the support it needed to become a world standard. The installed base is relatively small and is now mainly used in professional (industrial) situations.

Another advantage of using computers in IT applications is that they can easily keep track of a student's actions, record mistakes, and provide the teacher with information on the student's learning progress. A disadvantage of the computer is that it is often considered (and is experienced to be) difficult to access: if not by the deaf students, then by their teachers. Regardless of whether this is the truth or a myth, IT applications should always be designed such that they can be used by inexperienced or novice computer users once the system has been switched on and the program started.

IT design issues in deaf education

There is more to designing an educational IT application in general than simply 'the look and feel' of the program. Designing an IT application for deaf education brings along a number of aspects that are very specific for this type of application.

First of all, there is the aspect of deafness. This may seem self-evident, or even trivial, but the fact remains that the user's deafness poses serious problems for interactive training. Deaf users will use primarily visual information in an (interactive) application. Whereas hearing users are often informed about their actions or responses by beeps or other sounds – be they correct or incorrect – deaf users must be offered this information in a very clear, visual way. In the case of simple warning signals this will not be too serious a problem for designers. But if a sound signal functions as a means to let a hearing user know that an action has been recorded by the system, some subtlety must be added to the user interface to inform deaf users about this. An example of this would be to change the look of action/response buttons on the screen such that they seem to have been pressed or by changing their colour. This is to be preferred above having a hot-spot that can be clicked or double-clicked, but which does not change optically. However, use of colour can be a problem with a considerable number of deaf users, who have difficulty in perceiving various contrasts. It is important for graphical designers to be aware of this issue.

A second aspect is the problem of understanding the dialogue, which can be caused by a less proficient knowledge of the language used in the application. The interaction dialogue between an application and a user is usually presented in written language. As this is not the first language for many deaf people, the level of the language will have to be adapted to ensure that the deaf user will not have any doubts what actions to undertake and will understand the responses/assignments the system is giving. Language may also vary as a function of the intended end user group. There will be a definite distinction between the language used to young children (6–8 years), and to young grown-ups (18–20 years). Using icons wherever possible could be a satisfactory solution for all groups regardless of age.

A third issue is the possible use of visual information in the form of video sequences to present information in sign language, or to support auditory information for speech reading purposes. Although both are a very natural form of communication, sign language and spoken language are very different from written information, which can be read in the user's own tempo and with unlimited options of re-reading (parts of) it. The order in which texts can be re-read is free and determined by the user; it is hardly ever the complete text, but usually one or two sentences or a paragraph. In contrast, playing back visual or auditory information is generally established by clicking on a repeat button which triggers the complete message to be played back from beginning to end, thus repeating much more information than is usually necessary. As a result, frequent use of such an option will become annoying after a while, and will be discarded.

A fourth issue, which is becoming increasingly relevant with the growing use of Internet facilities, is whether a program should be designed for use on the Internet (*direct access*). Although the present rates of information that can be processed via telephone lines do not make such a program attractive to use, developments in this area go very quickly, and running an application directly from the Internet may become standard in the not-too-distant future. At this moment, a hybrid system could be a useful alternative: the educational program will be distributed on CD-ROM, and the training or learning materials such as sign language video sequences or speech files can be downloaded from the Internet (cf. the later section of this chapter on IT applications as a teaching tool). This will increase the flexibility of the application enormously. New lessons may be added by storing new data on a central computer system to be accessed from the Internet. Users could be charged for downloading this material – comparable to buying an addendum to a book – which would make it attractive for publishers to produce and maintain.

A final, more general, aspect is how to design an educational IT application such that users know where they find themselves in the program. Clearly, a menu can be of help here, but menus are not usually displayed continuously on each screen. One solution could be that the user is automatically redirected to the main menu or the latest submenu as soon as a particular part of the program has been finished. Another solution could be found in the graphical design of the user interface, which could display the different sections as tabs in a book.

In theory, the perfect educational IT application should come *without* a manual. Educational applications should be self-explanatory. When facing a new program, users will immediately start working with it, and will not start reading bulky manuals first.

In practice, however, it is advisable to have a manual with the program, so that learners can search for guidance when they are in doubt about what they or the program have been doing. The best manuals are written in such a way that they take the user through the program, step by step. To clarify how the program should be operated, screendumps explaining the functionality of buttons and showing results from a particular action should be used as much as possible. This way the user can always compare what is displayed on the monitor to what should be there according to the manual.

IT applications and the user

Users of educational applications can be roughly divided into two groups: students and teachers. Both will have different expectations of the application, and will need different options to be included. In order to produce a successful application, it is necessary to first define the end-user and to invite users to be involved in setting up the application requirements.

Defining the user group

Before starting the development of a new educational application, it is advisable to carefully define the intended end-user group. A (non-exhaustive) list of aspects to be considered are hearing capacity (e.g. whether only deaf users will work with the application or whether it will also be used by hearing relatives, friends, etc.), age (e.g. is it intended for a particular age group or a group covering a wide range of different ages), environment (e.g. whether it will be used in a classroom situation or at home), the type of user (e.g. whether it will be used by teachers, students, or both), and if used by teachers, their role (e.g. whether a teacher needs to be always present to help the student with any problem that is encountered, or whether the application is intended for independent student use).

User involvement

To increase the chances to develop a *successful* product, it is very important to consult representatives of intended end-users at the very beginning of an IT project. Educational IT applications are preferably designed incorporating the wishes and insights of the end-user, be they teachers or students. The functional specifications of the application to be used in deaf education especially requires much insight into the complex world of teaching deaf students, and knowledge about the way that deafness influences both user interface design and contents of the application.

It is also very important to get future users involved during the development phase. By showing them intermediate results (prototypes) they will be able to give their comments and point out any flaws that might have gone unnoticed. Having users involved in this stage of a development project will allow changes to be incorporated before the final version is completed, thus turning the development of the application into a re-iterative process. User involvement ensures that the ultimate application will be more readily accepted. As a result it will be easier to have it implemented and receive full support for it.

IT in deaf education: goals

There are two distinct types of IT: one is used as a learning tool, the other as a teaching tool. Each of these types of applications will put different demands on, for example, the user interface and the administrative facilities to be included in the application.

Basically, two equally important goals for IT in educational situations are that the application should:

- contribute to achieving the desired educational goals in an improved manner in comparison to existing methods and materials, and
- be ultimately used by teachers and/or students.

IT applications as a learning tool

IT applications can have a great number of advantages as a learning tool in comparison to 'old' information carriers such as books.

IT-based learning tools can range from teaching material which has been available for a period of time, but now with a little 'extra' added, such as sound or images, to intelligent tutoring systems that adapt the teaching material to the individual level of the student. Relatively simple IT applications based on existing teaching material with only images added are easy to design and produce. Intelligent tutoring systems require extensive research into the underlying educational problem: how can the student be certain that all topics to be learnt have been successfully covered, while at the same time the designer ensuring the optimal flexibility of the system? Aspects to be taken into account during the design phase of the application include the expected learning behaviour of the student, the types of mistakes that are likely to occur and the decision points that have to be built in the program.

IT applications as a teaching tool

First of all, it should be clear from the beginning that IT applications cannot, and never will, replace a teacher. IT designers and publishers should do their utmost to remove any fears that teachers might have in this respect. IT applications should be regarded as supplementary to 'regular' teaching. Removing this fear will additionally help to implement the application into regular teaching practice more smoothly.

In order to function as a satisfactory and effective teaching tool, the application should provide teachers with the same information, and preferably more, that would otherwise be obtained by working with traditional teaching methods. In order to monitor the student's learning process, the educational application could include built-in tests. As soon as a test has been successfully completed a student will be allowed to pass on to a following part of the program. More intelligent systems would be able to advise students which part of the program to study next, or give them a number of options to choose from.

The IT application should be flexible in the sense that teachers can easily redefine particular exercises or topics for individual students. The most advanced system should allow teachers to create their own exercises within a given framework by providing content materials. However, given the state of the art with respect to audio and visual technology in computerland, offering teachers the possibility to use their own sound and video material may turn out to be somewhat problematic. Audio signals such as sounds and speech can be recorded relatively easily, although sound quality very much depends on the recording conditions (e.g. microphone quality, room acoustics, voice quality, etc.). Sound recordings quickly suffer from reverberation as a result of room acoustics, but these are often only perceived when the recorded material is played back. High quality video recordings are even more difficult to produce.

A solution to these problems could be to have a (national) content provider, which could, for instance, be funded by all schools for the deaf. Teachers would request this organisation to provide them with material. Using a content provider would only slightly reduce the flexibility of the system.

Checking out the installed base

One mistake IT application developers might easily make is not to check out the market first to learn about the installed base. Developers are often tempted to use leading edge technology in the design of their application, while forgetting that this is not usually available at schools, institutions or the end-user's home.

It is recommended that a market survey be performed which checks for availability of hardware and program control software. IT technology in deaf education will nearly always be used by people who are computer laymen and who do not have the time nor the patience to deal with possible errors caused by hardware/software incompatibility. A simple rule of thumb would be that, for a two- or three-year development project, design and development should be carried out on systems that are new, but standard, at the research and development site at the start of a project. When the project has finished and an application realised, this would imply that the necessary hardware needed will have become affordable for most schools and individuals.

Issues in technological quality

There are a number of technological aspects to be considered during the IT design phase. Some of these aspects have to do with robustness of the system itself, others with the quality of its contents and how these will be presented.

When video images are to be used, it will not always suffice to use a frame rate which will make it possible for users to understand sign language sequences. Especially in bilingual applications which will also include the option of presenting a speaker's image for speech reading purposes, the frame rate will have to be higher for people to be able to follow the speaker. Research has shown that sign language video sequences can be understood by users when presented at a frame rate of ten frames per second, but that for speech reading a temporal resolution of 15 frames per second is needed (Woelders et al. 1997; Frowein et al. 1991).

Audio signals should at least cover the frequency range that is handled by a hearing aid. For training the perception of speech signals or environmental sounds, a direct connection of the hearing aid to the output of the computer system is to be preferred above using a set of loudspeakers. Apart from the fact that in some cases the loudness level will have to be relatively high – which will make it impossible to use the application for individual training in a classroom – users could be perceiving disturbing signals which will distract their attention from what they are doing. Additionally, in test situations it may be necessary to gauge the audio output level, which can be automatically controlled and adjusted by the system if a direct connection is available.

When users are requested to provide answers to the program, it is very important that response times are kept to an absolute minimum. If this cannot be realised, visual feedback must be given to make clear that the program is still running and further input from the user via mouse clicks or keyboard should be disabled.

Recent developments in IT applications for deaf education

A recently developed IT application in this area is the DICTUM[2] system, which is presently available as a prototype. The aim of this system is to train communicative skills, either in speech perception or sign language perception. It is the first system that incorporates sign language *and* spoken language. Skills can be practised in two different ways: there is an analytic approach, which addresses specific speech or sign language characteristics, and a global approach, which is more directed at understanding the language. The first has taken the form of a Workbook, the second the form of a Microworld, where the user can roam about to explore or to receive assignments generated by the system itself.

In the Workbook, users can define their own set of material for practising, by selecting on the basis of different aspects. At present, only spoken language is implemented, but the same algorithm can be applied to sign language material. The user can choose between, for example, vowels and consonants, and having selected this category, a narrower selection can be made on specific characteristics. When the selection has been made, different exercises are available to the user, such as discrimination and identification. After practising speech perception supported by speech reading in quiet, a selection of different background noises can be optionally added, with adjustable volume control. The user also can also benefit from extra support in the form of graphic displays, which show fundamental frequency variations, and presence or absence of frication. Each exercise is preceded by a familiarisation phase and automatically followed by a test if a particular level of proficiency has been reached. When the user 'passes' the test, the program advises on how to proceed. To make the program (even more) attractive, the user can choose to practise with the same material in an auditory memory game or a so-called 'Wordtris' game. The user may challenge the computer or play against another user.

Microworld of the DICTUM prototype consists of a kitchen, where the user can look around, click on objects, and answer questions. Two modes are available: the browse mode and the interaction mode. In each of these modes the user can choose from three levels of difficulty: in level I the material consists of words or glosses, level II of short phrases or a short sign language sequence, and level III gives complete utterances or a sentence in sign language. In the browse mode, the user takes control over the system. The program responds by playing an item as soon as the user has clicked on an object. In the interactive mode, the program asks the user to respond to the item played. At level III the program will give the user a description of a particular object, without actually mentioning it (e.g. What can you use to thaw frozen food?). Other prompts at level III include various series of questions where the user has to make a choice from four alternatives. The spoken language material is a translation of the sign language material.

Microworld offers the possibility of supporting sign language video sequences as well as speech reading to be supported by displaying what is being said in written language.

When sign language is presented, the grammatical order of the written language is maintained. It is felt that this will help the hearing sign language learners.

In order to introduce a competition element to this part of the program, learners will receive points for a correct answer, and lose half of that amount when an incorrect answer is given.

DICTUM provides the framework in which sign language perception and speech reading skills can be trained. The program is designed such that it will be able to handle any one sign language and spoken language. The program is stored on one CD-ROM. A second CD-ROM provides data for the sign language and spoken language. As mentioned before, the market for commercialisation is relatively small, particularly in Europe with its many different languages. In this way, production costs can be recovered more quickly, which may make it easier to turn the prototype into a commercial product. Also, deaf students wishing to train their perceptive skills in a foreign language can simply do so by replacing one language disk with another.

Evaluation of a new IT application

As there is an urgent need for educational applications, one may be tempted to distribute newly-developed products to the eager users, with little time spent (or no time at all) on evaluation and formal testing. This brings with it the danger that the products will eventually turn out to be less effective than was hoped for, which will cause disappointment to the user.

There are two aspects that need to be tested:

- the user friendliness of the program, and
- the effectiveness of the application.

Testing the user friendliness

User friendliness can be tested by inviting representatives of the intended user group(s) to work with the program, either for a short period, or for a prolonged period. By providing questionnaires which ask for opinions, ratings, etc., the application developers can acquire information about the user friendliness. When users are allowed to work with the application for a considerable period, questionnaires could be submitted both at the beginning and end of the evaluation period. It may well be that after the initial euphoria of being able to work with a new product that has been long awaited, users may find that parts of the application do not turn out to be what they expected. They may give different ratings or answers at the end of the period. Besides, they may provide useful suggestions for improvements. It is advisable to reserve funds that will allow a number of alterations being made to the application.

A different way of testing user friendliness could be achieved by giving users specific assignments, which they have to fulfil. Video recordings should be made of the users accomplishing their tasks, thus giving information about parts of the application that may cause problems or are unclear. However, this way of testing the user friendliness can be very time-consuming, especially with a large number of users participating or with complex assignments. One option might be to have no assignments at all, but simply record how users work with the program without any prior instructions being given. A drawback of this method is that it is not structured and may not cover all parts of the application.

Testing the effectiveness

The effectiveness of the application can be tested in two different ways, using a within, or between, groups design. In the first case, users will be given a formal test at the beginning of the training period to establish the baseline. At the end of the training period a second test can be given, which will provide new results. If the training period is long enough and results are unlikely to be influenced by the fact that users will remember it, the first test could be re-used. The difference between the second and first test will give an indication of the effectiveness of the application.

A between-groups design is to be used if the new application is to be compared with another application or with a traditional method of teaching or training. One group will be working with the new application, the other group with the old one. Baselines will have to be established for both groups at the beginning of the testing period. At the end of the period a second test must be given. Both groups should be receiving the same test. There should be no difference between the groups at the beginning of the testing period; if there is, the final results will not be reliable, and one should try to find out the cause of this difference. The outcome of the second test could show either a difference or no difference between the two groups. If no difference is found, it means that both methods are equally successful. A difference in favour of the group using the new application would indicate that it is an improvement in comparison to the method already in use. If a negative difference is found, it is an indication that the new method could do with some improvements or had better be discarded. Of course, this is not what one hopes for at the start of a new development, but it can never be excluded.

The DICTUM system (as described above) was evaluated using these methods of comparison. It was found to be a highly successful application, which showed large increases in sign language perception and speech reading skills at the various sites it was tested (Elsendoorn and Lampropoulou 1997), even after a short period of training.

Conclusions

The time between the start of an IT development project and the actual completed product can sometimes be quite considerable. To keep intended end-user groups informed about and interested in new developments, user involvement will be of vital importance. Only intensive interaction between users and IT application designers/developers, where both can function as sounding board to each other and where ideas can be discussed and tested on their viability, will be fertile ground in which to sow the seed of a new IT application to be used in deaf education.

Further reading

Elsendoorn, B. A. G. and Coninx, F. (eds) (1993) *Interactive Learning Technology for the Deaf.* Proceedings of the NATO Advanced Research Workshop held in Sint-Michielsgestel, The Netherlands, 4–7 June 1991. Berlin: Springer-Verlag.

Helander, M. (ed.) (1988) *Handbook of Human–Computer Interaction*. Amsterdam: North-Holland.

Notes

1. SFT is the German abbreviation for Sprach-Farbbild-Transformation (Speech-to-Colour Transformation).
2. DICTUM is the acronym for Development of an Interactive Communication Training system Using Multimedia. The research project was funded (in part) by the European Commission under the TIDE programme, and ran from 1994 to 1996.

AUDIOLOGY

Introduction

Audiology is an area which many teachers of the deaf find challenging. From the point of diagnosis a range of professionals become involved. Such professionals may include: the educational audiologist, audiological scientist, ENT consultant, medical audiologists, audiological technicians and the community medical officer. This concentration of specialists might suggest that teachers of the deaf can leave audiological matters to others. Professional effort could then be put into supporting the development of language skills and ensuring cognitive and linguistic access to the National Curriculum. Such an approach fails to take account of the fact that it is audiological science which allows us the potential for very early diagnosis and that sensory aids are only effective if the daily management is positive and rigorous. Audiology is one of the central aspects of the education of deaf children. Failure to attend to this aspect of deaf education is a failure to attend to the needs of deaf children and their parents. For this reason this section includes chapters on both new innovations technologically and the implications for services to deaf children and discusses children with special auditory needs who do not have a sensori-neural hearing loss.

Early detection of hearing loss has long been identified as a key feature of providing early sensitive support for families of deaf children. Peter Watkin discusses not only the technology which allows very early identification but also the implications of such an approach for both families and services. A growing awareness of the significant challenges that early identification has for the provision of services is discussed. The challenge is multi-faceted, demanding that health and education services work to provide a seamless service. While the importance of appropriate amplification is stated, the more important feature of parental preferences and readiness for intervention is stressed. The lack of appropriate training or a knowledge base of the ingredients which make up such a team are highlighted.

Sally Hind considers the research evidence on the effects of otitis media on development. This condition has been recognised as affecting a high percentage of children during the first six years of life, being the largest cause of hearing loss in children under the age of 12. As medical and educational service providers are asked to justify cost-effective outcomes, the need to clarify the potential effects of otitis media on the learning process and the most appropriate form of intervention become increasingly important. This chapter allows consideration of the studies to date on this controversial area and the potential implications for service providers. As health and education budgets come under increasing pressure a clear understanding of this area is essential for all those involved in delivering services to children.

The increasing speed of technological change within society is reflected in the range of amplification options available. The challenge to professionals is to take advantage of such developments on behalf of deaf children. This is not a simple task. Amplification aids are designed for adults and classically, research relating to new technology is trialled on deafened adults making any conclusions drawn suspect if related directly to a paediatric population. Russell Brett and Wendy McCracken look across some of the more recent technological developments, considering the possibilities offered by such developments and the problems faced in successfully accessing and applying such technology to meet the audiological needs of deaf children.

In expressing the perceived position of cochlear implantation for deaf children McCormick (1997) summarises that 'After years of cautious and gradual route finding, paediatric audiology and the practice of cochlear implantation for the very young are now ideally positioned to take off in the fast lane' (p. 307). The next few years will undoubtedly see a rise in the rate of cochlear implantation, particularly in the case of profoundly deaf infants. Whilst there are extensive reviews of the process of implantation and post-implant training elsewhere, Ken Robinson summarises some of the challenges presented by implant programmes, particularly focusing on research to date and the need for inter-centre pooling of information and long-term outcome measures to allow a clearer picture of the effects of implantation. It is likely that all teachers of the deaf will be responsible professionally for children who have cochlear implants. Information relating to neural plasticity, research findings and challenges yet to be met, ensure that a theoretical base is available on which to develop appropriate practice.

A much ignored group within the field of deaf education are those children who have no measurable degree of hearing loss in respect of a peripheral difficulty but who have specific difficulty in making sense of sound. The area of Central Auditory Processing Disorder is largely unrecognised within the UK. The lack of professional training, a clear definition of terms or an understanding of the implications for learning make this an area which demands the attention of professionals who have expertise in providing services for children with hearing loss. An understanding of this complex area, agreement on the use of terminology and a recognition of appropriate testing protocols which allow such children to be identified would allow authorities to develop appropriate services. At a time when effective schooling is firmly on the agenda such specialist needs should be recognised and met. Cara Wheeler provides an overview of current research and considers the possible implications for services. This is an area long recognised by teachers of the deaf although lack of information and training has meant this group have traditionally received scant, if any, attention.

From the point of identification of any measurable degree of deafness, be it permanent, central or transitory, teachers of the deaf are responsible for the daily management of the listening environment and for clear explanations of test results and their implications for parents and co-professionals. This section considers some of the most recent issues within the field of audiology and seeks to ensure such information is available to those actively supporting deaf children and their families.

Wendy McCracken

Chapter 4.1

Development in hearing screens – the implications for services

Peter Watkin

Introduction

Early detection is a starting point for improving the quality of life for hearing-impaired children, but is not an end in itself. It is worthless, and may even be harmful, unless appropriate habilitation is available. A national survey confirmed that the most common pattern of support in the UK 'falls on the teacher of the deaf from the time of suspected diagnosis' (Turner 1994). Rapid developments are occurring in methods of identification and fresh challenges are being faced. Seamless, multidisciplinary care requires a common understanding of these challenges.

The need for hearing screens

The 1944 Education Act, and subsequently Section 22 of the 1946 National Health Service Act, provided the impetus for identifying hearing-impaired children from birth onwards. Over half a century later the achievement of this aim remains elusive. Hearing impairment may be identified through *Reactive Referral,* made because of parental concerns about their child's hearing. These concerns initiate a clinical examination and specialist audiological assessment. By contrast, *Child Health Surveillance* consists of a set of activities, which are initiated by professionals at various pre-defined ages. They involve an important working partnership with the parents and require a complex diagnostic awareness. *Hearing Screens* are a separate component within Child Health Programmes. Simple tests, capable of being performed by less skilled personnel, are applied to identify previously unrecognised hearing impairments. They should be sensitive (i.e. able to identify those with the hearing impairment), specific (i.e. able to identify those with normal hearing), and acceptable to the public so that there is high coverage (the proportion of the cohort screened).

Preschool screens were first introduced in the UK following the Ewings' development of simple behavioural tests (Ewing and Ewing 1944). By 1952 the infant distraction test they had described was being implemented as a Health Visitor screen (Humphries 1957; Howarth 1958). Although widespread implementation of the Health Visitors Distraction Test (HVDT) followed, questions about screen validity were increasingly voiced

(Boothman and Orr 1978). McCormick (1983) highlighted poor screening techniques and recommended the more rigorous training of screeners. The National Deaf Children's Society argued that many parents held the HVDT in low esteem (NDCS 1983, 1989). More forthrightly, Robertson *et al.* (1995) reported that some parents frankly regard the screen as a joke. The National Children's Bureau (1987) articulated a commonly held belief that 'most parents are sensitive observers of their children, and abnormalities are more likely to be detected by them at an earlier stage'. In the light of such opinions, can hearing screens still be considered necessary?

Retrospective examination of the routes by which children's hearing impairments have been confirmed, suggest that they are. The Nottingham Children's Hearing Assessment Centre found that only 19 per cent of severely or profoundly deaf children were identified by reactive parental referral (McCormick 1990). Watkin *et al.* (1990) found that of 39 such children, only 26 per cent were identified as a result of parental concerns, with 19 per cent of 72 with a mild or moderate permanent hearing loss having been referred reactively. Only 44 per cent of the parents recognised the presence of a severe or profound deafness in infancy, with less than 10 per cent recognising a mild or moderate hearing impairment by this age. Although check lists alerting parents to the presence of hearing impairment (McCormick 1983) are now included in parent-held child health record books, a programme of 'vigilant' detection (Scanlon and Bamford 1990) had a sensitivity of only 29 per cent (Sutton and Scanlon 1997). These results give little encouragement to shifting the emphasis of detection away from screens. Parental concerns should always be treated seriously, but deafness presents very subtly. Such difficulties in early recognition are a precondition for screening.

When to screen?

Cochrane and Holland (1971) set out other preconditions for implementing screens and argued that they are only ethical if outcomes are improved. Although they agreed that screens for congenital hearing loss were justified, there is only now a gradually emerging, scientific evidence that early habilitation is beneficial (Markides 1986; Ramkalawan and Davis 1992; Eilers and Oller 1994; Robinshaw 1995). Markides (1986) found improved speech intelligibility when the hearing aid fitting of severely deaf children was within the first six months of life. Ramkalawan and Davis (1992) suggested that even those with milder losses may suffer detrimental effects if intervention is delayed. However there have been no convincing studies confirming that *additional* benefits result from very early habilitation. The study of Eilers and Oller showed a reasonably constant delay in the time taken for babble to emerge – irrespective of the age of habilitation. Despite this, they argued that earlier habilitation is likely to reduce cumulative deficits. This pragmatism is widely accepted.

Unfortunately even with a sensitive HVDT, *consistent* habilitation is often not achieved until the third year of life. Yet the unborn child hears from around the twentieth week of gestation. Most consider this habilitation delay unacceptable. The (NDCS) Quality

Standards recommend that 80 per cent of bilateral congenital hearing impairments in excess of 50 dBHL are detected within the first year, with 40 per cent being detected within the first six months of life (NDCS 1994). Detection through neonatal screening is the only way to meet such targets.

Neonatal screening methods

In the 1970s testing auditory behaviour with microprocessor-controlled devices had been developed in both the USA (Simmons and Russ 1974), and the UK (Bennett and Wade 1980). Bhattacharya *et al.* (1984) published an encouraging evaluation of the use of the *Auditory Response Cradle* – the device developed in the UK. However, neonatal tests of auditory behaviour inevitably have a reduced sensitivity for identifying lesser degrees of impairment (Tucker and Bhattacharya 1992). The statistical decision-making criteria of automated behavioural tests have also been questioned (Davis 1984), and reservations expressed about their use with premature neonates (Davis *et al.* 1991).

Other methods suitable for neonatal screening were explored. Since the 1970s the *Auditory Brainstem Response* (ABR) had become an established technique for threshold and neuro-otological diagnosis in adults and children. Unfortunately it is time-consuming and can only be readily used to selectively screen a small percentage of the birth cohort considered to be at risk of deafness. Hyde *et al.* (1991) and Galambos *et al.* (1994) have both reported long-term results from targeted screens employing ABR. In the UK smaller studies have been reported (Bradford *et al.* 1985; Rowe 1991; Watkin *et al.* 1991). Machines incorporating automated waveform detection and scoring have also been developed, but the test sensitivity of the device developed in the UK (Mason 1988) has only reached 82 per cent (Mason *et al.* 1997).

Although ABR is considered as a 'gold standard', difficulties in interpreting neonatal results require fuller appreciation. The ABR threshold to the usually employed click stimulus, correlates well with the degree of hearing loss between 2 and 4 kHz. It gives little information about low-frequency hearing. Even this correlation is not absolute (Hall 1992), and the relationship between neonatal ABR and the hearing loss present in later childhood is sometimes less predictable. Fjermedal and Laukli (1989) compared ABR thresholds measured in infancy with subsequently obtained pure-tone thresholds averaged between 2 and 4 kHz. In over one third of the ears, the ABR and pure-tone thresholds differed by as much as 40 dB. In a neonatal screen undertaken at Whipps Cross Hospital (Watkin 1996b) those neonates with an ABR threshold of 80 dBnHL or worse in the better ear, were all subsequently confirmed by the end of infancy to have a moderate or worse permanent hearing impairment. However the predictive value of a 70 dBnHL neonatal ABR threshold only achieved 66 per cent, with less than a third of those with a 60 dBnHL threshold and 10 per cent of those with a 50 dBnHL threshold having such an impairment. The accurate prediction from a neonatal ABR test is thus not always clear. Nevertheless the cost efficiency of selective ABR screening (Stevens *et al.* 1997) is beguiling, and this test methodology has now been adopted in some form or other, by a majority of districts within the UK.

The discovery of *Otoacoustic Emissions* has offered another objective method of screening the hearing of neonates. The cochlea emissions were originally described in the late 1970s at the Institute of Laryngology and Otology, London, by David Kemp (Kemp 1978). His further development, by 1987, of simple, quick, and non-invasive techniques to record otoacoustic emissions evoked by transient stimulation (Transient Evoked Otoacoustic Emissions or TEOAEs), made universal screening a possibility (Bray and Kemp 1987). The inner ear acts as a sound amplifier, with the outer hair cells contracting and amplifying sound vibrations which are transmitted to the inner hair cells for transduction into nerve impulses. This outer hair cell activity produces the emissions, which are transmitted back through the middle ear, and can be recorded as very low intensities of sound in the external canal. TEOAEs are absent if there is a dysfunction of the outer hair cells, or if transmission back through the middle ear is blocked. The absence of a recordable emission does not reveal information about the degree of hearing impairment, or indeed whether there is a middle ear or outer hair cell dysfunction. Test techniques are detailed by Baldwin and Watkin (1997), and the test set-up, and examples of TEOAEs, are illustrated in Figures 4.1:1 and 4.1:2.

Their use for neonatal screening was evaluated in the UK by Stevens *et al.* (1987, 1989, 1991). They reported a TEOAE test sensitivity of 93 per cent. However the test specificity was reduced to 80 per cent. A larger evaluation of the implementation of TEOAE testing as a universal neonatal screen was undertaken by the Rhode Island Hearing Project (RIHAP) (White and Behrens 1993). The results were so encouraging that in the same year the American National Institutes of Health (ANIH) recommended the maternity unit TEOAE screening of all neonates, with failure being followed by an ABR (ANIH 1993). The aim was identification and introduction of habilitation by 6 months. Reservations were expressed both in the USA (Bess and Paradise 1994), and in the UK (Curnock 1993). However, these issues are being resolved.

Universal or targeted neonatal screening?

The early implementations of the HVDT (Humphries 1957; Howarth 1958) suggested that only a neonatal sub-cohort known to be 'vulnerable' to congenital deafness needed to be 'targeted' or 'selected' for screening. This was also considered to be the case for other conditions, and during the 1960s 'Risk Registers' and a selective HVDT were employed in most districts. However by the end of the decade a large number of reservations were being expressed about 'targeted' screens (Richards and Roberts 1967; Oppe 1967, Hamilton and Richards 1968). Knox and Mahon (1970) concluded that 'they do no good and possibly do harm', and that the only sensible action to be taken was to abandon them. Universal screens were thus introduced – but this debate remains as pertinent as it did half a century ago. In 1973 the American Academy of Pediatrics recommended the hearing screening of only the neonatal sub-cohort at risk of deafness. Initially five risk factors were

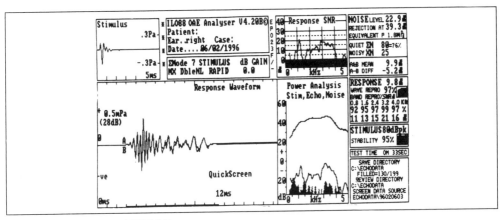

Example 'a' – A normal TEOAE

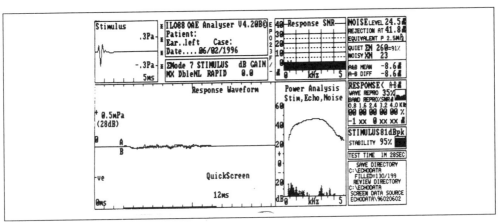

Example 'b' – An absent TEOAE

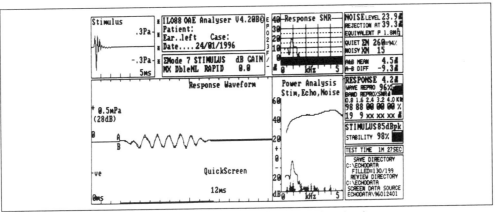

Example 'c' – An abnormal TEOAE – seen in high frequency hearing loss

Figure 4.1:1 Typical TEOAE recordings (Courtesy of Baldwin, M. and Watkin, P. (1997) 'Otoacoustic emmissions', in *Audiology in Education*. McCracken, W. and Laoide-Kemp, S. (eds) Whurr Publishers)

Figure 4.1:2 Neonate receiving TEOAE test (Courtesy of Baldwin, M. and Watkin, P. (1997) 'Otoacoustic emmissions', in *Audiology in Education*. McCracken, W. and Laoide-Kemp, S. (eds) Whurr Publishers)

included, but by 1982 these were expanded by the American Joint Committee on Infant Hearing to include the seven factors detailed in Table 4.1:1. Such selection could identify up to 70 per cent of severe or profound hearing impairments (Gerber 1990) by testing between 7 and 10 per cent of the birth cohort (Sancho *et al.* 1987). Davis and Wood (1992) demonstrated that admission for neonatal intensive care increased the relative risk for deafness by a factor of 10. They recommended that these babies, plus those with a cranio-facial abnormality or a family history of deafness be targeted for testing.

Selective neonatal screens identifying around two thirds of the hearing-impaired neonates would be extremely cost efficient (Stevens *et al.* 1997). But in practice there is not always such a high yield. Watkin *et al.* (1991) identified only 43 per cent of children with a moderate or worse degree of congenital deafness, by a selective neonatal screen. Cranio-facial malformations or syndromes may present subtly in early infancy. Inherited deafness may also be difficult to identify by simple questioning of the parents. A dominant family history may not be recognised within the family, and recessive deafness may not actually exist in any other family members. Congenital infections such as rubella may only be diagnosed once deafness has been confirmed. In practice, considerably less than half of those with congenital deafness may be selected for neonatal screening. Identification from risk factor registers therefore remains problematic. Universal neonatal screens offer an answer. However are they practical within post-natal wards in the UK?

Table 4.1:1 The 1982 American Joint Committee on Infant Hearing screening risk criteria for congenital or early onset deafness

1	Family history of childhood hearing impairment
2	Congenital perinatal infection (e.g. cytomegalovirus, rubella, herpes, toxoplasmosis, syphilis)
3	Anatomic malformations involving the head or neck (e.g. dysmorphic appearance including syndromal and non-syndromal abnormalities, overt or submucous cleft palate, morphologic abnormalities of the pinna)
4	Birth weight <1500 gm
5	Hyperbilirubinaemia at level exceeding indications for exchange transfusion
6	Bacterial meningitis, especially Haemophilus influenza
7	Severe asphyxia which may include infants with Apgar scores of 0 to 3 or who fail to institute spontaneous respiration by ten minutes and those with hypotonia persisting to two hours after birth

The practicability of universal neonatal screening

Haggard (1990) has pointed out the logistical difficulties of universal neonatal screening, cautioning that the main obstacle is the swamping of available assessment facilities with false positive results. Experience with the HVDT has shown that the success or demise of a universal screen is intrinsically linked to the coverage achieved (Brown *et al.* 1989). These difficulties have been investigated following the introduction of a universal neonatal screen in the East London district of Waltham Forest (Watkin 1996a). The aim was the identification of bilateral congenital deafness of moderate or worse degree in the better ear. TEOAEs were recorded in the Whipps Cross Hospital maternity unit, with failures being tested by ABR. An overall coverage of 92 per cent was achieved, with the cost per test being 25 per cent cheaper than the HVDT. Unfortunately neonatal ear canals are obstructed with vernix over the first couple of days, and thus a high initial failure rate is achieved by testing within this period. The failure rate by the age of the test is detailed in Figure 4.1:3. An ideal test age would be after the second day of life and up to the fourth week, but with increasingly early maternity discharge this would involve a logistically difficult community programme. However practicable universal TEOAE screens can be cost effectively implemented in the UK.

The sensitivity of universal TEOAE screening

High sensitivities of greater than 90 per cent have been reported for TEOAE screens by Stevens (1991), and from the US (White and Maxon 1995). In the Whipps Cross screen the yield of targeted hearing impairments was 1.25 per 1000. However by the time the youngest in the cohort was two years of age, there was an incremental yield of four children (0.28/1000) who had not been identified by the screen. Although none of the four was an actual false negative of the neonatal test, they illustrated well those children

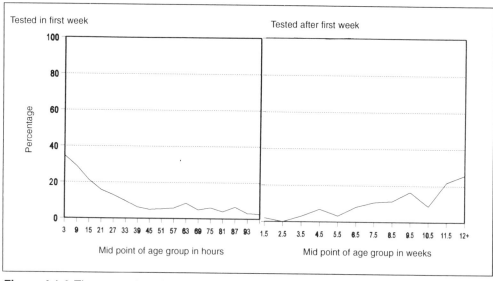

Figure 4.1:3 The proportion of maternity unit births failing the initial TEOAE test in both ears (data from Whipps Cross Universal Neonatal Screen, 1992 to 1995 cohort, 10,796 neonates tested in maternity unit)

likely to remain unidentified by neonatal screens. One was audiologically cared for out of district. Another failed the neonatal TEOAE test, but failed to attend for follow-up. A third had a degenerative neurological condition, and passed the neonatal TEOAE test, and the last child had a progressive deafness identified at just turned two years of age. Thus, however sensitive neonatal tests are, effective methods for the later identification of those hearing-impaired children missed by neonatal programmes need to be in place.

The worth of universal neonatal screening – measuring outcomes

Although ultimately the value of early identification must be assessed from improved outcomes in terms of the enhancement of a child's ability and improvements in 'quality of life', these indicators are difficult to measure. Bamford (1995) has pointed out the need to use intermediate outcomes as surrogate indicators of long-term benefit. Such indicators include the ages of detection and confirmation of the deafness, and the age at which habilitation is introduced. Haggard (1990) considered that the main objective of early infant screening should be to detect severe and profound pre-lingual deafness. Sancho *et al.* (1987) noted that a case exists for the early fitting of hearing aids to children with moderate degrees of deafness. The 1993 ANIH Consensus Statement also recommends the detection of infants with moderate and worse hearing impairment. However, outcomes differ according to the degree of impairment. A sensitive neonatal screen will identify twice as many infants with moderate impairments. However, the benefits of identifying such losses in early infancy are far from clear.

The cumulative distributions of the outcome indicators for the Whipps Cross Universal Neonatal Screen are illustrated in Figure 4.1:4. Those with a severe or profound deafness

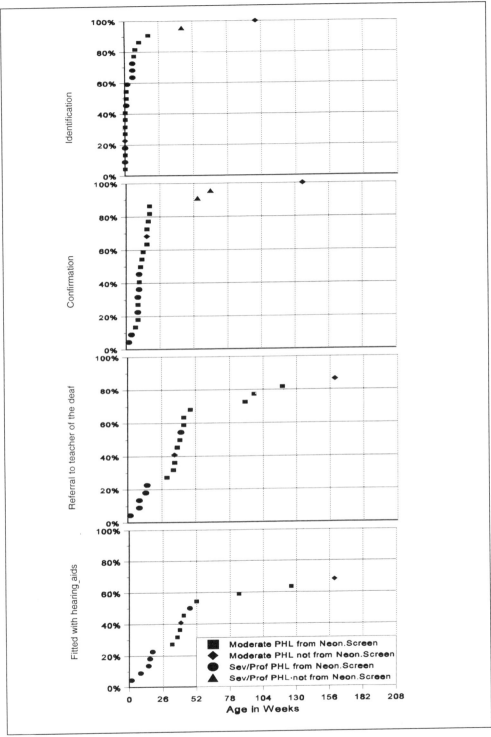

Figure 4.1:4 The cumulative distribution of the outcomes for children with a moderate or worse permanent hearing impairment in the better ear, identified from the Waltham Forest cohort of 14,353 born 1992–95 (number identified = 22)

had their hearing impairment confirmed at a median age of nine weeks. Following the neonatal tests the presence of deafness was evident to both the audiologists and, with a single exception, to the parents. Behavioural observation of the infants' responses allowed for early acceptance of the impairment with involvement of the teacher of the deaf at a median age of 11 weeks and hearing aid fitting at 16 weeks. The NDCS targets for the implementation of multidisciplinary habilitation were met in all but one.

The ABR confirmation of moderate impairments was at a median age of 13 weeks. However, there was not the same level of parental or professional concern following TEOAE failure and the confirmatory ABR was relatively delayed. Even after the ABR there were delays in recognising the need for habilitation. It was difficult to be sure early after the ABR that the hearing loss was permanent and that habilitation was required. Certainty grew during the second half of infancy. This allowed two thirds of those identified neonatally to be referred to the teacher of the deaf during the second half of infancy with one third being aided during this period. Continuing uncertainty was experienced by some of the parents, and one quarter of the children who had their impairment identified during the first weeks of life were referred for habilitation after infancy. Over 40 per cent of the moderately impaired children remained unaided at the age of two years. For those who were aided, the median age was delayed to 42 weeks. The NDCS targets were not achieved in any.

Such uncertainties are not surprising. Behavioural responses to sound in early infancy are difficult to evaluate even for the most experienced observers (Thompson and Weber 1974), and much diagnostic expertise is required to sort out those failing the ABR test. Reducing the age of audiological certainty is required to improve outcomes. Simple observations of behavioural response to sound (McCormick 1983) facilitate parental recognition of a severe hearing impairment. However, these behaviours are too gross to demonstrate lesser degrees of impairment and more subtle behavioural observations are required if habilitation is to be successful before disability becomes apparent. These should assist both the teacher and the parents to evaluate the validity of the clinic-based tests from observations within the home. The subtleties of neonatal ABR interpretation make this extremely important.

The implications of neonatal screening for habilitation

There can be little doubt that the worth of programmes of identification depend upon the availability of appropriate habilitation. Within the Whipps Cross programme, habilitation was commenced when the identified infants were referred to a joint clinic undertaken with the teacher of the deaf. There were significant implications for educational services (Watkin and Nanor 1997). The role of the teacher of the deaf is complex. For those children identified with a severe or profound hearing loss, counselling and guidance is necessary from early in the first half of infancy. The earliest age of educational referral was 12 days, with half of those identified with this degree of deafness being home visited by the time they were three months of age. Such skills are not necessarily available among teachers of the deaf. For those children with a moderate degree of deafness the role was markedly different. Not all the parents agreed to the involvement of a teacher of the deaf. For those that did, a major component of the educational input was observation of the infant's communication development and behavioural responses to sound within the home. There was always discussion about the benefits of hearing aid fitting, but where this was rejected, home visiting was continued. The problems of implementing appropriate habilitation for those with a moderate degree of deafness are clear.

Robinshaw (1995) reported the development of a small group of congenitally deaf infants. She concluded that programmes of habilitation additional to auditory stimulation required exploration. The present analysis would entirely support this view. If habilitation is centred exclusively around early hearing aid fitting, this will be rejected in early infancy by a majority of parents whose children have a moderate deafness. For such children habilitation programmes are required where amplification of sound is not perceived as the only habilitation strategy. Such programmes require evaluation.

The benefits to the children identified from the Whipps Cross Universal Neonatal Screen were considered to outweigh the difficulties of educational provision. Where educational habilitation was accepted at an early stage, confirmation of deafness and educational input from the first months of life was considered by the teachers to have been beneficial. 'Embedding' of the child within the family was facilitated, and the adjustment of the family to the hearing impairment was subjectively considered to have been achieved at an earlier stage. This is particularly important for the severely deaf infants not born into deaf families. Hearing aid fitting within the first months of infancy gives the parent(s) confidence in their management – and is often less problematical than fitting to children aged over one year. Early educational input achieves early consistent aid useage. When appropriate the parents can be introduced to manual systems of communication, and to deaf adults. Importantly, such parental education can be given while the child is at a pre-lingual stage.

In the UK teachers of the deaf are evolving management strategies for children identified in very early infancy. However, this is relatively virgin territory. Neonatal programmes in the USA often employ individual developmental plans, with stated goals and scored progress. As yet, there has been little debate about their use in this country in early infancy. Will the variables of development in the deaf neonate introduce educational failure even at this age? Much impetus to neonatal detection was given by the NDCS Quality Standards (NDCS 1994). Standards for those providing habilitation and support are also required.

The financing of habilitation services is also far from certain. The 1994 Code of Practice following the 1993 Education Act gave guidance to local education authorities (LEAs) on the Identification and Assessment of Special Educational Needs (DoE 1994a). For children aged two years and over assessment is statutory 'if the child is likely to have a particular condition or major health problem which has caused concern at an early age'. If the assessment leads to a statement of Special Educational Needs, funding is available for educational provision via the statement. The Code anticipated that very few children under the age of two would need a statement, suggesting for hearing-impaired children that home- or centre-based programmes from peripatetic educational services would be most appropriate. It may thus have been assumed that services for deaf children, under the age of two, would be quite readily available from LEAs. However this is not always the case, and there are 'vast discrepancies' in LEA interpretation. Some LEAs consider that all preschool provision is outside their responsibility and coherent programmes of support from birth are not funded. In some areas health visitors with special responsibility for audiological support are the key workers below the age of two years (Turner 1994). Interestingly, this is a reversion to the original model set up almost 50 years ago (Humphries 1957). There is now a theoretical model by which educational staff could be jointly commissioned by health authority purchasers to provide habilitation services for preschool children, but this practice is clearly exceptional. Earlier identification has made the question of educational support urgent, but even if adequately funded, the introduction of neonatal screens has considerable implications for educational services. These are summarised in Table 4.1:2.

Table 4.1:2 The Implications of Universal Neonatal Screens for Educational Services (see Watkin and Nanor 1997)

---

1 Infants with severe or profound hearing impairments usually have their deafness confirmed within the first weeks of life. On occasions this is very shortly after birth. Habilitation and family support is required from this age

2 Infants with a moderate degree of hearing impairment usually have their deafness confirmed during the second half of infancy despite neonatal detection. Teachers need to be involved in the confirmatory process, accepting the need to work alongside parents, jointly assessing behavioural responses in the home and the effects of the impairment on the infants' development

3 Habilitation strategies which do not solely involve hearing aid fitting and which are available for young infants with moderate degrees of impairment require further research and development

4 The place of Individual Development Plans for hearing-impaired infants requires further development and debate

5 Children with a moderate or worse degree of congenital hearing impairment may all be identified in infancy. Educational services need to be adequately researched and in a position where they can respond to this need

---

Conclusions

Since the early implementations of infant hearing screens, programmers of detection have travelled a long way – albeit somewhat slowly and falteringly. Identification in early infancy for the majority of children with a bilateral, congenital hearing impairment of moderate degree or worse is now possible. However, it is worthless and possibly harmful unless habilitation services are available. In the past the development of educational services and methodologies for identification have been inextricably linked. However, the climate of service growth has changed. The educational services for children with congenital hearing impairments, identified neonatally, need to develop alongside the screens. This is only one of many responsibilities assumed by educational services for the hearing impaired. It does not in any way negate the numerically greater needs of children with other permanent or temporary hearing impairments. However, to be worthwhile, educational resourcing needs to be included as a component part of neonatal hearing screens and successful habilitation methodologies, appropriate for use in very early infancy, need further development.

Implications of otitis media for development

Sally Hind

In discussion of the education of deaf children, one might question the inclusion of otitis media; even the most persistent cases of otitis media with effusion (OME) mostly present with only a relatively mild and fluctuating hearing loss which is generally of limited duration. Furthermore, in most cases, the disease resolves early in the school years, with or without intervention. Nonetheless, various linguistic, cognitive and behaviour problems are associated with this extremely common, but not well understood, condition; the discussion of their mechanisms and the extremes of impact have a place in this book. The main issues will be discussed under the following broad headings: definition of OME, efficacy of approaches to treatment, developmental effects/sequelae of OME and implications for effective service delivery. It is timely to be considering the effects of OME on the developing child, as pressures in the NHS have led some Educational Health Services to consider withdrawing or reducing school hearing screening and many NHS Trusts already ration surgical treatment for this disease. It is important to quantify with well-controlled data the concurrent impact and sequelae (problems associated with the disease after resolution) of OME. If the developmental sequelae are material, can we justify investing resources in minimising those effects?

Definition of OME

Lack of a single definition for OME in the literature leads to difficulties with cross-study comparisons for epidemiological studies, though individually useful determinations of prevalence and incidence do exist. The problem of definition arises partly because there are various forms of OME. However, for purposes of screening and consideration of risk for cognitive sequelae, Haggard and Hughes (1991) suggest that it is acceptable to regard OME as unitary, as the risk factors for the various forms are so similar, the histories overlap, and the differences in effect within forms diagnosed at one time point are likely to be as large as those between (e.g. recurrent acute otitis media versus OME).

Taking this stance enables cross-study assessments of prevalence. This is defined as the number of cases of a specific condition in a specified population (at a specific period in time). Prevalence rates usually represent the number of people who have the condition divided by the population at risk at a specific point in time. Haggard and Hughes (1991) propose as a working estimate that at a given time nearly 20 per cent of children in the age range 2–5 years are affected by OME. However, though this is an extremely common disease, the number of severe/persistent cases is relatively few. Haggard and Hughes (1991) provide more detailed discussion on prevalence and other epidemiological factors.

From a review of 23 studies, Zielhuis *et al.* (1990) found a bimodal distribution of prevalence in childhood, with prevalence rates rising from birth onwards until they reach a maximum at around 2 years. The rates then decrease but rise again to a lower peak at around 5 years. The initial increase could be partly due to the delayed development of the immune system and the decline of maternally conferred immunity; reduced protectiveness and increased social contact probably also raise prevalence via increased exposure to infection during this period. The second peak appears to correspond to the period of time when the child first starts school and is thereby exposed to greater risk of infection. The consequent perception of a need to screen for hearing impairment at school entry is based on this observed prevalence.

Incidence is defined as the number of new instances of a specific condition occurring during a certain period of time in a specified population. Longitudinal studies suggest that the majority of children will suffer at least one episode of OME during their infancy.

Another epidemiological issue of interest is risk factors for OME. Knowing them would help us to understand the cause and how best to prevent or treat the condition. Furthermore, such knowledge could facilitate appropriate selective screening. Known or suspected risk factors may be categorised as intrinsic or extrinsic to the child. Intrinsically, certain syndromes such as Turner's and Down's are commonly associated with OME, as is a family history of OME. Small head size at birth may also be associated with a greater risk for persistent OME. Extrinsically, factors such as socio-economic status (SES) of the family may constitute a risk factor or exacerbate an existing condition. The season significantly determines incidence and recurrence of the disease; figures are higher for late autumn, winter and early spring. There is an association between attendance in day-care and incidence of OME, probably attributable to the increased risk of exposure to upper respiratory tract infections. Children with smoking mothers are at greater risk of OME. This is probably due to the smoke exacerbating the mucosal response to any infection, though there are other explanations.

It is not possible fully to explore the epidemiological issues of OME here. For more in depth discussion the reader should consult Chalmers *et al.* (1989) or Haggard and Hughes (1991). The important point is that this disease is extremely common in the child population, although the number of persistent cases is relatively few.

Efficacy of approaches to treatment

OME is the most commonly surgically treated childhood disease and yet there is little direct scientific evidence on which to base choice of the best treatment method in the individual case. The consequent disagreement on treatment policies leads to large differences in the intervention rate from district to district. There are various options for treatment which fall under one of two broad headings: surgical or non-surgical intervention.

Considering the former approach, the child can be surgically treated in one of two ways. By far the most common surgical treatment is a myringotomy with the insertion of ventilation tubes (VTs) into the tympanic membrane. The VTs, or grommets, serve to keep the middle ear ventilated. If not blocked by wax, pus or debris they will continue to do this until they naturally fall out 6 to 18 months later. This keeps the effusion at bay and hence maintains near-normal hearing. Some clinicians advocate performing an adenoidectomy at the same time as insertion of VTs, claiming that this reduces the likelihood of recurrence of the disease or at least extends the period of remission and has effects beyond those upon fluid persistence and hearing levels. There is less by way of controlled scientific support for this practice. The issue here concerns the size and quality of the clinical trials conducted (not the number of them to date), and the nature of the outcome measures used. In permanent hearing impairment, the hearing level in the better ear is the simple most useful piece of knowledge about the child, however imperfect and incomplete. In OME the usefulness of a hearing level in assessment of both disease and outcome is less clear because of fluctuation. Hearing level and middle-ear fluid status are able to test the validity of a therapeutic hypothesis (efficacy of surgical treatment) but are not necessarily what matter most to people; indeed, they correlate only moderately with what does matter, such as health indices, behaviour problems and parental quality of life (effectiveness).

There are two main non-surgical approaches in treatment. One involves minimal intervention by instigating the regimen of 'watchful waiting'. With this approach, the child receives ear and hearing checks and is treated medically by the administration of antibiotics if acute ear infections occur. This has, of course, always been part of the approach to treatment; most children who are treated surgically will have undergone such a period of watchful waiting before intervention, the amount of waiting constituting the main variation between districts. As a treatment policy watchful waiting is a bit of a sham as the standards for watchfulness and the criteria for stopping waiting have not been specified. Active treatment of OME with antibiotics is possible but requires medium-length courses. Although this reduces the impact of OME, the cure rate is very modest, the effect short lived, and the contribution to growth of antibiotic-resistant bacteria is deleterious.

Alternatively, the child may be fitted with hearing aids. The requirement for parent training and support in the management of the aid does not make this the inexpensive option it appears. Nonetheless some Health Districts are introducing this method of intervention. The idea of maintaining good hearing levels is appealing although there are two main arguments against this approach: children will receive unnecessarily amplified input during unacknowledged periods of remission and a few of them may come to rely on the aid when they do not need it.

Because of the high cost of surgery and the lack of scientific support for this type of treatment, some Health Authorities have been reducing the rate of surgical intervention. Clearly, it is necessary to establish some general guidance on appropriate intervention rates and, if possible, a way of determining the most effective treatment regimen for a given child. The MRC Institute of Hearing Research, having argued for the need of a well-designed randomised clinical trial to assess overall effectiveness of treatment, is currently conducting such a study: the Trial of Alternative Regimens for Glue Ear Treatment (the TARGET study[1]). The TARGET study is assessing true effectiveness outcomes of intervention rather than simply quantifying resolution of OME from the treatment regimes.

Developmental effects/sequelae of OME

The possibility of developmental effects of OME has been the main reason for interest in the condition and the justification for intervention. Before discussing any language, cognitive or behaviour sequelae, however, it is appropriate to consider the possible auditory developmental effects of this disease. Recurrent OME and the associated fluctuating hearing loss, experienced before 2 years of age, may impinge on the developing auditory system.

Inconsistent and decreased auditory stimulation during the sensitive period of auditory pathway maturation may lead to permanent disturbance, damage or changes of these pathways. This has implications for the young child with OME, attending nursery or school. One possible consequence is an over-sensitivity to loud sounds and poor speech discrimination in everyday situations. Scholastic achievement could be compromised if performance on competitive listening tasks is materially affected. Children with well-defined OME have thresholds for identifying speech in noise that are about 3 dB S/N worse than controls; this is a large difference and the effect applies even when the speech is far above threshold, so the danger is real.

Hearing difficulties may not be the only cause of problems associated with this disease. The *illness effects* could be sufficient alone to have a substantial impact. During episodes of OME the children may be irritated by the symptoms of the disease and show reduced attention spans. Where irritability with no fever accompanies an episode, this may present, and be interpreted by others, as bad behaviour. The children may be labelled as disruptive. Alternatively, rather than be irritated, some children become confused by the condition and tend to withdraw which can lead to labels of 'dreamer' or 'inattentive'. Such behaviour could ramify in at least two ways: reduced learning and a negative effect on teachers' or parents' expectations. In addition when episodes of OME are severe, the child may miss a considerable amount of schooling which may have implications for educational achievement.

Nonetheless OME, be it the associated hearing loss, the illness effects or an interaction of the two, could impact on early language development (Ruben *et al.* 1997) which may impinge on cognitive development (Hind *et al.* 1996). There are clearly other factors which could influence the impact of OME. Studies (e.g. Hind *et al.* 1996) suggest a synergistic effect between OME and SES; children with low SES and OME have a greater risk of subsequent problems. Furthermore, the child who attends a school where class sizes are large and the school environment very noisy, typical of many schools in the UK, may experience greater problems.

There is disagreement in the literature as to the presence of sequelae effects of OME. Haggard *et al.* (1994) reviewed the findings from 13 large studies looking at language and categorised them into two groups, those which showed some adverse effects of OME on language performance and those which did not. The majority of studies (n = 9) found some effect of OME. Effects occurred between two and four years but not beyond. The language measures assessed varied between expressive and receptive language and covered skills such as vocabulary, articulation, verbal comprehension and the structural aspects of language. Haggard *et al.* (1994), like Chalmers *et al.* (1989), were critical of the design of many of these studies but concluded that there appears to be an effect of age at onset, length of duration of episodes and number of bouts of OME. These two publications offer clear explanations of the typical type of weakness in many studies of OME sequelae.

Several further studies have been conducted since though most of them continue to be poorly designed in terms of poor controls or restricted samples. Table 4.2:1 shows the studies reviewed here and their findings. It is generally accepted that OME in infancy impacts on expressive and to some extent receptive early language skills. Interestingly, however, the majority of the studies shown in Table 4.2:1 (five out of seven) failed to find any deleterious effects on language in children over 5 years of age, suggesting that the measured OME sequelae have generally resolved by early school age. The study by Hind *et al.* 1996 was designed to avoid the shortcomings in earlier studies. Children with reported OM histories were assessed on their performance measures across various aspects of language and cognition, as were closely matched controls. The controls had a reported OM-free history and no abnormalities of tympanograms throughout the testing period. This study found evidence of differences in some cognitive tasks between the two groups but not in language tasks.

As the effects are relatively small, it is inappropriate for performance measures to be used as outcome measures in trials of treatment on children with OME who are over 5 years old. Haggard *et al.* (1994) conclude that variables, such as aspects of cognition and behaviour are likely to be affected by OME. Findings from recent studies (e.g. Hind *et al.* 1996; Vernon-Feagans *et al.* 1996) support this conclusion. These will be discussed over the next few paragraphs.

As with language, there is no firm agreement in the literature on the existence of cognitive sequelae. Table 4.2:2 lists some of the more prominent or more recent studies looking at cognitive effects of OME. Again some of these studies were poorly designed, leaving conclusions open to doubt. As expected, the more rigorous studies (e.g. Chalmers *et al.* 1989; Teele *et al.* 1990; Hind *et al.* 1996) produce definite but rather restricted findings. This last study controlled for many known potentially confounding variables (e.g. age, SES, school type, hearing level during test session, age at onset), and found no effect for reading,

Table 4.2:1 Effects of OME on later language skills

Author/s	Publication	Subjects	Outcome measures	Results
Gravel, J. S. and Wallace, I. F. (1992)	*Journal of Speech and Hearing Research*, Vol 35, 558–595, June 1992	OM+ (n = 10) i.e. bilateral OME during ≤30% of first year of life; OM- (n = 13) i.e. bilaterally normal ME status during ≥80% of first year of life. All of low SEG	Speech intelligibility (speech-in-competition task), IQ, and receptive/ expressive language	OME effect on speech intelligibility. None on receptive or expressive language
Grievink, E. H. *et al.* (1993)	*Journal of Speech and Hearing Research*, Vol 36, 1004–1012, October 1993	7 year olds screened for OME × 9 from age 2–4 years grouped: 82 OME-free, 151 early bilateral OME and 37 VTs at preschool age	Language production and perception, phonological ability, reading, spelling, auditory discrimination	No OME effect on later language nor any benefit from intervention
Harsten, G. *et al.* (1993)	*Journal of Laryngology and Otology*, Vol 107, 407–412, May 1993	OM+ (n = 13) i.e. ≥ 6 episodes of acute OM during a 1 year period; OM- (n = 29) i.e. no acute OM episodes. Assessed at 4 and 7 years of age	Phonology, grammar, interaction and auditory discrimination	No differences between groups on any of the linguistic analyses at 4 and 7 years
Schilder, A. G. M. *et al.* (1993)	*Clinical Otolaryngology*, Vol 18, 234–241, 1993	Follow-up at 7–8 years of children (n = 47) studied by Grievink *et al.* (1993)	Expressive/receptive language and phonological ability	No OME effect on language development at school age
Hind, S. E. *et al.* (1996)	*XXIII International Congress of Audiology/Abstracts*, June 1996	71 OM+ and 64 OM- aged 5–7 years (Stratified by parental report)	Expressive and receptive language	No OME effect on expressive or receptive language
Peters, S. A. F. *et al.* (1997)	*Developmental Medicine and Child Neurology*, Vol 39, 31–39, 1997	Same subjects as Grievink *et al.* (1993)	Production, perception, phonology, reading, spelling, auditory discrimination	OME, even when combined with other risk factors, produces only minor effects on later language, reading and spelling
Ruben, R. J. *et al.* (1997)	*Acta Otolaryngol* (Stockh), Vol 117, 206–207, 1997	18 OM- and 12 OM+ 9 year olds from sample studied by Gravel and Wallace (1992)	Expressive language at 1, 2 and 4 years, receptive language at 4 years, comprehension at 6 years and recall of narrative at 9 years	OME effects observed across the listed language outcomes

spelling, memory, reception of grammar or auditory discrimination and attention. It did find consistent effects on verbal and non-verbal reasoning and on phonological awareness. Overall the results suggest very restricted effects of OME on cognition and educational achievement measures remaining at ages 5 to 7 years.

There is some general agreement across studies that where effects of OME on performance are significant, they tend to be small, of the order of one third of a population standard deviation. This applies to clearly defined histories which (while not exactly extreme) are of low prevalence, of the order of 1–3 per cent. Lous (1995) reports no practical effect on reading achievement, but acknowledges that many professionals from various disciplines are convinced of an association between OM and cognitive disabilities in some children. The probable mechanism for this is synergy, i.e. children with both an inherited predisposition to language disorder and the impoverishment of early auditory experience from OME will produce more and more serious cases of speech delay or reading disorder. In a prospective study (i.e. one stratified on OME history not clinic attendance) these cases are too few to influence the results. The process of selective referral into health care or remedial education has the precise aim of finding only such rare cases.

OME is considered to be a possible explanation for individual differences in the behaviour of young children. Anecdotal but widespread claims from ENT clinicians refer to parental reports of behaviour improvement following successful intervention. Our understanding of the possible pragmatic link between cognition/language and behaviour is growing. Vernon-Feagans *et al.* (1996) studied the social behaviour of children in day care. They found that children who experience chronic OME from early infancy more often play alone and have fewer positive or negative verbal interactions with peers. This process probably contributes to the 'socially withdrawn' part of the OME behaviour syndrome. Again the noise level of day-care settings may contribute to this behaviour pattern. Using withdrawal as a coping mechanism may have deleterious long-term consequences. Longitudinal studies have found significant behaviour effects of OME, chiefly in the social domain, as reported by either or both teacher- and parent-ratings up to 11 years of age (e.g. Chalmers *et al.* 1989, Bennett and Haggard 1996); this suggests that the impact of OME on behaviour evolves through childhood without disappearing completely, impinging on the child's and family's quality of life as they go.

We can conclude that developmental effects of OME are real but unlikely to be of major magnitude. Nonetheless, they may have consequences at the individual level, especially for children from impoverished backgrounds or for those having other predispositions to ill health, cognitive delay or behaviour disorder. Because of the ubiquitousness of OME, it is important to consider how these effects may be further minimised.

Implications for effective service delivery

It should now be quite clear that we need to know more about the best way to respond to OME. It is envisaged that the TARGET study will fill the gap in pragmatic cost-

Author/s	Publication	Subjects	Outcome measures	Results
Chalmers et al. (1989)	Mac Keith Press. Oxford, Blackwell Scientific Publications Ltd. Philadelphia. J. B. Lippincott Co.	Cohort of 1037 assessed at 3 years (536 boys and 501 girls), and follow-up at 5, 7, 9, and 11 years	Language, articulation, reading and teacher-reported behaviour problems	Bilateral OME had effect on language development, speech articulation, reading and teacher-reported behaviour problems
Teele, D. W. et al. (1990)	Journal of Infectious Diseases 162, 685–694, 1990	207 × 7 year olds with 7 years full observation, ranked re number of days spent with OME in first 2 years of life	Intelligence, reading and mathematics	OME effects on verbal and performance IQ, mathematics and reading
Updike, C. and Thornburg, J. D. (1992)	Ann Otol Rhinol Laryngol, 101, 530–537, 1992	OM+ (n = 24) and OM- (n = 24) pair-matched for age, gender, grade and vocabulary	Auditory processing and reading ability	OME effect on all tests
Roberts, J. E. et al. (1994)	Journal of Pediatric Psychology; Vol 19, 347–367, 1994	55 × 8 year olds with at least 7 years observation and OME during first five years of life (32 boys and 23 girls)	Intelligence, reading, mathematics and classroom behaviour	OME is a negative predictor of teachers' ratings of child's task orientation/distractability. No OME effect on intellectual development between 3–8 years
Peters, S. A. F. (1994)	Journal of Learning Disabilities, Vol 27, No 2, 111–121, February 1994	Cohort of 1,439. 1,328 screened for OME between 2 and 4 years. Follow-up at 7–8 years (n = 946). 270 participated (OME+ n = 151; OME- VT n = 37; and OME- n = 82)	Reading and spelling	No OME effect on reading but an effect on spelling at 7 years
Roberts, J. E. et al. (1995)	Journal of Pediatric Psychology Vol 20, No 5, 645–660, 1995	Follow-up at 12 years children studied by Roberts et al. (1994)	Intelligence, reading, mathematics, written language and attention and behaviour	No effect on intelligence, academic achievement, behaviour or attention
Lous, J. (1995)	International Journal of Pediatric Otorhinolaryngology, Vol 32, 105–121, 1995	10 non-cohort and 10 cohort studies	Reading	Correlations between OM and reading too small to have practical importance
Hind, S. E. et al. (1996)	XXIII International Congress of Audiology Abstracts, June 1996	OM+ 71 and OM- 64	Reading, spelling, IQ (verbal and non-verbal reasoning, memory and vocabulary) and phonology	OME effects on reasoning and phonology. No OME effects on reading, spelling, memory or vocabulary
Nittrouer, S. (1996)	Journal of Speech and Hearing Research, Vol 39, 1059–1070, October 1996	4 groups: OM+ and low SEG (n = 5), OM- and low SEG (n = 12), OM+ and mid SEG (n = 12) and OM- and mid SEG. Aged 7:10–8:11 years and months	Phonemic awareness and labelling of fricative-vowel syllables	Effect on speech perception and phonemic awareness: OM+ worse than OM- but Low SES (OM-/OM+) worst

effectiveness trials. Subject to the clarity of its conclusions (i.e. a message, favouring or not favouring, intervention that is consistent across the diverse outcome measures), it should point to rational strategies for intervention that can be agreed between Health Authorities and ENT clinicians and practised in a standardised way.

The realities of noise levels in schools suggest that children with OME may be disadvantaged, particularly during episodes, and so need to be identified by their nursery/school. Reducing noise levels in mainstream schools may not be a practical solution but enhancing the speech-to-noise ratio could prove cost-effective. Sound-field amplification improves speech recognition for all children in primary school classrooms (Crandell *et al.* 1995). If it were routinely introduced into mainstream schools, this could be of benefit to teachers' voices and to children with OME. This type of amplification is discussed more fully in the following chapter.

This system of amplification is not yet available in mainstream schools so parents and children must be encouraged to divulge information on ear problems to the nursery/school. Teachers can be made reliably aware of a shortlist of practical consequences. It is not clear that this action (one of the purposes of school screening) is being reliably followed by schools. Gdowski *et al.* (1986) report that children with conductive mild–moderate hearing losses have problems in the classroom such as misunderstanding short words in connected speech or the reflexive endings of words. Consequently nursery staff and school teachers should be well informed about the optimum practices for enhancing hearing. In the classroom, tactics such as encouraging the child to work with one or two other children in a relatively quiet area during episodes could be useful. It may be helpful to inform day-care staff to be alert to the possible 'social withdrawal' effect of OME. Two new products are currently available: a 'glue ear' leaflet[2] for parents and a 'glue ear' video[3] for primary care; both provide useful information for nursery and school staff.

A child who is identified as having OME may need to be given more careful consideration in discipline issues. Identifying the likelihood of such problems via notification of disease permits providing the child with appropriate work and workspace, so minimising the risks of 'bad' behaviour. Inappropriate punishment for something beyond the individual's control carries a long-term social cost that justifies a behavioural strategy for OME.

The suggestions put forward to enhance the school environment also apply in the home. The risk factor associated with smoking further suggests that mothers should be discouraged from smoking when their children are present to avoid exacerbating the disease.

Conclusion

It should now be evident why OME deserves consideration in a book about education for hearing-impaired children. The hearing loss associated with this disease is transient and usually only mild–moderate but the presence of other aspects of the disease, plus external environmental stressors or lack of environmental compensation, leads by synergy to significant impact. The developing child, struggling to make sense of the nursery and school environment, faces difficulties similar to those of children with permanent hearing loss. Furthermore, some of these effects, although relatively small, seem to be long-term.

Further reading

Chalmers, D., Stewart, I., Silva, P., Mulvena, A. (1989) *Otitis Media with Effusion in Children in the Dunedin Study.* Oxford: Blackwell.
This book provides an accessible account of the study of OME with more in-depth information on the main points discussed in this chapter.

Haggard, M. and Hughes, E. (1991) *Screening Children's Hearing. A Review of the Literature and the Implications of Otitis Media.* MRC Department of Health, London: HMSO.
This book also provides more in-depth information on many of the topics discussed in this chapter. Intellectually, it is quite demanding but the reader's effort is well rewarded.

Notes

1. The TARGET study is a multi-centred randomised clinical trial, on children (aged 3.5 to 7 years at recruitment) from 12 ENT clinics across the UK. There are three treatment arms: medical management (controls), insertion of VTs, and insertion of VTs with adenoidectomy. About 150 children with persistent OME are being randomly allocated to each of these three treatments. Assessed outcomes include middle ear function, hearing level, specific and non-specific health, behaviour and quality of life (child, carer and family). Information from this study should be available around the year 2000.
2. *Glue Ear. A Guide for Parents.* Institute of Hearing Research and Defeating Deafness (The Hearing Research Trust) 1997.
3. *Otitis Media with Effusion – Glue Ear.* MRC Institute of Hearing Research.
   Available from: MRC Institute of Hearing Research, University Park, Nottingham, NG7 2RD.

Recent technological innovations within paediatric audiology

Russell Brett and Wendy McCracken

Introduction and overview

There have been many useful developments in paediatric audiology within the past decade which are worthy of consideration. Most paediatric technological innovations continue to be spin-offs from work within the electronics industry at large. There is still comparatively little hardware that is new within the paediatric field which does not have some correlation within the adult world.

There is a tendency for the paediatric population to be relegated to the class of small adults without any specific needs of their own. For a paediatric population amplification allows access to the acoustic environment. Amplification can allow access to the spoken word for children acquiring language. For the majority of the adult population amplification allows access to language already learnt. Adults have a wealth of linguistic and world knowledge which allows them to use amplification in a specific way and to have opinions on the quality of amplification being provided. For a pre-lingually deaf child the situation is markedly different. This chapter considers some of the recent advances made and the challenges that need to be met if professionals are to take advantage of these possibilities on behalf of deaf children.

Basic needs

Today's technology is able to address some of the following specific needs of the child who wears hearing aids. The child needs to:
* have a well-fitted hearing instrument which fits audiological needs;
* be free of acoustic feedback (whistling hearing aids);
* be able to hear effectively in a variety of listening environments;
* have a consistent, good quality hearing aid prescription regardless of hearing aid type or clinician;
* have access to a wide frequency range;
* have available a personal FM system which is discreet and which automatically adjusts to accommodate for speaker/listener variables.

While amplification has classically be seen as appropriate for individuals within specific audiological groupings research also suggests that there are many children with audiologically minimal degrees of deafness who stand to make considerable gains from the application of sound field amplification. (See later in this chapter.)

Verification of hearing aid fitting

The availability of probe-tube measurements is particularly useful in identifying the difference in ear canal characteristics of infants. The considerable difference in size and shape of ear canals gives rise to different resonant peaks, that of an infant being considerably higher than an adult (Kruger and Ruben 1987). In addition the ear canal volume differences can result in considerable differences in the sound pressure level generated within the ear canal (Feigin *et al.* 1989). To complement these systems there are couplers which may be used to channel sound to the ear through the child's earmoulds rather than via headphones. Systems are progressing now from the use of composite noise stimulus, allowing multiple pure tone measurements to be taken simultaneously. This gives increased flexibility, allowing for constant adjustments to be made to accommodate for child movement, changes in the measuring environment in real time and for the use of live voice. Digital technology has now made 'live voice' presentation a real possibility for probe-tube measurements and there is progress currently within the industry on this front.

The use of probe-tube measurements has brought about direct changes to the hearing aid prescription formulae which now make use of real ear to coupler difference (RECD) measurements, hearing aid microphone positions, head diffraction/body baffle effects and most of these formulae are available as installed software on new probe-tube microphone systems. Probe-tube measurements are valuable in verifying hearing aid fitting, particularly within a paediatric population where individual differences are likely to be greatest. In the survey of practice in the USA between 15 and 39 per cent of respondents always used probe-tube measurements to verify paediatric hearing aid fittings (Hedley-Williams *et al.* 1996). It is important however, to note that such measurements were most likely to be used with the older age group (5 years–11 years 11 months) and were least likely to be used with the infant age group (0–6 months). Thus, as with the initial fitting procedure, the approach which is supported as most appropriate for use in verifying a hearing aid fitting for infants and young children is not as yet being routinely applied within the USA. There is no comparable information regarding practice within Europe but practice is likely to show a similar findings.

For a detailed consideration of the amplification selection considerations in the paediatric population the interested reader is referred to Bess *et al.* (1996).

Issues relating to the fitting of amplification to a paediatric population

A deaf child is dependent upon well-fitted hearing aids to maximise the use of his residual hearing. A definition of what is meant by the term 'well-fitted' is, however, unclear. The settings made to the instrument depend not only on the skills and knowledge of the clinicians fitting them, but also on the methodology adopted by them, the hearing aid prescription formula chosen and the rationale behind this choice. Fundamental to any hearing aid prescription formula is the way in which the Long Term Average Speech Spectrum (LTASS) is defined. This will have a direct effect on the gain across the frequency range stipulated as appropriate for a specific hearing instrument and in turn govern the listening experience of the child. The further the microphone is away from the speaker when the LTASS is recorded the higher the prescribed gain requirements will be. How many clinicians are aware of the source of the LTASS within the prescription formula they are using?

There is a marked paucity of research into the specific needs of a paediatric population with regards to amplification. Of the few hearing aid prescription protocols the Desired Sensation Level (Seewald 1992) is specifically designed for this population.

There is a specific need for such formula for a number of reasons:

1. It is clear that the average speaker interaction distances for baby–adult, child–child are different from that of adult–adult and the resultant LTASS changes considerably. In addition the interaction distance between mother and baby varies considerably between 2 and 12 months. Stelmachowicz *et al.* (1993) showed a variation of 10–18 dB in gain and a variation in spectral response of 12 dB in low frequency (LF) regions to 6 dB in the high frequency (HF) regions.

2. A child is not able to make adjustments to hearing aids and unlike a deafened adult has no frame of reference anyway with which to decide the level of gain required by the hearing instrument. Thus the child is at the mercy of the clinician and the settings defined by them. The settings therefore need to be more precise for children than for adults.

3. A child is in the process of acquiring spoken language and there is no redundant information available to him or her. As much speech information as possible is required – within a comfortable range – in order to develop spoken language and self-monitoring skills.

4. There is very little audiometric information available on neonates when they are first diagnosed as having a hearing impairment. Pre-6 to 7 months this information is inevitably solely Auditory Brainstem Response (ABR) and confined to one or possibly two frequency regions. What little information there is to define the child's unique auditory status must be utilised as accurately as possible for all of the aforementioned reasons.

5. As the child is growing rapidly there will be changes which take place within the outer ear and ear canal that will alter the response to sound. The external ear resonances will make all measurements change with age – the real-ear-unaided response will not become stable (i.e. reach average adult values) until post-37 months and even then the child may show considerable individual differences. Down's Syndrome children typically have much smaller pinnae and external canals for their chronological age. In addition to a hearing impairment the child may also have dysmorphic features which affect ear canal resonances.

A survey of practice procedures concerning the fitting of hearing aids to this population was carried out in the USA (Hedley-Williams *et al.* 1996). When asked about the fitting rationale almost half of the respondents reported that their most common fitting approach was 'a personal fitting strategy' i.e. they utilised their own fitting criteria, regardless of the child's age. In excess of 90 per cent of the respondents seldom used the desired sensation level (DSL) approach when seeking to meet the amplification needs of children. In itself the DSL formula does raise the interesting questions regarding the suitability of today's hearing aids to the paediatric population, specifically with regard to the frequency gain characteristics of these instruments.

Advances in conventional analogue technology

Directional microphones – multi-microphone technology (MMT)

Directional microphone technology has been in use for many years now in hearing instruments. They function by introducing a delay into the acoustic network (see Figure 4.3:1). They can act upon an input and eliminate some of the unwanted noise before arrival of the sound at the amplifier stage. The use of multi-microphone technology (MMT) is a further attempt at reducing background noise by creating a highly directional microphone system (see Figure 4.3:2). The user can switch, remotely, between an omni-directional microphone, where an awareness of surrounding sounds is important, e.g. traffic noise, and a directional microphone. Thus these systems could be used within the paediatric population by an older sophisticated listener. Background noise is known to be a more significant problem for children than for adults and is probably the single most crucial factor to the recognition of speech by hearing-impaired children. A child will require a signal to noise ratio (S/N) in excess of +20 dB for residual hearing to be maximised (Ross and Seewald 1988). Phonak, who have designed the Audio Zoom system, have suggested from their 1994 research an average 8.5 dB improvement in S/N with MMT (Valente *et al.* 1995).

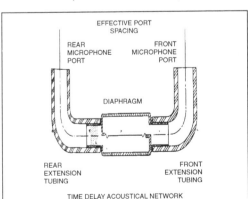

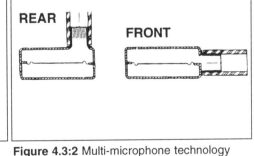

Figure 4.3:1 Conventional directional microphone

Figure 4.3:2 Multi-microphone technology

The use of multi-channel hearing aids

Multi-channel hearing aids have to some certain extent been superseded by digital hearing aids. They evolved to circumvent one of the problems with conventional hearing instruments – the inability to adapt to a multiplicity of listening environments. It may be possible to adjust and set a hearing instrument to provide a child with good access to speech sounds in the 'ideal' listening environment of the Hearing Assessment Clinic but this does not mean that the child will obtain any benefit at all from the hearing aid when it is used in the classroom, on the playground or at home. Providing a suitable frequency response is a compromise between optimal listening in quiet and best discrimination in noise, the former necessitating a relatively flat frequency response the latter a greater HF emphasis.

Widex was the first to produce the first multi-program remote-controlled instrument, Quattro, with four separate listening programs. Widex advertised this hearing instrument as suitable for children's use, and suggest that programs for use in assembly, playgroup, classroom and home situations could be set up. This hearing aid is fitted with directional microphone and direct input facility for use with personal FM systems and ancillary input devices.

One reasonable argument for using programmable hearing aids with children is that very little audiometric information is readily available when a hearing aid is first fitted – often only ABR results. Repeated adjustments are required to the time when a reliable audiogram is obtainable from the child, and often beyond this due to fluctuations and changes in Real-Ear Unaided Response (REUR) due to ear canal growth changes. The difference between measurements taken in the test box and in the child's ear (RECD) are greater for children than adults and they also show a greater inter-subject variance. It can be argued that programmable hearing instruments offer the greatest degree of hearing instrument flexibility available. They can provided a greater number of filters, finer filter control, a wide range of gain and output, a choice of output limiting mode. A second reason for providing a choice of several alternative programs is that the infant's listening environments vary to the extent that both gain and frequency spectrum change (Stelmachowicz *et al.* 1993). Change from cradle (2–4 month), to hip (5–7 month) to floor (6–12 month) positions showed a variation of 10–18 dB in gain and a variation in spectral response of 12 dB in low frequency regions to 6 dB in the high.

Other advantages include no need for volume covers or sticky tape over volume control on child's hearing aid – gain can generally be 'locked' via the remote control or programmer, binaural adjustment of hearing aids is often possible via the remote control – ensuring a balanced input of sound.

There is very little data relating to paediatric use of programmable aids, despite the potential advantages such aids have to offer. It is reported that within the USA less than 10 per cent of the audiologists working within the paediatric field ever offer a programmable hearing aid as an option (Hedley-Williams *et al.* 1996).

Digital technology

Digital technology is of such significance to the recent advances made in paediatric amplification that it is worth spending some time explaining what it is.

The term 'digital' has been used in relation to hearing instruments for nearly ten years but has become increasingly prevalent of late. For many professionals working with hearing-impaired children there has been considerable confusion as to what it is that this technology offers. The manufacturers have not always added to the clarity of the situation. Terms such as 'quasi-digital', 'true digital', 'digital programming', 'analogue to digital conversion' are in common usage.

What is digital technology?

Digital technology indicates that at some point in the hearing instrument chain, be it the receiver, the processor or at hearing aid programmer level, a digital microprocessor is employed. At the start of the previous decade the words 'digital technology' indicated that it was possible to programme a hearing instrument via an external programming unit, e.g. Bernafon Phox range, not that the hearing instrument itself had a digital audio processor within it. 1995 saw the introduction of the first truly digital hearing aid. A digital hearing aid makes use of an Analogue to Digital Converter (ADC) and a processor which is capable of making adjustments to a digital signal in 'real-time'. The signal is processed and output sufficiently fast for the wearer to not perceive any dis-synchrony while listening to speech.

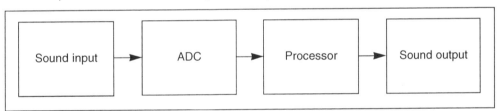

Figure 4.3:3 Digital hearing aid – simplified overview

What is an ADC?

An ADC is a circuit which allows an analogue signal (one that is continuously variable) such as a speech wave to be represented by a series of binary digits, in reality electrical pulses i.e. ons and offs. In the world of hearing aid technology this corresponds to representing sound waves in the form of a train of pulses rather than as a continuously variable voltage.

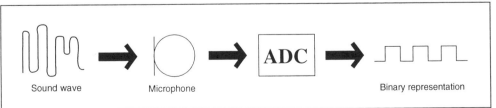

Figure 4.3:4 Analogue to digital conversion

Immediately after the microphone stage the ADC samples the analogue signal at regular time intervals – termed the sample rate. The resultant string of binary digits then represents the analogue signal (or the change in the analogue signal) at that specific point in time. The sampling rate of the ADC is extremely important since it governs the amount of information recorded. Typical sampling rates for Digital Hearing Instruments are 32 kHz. This can be compared to a modern CD recording which is at 44.1 kHz.

Digital technology does theoretically offer an infinite control over the frequency range. In practice the frequency spectrum is divided into discrete bands – today a typical digital hearing aid supports seven such bands (Oticon: Digifocus). The hearing aid gain can be contoured more effectively to suit the child's needs with a digital system than with an analogue.

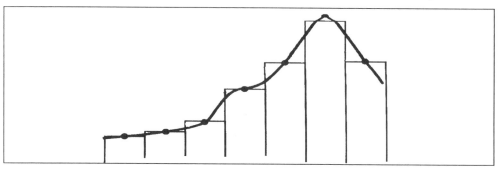

Figure 4.3:5 Matching gain requirements with digital technology

Reducing unwanted noise
Environmental noise
Using digital technology it is possible to analyse the 'type' of sound input to the processor. It is possible to distinguish between a speech type sound and noise and to then reduce the noise component of the input wave form. A popular digital hearing aid achieves this by dividing the sound input into three frequency bands and analysing the waveform in each, in real time, over a time period. A comparison of how the sound varies within that period results in the processor making adjustments to the combined output waveform by reducing the background noise and increasing the sensitivity to speech sounds.

There are two *main* methods of reducing background noise:
1. electronic filtering or Automatic Signal Processing (ASP) (although these techniques are discussed under this section they may also be analogue technology);
2. directional microphone technology or beamforming.

The former technique involves processing the signal, the latter technique aims to provide the 'desired' signal, not the background noise, to the hearing instrument – thus making the amplification and processing much simpler.

While such amplification options continue to develop the application of such technology is little researched amongst the paediatric population. A linear hearing aid will not provide every child with an appropriate sound experience. For children who have a mild to moderate degree of hearing loss, a linear hearing aid is unlikely to provide access to quiet sounds while providing comfortable access to intense sounds. With linear technology the required frequency response is only likely to be gained by continual adjustment of the volume control. Automatic signal processing provides a number of alternatives which can be used to increase the level of electro-acoustic flexibility. In the case of children with a mild to moderate hearing loss, level dependent frequency response or wide dynamic range compression (WDRC) theoretically offer this group access to quiet sounds while avoiding amplification of intense sounds. These findings have been endorsed by Stelmachowicz (1996) in case studies.

Although this type of WDRC appears to offer benefits to certain paediatric groups, the technological possibilities do pose many questions regarding sensitive application which remain to be investigated. For further information on WDRC hearing aids, including BILL, TILL, PILL, the K-AMP© and the rationale behind their selection and use, the interested reader is referred to Killion in Chapter 8 of *Hair Cells and Hearing Aids* (Berlin 1995).

Amplifier noise

The components in a traditional analogue amplifier have to function to extremely high tolerances in order to keep noise levels low within a circuit. In traditional high-gain push-pull amplifiers a considerable amount of 'hissing' is created by the amplifier. Any distortion of the current flowing through a circuit may be perceived as interference. In addition individual components, such as resistors, themselves generate noise (due to random movement of electrons). It is extremely difficult to achieve these demanding tolerance levels within the confines of an integrated circuit where thousands of transistors are crammed onto a 2–3mm square silicon chip.

With digital circuitry it is possible to manipulate the signal and to reduce the unwanted noise created by the amplifier. A digital signal is very robust to corruption and therefore much lower tolerances can be utilised in circuit design. Any noise generated can be reduced to below the child's hearing threshold as it occurs.

Control of acoustic feedback

Oticon method

Acoustic feedback is a problem well-known to all professionals working with children with severe and profound hearing losses. The characteristic whistling, caused by the sound leaking between the input and output stages of the amplifier, can be very difficult to control when high gain is required from a hearing instrument – particularly when the microphone and receiver are in close proximity. Unfortunately a regular solution to this problem is to attenuate the output of the hearing aid either by cutting the high frequencies, or more often by turning down the volume of the hearing instrument. In either case a loss of gain results frequently making the hearing aid useless to the child.

Digital technology does offer a more sophisticated and useful solution. It is possible to attenuate the frequency band which contains the feedback frequency. By attenuating this specific frequency or frequency band it is possible to maintain the required gain at other frequencies. See Figure 4.3:6.

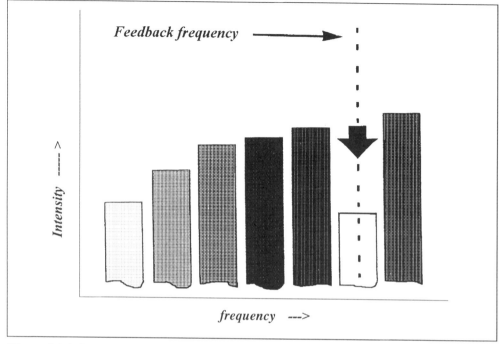

Figure 4.3:6 Controlling 'feedback' through digital technology

Widex method

Other types of digital instrument have been produced recently which provide additional gain by suppressing feedback but in an alternative way. The Danavox Genius does not reduce the frequency or frequency band where the feedback occurs but rather functions by continuously analysing the feedback situation and creating a correction signal to cancel any detected feedback signal. This cancellation signal is present at all times, although weak compared to the input signal. A white noise test signal is introduced to the input signal at either –18 or –24S/N dependent upon whether the volume control is above or below the mid setting.

To control compression amplification

The idea of compression amplification in hearing instruments is not a new one. The theory is that sounds are placed within the most comfortable listening range (CLR) of the child by squeezing them between the desired sensation level (DSL) and the uncomfortable listening level (ULL) as opposed to 'clipping' the peak of the sound wave above a predefined ceiling threshold and adding distortion to the received signal. With conventional analogue instruments this can be a haphazard exercise. While paediatric hearing aid prescription programmes, such as Seewald DSL, now state precise figure at inter-octave frequencies for both target gain and Saturation Sound Pressure Level (SSPL)90 or Real Ear Saturation Response (RESR) the output to the child's ear is governed by the limitations of the hearing instrument. It is not possible to contour the SSPL90 curve to match the targets the whole way across the frequency range since the maximum output across the frequency range will be governed by the setting of the low or high frequency filters.

With digital technology more flexibility is allowed. To date hearing instruments exist which will separate the HF and LF ranges and provide control over the compression within these two sectors in real time (see Figure 4.3:7). It is thus possible to ramp down the response of the LF range and ramp up the response of the HF range, thus ensuring that an upward spread of masking does not obliterate the HF consonant sounds and adding further gain to them within the CLR.

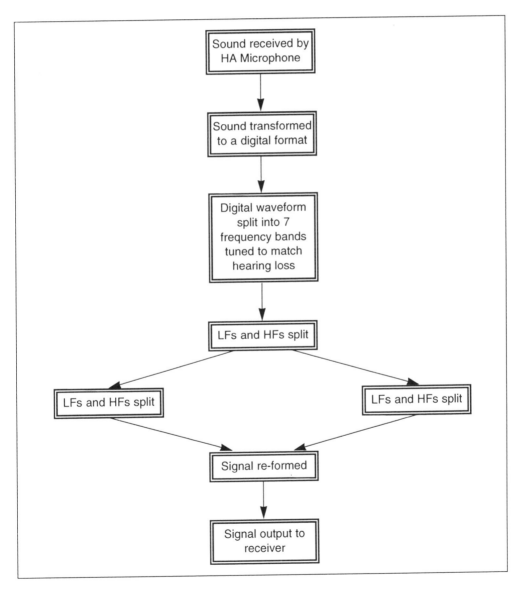

Figure 4.3:7 Functioning of a 7-channel digital hearing aid

To lend themselves to computer programming

The logical development of the digital hearing instrument is that it can be set up and programmed either via an external programmer or through connection to a personal computer with appropriate interfacing hardware and software. This may now be achieved via the NOAH platform.

The NOAH Platform and programmable hearing aids

Programmable hearing aids have been around for the last decade. There is one major advantage associated with the use of these systems with the paediatric population: the hearing instrument can be adjusted *in situ*, without any interference to the hearing instrument or the child while measurements are verified, either via a probe-tube microphone system or in the Sound Field. There are disadvantages too – the largest of these is that the hearing instrument cannot be adjusted without a programming unit. All audiologists cannot adjust all hearing aids, furthermore spare hearing aids cannot be provided for a hearing-impaired child without a technician present who can programme the instrument.

A further initial disadvantage of these systems used to be that each individual programmable hearing instrument required its own specific programmer. This led to the audiologist/dispenser either not using programmable hearing aids, using one type of programmable hearing aid only or having to speculate and purchase a variety of different programming units. There was no accepted protocol within the industry. In October 1993 a group of leading hearing aid manufacturers agreed to establish a joint development group the Hearing Instrument Manufacturers' Software Association (HIMSA) whose brief was to establish a software standard for fitting programmable hearing aids. Later in 1993 NOAH was introduced. NOAH is a personal computer-based system for fitting programmable hearing aids that provides a standard agreed by all hearing aid manufacturers. Each hearing aid manufacturer produces its own hardware (interface box – such as Hi-pro™) and software module, using a common programming language, to interface with the computer system. Not only has this system been agreed by hearing aid manufacturers but also by manufacturers of audiological test equipment and makers of office systems. Thus insertion gain measurements can be uploaded to the program hearing aids set appropriately and reports output to a chosen database or report generator.

Other advantages offered by NOAH include:

- a visual representation of fitting procedure;
- a standardised database for storing children's records;
- one common interface for all programmable hearing instruments;
- a technology which lends itself to digital hearing aid technology (forward compatibility);
- an interfacing of all equipment within the audiology room;
- reduction of prescription calculation errors;
- *in situ* measurement and adjustment of hearing aids.

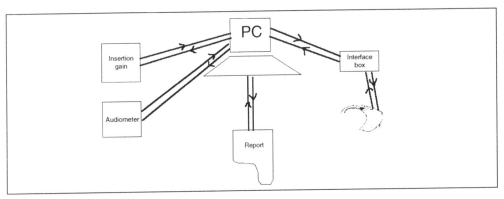

Figure 4.3:8 Schematic of component parts in Noah programming system

Advances in Personal FM Systems

Personal FM systems are able to improve S/N by bringing the speaker's voice, usually the class teacher's, to within the *critical distance*, i.e. where the child is within the teacher's 'direct' rather than 'reverberant' field. This theory is sound, but the practice often leaves much to be desired. A misused FM system may place the child at an actual disadvantage and the systems are easily misused. Experience has shown that there are at least three main problems associated with the use of personal FM systems:

1. The class teacher forgets to turn the system on and off at the appropriate times – thus the child hears high-quality irrelevant material or nothing
2. The child is too young to control the environmental microphones on his personal hearing aids and thus they are either permanently switched on or off. In the former case the child will continue to be troubled by the background noise in the classroom even though the FM system is functioning correctly since hearing aid microphones are live. In the latter, the child will not be able to hear the other children around him when they have something worthy of note to say.
3. The FM system is too obtrusive and bulky and many children take an active dislike to the systems. The negative feelings of the child towards the system can sometimes be so pronounced that they outweigh any acoustic advantages offered or put at risk the wearing of the personal hearing aids.

Unfortunately, there is no solution to the first problem. No electronic device can anticipate what a teacher is going to say and make a decision as to whether it is going to be of relevance to the hearing-impaired child or not. In-service training is the only retort. However the latter two problems have seen significant recent developments.

Automatic Volume Control systems (AVC)

There are at least two systems currently on the market which have a long-term Automatic Volume Control (AVC). This is not a new technology. It is the type of system which has long been used by DJs' 'speak-over system' to automatically reduce the volume of a record playing when they speak into their microphone.

For the child the parallel is when there is any input from the teacher's FM transmitter the microphones on the child's personal hearing aids are ramped down by a pre-determined amount. When the teacher ceases talking the environmental microphones ramp up to their former levels. Thus an S/N is maintained and is not subject to the level of noise immediately surrounding the child.

There have been criticisms levelled at these systems – the major one being the attack and release times of the AVC. The author is of the opinion that even if some morpheme information is clipped by these systems the child continues to be at an enormous advantage when using them compared to the alternative scenario described for the following reason. A good teacher will obtain the children's attention before imparting information and repeat herself in a variety of ways – thus the initial missed information is most generally redundant. The child is, at the very least, afforded a guaranteed good S/N ratio for the majority of the dialogue.

Size

Most hearing-impaired children, understandably, become very conscious of their radio FM systems when they are approaching adolescence. They have always been indiscreet. Phonak have recently developed a system, the Microlink (TM) which will fit on to the 'shoe' at the bottom of the child's personal hearing aid. There are no other components required. The receiver is able to take its current from the battery in the hearing aid through a tiny hole in the battery compartment. There is an FM/M and FM-only switch on the shoe (similar to the Phonak Super Front PPCLA) which will allow the user to switch off any surrounding noise if required.

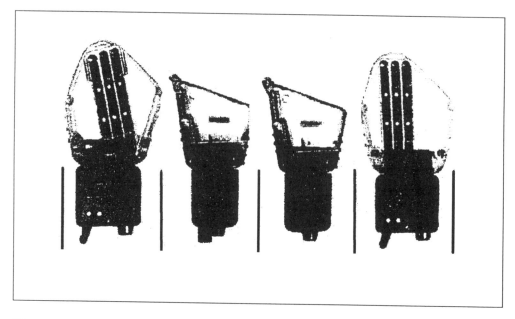

Figure 4.3:9 Phonak Micro-link system – variety of shoe sizes to fit Phonak range.

These systems do not have AVC and as such are perhaps more suited to the secondary-aged child who is likely to be more grateful for the system and who is also able to decide when to switch environmental microphones on and off.

The system does have the advantage that it can be used with old transmitters, although there are a limited range of frequencies available on the system, and of course there are no expensive batteries or charger units to purchase.

Recently systems which incorporate an FM system with a behind the ear (BTE) or post-aural aid have come onto the market. The BTE FM systems incorporate the FM receiver within the housing of the BTE aid, making it cosmetically preferable to the traditional body-worn FM receiver. These aids are not currently available for use within the UK. One of the major benefits in addition to the cosmetic advantage is the elimination of coupler components. These components are classically weak links in the amplification chain. An FM system should be acoustically transparent, having no effect on hearing aid performance *per se*. In fact, several researchers have suggested that this is far from the case and that carefully selected and verified hearing aid settings are frequently compromised by coupling to an FM system (Hawkins and Schum 1985; Lewis *et al.* 1991; Thibodeau *et al.* 1988). A review of the FM-related variables related to use of FM systems is provided by Seewald and Moodie 1992.

While the American Speech-Language Hearing Association (ASHA) have published guidelines for fitting and monitoring of FM systems (1994) no similar standardised guidelines are followed within the UK. There is little evidence that audiologists are employing probe-tube measurements in verifying FM fittings, despite the fact that the majority of a child's listening experience during a school day may be via an FM system. Similarly, the use of measurements in quiet as predictors of a child's performance in the everyday noisy environment must be questioned, whether in relation to personal hearing aids or personal FM systems.

The challenge of meeting the audiological needs of profoundly deaf children has seen rapid advances over the past decade. The increasing use of cochlear implants within the paediatric population appears to be inevitable and raises a number of issues (see Chapter 4.4). In addition to the developing technology related to cochlear implants, other audiological aids have seen a revival. Tactile aids and transposition aids are being employed and raise a number of issues related to fitting protocol, verification and what constitutes appropriate habilitation. Both have a long history with the first tactile aid being reported in the 1920s, and transposition aid developed by Johansson in the early 1960s. Cochlear implantation provided the spur for these instruments to be developed and exploited largely for deafened adults or children for whom implantation was not an option. For a review of current research the interested reader is referred to Gravel and Chute 1996; Osberger *et al.* 1996.

Sound field FM systems

Sound field FM systems (SFFM) merit a scant mention in this chapter, not because they are a recent technological innovation as such, but in view of the fact that their introduction into the UK has been so tardy. Few authorities make use of them routinely as part of their audiological remediation package, yet they are a practical and cost-effective way of dealing with the problems encountered by hearing-impaired children in acoustically poor primary classrooms.

SFFM systems are nothing more than miniature public address systems. Speakers are mounted in the corners of a classroom or suspended from a central pod in the ceiling. The class teacher is equipped with a radio microphone, and the system is generally set such that the teacher's voice is a constant 10–15 dB above average background noise levels (bearing in mind that the effect of the SFFM system is to reduce some of the 'controllable' aspects of background noise within the classroom effectively the S/N maintained is usually better than this).

SFFM systems are thus improving S/N for all children within the classroom. Is this necessary? Typically an average infant class will contain two or three children with a fluctuating hearing loss, due to glue ear. In addition there may be children with unilateral hearing losses. In addition to children with hearing losses an improved S/N is known to be advantageous to children to whom English is a second language (non-native speakers). Furthermore it has been proven to be of advantage to *all* children *per se* since they are in the process of acquiring a fluency of spoken language (Nabalek and Nabalek 1985).

An SFFM system is a way of providing benefit to all children in the primary class, vocal relief to a tired class teacher and at the same time improving the S/N for the hearing-impaired child without any stigmatisation. The interested reader is referred to Flexer (1994) for further details.

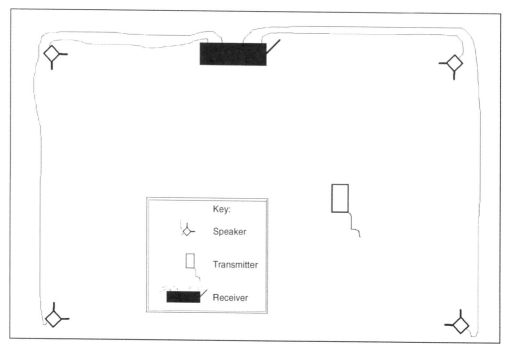

Figure 4.3:10 SFFM system

Summary and caveat

Before a hearing aid is fitted or any instrumentation is used to take a measurement from a child there must be a clear rationale behind its use. All the instrumentation and techniques described are subject to individual professional evaluation. There has been considerable research in recent years relating to the use of probe-tube microphone systems with young children. There are prescription formulae which take into account head diffraction, body baffle, position of hearing aid microphone, etc. However, one must be cognisant of the fact that the only hearing results available to the clinician, pre-7 months, are via auditory brainstem response (ABR) with a centre frequency of 3kHz. Where does all this theory fit with this dearth of data? The splitting of the decibel, at this stage, could be seen as a rather pointless exercise. Similarly what is the point in using real-ear coupler difference measurements, either actual or age-appropriate averages when the starting point for the air and bone conduction thresholds is the pure-tone audiogram (PTA)? The audiogram does not make allowances for age differences/ear canal differences – its zero line is based on average adult figure. The caveat with all of this technology is that it can be easy to use the hardware with little thought to the processes behind its implementation. Audiology and hearing aid fitting is not altogether a scientific affair. There are philosophical issues which each individual must resolve. The choice of LTASS is a case in point.

When a hearing aid is fitted is one aiming to provide the hearing-impaired child with a consistency of auditory input from birth onwards? Yes? – well this is not what the hearing child experiences. If 'yes' then what is this consistency? Is it the average adult auditory experience, or is it the auditory experience that the child would probably have had as an adult? The changes in ear canal and pinnae size provide the child with a different experience of sound as the child grows – being more sensitive to higher frequency sounds as a baby. Should we not, as clinicians, be continually adjusting the child's hearing instrument so as *not* to provide him with a consistency of auditory input? In any case is there sufficient audiological information available in the early months, when ear-canal changes are the most dramatic, to make this practicable anyway? An informed approach which sensitively incorporates technological change into the ecological setting of the child is the only way forward. To have a chance of achieving this parents, teachers of the deaf and audiologists must work together.

Chapter 4.4

Cochlear implants: some challenges

Ken Robinson

Overview

This chapter briefly reviews the literature on developmental plasticity and what is known about sensitive periods for language development, with specific reference to the implications for paediatric cochlear implantation. The data show that the earlier that profoundly deaf children receive a cochlear implant, the better the outcome, whether it be speech perception or production. Age at implantation, however, is not the only important factor in determining outcome, and other factors play as important a role. Some of these other factors are identified, for example, communication mode, educational setting, quality of acoustic environment and degree of residual hearing. The challenge for research is to study large enough numbers of children to show clear and systematic effects for each of these, and other, factors. Large numbers are required to perform appropriate statistical analysis, and so it is argued that cochlear implant centres need to standardise on surgical, audiological, psychological, speech and language therapy and education outcome measures to enable pooling of data.

Auditory deprivation and the sensitive period

The physiological literature on the effects of auditory deprivation shows that major anatomical reorganisation occurs as a result of insults such as cochlear ablation and neonatal deafening from ototoxic drugs. The general result is that early insult to the auditory nervous system has a far greater effect than an insult suffered during adulthood. Hence, sustained effects of sensory deprivation can lead to a loss of responsiveness and selectivity in the auditory system, and these effects are more marked during infancy than in adulthood. A brief review may be found in Lustig *et al.* (1994), as well as studies showing that the effects of auditory deprivation may be reversed by the subsequent provision of electrical stimulation by a cochlear implant.

Despite the advances made by animal researchers, the linkage between the physiological studies of auditory deprivation, and subsequent effect of chronic electrical stimulation and language development in children remains tenuous. It is now clear that chronic, long-term electrical stimulation is safe at the levels provided by cochlear implants, and much is now known about the anatomical reorganisation that occurs following neonatal cochlear insult. However, relatively little is known about the behavioural effects of auditory deprivation in animals. A major challenge for researchers in this field is to perform experiments that examine the behavioural effects of auditory deprivation on tasks such as frequency discrimination, and possibly phonetic contrast discrimination such as /sa/ and /sha/, and the potentially reversing effects of cochlear implantation.

Turning to language development, the literature on extreme language deprivation in children reared in isolation has recently been reviewed by Bench (1992, ch. 2). This literature is poignant, but is difficult to interpret because it is based on case studies. For example, Bench cites the well-known study of Genie, who was discovered at 13 years of age, after having been isolated since the age of 20 months. Even after seven years of rehabilitation, Genie never achieved good language acquisition. In comparison, other studies of children isolated at birth, but discovered during childhood have shown large improvements in the rate of language acquisition. Generally, it is accepted that the acquisition of language is relatively robust, in that recovery occurs even after many years of isolation during childhood. However, should isolation persist until adolescence, then language acquisition becomes more difficult.

A persistent theme in the language development literature is the notion of a critical period. Lenneberg (1967) is generally credited with the suggestion that language acquisition could be seen to be limited by biological considerations in the form of a critical period occurring between 2 years and the onset of puberty. Today, physiologists write about 'sensitive' rather than critical periods, as there is recent evidence that the adult brain continues to adapt and reorganise. Nevertheless, all agree that there is an increased sensitivity during childhood.

At the time of writing, Lenneberg (1967) had little direct evidence for his thesis of the importance of the sensitive period of language acquisition. He relied on cognitive neuropsychological evidence showing that children recovering from traumatic aphasia were more likely to relearn language than adults. Since the publication of the book, there have been a number of reports which provide further evidence for a sensitive period of language acquisition. For example, Ruben (1986) has noted that the earlier and greater the deprivation of speech perception, the greater the effect on language acquisition. His research has concentrated on children who have had severe to profound sensori-neural loss, and also children with conductive loss through otitis media with effusion (glue ear). He has shown that children who are profoundly deaf generally show poor oral language skills, those who are moderate to severely deaf have significant delays in language acquisition, and those with mild to moderate losses tend to show a lesser delay. Moreover, children with glue ear are more likely to demonstrate reduced auditory sensitivity as measured by auditory brainstem response, and poorer expressive language abilities than children who have not had the disease. Ruben has suggested that the sensitive period for initial language acquisition may last up to around 2 to 3 years of age.

In addition, however, Ruben (1986) has added an important voice to the theoretical debate, in that he has suggested that there were different sensitive periods, with differing periods for voice and speech production. Hence, his view is that a single sensitive period of language acquisition stretching from birth to the onset of puberty probably does not exist; rather, it is made up of a cascade of sensitive periods, including those for spatial discrimination, temporal resolution, consonant discrimination, voice production and language production. The challenge for future research in auditory developmental plasticity is to show differences in sensitivity for these differing aspects of auditory processing and language acquisition.

It is now clear that the provision of a cochlear implant to a profoundly or totally deaf child can reverse the effects of auditory deprivation. This research provides a direct test of Lenneberg's (1967) hypothesis of language acquisition, as prior to implantation, these children have been unable to perceive speech even with the most powerful hearing aids available. Recently, Dowell *et al.* (1997) studied 52 profoundly deaf children and adolescents who first received a cochlear implant at ages ranging from 1;9 to 19;9 years. On an open-set sentence task using audition alone, 86 per cent of the children were able to perform significantly, with half of the group exceeding a score of 25 per cent. It is important to note that without an implant, none of the children would have been able to complete the task. Dowell *et al.* also show that age of implantation is a significant factor that affects subsequent speech perception. For profoundly deaf children with cochlear implants, there appears to be a sensitive period for speech perception from birth to approximately 4 to 6 years of age; performance plateaus about 12 to 14 years of age. Dowell *et al.* note, however, that large individual differences occur and this review will later attempt to deal with why some of these differences are found. Similar data have been collected in the author's centre at Nottingham, where children implanted under the age of 5 years show better auditory perception than children implanted at older ages (Nottingham Paediatric Cochlear Implant Programme 1997, Figure 9). These data study 63 children on whom an auditory performance rating, known as the Categories of Auditory Performance, had been made at 2 years post-implantation, and 39 children on whom the same rating had been made at 3 years post-implantation. Results show that 57 per cent of children implanted before the age of 5 years are able to understand conversation without lip-reading, whereas 22 per cent of children implanted at ages of 5 years and over can achieve this same level of performance. Further data in the same report show that children who are implanted at an age prior to school placement are more likely to be in mainstream schools, compared with those children implanted following educational placement (Nottingham Paediatric Cochlear Implant Programme 1997, Figure 14).

Similar effects of age at implantation have been noted for speech production. Tye-Murray *et al.* (1995) reported on 28 pre-linguistic children with about three years of implant experience. Children were divided in a group implanted at 2 to 4 years of age, 5 to 8 years and 8 to 15 years, and phonetic transcriptions for phonemes and for words were used. They found that children who were implanted at under 5 years of age showed better performance than children implanted at older ages.

The combined data show that a cochlear implant can reverse the effects of auditory deprivation, and that implantation at younger ages is likely to result in better speech perception and speech production performance in the longer term. However, there may also be structural influences from the educational setting in which the child or adolescent is placed. For example, it may be that the acoustical environment for a child in a primary school setting is more favourable than that of an adolescent in a secondary school setting, which could be expected to affect the degree of benefit from the cochlear implant. Nevertheless, there is agreement in the literature that older children still benefit substantially from a cochlear implant, and that it is possible for older children to continue to improve their performance with continued experience of the implant. Secondly, there is agreement that the individual variability in performance is large, and that there are many other factors that are important in mediating benefit from a cochlear implant.

Some mediating factors that enhance performance from a cochlear implant

Communication mode

This is an important mediator of benefit from cochlear implant. For example, Somers (1991) studied children with hearing aids and children with cochlear implants who used either oral or total communication. There were five groups of children in the study: 16 children with hearing aids who used total communication, 14 children with hearing aids who used oral communication, 13 children with cochlear implants who used total communication, 13 children with cochlear implants who used oral communication, and a control group of 12 children with hearing aids who demonstrated no usable hearing. Each of the groups were matched for age, and the residual hearing for the hearing aid groups was between 100 and 110 dBHL and greater than 110 dBHL for the cochlear implant groups (unaided, better-ear three frequency average of 0.5, 1 and 2 kHz). A number of speech tests were employed ranging from discrimination of time and intensity changes in speech to open-set speech perception. The results from this study showed that children with cochlear implants performed better than children with equivalent hearing loss provided with hearing aids. Moreover, the totally deaf children with cochlear implants performed as well as the profoundly deaf children with hearing aids. It is important to remember that this result was obtained using a majority of single-channel devices, and that preliminary data from the author's programme shows that totally and profoundly deaf children provided with cochlear implants can perform as well as, and sometimes better than, severely deaf children optimally fitted with hearing aids.

Somers (1991) also found an overall effect of communication mode, in that all children using oral communication performed better than those using total communication. In interpreting this result, it is important to remember that in the USA total communication educational programmes tend to use sign language (manually coded English) in addition to oral language. Nevertheless, there have now been a number of US papers that have replicated this result, together with one study that has failed to replicate. This failure to replicate may have occurred due to the wide variation in aural input that is likely to occur in a group of total communication programmes. A recent Australian paper by Dowell *et al.* (1997) of 52 children with cochlear implants has also shown that an oral/aural mode of communication is likely to result in improved open-set speech perception (Bench Koval and Bamford (BKB), sentence test and Phonetically Balanced Kindergarten test (PBK) word lists). In the UK, schools using total communication tend to span a wide spectrum from being manual-dominant to being oral-dominant, and so such a result may not be as apparent in the UK. Given the data on developmental plasticity reviewed in the earlier section of this chapter, it is clear that continued auditory input is essential for children with cochlear implants. It is therefore cautiously and provisionally concluded that an oral/aural mode of communication, or aural-dominant mode of communication is likely to enhance performance in children with cochlear implants. We must remember, however, that the communication needs of young children differ widely, and that these must be considered carefully in addition to the development of audition. It is clearly a challenge to UK researchers interested in cochlear implants and in hearing aids to replicate this result, and again, one potential solution is to pool data across implant centres.

Educational setting

The educational setting of the child with a cochlear implant is also likely to mediate benefit. Nevins and Chute (1996) have recently reviewed aspects of US education programmes, and cite studies indicating that the academic achievements of deaf children in mainstream schools are likely to be higher than their non-mainstreamed peers. Moreover, improved speech intelligibility is also noted in deaf children placed in mainstream schools. However, as Nevins and Chute mention, it may be that this occurs because children with residual hearing tend to be mainstreamed, or that a higher level of speech intelligibility is part of the selection criteria for mainstream schools. Moreover, the population of children in special schools and in mainstream are very different, and it is therefore difficult to make meaningful comparisons.

With respect to children with cochlear implants, Nevins and Chute review data from their own programme. Results show that about 75 per cent of children with five years' experience with a cochlear implant tend to shift their educational placement from a special school or unit to a mainstream school. In addition, their most recent data shows that children receiving an implant at a younger age tend to proceed to a mainstream school. As mentioned earlier in this review, data from the author's programme also support this conclusion (Nottingham Paediatric Cochlear Implant Programme 1997). Children who are implanted at preschool ages are five times more likely to subsequently attend mainstream school than the general population of profoundly deaf children with hearing aids. Despite this encouraging result, both Nevins and Chute (1996) and members of the author's Programme advocate that all children with cochlear implants require regular follow-up. Those in mainstream education continue to require constant monitoring to ensure success. This requirement represents a considerable challenge to all implant centres now and for the future.

Quality of acoustical environment

The data reviewed above show that preschool children with cochlear implants are more likely to subsequently enter a mainstream school than children with hearing aids. However, in some cases, it is possible that the acoustical environment in a mainstream school is hostile to the continued use of a cochlear implant. The importance of a favourable acoustical environment may be an additional factor affecting benefit from a cochlear implant. It may be that the signal to noise ratio may be worse in a secondary educational setting with a wide range of acoustical environments compared with a primary school or nursery setting, which could therefore affect an age-at-implantation study, or that acoustical environment may interact with communication mode. It is a challenge to implant centres to address the potential effects of hostile acoustical environment, and the degree to which it impairs performance. Potential avenues for research are an emphasis on measurements in noise, and the impact of hostile acoustical environments on performance. In pursuing this research, the importance of the mediating factor of FM systems must also be taken into account.

Residual hearing

A strong factor in determining eventual performance from a cochlear implant is the degree of residual hearing. A retrospective study of 192 children by Cowan *et al.* (1997) showed that 65 per cent of all children were able to complete a test of open-set speech perception using electrical stimulation alone. When children have residual hearing at the time of implantation (aided thresholds in 70 dB speech spectrum up to 1 kHz), over 85 per cent were able to complete a test of open-set speech perception. Hence, the results showed that children with higher levels of residual hearing are good candidates for cochlear implants. The study is also important because it represents an example of pooling of data between two major implant centres (Melbourne and Sydney). Cowan *et al.* (1997) used category tables to group children according to their pre-operative aided residual hearing thresholds, and to group children according to their speech perception category. This method is effective, and shows the importance of pooling data to overcome the problem of comparatively small numbers of children available to individual implant centres.

Conclusion

This chapter has provided an brief introduction to the challenges that face clinicians and researchers interested in profoundly deaf children with cochlear implants. A considerable weight of data now exists that indicates that the earlier a deaf child receives a cochlear implant, the better the outcome. However, wide individual variation remains a hallmark of the literature. This variation indicates that there are other factors, both restrictive and assistive, that determine performance. Some of these factors are likely to include communication mode, educational setting, acoustic environment and degree of residual hearing. This is by no means an exhaustive list, and editorial space restrictions preclude a discussion of effects such as the communicative competence of the child prior to implant, the degree and nature of parent–child interaction, amount of family support available and socio-economic status. Moreover, the effects of identity resolution and personality in longer term outcomes in adolescent and young adult cochlear implant users are important as potential mediators of benefit.

The pursuit of a clearer understanding of the mediators of eventual performance represents a major challenge for both clinicians and researchers working in this field. To assist in that challenge, larger numbers of children will need to be studied. Hence, there is a necessity for implant centres to standardise on outcome measures so that pooling of data is possible to provide better purchase on the relative importance of the mediating factors, and therefore understand why large differences in individual performance occur. The standardised outcome measures should embrace the requirements of all of the disciplines involved in cochlear implantation: surgery, audiological science, psychology, speech and language therapy, and education.

Chapter 4.5

Central Auditory Processing Disorder

Cara Wheeler

Introduction

The phenomenon of 'Central Auditory Processing Disorder' (CAPD) is not a recent one, and in the USA, research and practice in this field is now established. However, at present in the UK, both health and education professionals in the field of audiology and education of the deaf are just beginning to be aware of the existence of CAPD and its implications for clinical audiological practice and educational provision. Consensus has been lacking on a clear definition of CAPD (Jirsa 1992) but it is generally used to denote an individual's difficulties in discriminating, recognising, or comprehending auditory information despite normal peripheral hearing sensitivity. Individuals with CAPD are not a homogeneous group and may present with many different symptoms, and this makes the entire area a complex issue for professionals involved in assessment and remediation .

This chapter will attempt to offer some insights into the nature of CAPD, the confusion regarding terminology and its association with speech, language and learning difficulties. One of the major issues also to be addressed in this chapter relates to the implications of CAPD for future research and for professionals involved in deaf education.

There is still much to be learned of CAPD, particularly in the UK, and this chapter does not aim to provide a definitive guide: it hopes merely to outline current thinking in the field and to provide some insight into how provision for CAPD may develop in the future.

Terminology

The term CAPD originated in the US. It has been used interchangeably with other terms such as:

Auditory Perceptual Disorder
Central Auditory Perceptual Disorder
Auditory Processing Problems
Auditory Language Learning Disorder
Central Auditory Dysfunction (CAD)

(Keith 1981 p. ix)

The most frequently-used terms are CAPD (Jerger *et al.* 1987) and CAD (Keith 1977) which tend to be used synonymously. For the purposes of this chapter, CAPD will be used.

Most researchers agree that the central auditory pathway begins at the cochlea nuclei and terminates in the auditory cortex of the brain (Bamford and Saunders 1992). In this sense, 'hearing' and 'hearing sensitivity' relate only to the operation of the peripheral parts of the auditory mechanism, starting at the outer ear and ending at the auditory nerve, whereas 'central processing' refers to the use made of the auditory signal by the central auditory pathways.

The use of the words 'central' and 'disorder' could imply the presence of physical neurological damage or lesion. However, CAPD is more commonly used to describe a functional deficit of one or more areas of central auditory processing with normal functioning of the peripheral hearing mechanism, and in the contexts in which it is used does not usually imply the presence of a central lesion. Indeed, actual damage to the central auditory nervous system is the exception rather than the rule and there is usually clear medical evidence to the contrary. With this interpretation in mind, although CAPD has clinical implications from an audiological point of view, it is considered to have educational rather than medical implications for management and remediation.

Clinical description

Until recently, the term CAPD has been used to denote a wide range of auditory and language learning problems. Usually however, individuals will experience greatest difficulty in listening to and comprehending auditory information when the auditory signal is compromised by distortion, competition, poor acoustic environment or other reduction in signal clarity, strength or information content. Individuals who have CAPD are a heterogeneous population, presenting with different behavioural manifestations of auditory processing difficulties and with varying degrees of severity.

In an attempt to clarify the use and definition of the term CAPD, a technical report was published in 1996 by the American Speech-Language-Hearing Association (ASHA) Task Force on Central Auditory Processing Concensus Development. As part of this consensus statement, the following behavioural responses which are governed by central auditory mechanisms were noted:

Sound Localisation
Auditory Discrimination
Auditory Pattern Recognition
Temporal Aspects of Audition including:
    temporal resolution
    temporal masking
    temporal integration
    temporal ordering

Auditory Performance decrements with competing acoustic signals

Auditory Performance decrements with degraded acoustic signals

According to ASHA, a deficit of behavioural functioning in *one or more* of these areas would indicate CAPD. Each of these areas is measurable by central auditory testing which is discussed later in this chapter.

Association with other disabilities

As central auditory processes may be responsible for functioning in other areas, such as speech and language functioning, CAPD has been associated with specific speech, language and learning disabilities.

Many researchers take the view that auditory processing is synonymous with speech processing. It is known that the development of spoken language closely parallels the neurological maturation of the auditory system (Young 1983) and that the left and right cerebral asymmetry for language is related to the structural asymmetry of the auditory cortex. Keith (1981) believes CAPD to be associated with an immature central auditory system and that in immature pathways, a plateau of language development is reached which leads to speech, language and literacy learning problems. According to this thinking, the distinction between auditory and speech processing is therefore an unnecessary one. There is evidence to support this view: Devens *et al.* (1978) found that children with language learning and reading disabilities generally have difficulties with non-linguistic, non-cognitive auditory functioning in areas such as binaural fusion/separation and auditory localisation. Tallal *et al.* (1993) found that children with language impairment have difficulties in the temporal processing of auditory signals, atlhough it is unlikely that temporal processing difficulties alone would be sufficient to produce specific language impairment.

An alternative view is that audition and speech processing have differentiated areas within the brain and that the two processes are not in fact interrelated at all (Efron 1985). Unfortunately, this issue remains largely unresolved.

A further confusing issue is the existence of possible links between central auditory processing and general learning difficulties. The evidence for this link is fairly well documented. Learning disabled children have been shown to perform poorly on tests of binaural integration (Berrick 1984) but such behavioural measures of auditory processing should be viewed with caution particularly where children have language/learning/attention control problems as the test themselves are invariably influenced by linguistic, cognitive and attentional variables. However, there *is* physiological evidence to support this finding: Arehole (1995) found that children with learning disabilities show prolonged Middle Latency Responses (MLR) using Electric Response Audiometry, and in contra-lateral recording, the responses were asymmetrical. An abnormal Long Latency Response has also been noted (Arehole *et al.* 1995). Caution should perhaps also be observed in interpreting this data as the MLR develops and matures throughout the first decade of life, and in children different generators than in adults may well be operating (McGee and Kraus 1996). In children with developmental delay, these maturational effects may be even more problematic.

CAPD is also considered to be closely related to Attention Deficit Disorder (ADD). Children with ADD have been shown to perform poorly on tests of central auditory function: Cook *et al.* (1993) found that 12 out of 15 children with ADD met the criteria for CAPD. It is thought that attentional problems cause these children to lose auditory information presented at fast rates. The current diagnostic criteria for CAPD makes clinical separation of the two disorders problematic.

While central auditory testing has been shown to differentiate sub-groups of the heterogeneous population of children with learning/language difficulties who have a central auditory component to their problems, one cannot assume that a central auditory deficit is the causative factor, it may merely compound the child's difficulties.

Aetiology

The presence of a CAPD in a child is usually determined by deviant results on one or more tests of central auditory function when hearing sensitivity has been found to be normal, and in this sense investigations into aetiology are not relevant for remediation purposes. Moreover, as the population of children with CAPD is so diverse in terms of behavioural manifestations of auditory processing difficulties, it is likely that the causes of those difficulties in each individual may be different. There is little consensus at present and the causes of CAPD remain elusive.

Research into aetiology is complicated by the fact that behavioural central auditory testing may be affected by peripheral pathology. Moreover, where abnormal peripheral functioning demonstrated by raised pure-tone thresholds and/or impaired speech discrimination is evident, one can not necessarily preclude the involvement of central auditory mechanisms. Physiological testing using Electric Response Audiometry and Otoacoustic Emissions may be of value in providing differential diagnosis, but this is an area which requires further research. Although many other variables exist, the co-existence of a central processing disorder with a peripheral hearing loss may account in part for the variations in the progress made by children with the same degree of peripheral hearing loss.

It is beyond the remit of this chapter to discuss individual research into aetiology in detail, but readers may find it useful to refer to the following for insights into the aetiology of specific areas of deficit associated with CAPD: Ferman *et al.* 1993, Noback 1985; Narula and Mason 1988; Lynn and Gilroy 1972; Downs 1985; Keith 1981.

Identification

Although many children affected by CAPD will have obvious learning, speech, language or attention control difficulties, a large number will in fact not present with such obvious 'symptoms' but may be working below their ability at school and/or having difficulties at home.

Typically, this group of children demonstrate difficulties in learning through the auditory modality and may have deficits in various areas of auditory functioning. Auditory figure ground problems may be evident which are characterised by poor learning or listening behaviour in the presence of background noise. Poor auditory memory may be indicated by difficulty in recalling verbal information, including the following of instructions or directions. Impaired auditory discrimination skills are often presented as difficulties with literacy and phonics. Auditory attention problems may be evident which result in the child's inability to maintain focus for listening. At a higher level of auditory processing, auditory cohesion problems may exist which are demonstrated by the inability to draw inferences, to interpret abstract information or to problem solve. There may be problems in all or just some of these areas. Children exhibiting these types of behaviour may be candidates for further assessment and remediation.

The audiologist is likely to be a key worker in providing a comprehensive audiological assessment of both peripheral and central auditory functioning. He or she must also be skilled in interpreting assessment information from not only the family/caregivers, but also from professionals such as psychologists, medical professionals, speech and language therapists, teachers of the deaf and the child's school teachers, in using that information to influence decisions about testing, and relating it to the results obtained. The audiologist should also be aware of the linguistic, cognitive and attentional variables which can affect interpretation of the test results. Without a clear coordination of skills and professional knowledge, the area of assessment could become a minefield of misinterpretation of test results and inappropriate identification.

The ASHA Consensus document (1996) describes the purpose of testing as being 'to confirm the presence of a CAPD and to describe its parameters in terms of functional auditory performance deficits'. Therefore, use of the term CAPD must be accompanied by a full explanation of the child's functioning in areas of central auditory processing which are causing difficulty.

A test battery approach is advisable which should include full history-taking of details relating to the child's health status, psychological, educational, social and communicative development. The child's cultural and linguistic background should be considered, along with any relevent family history details. Auditory behaviour should be enquired about and observed. Audiologic test procedures may include the usual behavioural and physiological tests of peripheral auditory function, and if the results are within normal limits, then central testing may be relevant, including both behavioural and if necessary, electrophysiological testing using the Middle Latency Response and Late P300 evoked potentials. A number of behavioural tests of central auditory function which form a test battery should be implemented according to the referring complaint/s of the child and should examine different central processes at different levels. A behavioural screening test battery for CAPD exists in the USA, the 'SCAN Screening Test for Central Auditory Processing Disorders' (Keith 1995). This test battery comprises the following tests of central auditory function:

- filtered word subtest (for auditory closure/blending);
- auditory figure ground subtest (for assessment of speech in noise processing) (performance intensity measures of speech discrimination in noise may also be used with children who are sufficiently linguistically mature);
- competing words subtest (to assess binaural integration).

The test battery may be used from 3 years of age for screening purposes, along with other tests of central auditory processing including the Auditory Continuous Performance Test (ACPT) (Keith1994). This test may be used from 6 years of age. It measures attention and impulsivity errors.

The Auditory Fusion Test-Revised (AFT-R) (McCroskey and Keith 1996) may be used from 3 years of age. It measures discrimination of temporally separated auditory signals.

The administration of the ACPT and the AFT-R tests depend particularly on verbal instruction. The ACPT relies on the vocabulary repertoire of the child as it consists of lists of single words. The linguistic level of the child will therefore inevitably determine whether such tests may be used successfully.

It should be noted that the SCAN test battery, the ACPT and the AFT-R are not standardised for use with children in the UK. At present there is no standardised test battery of central auditory function available for use in the UK.

In addition to tests of central auditory function, speech and language assessments should be implemented by a relevant professional to assist in the differential diagnosis of CAPD.

Approaches to remediation

The remediation of CAPD should be inherently linked with the process of assessment and identification and as such needs to be multidisciplinary. Although the *individual* needs of the child must be addressed and remediated, it is helpful to consider the broad model for remediation proposed in the USA which is based on the belief that 'for many cases there may be no way to isolate the relative contributions of a) language limitations and b) signal processing limitations' (ASHA 1996). Management of CAPD therefore involves the use of intervention procedures which enhance the acoustic signal *and* which develop central resources such as language skills. Individuals are encouraged to improve their language processing skills in a number of ways: by fostering the development of auditory comprehension skills, by improving attention to individual speech sounds, and finally by developing the use of prosody and sentence structure to predict degraded message elements. It is vital that direct professional intervention in these areas of remediation is carried over to the home and school environments. Professionals working with a child with CAPD should provide training to parents, caregivers and schools on the nature of CAPD as it exists in that individual child and should offer advice on improving the home and school acoustic and listening environments. Information regarding practical management techniques, many of which are similar to those for children with a peripheral hearing loss, should also be offered. Such techniques may include preferential seating for the child, use of visual cues to support spoken language, modification of spoken language in terms of rate of utterance and complexity and gaining visual attention before imparting information. Some children may also require linguistic modification of the school curriculum and may benefit from auditory training programmes. There is evidence that this type of direct intervention is effective for children with CAPD. Jirsa (1992) used Electric Response Audiometry to measure the latency and amplitude of the P300 response in a group of children with CAPD following a treatment programme to improve auditory skills. While a control group showed no change in the P300 response, the children who had undergone therapy showed a significant change. Improvements were also noted on behavioural tests of auditory processing. Neuroplasticity is a further argument for the implementation of direct remediation: it is known that the auditory system can resume normal development following a period of auditory deprivation (Ponton *et al.* 1996).

Procedures employed to improve signal quality are based on the knowledge that individuals with CAPD have difficulties in processing auditory information when that information is degraded by interference from noise or in terms of intensity or clarity. The masking effects of noise and reverberation in the school and home settings can be reduced through acoustic modifications to rooms. Assistive listening devices have also been shown to be effective in improving the signal to noise ratio and reducing the speaker/listener distance. Sound field amplification provides an improvement in signal to noise ratio of 10–15 dB and a uniform sound field in the room. There is no evidence to support the use of such systems with CAPD individuals in particular, but as SFFM amplification has been shown to benefit a wide population of children with and without classroom learning difficulties including attention control (Flexer 1994), there is no reason why such a system should not benefit CAPD individuals who experience specific problems with auditory processing in noise. Personal FM systems have been successfully used with children with CAPD (Stach *et al.* 1991) but very little information has come to light which fully explains the gain, coupling methods and circumstances under which the equipment was used. Indeed, ASHA (1991) pointed out that caution should be exercised in the use of amplification devices with children with normal peripheral hearing owing to the potential for noise induced hearing loss. They noted that 'it is not uncommon for personal hearing aids and amplification systems to produce 135 to 145 dB SPL at the tympanic membrane' and that although low gain may be used, the actual peak output of the instrument will vary depending on factors such as input level, distance from microphone and receiver coupling. It is therefore essential that if such instruments are to be routinely used with CAPD individuals, then real ear measures of sound pressure level (SPL) delivered to the ear and discomfort levels should be ascertained.

Recognition of CAPD: the challenge to services

CAPD is a term which until recently has not been acknowledged or used in the UK. There is some personal concern that as the existence of CAPD becomes a more familiar phenomenon, it may be confused with a term currently used in the UK to define auditory processing problems in adults. The term 'obscure auditory dysfunction' (OAD) is widely used in the UK to refer to 'self report of auditory disability accompanied by normal hearing thresholds ... for an individual aged between 15–55 years' (Saunders *et al.* 1992). OAD shares many of the symptoms of CAPD, including poor discrimination of speech in noise, poor dichotic listening ability, and poor linguistic ability. Despite the fact that OAD does not refer to individuals below 15 years of age and that the determinants of OAD in children are likely to be different from those in adults, a recent unpublished survey of 69 audiology departments (Wheeler 1997) revealed that the majority of departments with provision for children in this area are in fact using the term OAD. In addition, there was found to be no discernible difference between the significance given to clinical presenting factors by those using OAD and those using CAPD as a term. There is a clear need to clarify this issue in the UK. Is OAD in children akin to CAPD in children? A clear delineation of terms is needed to avoid confusion, not only in the field of clinical audiology but also across professional domains in health and audiology. There is not enough evidence to equate the two terms and the author does not wish to suggest that they are synonymous, but sufficient overlap exists for research in this area to be of vital importance.

If, in the near future, CAPD becomes an accepted and routinely used term both in health and education domains, professionals still have a long way to go before provision for CAPD can be complete and coherent. There are many areas of CAPD research which are as yet unfulfilled: the exact nature of CAPD is still not consolidated and effort needs to be directed in several areas. The aetiological foundations of CAPD remain unclear: the catalogue of indicators of CAPD is so broad that to ascribe aetiological foundations for each specific processing problem seems to be an almost impossible task, especially as the causes may well be different in individuals. It is an area where researchers should continue to seek explanations, perhaps investigating the involvement of genetics, family history and developmental delay in the aetiology of CAPD.

Testing for CAPD is a huge area for concerted effort. Tests need to be standardised for use with the UK paediatric population and until this occurs, provision for CAPD in terms of assessment and remediation is problematic. Furthermore, it would be unwise of professionals to assume expertise in the area of CAPD and to embark on a programme of assessing children without training in the area. They must first be able to discriminate those children who are appropriate candidates for CAPD assessment: this requires an in-depth understanding of CAPD and the many forms in which it may manifest itself. If professionals are not knowledgeable about CAPD in detail, then audiology departments are likely to be overun with demands for central auditory testing which may be inappropriate and which will inevitably drain resources.

The question remains as to which services or establishments will be responsible for training in CAPD. Logically, training should become part of courses for audiologists, teachers of the deaf, speech and language therapists and educational psychologists. Short courses to promote awareness of CAPD should also be offered by those establishments involved in training professionals in the field. Trained professionals are then in a position to raise awareness of CAPD and to deliver in-service training to schools, not merely when a child has been identified as having CAPD, but also to help schools to use their knowledge of CAPD to make appropriate referrals to audiology departments for assessment.

The links between CAPD and other associated difficulties seem to warrant futher investigation, as does the whole area of remediation. Which approaches result in the most positive outcomes? This may indeed be an impossible area to research: different methods may be beneficial for individuals. There is a need for both the assessment and remediation of CAPD to be individualised as far as possible: professionals should provide the child and family with a comprehensive overview of the child's individual functioning in areas of importance and set goals for achievement which are achievable in both the long and the short term. This may be best achieved through interdisciplinary professional and family collaboration using the child's Individual Educational Plan as the basis for that coordination. In order for health and education authorities to provide comprehensive provision, collaboration in formulating a working policy on CAPD in each authority will be essential.

Conclusion

CAPD is an issue for a wide variety of professionals, but it is clearly a major issue for deaf education. Educational audiologists are able to provide or to collaborate in comprehensive audiological assessment but also have the advantage of an educational background in the education of deaf and usually, hearing children. As many educational audiologists are already involved in working with schools, they are in an advantageous position for implementing acoustic assessment of classrooms, advising on acoustic modifications and for the provision and management of FM/amplification devices. Teachers of the deaf are similarly skilled, with a knowledge of acoustics and audiology, and have specialist skills in working with hearing-impaired children, families and schools, teaching speech and language, modifying the school curriculum and managing amplification devices. Both professional groups, it is argued, should be integral parts of a multidisciplinary team for CAPD intervention. However, as with other groups, specific training in CAPD will be required.

THE CONTEXT OF THE EDUCATION OF DEAF CHILDREN

Introduction

The four chapters in this final section of the book provide the context for the discussion in the previous four sections. It does this under four broad themes; different views on deafness, the educational attainments of deaf pupils, the relationship between policy and provision and the international perspective on the education of deaf children. This final section does not consider the detail of professional practice but is essential reading for those wishing to understand the wider context.

For many people the question 'Is deafness a disability?' is central to both their understanding of deafness and their views on the education of deaf children. The topic of deafness and disability is an important one in that it strikes at the core of what the aims of deaf education should be and helps to explain the very different views there are on how deaf children should be educated. Pamela Knight addresses this complex question of deafness and disability in the context of the wider discussion on disability in general. She first describes the medical model of disability, argues that this has been the dominant model and explains why many disabled people claim that this way of thinking has resulted in a dependency culture, leaving them disempowered. She then describes how the disability movement has grown out of a reaction to this and presents the alternative social model of disability as well as a third, educational model. Knight then discusses the fact that many Deaf people may choose to reject these models and view their deafness in linguistic–cultural terms. Knight draws out the differences and tensions that exist between Deaf organisations and the disability movement, especially the issue of Deaf culture and disability culture and the different views on inclusive education.

Stephen Powers reviews the recent research from this country and the USA on the educational attainments of deaf children and places this in the context of the rise in accountability in education. He argues that we have very little information on the attainments of deaf children and that teachers and parents urgently need some bench-marks by which to begin to evaluate the effectiveness of different educational programmes. He also briefly summarises the lessons that can be learnt from the research literature on general school effectiveness and emphasises the difficulties in gaining true measures of effectiveness.

Margaret Kumsang and Ted Moore bring the perspective of two very experienced educators of deaf children to their analysis of how recent legislation and other factors have determined the policy and influenced the practice of deaf education. They present a broad-brush picture of current provision, explaining the influence of government policy, political ideology, educational philosophy and international directives on a range of issues including the educational placement of deaf children and the training of teachers of the deaf. Although identifying and commenting on a number of apparent threats to current provision for deaf children, in the end the view is not pessimistic, and the chapter ends with a positive vision of the future.

It is fitting that the final chapter of the book places the previous chapters in the wider context of a number of international issues. This wider perspective is important because it goes beyond a narrow national focus and allows us to understand better why we are where we are, as well as drawing attention to the difficult situation faced by the majority of the world's deaf children. Lesley Barcham chooses three themes to explain the international dimension to the education of deaf children; globalisation, conflict and struggle, and the changing role of the Deaf community, mentioning specifically the role of international organisations such as the United Nations and the United Nations Educational, Science and Cultural Organization (UNESCO). She chooses one developed country, Finland, and one developing country, Zimbabwe, as two case studies to illustrate the very different situations that now exist between countries, and in the case of the latter she draws attention to the dilemmas in developing countries in general especially over policy and on special school or mainstream placement. The proceedings of the International Congress on the Education of the Deaf, held every five years, should provide one of the most useful sources on this topic, but, as Barcham points out, it is unfortunate that these are not always published.

Stephen Powers

Chapter 5.1
Deafness and disability

Pamela Knight

Introduction

The issues of disability are not straightforward for the factors involved are complex and contentious. They are complex because they are affected by social, political, and economic issues and contentious because disabled people perceive that much of the practice for managing disability has evolved from the dominance of professional and medical opinion. This chapter will first consider the different models of disability and then look at deafness in this broader context. Terminology linked to disability issues will be discussed and the growth of the disability movement will be traced together with an exploration of current responses to the disability movement by the Deaf community.[1]

Models of disability

The term 'model' is used to describe the social construct or framework within which society's understanding and interpretation of its own behaviours are explored (Cunningham and Davis 1985).

The medical model
The view that members of society in general have of disabled people is largely influenced by past experiences or encounters with disability. Drake (1996) and Barton (1986) suggest that in advanced western societies the predominant view of disability is one informed by the medical profession. Drake claims that, from a medical perspective, 'people are disabled as a result of their physiological or cognitive impairments' (Drake 1996, p. 148). The medical response to this is to seek a cure and the aim is to rehabilitate disabled people into the wider society. Barnes and Mercer (1996) see the medical model as a deficit one focusing on personal limitations which are the responsibility of that person. It is *their* functional limitation which is the root cause of the disadvantages experienced, and these disadvantages can only be rectified by treatment or cure. The medical model emphasises *individual* loss and inability contributing to a model based on dependency on the wider society.

It is claimed (Campbell and Oliver 1996) that this model of dependency has an impact on the identity of many disabled people. Ann MacFarlane in Campbell and Oliver (1996) describes her disability as being very much illness based.

> I was perceived to be ill by everybody including the professional people and other people that visited me. I think I perceived myself as being ill, though in retrospect I certainly wasn't most of the time ... I was kept very much where they wanted me kept (p. 36).

Drake (1994) argues that the basis of support from a high proportion of the traditional voluntary agencies subscribes to this model of dependency. It is claimed that an infrastructure of complex, confusing and dependency-creating services has resulted in many disabled people being placed in positions of passivity and disempowerment (Campbell and Oliver 1996)

The social model

Disabled people themselves have come to challenge the medical perception of disability and view their disabilities in terms of the society in which they live. The social model of disability focuses on an environment which has been designed by, and for, non-disabled people. From this perspective people are disabled not by their physical or mental disability but by their social environment. Brisenden (1986) argues that he and other people with impairments are 'disabled by buildings that are not designed to admit us, and this in turn leads to a whole range of further disablements regarding our education, our chances of gaining employment, our social lives and so on' (p. 149). The social model, which focuses not on the individual disabled person but on society and the environment, explains the discrimination experienced by disabled people and implies an urgent need to address economic and resource issues. The social model questions whether resources should concentrate on supporting individuals with disabilities and implies that money would be better spent on adjusting social and physical environments (French 1993).

The social model challenges the assumptions of the medical model (Drake 1996). It questions the medical model's focus on person-centred illness, with remediation as the cure. However, the social model itself is also criticised for having the goal of 'normality' for disabled people (Oliver 1996). Each society has expectations, beliefs and values of its own which constitute a concept of normality for that particular society. The social model incorporates the assumption that all members of that society must aspire to the same norms.

The educational model

Dale (1996) suggests that there has been a major shift in many western societies away from a medical model of disability to an educational model linked to 'a human rights, sociological approach' (p. 49), and the educational model that has emerged has implications that spread beyond the classroom.

The educational model of disability is enshrined in the Warnock Report (DES 1978) which, in the UK, was largely responsible for the change in perception and official thinking away from a child with a category of handicap to one with a special educational need (Riddell 1996). The concept of special educational need was a relative and interactive one incorporating both child and environmental factors and was derived from a model which draws from both medical and social models. For Norwich (1996) it is the educational model which respects the distinctiveness of the individual but which is also inherently connected to all other areas of education and avoids the fixed dichotomies presented by the two discrete medical and social models.

The deaf perspective

The medical model of deafness

A well-documented and significant factor in any discussion of deafness is that approximately 90 per cent of deaf children are born into hearing families. For many hearing parents this is their first contact with a deaf person or child. Although they may bring to the situation a view based on past experiences or encounters with deafness, it is likely that they will have had no previous direct contact with deaf people.

The diagnosis and degree of deafness in a child is a medical issue. Efforts are made by the medical profession to find the cause of deafness and if possible a cure. If no cure is possible then provision of appropriate amplification devices is made to compensate for the degree of deafness. This medical scenario is the first experience of deafness for most parents. Deafness is presented as an illness where, at best, a cure is sought or every effort is made to minimise the effects. Reagan (1990) suggests that this medical or 'hearing view' of deafness is concerned almost exclusively with 'the audiological features of deafness and, as a result, emphasises what a deaf person cannot do (or cannot do as a hearing person would do)'(p. 74).

It can be argued that the principle focus of a medical model of deafness is to minimise the effects of deafness which is viewed as a deviation from the hearing norm. The aim then becomes the 'assimilation' of the deaf person into the hearing society.

The social model of deafness

Deaf people who have sign language as a first language may have limited access to the spoken language of the hearing community. This can restrict social and professional interaction with hearing people and also access to some of the technology of modern society. The social model explains the disablement of deaf people in terms of being second language users and people with reduced access to the majority language (Higgins 1980). This in turn leads to further disablement with regard to education and employment opportunities. Deaf children are portrayed as having to fit into and function in a hearing world with hearing people making educational and social decisions on their behalf (Reagan 1990).

The linguistic model of deafness

An alternative model of deafness is one which focuses on the languages used by deaf people, while not denying the medical aspects of deafness. There are many influences affecting the initial language acquisition of deaf people including the hearing status of the family, the degree of deafness and social, environmental and economic factors. For many deaf people whose degree of deafness falls into the slight or moderate category spoken language is likely to be their preferred language, the language in which they communicate most comfortably, socially and professionally. They may also develop sign language skills in order to interact socially with other deaf people. Those with severe or profound deafness are likely to develop sign language, the visual gestural language of the deaf community, as their preferred language, but will also develop skills in the majority language in order to access the literacy of their society.

It is the acceptance and acknowledgement of the preferred or first language of the deaf person that allows for their identification in terms of language use. In this context the focus is not on deaf people as having a particular pathological, medical condition but as members of one of two identified linguistic groups. It is the move towards identifying deafness in terms of a linguistic model which has led to the recognition of deaf people who use sign language as the linguistic minority group who constitute the deaf community (Jones and Pullen 1989). Skutnabb-Kangas (1994) argues that the deaf community is a linguistic minority group in every country in the world.

The term Deaf rather than deaf is currently used to identify this group of people whose communication is through sign language from positive personal choice and who share the culture centred round this language (for full discussion see Gregory (1992)). This convention will be used throughout the remainder of this chapter.

Terminology

The power of terminology in reflecting beliefs and attitudes is well documented (Emanuel and Ackroyd 1996). In the wider world of disabilities it is important to understand there may be conflicting opinions about, and interpretations of, terms used. Campbell and Oliver (1996) claim that in studies of new social movements the problems of disabled people 'rarely get a mention' (p. 22) and when they do, categories such as 'the disabled', 'the deaf' or 'the handicapped' are used, reflecting a lack of interest and a dehumanising of a group of people. In response to the difficulties of explaining the complex relationships between impairment, disability and handicap, definitions have been drawn up by both the World Health Organization (WHO) and the Disabled People's International (DPI).[2]

The WHO definition implies that illness is the cause of the disabled person's experience, whereas the DPI definition implies that disability is an exclusively social phenomenon (Oliver 1996). In response to these extreme views further guidelines were developed by the Greater Manchester Coalition of Disabled People (GMCDP), a group which was influenced by disabled people's organisations from the beginning.[3] Their definition embraces aspects of both the medical and social models.

For people who are disadvantaged in their access to resources and opportunities, their disabilities become handicaps in certain social and employment situations. Biklen and

Bogdan (1977) regard the term 'handicap' as referring to 'a set of assumptions and practices that promote the differential and unequal treatment of people because of apparent or assumed physical, mental and behavioural difficulties' (p. 14). The term relates to the demands of a society where the majority are non-disabled and is not inherent in the person's disability.

The term 'impairment' as in physical, intellectual and sensory (visual and hearing) impairments is commonly used. Many groups consider this to have a negative connotation and the term 'disability' is preferred, certainly in the context of physical and learning disabilities. The sensory organs of sight and hearing can be described in terms of their social/personal condition, that is blindness and deafness. Deaf and blind people often prefer to describe themselves in this way, reflecting the degree to which they *are* deaf or blind, rather than the degree to which they are *not* hearing or sighted. Swisher (1989) suggests that deaf people themselves prefer the term 'deaf' as they see it as invested with a positive value. Deaf people use the terms 'deaf' and 'hard of hearing' in a quite different way to hearing people (for a fuller discussion see Padden and Humphries 1988).

Growth of the disability movement

> The disability movement is obviously a set of ideas that presents a challenge to dominant ideology that says disabled people are burdens on society and that they should be taken care of (Lisick, in Campbell and Oliver 1996, p. 21).

The disability movement is defined as a new social movement that offers disabled people a democratic and political voice, 'something we have never had before' (Campbell and Oliver 1996, p. 23). The current disability movement in the UK started during the 1960s. Prior to that there had been many voluntary organisations committed to supporting disabled people, developed during the late nineteenth century as a reflection of the social ethos of the time. There were also organisations emerging in the first half of the twentieth century, largely middle class, and organised by the parents of disabled children. The Second World War led to the formation of further organisations whose primary aims were to resource medical research into particular impairments with the specific focus on identifying cures. By the 1960s disabled people were faced primarily with a choice from a range of dependency-creating services developed to meet their perceived needs. Campbell and Oliver (1996) describe this situation as a massive infrastructure of complex, confusing and dependency-creating services and a body of disempowered disabled people.

Social movements emerge in response to several factors. Marx and McAdam (1994) suggest there are four. The first is the combination of problems and conflicts that exists for certain groups within society giving rise to collective action by that group. Secondly, collective action is brought about by groups when they are excluded or disempowered by times of rapid social change. Thirdly, a time of economic growth makes financial support possible. Fourthly, movements emerge as a reaction to existing political institutions which appear unresponsive to the needs of a particular group.

All these factors were apparent in the 1960s which reflected the growth of the Civil Rights Movement, growing affluence and rapid social change. While the mood of this time raised the expectations of disabled people, it also highlighted the fact that existing political institutions were not providing sufficient resources for them to lead a life style comparable with non-disabled people.

An additional factor at the time was the large number of residential institutions for disabled people, including special schools, which had been established over a long period, particularly immediately after the Second World War. There was a reaction to this segregation with a subsequent move towards the type of support which would allow for independent living in the wider society. There was a growing realisation that neither charitable organisations nor political institutions were meeting the needs of disabled people appropriately, and many saw the need for disabled people to be empowered to act for themselves. This was a key factor in the emergence of the disability movement. Davis and Davis (1996) describes the impetus for change as a

> mass movement amongst disabled people, controlled by disabled people themselves. Within this, the role of non-disabled people, professionals, experts and anybody else would be to support disabled people to articulate and to take the lead in their own emancipation (p. 63).

From these pressures there was dramatic growth in the number of organisations controlled and run by disabled people.

The disability movement continued to develop. In 1975 the United Nations Declaration of Rights of Disabled Persons was passed to ensure the full economic and social integration of disabled people, with a stated declaration that disabled people should be consulted in all matters regarding their rights. The 1980s led to a greater understanding of the nature of disability, and issues of policy and support began to change. The concept of self-help and self-empowerment provided the focus of much of the activity of that period. By the 1990s both national and international organisations had been established with the aim of coordinating the many constituent organisations that had evolved from the disability movement. In 1993 the United Nations Standard Rules on the Equalisation of Opportunities for Persons with Disabilities were adopted by the General Assembly. In the UK constituent organisations of the British Council of Organisations of Disabled People had risen to over one hundred in number, reflecting the phenomenal growth of individual and collective organisations and the move towards the empowerment of disabled people.

It is through the acceptance by disabled people themselves of the disability movement as a developing political force that it can continue to make an impact on a non-disabled society. Begum (1996) describes her emerging consciousness of disability as a political issue and links it to her growing perception of disability as an external issue. Disabled people describe the need to transform their personal consciousness as disabled people, to a growing political consciousness as a disabled group which can affect the society in which they live (Campbell and Oliver 1996). At the core of this transformation is the rejection of disability as a personal tragedy. Wood (1996) claims that it is through the development of disabled people as a distinct group in society with a unique position, that they have an identity, both as a group and individually.

> Discovering our identity as disabled people is very, very important ... I think it is probably the greatest success that the movement has been able to point to. It is our movement, nobody else owns it. We know who we are (p. 124).

Disability culture and deaf culture

Disability culture

There is a disability culture which has been born out of disabled people's common experiences of dependency, their oppression from a majority culture and their wish to create a positive identity of disability. For the most part, disabled people share a common language with the hearing speaking world and because of this they have been able to develop socio-cultural activities which are different from, but appreciated by, the hearing majority. Cultural activities have been described as a way of fighting against a disabling culture. Mason (1996) sees the need for disabled people to become involved in cultural production. 'Disability arts and culture came flooding onto the disability movement's agenda in the mid 1980s, providing a very important channel to promote our newly discovered identity' (p. 111).

   Finkelstein (1996) sees a contradiction in the disability movement's impetus for integration into the non-disabled society compared with a desire to promote differences and a separate identity as expressed through cultural arts. He acknowledges, however, that a cultural identity will play a vital role in developing the organisations needed to promote social change. 'There should be creative interaction between disabled people involved in the arts and those in the politics of disability' (p. 112). This view is shared by Shakespeare (1996) who also sees disability arts as a context for disabled people to get together, enjoy themselves and consider issues of common concern. He goes on to say that disability arts and culture offer people 'a key to the basic process of identifying as a disabled person, because culture and identity are closely linked concepts' (p. 102).

Deaf culture

Following research by Jones and Pullen (1989) it is clear that Deaf people themselves, wish to be accepted as a linguistic and cultural minority group rather than a disabled group. Corker (1994) suggests that Deaf people have a perspective and an identity of their own as a minority group and are 'not as a rule happy about identifying with disabled culture' (p. 26). She also points out, however, that people from the part of the deaf community who are deafened, do tend to identify themselves as a disabled group.

   The concept of Deaf people as a linguistic minority group has many commonalities with other minority and disabled groups. They share similar experiences of dependency, oppression from a majority culture and a wish to create a positive identity for themselves. There is a common need for equal rights with the majority through empowerment at individual and collective levels.

Deaf people are also involved in the creative arts. There are Deaf actors, artists, painters and musicians. However, as Ladd (in Campbell and Oliver 1996) succinctly says 'Culture as in art is one thing. Culture as in Deaf culture is another' (p. 121). Two fundamental differences, separating Deaf people and their culture from other disabled groups, spring from institutional and linguistic foundations (Corker 1994, p. 26). Institutional issues are based primarily around the educational placement of deaf pupils. The Deaf community is not generally in favour of the inclusion of deaf pupils into mainstream schools, whereas inclusion is an important focus for other disability groups. Segregated schools for the deaf are considered by many to have been, and that they should remain, the cornerstone of Deaf culture and history. Ladd (1996) argues that it is in schools for the deaf, which go back to the 1790s, that deaf children are socialised into their language and culture. The issue of segregated versus inclusive education has continued to divide the Deaf community from other disability movements.

Deaf people whose first language is a sign language are a linguistic minority whose culture is a natural extension of that. Traditions, customs, poetry and stories have been passed through the generations.

> It is those together with their values and beliefs that constitute their culture. These parallel closely with other linguistic minority groups rather than disability groups. The whole definition of culture is so much wider than the one espoused by the disability movement (Ladd, in Campbell and Oliver 1996, p. 120).

Kyle and Woll (1985) see the Deaf community themselves as wishing to be perceived as a linguistic minority group with a unique cultural identity to be preserved rather than a disabled group to be normalised.

Conclusion

The focus of this chapter has been to address, in general terms, the issues relating to deafness and disability. It is only through an awareness of the issues facing disabled and other minority groups that the majority society can respond both politically and positively to their needs and rights as identifiable groups in society. As part of this the use and influence of terminology must be understood as a reflection of individual and society's knowledge, beliefs and attitudes towards disability and other minority groups.

An understanding of deafness and disability according to medical, social and educational models is important in that it highlights many of the implications of being deaf or disabled in a hearing, non-disabled society. These models are relevant when addressing the practicalities of disability and they reflect the society in which deaf and disabled people live. However, what is crucial is that Deaf people are recognised as a group within society, with its own identity as a minority, linguistic group and its own culture.

The fact that the disability movement is described as 'a movement' is significant, whether it is a movement, a new movement or an emerging movement. Whatever term is used it remains an element in the considerable force which allows deaf and disabled people to become more self-organised and politically conscious. The movement will be judged by the extent to which Deaf and disabled people themselves become more politically conscious and empowered, the extent to which disability issues are raised nationally and internationally and the promotion of deafness and disability as a human and civil rights issue.

Notes

1. It is interesting and relevant to note here at the beginning of the chapter that Campbell and Oliver (1996) consider the formation of the British Deaf Association (BDA) in 1890 to be the first important historical landmark in the formation of this movement.

2. **The World Health Organization (WHO):**
   International classification of impairments, disabilities and handicaps:
   IMPAIRMENT: In the context of health experience, an impairment is any loss or abnormality of psychological, physiological or anatomical structure or function.
   DISABILITY: In the context of health experience, a disability is any restriction or lack (resulting from an impairment) of ability to perform an activity in the manner or within the range considered normal for a human being.
   HANDICAP: In the context of health experience, a handicap is a disadvantage for a given individual, resulting from an impairment or a disability, that limits or prevents the fulfilment of a role that is normal (depending on age, sex, social or cultural factors) for that individual.

   The Disabled People's International (DPI) definition:
   IMPAIRMENT: is the functional limitation within the individual caused by physical, mental or sensory impairment.
   DISABILITY: is the loss or limitation of opportunities to take part in the normal life of the community on an equal level with others due to physical and social barriers.

3. **Greater Manchester Coalition of Disabled People (GMCDP)**
   IMPAIRMENT: occurs where part of the organ or mechanism of the body is unable to function fully (while recognising deaf members' preference for the term 'difference').
   DISABILITY: occurs where society is structured or organised in such a way as to prevent or restrict activities being undertaken or potentially being realised because of an impairment.
   A DISABLED PERSON: is someone who has a physical, sensory or mental impairment (or difference) and who is, as a result, prevented from undertaking a range of activities because of environmental or attitudinal constraints imposed by societies or individuals.
   ACCESS: was defined as referring to a fully accessible society. This included addressing all barriers which could be physical/structural/environmental; emotional/psychological; communication/information; and functional.

Further reading

Campbell, J. and Oliver, M. (1996) *Disability Politics: Understanding our Past, Changing our Future.* London: Routledge.
This book explores the growth of the disability movement including the perspective of disabled people themselves.

Reagan, T. (1990) 'Cultural considerations in the education of deaf children', in Moores, D. and Meadow-Orlans, K. (eds) *Educational and Developmental Aspects of Deafness.* Washington, DC: Gallaudet University Press.
This chapter provides a comprehensive overview of the issues from a perspective which accepts the cultural and linguistic diversity of deaf pupils.

Skutnabb-Kangas, T. (1994) 'Linguistic human rights – a prerequisite for bilingualism', in Ahlgren, I. and Hyltenstam, N. (eds) *Bilingualism and Deaf Education.* Hamburg: Signum Press.
This chapter presents the case for bilingualism as an extension of linguistic human rights .

Gregory, S. (1992) 'The language and culture of deaf people: educational implications', *Language and Education* 6 (2), 183–197.
This article explores the linguistic and cultural issues for deaf people and the implications for education.

Chapter 5.2

The educational attainments of deaf children

Stephen Powers

'to live effectively is to live with adequate information'
(Norbert Wiener, originator of cybernetics, from Fitz-Gibbon 1996, p. 4).

One could argue that 'the originator of cybernetics would say that, wouldn't he?' However, when we see 'information technology' as a compulsory subject in schools we realise, despite the cliché, that we really do live in an information age. It is also clear, not least to teachers, that we live in an age of demands for greater accountability, and it seems no accident that these two developments have occurred together.

However, up till now parents and teachers of deaf children in the UK might easily have thought that the latest information revolution was passing them by. Parents might have wondered in what ways educational programmes for their deaf children were being held to account, where they could find the information that evaluated different educational programmes. Teachers of deaf children might have wondered what measures there were by which they could evaluate their effectiveness as teachers. The fact is that there have been some published data but far too little.

This chapter aims to review some of the main data available on the educational attainments of deaf children and to place the discussion in the wider context of both the rise of accountability in education and the general literature on school effectiveness. It is hoped that this wider perspective will provide some insight into deciding what is needed, what is possible and where research needs to go from here.

Of course, any demand for more information must be done with some caution. Fitz-Gibbon (1996, p. 23) has wisely warned us against the 'corruptible' and 'corrupting' performance indicators currently used in education. Teachers, parents and policy makers all need performance indicators but, of course, the decision about what performance indicators are required needs careful consideration.

The move towards greater accountability in education

Pupil achievement has always been a primary concern of parents, educators and policy makers but in recent times interest in measuring achievement has become even greater. One reason is that the power of modern computers has massively increased our data-handling capability (Fitz-Gibbon 1996). Another reason is the recent common popular assumption that schools and teachers have 'failed' their pupils (Thomas 1990). A third reason is economic. The 1960s and early 1970s are now characterised as boom years which saw massive increases in the money spent on education, health and other social services, but the 1980s and 1990s have been a time of economic stringency. With the need to keep much tighter control over spending, issues of cost and efficiency have become central to educational thinking and planning. This was very clearly reflected in the Coopers and Lybrand Report on Local Management of Schools (1988). There is now a preoccupation with getting value for money in education, as indeed in all spheres of public spending. This call for improved efficiency inevitably emphasises the need for accurate measures of pupil achievement.

Prime Minister Callaghan's speech at Ruskin College, Oxford in 1976 is often said to mark a watershed in education in the UK. The speech took place at a time of increasing concerns about the performance of British pupils and schools. It was followed by the 'Great Debate' on education which led to increasing central government control over the curriculum, culminating with the National Curriculum introduced in the Education Reform Act of 1988. Over the same period and continuing to this day there has been an increasing emphasis by the governments of the day on standards and accountability. The results of national examinations and National Curriculum tests are now used both to monitor the progress of individual pupils and to evaluate the performance of schools.

However, on both counts these measures have been subject to criticism. As a measure of individual pupil attainment it is clear that exam and curriculum test results do not inform us about how the broad aims of education are being met. As a measure of individual school performance the obvious criticism of using raw exam scores is that they are an unfair measure on which to compare schools. In this context the widespread acceptance of the need for 'value added' measures is a welcome development (SCAA 1996c).

Value added measures

In evaluating the performance of a school we need information about how well pupils have progressed during their time there rather than simple measures of their final attainment. To do this we need to have both a measure of pupils' 'prior attainment' on beginning a school as well as their final attainment, the difference between these sometimes being called the 'added value'. (However, there is a more useful measure, more properly called 'relative value added'. See Fitz-Gibbon 1996, p. 119, for a detailed discussion of the different ways of calculating value added.) The notion of value added can be applied to progress across any period of schooling.

Of course, it is perfectly possible that pupil progress has very little to do with the school and is largely explained by pupil and family background factors. This is the old view on school effectiveness, enshrined in the Plowden Report (1967) on primary school education in Britain which argued that schools had little effect on their pupils, and that the key determinants of pupil achievement were parental factors such as social class and attitudes (Reynolds 1992). According to Barber (1996, p. 127) this is a view that 'drives teachers ... into demands for social and political change since, if schools make no difference, only this will change things'. This pessimistic view of the potential of education as a force for social change is in complete opposition to the commitment of the present Labour government to its three priorities of 'education, education, education'.

It appears that the current majority view among both politicians and researchers is that schools do have a significant effect on pupil outcomes. Recent research into school effectiveness seems to have provided sound evidence for this (Reynolds 1992; Mortimore *et al.* 1988) although there have been wide variations in estimates of the size of the effect that schools have (Reynolds 1992). In one recent report from the UK the difference between the most and least effective schools was said to be of the order of 12 points in the General Certificate of Secondary Education (GCSE) examinations, ie. the difference between six D grades and six B grades (Sammons *et al.*, British Education Research Association paper 1995, quoted in Barber 1996).

Much of the research on school effectiveness has attempted to identify those factors associated with the more effective schools, but this body of research has had little success in identifying the key factors that operate at class and departmental level. There is a further problem when it is recognised that descriptions of effective schools do not necessarily provide any clear guidelines for improving the less effective ones. Tymms (1996, p. 122) has even suggested that 'The answer to the essential question "How can we improve our schools?" is little clearer than it was a decade ago'.

Not everyone would agree with Tymms and a number of recent government initiatives, including the introduction of training for head teachers, can be seen to be coming directly from the work on school effectiveness. However, the widespread expression of disappointment amongst researchers over what the effectiveness research has taught us provides a salutary lesson for those who think that this type of research will provide a straightforward answer to improving educational programmes for deaf children.

Quality of life

One of the positive features of the research into school effectiveness in the UK is that it has provided a broad approach that has included measures of non-cognitive pupil behaviours (e.g. self-concept, attitudes to learning). The debate has now extended even further to include discussion about pupils' 'quality of life'. This discussion inevitably leads to recognition that educational measures themselves are only proxy measures of school effectiveness, that the ultimate aims of education include maximising adult life opportunities and adult quality of life (Thomas 1990).

Unfortunately, quality of life is very difficult to define although a number of writers have attempted this. For example, Bullinger and Ravens-Sieberer (1995) define quality of life (albeit from a health perspective) as:

> how a person feels, psychologically and physically, how he or she gets along with other persons and how he or she copes with everyday life ... a multidimensional construct covering physical, emotional, mental, social and behavioural components of well-

being and function as perceived by patients ... [including] ... the ability to fulfil age related activities (p. 245).

Of course, the problem in defining quality of life is that the list of components could be almost endless, and even if we were able to agree on a definition there would then be the problem of agreeing on the criteria for assessment. Some see the problem of definition as an inherent difficulty and conclude that quality of life is not therefore measurable (Taylor 1994, in Goode 1994, p. 10), but despite the difficulties many would agree that the quality of life debate has introduced an essential dimension into education.

However, with regard to the educational outcomes of deaf children this discussion is anticipating future research. It is time to look at what we already know.

The attainments of deaf pupils

Although there has been some important work on the educational achievements of deaf pupils in the UK, most research on this topic that appears in English has taken place in the USA. Without reference to the US literature our sources would be very limited. However, the following discussion begins by looking at research in the UK.

Research in the UK

Despite the rapid and significant changes in the education and health provision for deaf children in the UK in the last 20 years (which are described in other chapters of this book) there has been little research to evaluate how these changes have affected the performance of deaf pupils. There has been little research into their educational attainments since the major work of Conrad on school-leavers almost 20 years ago (Conrad 1979).

The last major report on deaf education from government inspectors, which concerned deaf pupils in special schools and units in Scotland, reported in only general terms (HMI 1987). The report claimed that 'considerable progress' had been made and that 'overall the gains have exceeded the losses' (section 4.1). No substantial evidence was provided to support these claims, and one must wonder how the inspectors reached their conclusions, especially when they admitted that the criteria for judging success were perhaps 'not always clearly perceived'. Perhaps the most useful comment to come from this report was the urge for schools and authorities to carefully monitor the achievements of deaf pupils. Central government was clearly not going to do this itself. Unfortunately, it appears neither did the local authorities.

The study by Conrad (1979) deserves special mention for two reasons, first because no other study of deaf pupils' achievement in the UK has been so detailed and second because of the impact it has had on educational thinking and practice. Conrad found that his sample of deaf children of school-leaving age (n = 468) had low expressive and receptive skills in spoken language and low literacy levels. Half of those with a hearing loss greater that 85 dBHL were totally illiterate. Conrad's main conclusion was that the majority of very deaf youngsters were not able to make use of spoken language to develop the inner language necessary to develop their cognitive potential and that most deaf youngsters would benefit from the use of sign. Conrad's work is a seminal one but is open to a number of major criticisms and a useful critique of the study is provided by Lewis (1996).

For Conrad, degree of hearing loss was crucially related to pupil performance. However, two studies reported in 1986 found that degree of hearing loss did not appear to be a major determining factor in academic performance (Wood *et al.* 1986; Abel 1986). This finding might be counter-intuitive to many people but, as the rest of this chapter will show, it is one that has been repeated a number of times.

Two recent reports on deaf pupils' attainment have concentrated on exam results. In the first Powell (1995) collated the published 1993 and 1994 GCSE results of pupils in special schools for deaf children in England and Wales. Table 5.2:1 shows figures derived from Powell's report using the Government codings for exam success presented against Government figures on the whole school population for 1994.

Table 5.2:1 GCSE results: deaf pupils in special schools against the whole-school population

	Pupils achieving 5 or more A–C grades %	Pupils achieving 5 or more A–G grades %
All 16-year-old pupils in special schools for deaf children in England and Wales, 1993 and 1994 combined (n = 471)	8	29
England Average (all schools) 1994	43	86

The second report was of a questionnaire study of Year 11 (16-year-old) deaf pupils in mainstream schools in England in 1995 (Powers 1996a). This is the only recent research in the UK that has attempted to investigate the effect of a range of background variables on pupils' attainments. Powers collected data on some academic and non-academic outcomes and analysed these data against a number of background factors (including social and audiometric descriptors, but not pupils' intelligence). He repeated the exercise in 1996 to improve the response rate (Powers, in press). Table 5.2:2 shows the 1996 results on exam success again using the government codings and against the figures for the whole school population.

Table 5.2:3 shows Powers' results analysed according to pupils' degree of hearing loss and includes a total points score coding. This would seem to be a better coding for GCSE success, but unfortunately the Government does not code in this way therefore a comparison with the whole school population is not possible. One important point to note from Table 5.2:3 is that whether the association between degree of hearing loss and exam success is statistically significant depends entirely on the choice of coding.

Table 5.2:2 GCSE results: deaf pupils in mainstream schools against the whole-school population

	Pupils achieving 5 or more A–C grades %	Pupils achieving 5 or more A–G grades %
Year 11 deaf pupils in mainstream schools in England in 1996 (n = 403)	18	75
England Average (all schools) 1996	45	86

Table 5.2:3 GCSE results of Year 11 deaf pupils in mainstream schools in England in 1996 by degree of hearing loss (n = 387)

Degree of hearing loss	Pupils achieving 5 or more A–C grades %	Pupils achieving 5 or more A–G grades %	Pupils achieving 25 GCSE points or more %
Moderate	22	80	48
Severe	13	80	44
Profound	18	75	42
All three categories	18	75	42
	ns	p<0.01	p<0.05

Multiple regression analysis on the 1996 data showed that the factors included in the study were able to account for an effect of about only 20 per cent on GCSE results, that is, that much of the variance was left unexplained. Relatively strong predictors were age at onset of deafness, the socio-economic status of the family and the presence of any additional learning difficulty. The hearing status of the parents and the language used in the home were less important but nevertheless significant factors. In this study any effect due to the degree of hearing loss was not statistically significant.

Other studies in the UK of deaf pupils' achievements have included a study of deaf pupils' speech skills (Markides 1989), and the reading abilities of pupils taught in oral programmes (Lewis 1996).

Research in the USA

Since its inception in 1968 as the Office of Demographic Studies (ODS), and later as the Center for Assessment and Demographic Studies (CADS), the Gallaudet Research Institute (GRI) at Gallaudet University (which is the only university in the world established specifically to serve deaf students) has conducted national investigations into the educational achievements of all deaf students in special educational programmes in the USA and has analysed measures of achievement against a range of pupil, family and school factors. The early exercises were preparatory studies that resulted in a version of the Stanford Achievement Test (SAT) specially adapted for use with deaf students. This test in its ordinary version has been used for over 50 years to test achievement in all schools across the USA. Later editions of the SAT were not adapted but were normed on deaf students allowing for comparisons with hearing students of the same age.

As well as conducting these investigations into pupil performance, GRI has also conducted an annual survey to gather simple demographic information on deaf pupils, the Annual Survey of Hearing-Impaired Children and Youth.

One shortcoming of the GRI studies is that data have been collected only on those hearing-impaired students in special educational programmes therefore excluding hearing-impaired students in regular schools receiving no special education.

The early GRI studies did little more than confirm what teachers already knew about deaf pupils' poor attainment levels in reading and maths (Trybus and Karchmer 1977). However, Allen (1986) looked again at the data from the 1974 and 1983 studies and used regression analysis to measure the size of the effects of a number of demographic variables on deaf students' achievements in reading and maths computation. The strongest predictors were having an 'additional cognitive–behavioural handicap' and ethnic group (which Allen argued was almost certainly the result of factors that included the economic status of the family and language used at home, factors not included in the study). Degree of hearing loss and age at onset were only weak predictors. There are similarities but also some differences between these findings and those of Powers in the UK.

The 'integration effect'

In later GRI studies particular attention was given to investigating the 'integration effect'. This has been a major theme in deaf education for many years both in the UK and the USA as deaf educators have asked the question 'Does integration work?' In two separate reviews of the literature Kluwin and Moores (1985) and Lynas (1986) found that integrated pupils appeared to perform better academically than pupils who were not integrated. However, Kluwin and Moores pointed out that many studies had not accounted for obvious confounding factors such as intelligence and factors associated with family background.

To isolate the effect of the different factors Allen and Osborn (1984) used an analysis of covariance on a random stratified sample of 1,465 from the Annual Survey of 1980–81 of approximately 54,000 pupils and showed that the integration effect accounted for only 1 per cent of the variance on academic achievement. Other factors emerged as much more influential, especially ethnic background and additional handicaps. Degree of hearing loss was not found to be one of the most influential factors determining achievement.

In his recent investigations into deaf students' achievements Kluwin has concluded, like Allen and Osborn, that mainstreaming itself has almost no effect on academic achievement (Kluwin 1993).

One main difficulty here is that large scale studies that look at *types* of educational programme fail to account for the differences between *individual* programmes. As Hegarty has pointed out, integrated and segregated situations are not sharply contrasting but both are umbrella terms that conceal within each of them wide variations in practice (Hegarty 1993). Hegarty's implication is clear that rather than attempting to compare different *types* of programme research would do better to look at the differences between *individual* programmes. This point was made by Wood and his colleagues over ten years ago (Wood *et al.* 1986, p. 171).

Mode of communication

For some people mode of communication is the most important factor determining deaf pupils' attainment (Powell 1995) despite some evidence that it is not a major influence (Jensema and Trybus 1978, in Wood *et al.* 1986, p. 170). Clearly there a number of factors that complicate interpretation of the research evidence on mode of communication: first, is the point we have just made that the unit of investigation should be the individual school rather than type of school; secondly, there has been no published evaluation of the outcomes of bilingual programmes, and thirdly it would seem that the factor of mode of communication cannot be investigated properly without inclusion of other potentially equally important instructional factors, such as the amount and nature of preschool provision.

Identifying family variables

A number of studies in the USA have looked specifically at family social–psychological influences on the achievements of deaf students. Those factors reported as being associated with high achievement include parental expectations, fluency of communication in the home (Ritter-Brinton 1993) 'adaptation to deafness' (which included acceptance of the deaf child and a positive orientation to the deaf community) and 'press for achievement' (which included high educational and occupational expectations) (Bodner-Johnson 1986, p. 447). One major review of the literature found that the hearing status of parents *per se* did not emerge as a major factor (Ritter-Brinton 1993).

Theoretical models

One of the main features of the recent literature has been the adoption of more sophisticated theoretical models of achievement. In their model of *family* effects on deaf achievement Kluwin and Gaustad (1992) incorporate 'global factors' such as family income and family size along with social–psychological factors related to family functioning. The influence of the family is described according to four main classes of variable: first, family resources, including maternal education levels and overall measure of resources (according to the authors the two most consistent predictors of achievement in non-deaf research) and the presence of a second adult; secondly, family environment, which refers to such things as emotional climate, cohesiveness and parenting style; thirdly, parental expectations, and fourthly, parental behaviours that directly support school learning, for example, reading with the child and checking homework.

   In their model of the possible *school* effects on achievement O'Donnell and colleagues (1992) take a broad view that includes four categories of variable: population traits (including student background factors and attitudes to school); physical plant characteristics (classroom space, etc.); personnel, and procedures (pupil grouping, amount of integration, etc.). The value of this model is that it begins to incorporate in some detail some of the possible school-based factors influencing achievement. However, what becomes obvious when we consider models such as this is the extent of our ignorance about what the important factors actually are.

Conclusion

Identifying 'effectiveness' to help bring about improvement in schools is, of course, one of teachers' main concerns. However, one main lesson from the literature is that research and intervention in school effectiveness and school improvement is not an exact science (Fitz-Gibbon 1996; Tymms 1996). Also, it is now recognised that what we know from looking at successful schools is not necessarily going to help us in improving poor ones.

In the education of deaf children the search for effectiveness is perhaps even more difficult. It has been well accepted among teachers of the deaf for a long time that what works well for one deaf child will not necessarily work well for another and that a range of educational approaches is needed. This inevitably complicates further the search for effectiveness.

One response to the difficulty in identifying effective practice is to argue that in fact we don't need to do it and that simply providing information to schools and teachers about their pupils' attainments will in itself bring about school improvement. This appeared to be the view of the previous Secretary of State for Education, Gillian Shephard, for whom the crucial step in improving schools was to publish school exam and National Curriculum test results in tables. In her announcement at the time of the press release of the 1996 school tables she stated 'we can see over ... five years how tables have consistently driven up standards, school by school, college by college' (press release by DfEE, 20 November 1996).

Like Shephard, Fitz-Gibbon (1996) also believes in the need to report results but not, she crucially argues, in the form of published lists. Fitz-Gibbon disapproves of the 'misinformation' of the raw results published in tables and argues that any improvement brought about through these tables has only happened because of the climate of fear. For her the key to school improvement is *self-regulation* through regular feedback to schools of *high quality information* (i.e. value added measures).

> in response to the question 'how do we get quality into education?' ... our best strategy lies in improving the information in systems particularly by defining and measuring the many outcomes that we care about and feeding back the measurements to the *units of responsibility* [i.e. the schools and teachers] (Fitz-Gibbon 1996, p. 4).

Whether this is sufficient, whether our aim to improve the education of deaf pupils can be met in this way, it is too early to say. I would suggest that many people would be doubtful. However, it does seem that the regular monitoring of the academic and non-academic attainments and progress of all deaf pupils is a crucial first step.

It might be that we are still some way off providing soundly researched answers to questions of effectiveness in deaf education. Fortunately, measuring attainment and progress is easier and in fact is an urgent necessity at a time when many see threats to the education of deaf children. We have seen that there has already been some recent research into deaf pupils' attainments in the UK but more comprehensive information is now needed in order to provide benchmarks for parents, educators and policy makers. It is encouraging to see two large-scale research projects already underway, one led by a consortium of deaf organisations and the other based at the Institute of Hearing Research in Nottingham, which between them should be able to provide the benchmarks we need.

Policy and practice in the education of deaf children and young people

Margaret Kumsang and Ted Moore

Introduction

This chapter looks at how educational policy in particular, as well as other related factors, have affected the education of deaf children in the UK. In the majority of cases, changes in the provision for deaf pupils have followed general educational legislation or been subsumed under the heading of Special Educational Needs (SEN). However, the field of deaf education has still maintained its own uniqueness and been constantly surrounded by controversy.

The current situation is a result of a range of influences. The privileged and powerful, those with religious zeal, the humanitarians, and those seeking commercial opportunity have all made their mark. Nor should one forget the significant influence of the undoubted powerful practitioners within this specialist field. There has been, too, an impact from changing ideas in educational philosophy, from shifts in social attitudes and from technological and medical advances. All these influences have led to variations in provision over time and by region.

Notable landmarks include the first School for the Deaf (Braidwood School, established during the 1760s), the Milan International Congress of 1880 which passed a resolution promoting oral educational methods for deaf children, the foundation of a professional association for Teachers of the Deaf, the introduction of a mandatory qualification for Teachers of the Deaf (TOD) (1907/8), the application of electronics for amplification, National Health Service hearing aids (1948), transistors (1950s), the Civil Rights movements (1960s), radio hearing aids (1970s), the recognition of sign languages as true languages (1970s), and cochlear implants (1990s).

Government legislation obviously has also been a major influence and this is considered separately in the next section.

Legislation

Major influences before 1978
The twentieth century has seen the introduction of Local Education Authorities (LEAs) (1902), and thereby local accountability, compulsory education for an increasingly greater age range, and in 1944 the introduction of a responsibility on LEAs to make provision for

the assessment and education of children with disabilities.

For most of the twentieth century deaf education has meant education in special schools, but this began to change in 1947 with the integration of hearing-impaired pupils attending 'partially hearing units' attached to ordinary schools. This was at the vanguard of the integration movement which developed rapidly in the 1950s and 1960s (Lynas 1986). The 1960s also ushered in the beginning of a period of increased expenditure, optimism and expansion with the introduction of comprehensive schooling (Chitty 1989; Ranson 1990; DES 1965). The Civil Rights campaigns of the time also affected disabled and deaf people, and the beginnings of a change from a dependency culture to self-advocacy could be detected. It was not, however, until the Education Act of 1970 that all children, whatever their level of disability, were deemed educable and LEAs were required to provide appropriate education for all.

The impact of the Warnock Report

There have been many important policy developments within the field of special education since the publication of the Warnock Report in 1978 (DES 1978). The report greatly influenced the development of policy and practice for hearing-impaired pupils by giving greater impetus to their integration into mainstream schools and by promoting the integration of all pupils with SEN (Hegarty *et al.* 1982; Lynas 1986). Subsequent policy changes enacted through the Education Acts of 1981, 1988, 1989, 1992, 1993 and 1996 and the Children Act of 1989 have all contributed towards a reconstructed system of special education. The two main changes have been, first, a move from categorisation based on medical diagnosis to the concept of a continuum of SEN and multi-professional assessment, and secondly, a move from segregated to integrated provision through to the concept of inclusion based on issues of civil rights, equal opportunities and curriculum entitlement. Parental rights to involvement in their children's education have also gradually been extended (Wolfendale 1992). In addition there has been an increased awareness and recognition of children's SEN in ordinary schools and a move towards differentiation of the curriculum to meet individual needs (Visser 1993). As a result of the introduction of the National Curriculum many previously segregated 'units' have become resource bases, with hearing-impaired and other SEN pupils on class registers receiving much of their support within the classroom situation (Dyson 1993; Mittler 1993).

The 1981 Education Act, described by Baroness Mary Warnock as the 'last gasp of the welfare state' (Peter 1997, p. 11), reinforced professionalisation and increased bureaucratisation through a complex process of assessment (DES 1983). The requirements of the 1981 Education Act ensured that peripatetic (visiting teacher) services for hearing-impaired pupils and other SEN support services flourished and expanded following its implementation in 1983 when 'LEAs were the planners, providers and dispensers' (Bowers 1993, p. 60). It would have been difficult to predict then that SEN services were to become a significant part of what would be left under the direct control of LEAs by the 1990s. Many argue that the real agenda of the Conservative Governments of the 1980s and 1990s was the removal of power from LEAs followed by their eventual demise (Bash and Coulby 1989;

Chitty 1989; Ranson 1992; Lawton 1994). The Centre for Policy Studies certainly promoted that view (Lawlor 1988).

The New Right

A new ideology emerged in the UK in the 1980s and early 1990s as the views of the New Right became increasingly influential (Chitty 1989). The New Right asserted that the control of education was held by those with vested interests (i.e. the providers, comprising the LEAs and teaching professionals) and argued for a move from a 'producer'-led to a 'consumer'-led system with more accountability. Under the influence of the New Right the education service was to be reorganised as part of a wider ideologically based political movement which called for the privatisation of all public sector services. The views of parents as 'consumers' were to become paramount. This 'choice and diversity' through increased parental choice of schools and greater influence on school governing bodies was intended to drive up educational standards. Some claim that the government-led changes in education at this time were part of a more general move away from a society based on consensus to a more fragmented society based on the principle of competition and individual rights (Lawton 1994).

Changing the balance of power

The 1988 Education Reform Act was based on these principles and its implementation dramatically altered the balance of power between central and local government (Maclure 1988; Ranson 1990). The main measures brought in were a centralised National Curriculum with associated testing and assessment; open enrolment for schools aimed to ensure increased parental choice and thus competition between schools; Local Management of Schools (LMS) to shift the power from LEAs to schools through the delegation of financial management; and the creation of grant-maintained schools, independent of the LEA but receiving a direct grant from central government. The 1988 Education Act further reduced the influence of LEAs through the self-government of Further Education colleges and the abolition of the Inner London Education Authority, which at the time was the largest LEA in the country. The principles and values of the 'new liberalism', those of freedom of choice and the opportunity to pursue self-interest, underpinned the legislation. A scenario was predicted where the rhetoric of choice would result in a large number of pupils competing for limited places in 'good' schools and where there would be selection by the 'backdoor' resulting in the pupils that nobody wanted being educated in 'sink' schools.

The National Curriculum

The 1988 Education Reform Act deemed that all children were entitled by law to the same broad and balanced curriculum, and anecdotal evidence suggests that the introduction of the National Curriculum has led to wider, more structured and probably better balanced syllabuses for deaf children. However, on the other hand, this entitlement has brought with it pressures to follow particular Programmes of Study irrespective of perceived need.

The effects of Local Management of Schools (LMS)

Policies often have unintended outcomes and it is important not to underestimate the 'politics of policy making which follow government policy' (Fulcher 1989, p. 9). The effect of LMS led to the delegation of the funding for many units to their host schools. Although not required by law 'delegation is not ruled out if that is what LEAs and schools wish' (DoE 1994b, para 4). As a consequence, an unintended policy outcome was that teachers in peripatetic services managed by LEA central services became separated from their erstwhile unit colleagues, and more head teachers of mainstream schools then became responsible for policy development in place of heads of service (Eatough 1995). Mainstream head teachers were advised by their heads of units, or in some cases individual TODs, on issues such as communication policy and placement decisions. This necessarily *ad hoc* approach appears to have resulted in uncoordinated provision across some LEAs and lack of clear policy direction. Thus the organisation and structure of services for hearing-impaired children has gradually fragmented, and in some cases peripatetic services have become subsumed as part of generic SEN support services, a change predicted by Kumsang (1987). The introduction of LMS caused a reduction to LEA central budgets and consequently a loss of flexibility to appropriately fund low incidence SEN services. Smaller hearing-impaired service budgets have led, in some instances, to an inability to purchase essential equipment or to provide appropriate levels of support. The particularly vulnerable groups appear to be those at preschool level, those who do not have the protection of a Statement of SEN and those with additional learning difficulties (South East Region Heads of Schools and Services for the Hearing Impaired Meeting, 9 February 1996).

The competitive environment brought about by the 1988 Act presented head teachers and governing bodies with ethical problems. Planning and decision making became increasingly budget-driven as schools were now responsible for their own budgets. Choices had to be made between spending money on the appointment of an experienced but expensive teacher or one who was newly trained and cheaper which would leave some funding for other purposes. Budget management had implications for the admission of sensory-impaired pupils; they were expensive in terms of resources and they could be perceived as lowering overall test results and thereby seen as affecting the ability of the school to attract able pupils. Schools in England and Wales are now judged on published league tables of exam and curriculum test results and this may well begin to work against the 'inclusion' of pupils with SEN including those who are deaf. This would be a denial of equal opportunities. There is also continuing concern that SEN central support services will be cut or reorganised into independent agencies (Bangs 1993; Lunt and Evans 1994), although economies of scale will make this difficult to carry out equitably for peripatetic services for hearing-impaired pupils.

The 1993 Education Act

By the early 1990s proposals to amend the 1981 Education Act had been long overdue. The 1993 Act provided for the establishment of a new Funding Agency for Schools (FAS) to support the distribution of resources to grant-maintained schools and to take over from LEAs where a high percentage of schools became grant-maintained. LEAs would continue to be responsible for pupils with Statements of SEN whether they attended a grant-maintained or local authority school. Special schools could apply for grant-maintained status. Statements had to be issued within 26 weeks from commencement, be more specific in the way they were written and were to include measurable learning or behavioural objectives. Parents' rights were extended and a new independent Special Educational Needs Tribunal set up. An unintended outcome of the tribunal system, if considerable anecdotal evidence is to be believed, is the widening chasm between the special school sector and LEA peripatetic services, with parents and hearing-impaired pupils caught in the middle of increasingly acrimonious disputes about appropriate placements.

The Code of Practice

The Code of Practice on the Identification and Assessment of Children with Special Educational Needs (Education Act 1993, part 3) came into effect in September 1994 and LEAs were required to 'have regard' to it. Unfortunately it did not specify national criteria for assessment but significantly it did specify that *qualified* teachers of the deaf were required to assess hearing-impaired pupils. The Code of Practice provided a framework for a more effective partnership to be established between parents and professionals and between professionals themselves. Curriculum differentiation, implied through the formal requirement for Individual Education Plans, has led generally to a more focused educational approach based on careful assessment. More educators are aware that different communication methods may be necessary for children with different needs. Registered government inspectors, through the Code of Practice, were obliged to look closely at schools' SEN policies and importantly 'at the impact of special educational needs support services' (Education Act 1993, p. iii). Schools could now procure support from either the LEA or independent agencies. There was, however, no indication of who would ensure that services, from whatever source, met an acceptable quality standard, but it seems clear that those judgements were not to be left to individual schools (Fish and Evans 1996). However, the programme of inspection of LEAs to be carried out by Her Majesty's Inspectorate (OFSTED 1996) should go some way to examining the quality of an LEA's contribution to supporting schools in improving access and achievement as well as looking at the management of such support services.

Looking back over the 1981, 1988 and 1993 Education Acts it is apparent that the process of assessment of SEN has become increasingly bureaucratic. Although schools now make their own policies the bureaucratic procedures required by the LEA, for example the stages of assessment in the Code of Practice, direct to a considerable degree that policy-making process (Fulcher 1989). This has resulted in the LEA regaining some of the ground lost to central government during the 1980s and 1990s.

Towards inclusion?

It could be argued that the Labour Government's White Paper *Excellence in Schools* (DfEE 1997b) has brought about a sea change to the policy climate. A range of literacy and numeracy targets has been set for the year 2002 together with extra support for schools for children with behavioural problems. The subsequent Green Paper *Excellence for All Children: Meeting Special Educational Needs* (DfEE 1997a) is likely to affect SEN policy development for the next decade and more with its emphasis on 'inclusion'.

The Salamanca Statement and the Framework for Action (UNESCO 1994a) was the impetus for the movement towards inclusive education for all children. However, there is currently controversy over the definition of 'inclusion'. Ainscow (1997, p. 5) describes the difference between 'integration' and 'inclusion' thus:

> Whereas the idea of integration was seen as preparing children perceived as being special to fit into a school that remains largely unchanged, inclusive education starts from the assumption that all children have a right to attend their neighbourhood school. Therefore, the task becomes one of developing the work of the school in response to pupil diversity.

The Centre for Studies on Inclusive Education (CSIE) suggests that integration is where disabled and non-disabled people share a common space or activity, usually initiated and controlled by non-disabled people. Inclusion, says CSIE, is different and involves a philosophy which 'views diversity of strength, abilities and needs as natural and desirable ... and giving each and every member a valid role. Inclusion requires the restructuring of schools and communities'. Another view is offered by Powers (1996b) who suggests that inclusion is best thought of as 'an attitude not a place'.

In one sense it can be viewed as most commendable that all children within a particular community have the right to be educated with their peers (but perhaps not if this means a child is present in a class but is taught, or has instruction communicated, separately from class mates). A cynical view is that inclusive provision has been seized upon by the bureaucrats as being sufficiently high principled but essentially a good way to save money.

It should be noted that the Green Paper (DfEE 1997a) selectively quotes from the Salamanca Statement in its reference to inclusion as the way forward for all pupils. In fact the Statement specifically asserts that 'owing to the particular communication needs of deaf and deaf/blind persons, their education may be more suitably provided in special schools or special class and units in mainstream schools (UNESCO 1994a). This statement could of course be seen as a civil rights or equal opportunities issue.

At the crux of the issue lie questions of resourcing. Inadequate numbers of specialist SEN staff or lack of equipment may be major factors in preventing a pupil gaining appropriate access to both curriculum and peer group. Yet, even then, although the support may be excellent, pupils must still feel valued by all, perceive themselves as successful achievers within their teaching group, and hence feel, and become, fully included.

It is important that if there is to be a change of policy from integration to inclusion then the change should be reflected in practice and not be purely a cosmetic change of name. For example, in a contradictory move the proliferation of segregated pupil referral units can be seen as a return of the special school structure to LEAs under another guise (Bowers 1995).

Local government reorganisation and service structure

Local government reorganisation and the effects of LMS is causing the break-up of many peripatetic services for hearing-impaired pupils into smaller and less effective groups. Low-incidence SEN services need to be of sufficient size to enable them to respond flexibly to changing patterns of need. The Green Paper (DfEE 1997a) recommends regional rather than local planning for all low-incidence SEN. Regionalisation, if adequately funded and structured, could be the mechanism to facilitate more efficient and effective support for hearing-impaired pupils in the future. Reorganisation through regionalisation may also prevent the 'ambivalence of place' that can be experienced by some support services as they operate in that grey area between local government and schools. Unfortunately these services are often seen by the LEA as belonging to the school culture and by schools as belonging to the LEA structure.

Influence of policy on provision

It is apparent that as a consequence of legislative and policy changes outlined above, which have powered the integration movement since the Warnock Report (DES 1978), a number of trends have emerged within the field of deaf education. The largely segregated provision of the nineteenth and first half of the twentieth century has been supplanted by a greater emphasis on, and entitlement to, more local, integrated settings. There has, however, been a slow realisation that this can, in fact, be an expensive option. There has also been an acceptance that some deaf pupils need an education with deaf peers which involves specific communication methods.

Trends and statistics

The British Association of Teachers of the Deaf (BATOD) has conducted a number of surveys (from 1979 onwards) to ascertain statistics relating to the number of TODs, and the number and educational placement of deaf children. Although there has not always been a total response it is apparent, in conjunction with other sources, that there have been a number of trends.

1. There has been a significant increase in the age range of deaf children and young people who are receiving teaching support to now include extensive provision both preschool and post-16. Particular importance is now placed on early intervention, now more possible as a result of improved assessment, more advanced technology, and a better understanding of early language development (including sign language).

2. There has been a shift from placing deaf children in schools (mainly residential), to placing them in units. The advent of the radio hearing aid and the philosophical drive for integrated and inclusive provision created a further impetus towards local mainstream education.

3. There has been a reduction in the number of schools for the deaf. Jordan (1982, in

Child 1991) indicated that there were 75 schools for the deaf in the UK in 1980–81. The BATOD surveys then state that there were only 48 in the UK in 1991 (38 in England and Wales in 1987, 37 in 1991, 32 in 1994 and 30 in 1997). This situation has stemmed partly from a reduction in the profoundly deaf population, and partly from LEAs having to make tough choices about the equitable use of scarce resources. An 'out-county' place in a special school for deaf pupils is seen as an expensive and perhaps privileged option. This has led in some cases to an increased tension between such schools, LEA services for hearing-impaired children, LEA officers and parents, often culminating in SEN Tribunals.

4. Anecdotally, there have been reports of a reduction in the number of profoundly deaf children. However, the BATOD surveys do not provide sufficient detail to support this notion. What is of significance is that the number of profoundly deaf children is very small, equating to only about two to three pupils per year per LEA.

5. There has been a significant increase in the numbers of children receiving cochlear implants since the first child was implanted in 1989. By 1997 numbers had grown within the UK to about 750. This equates in 1997 to between 150 and 200 implantees per year. There has been a change in emphasis towards implanting more young children, i.e. under five years (Archbold 1997, personal communication). It is currently unclear as to the impact this will have for TODs but perhaps more deaf pupils will have access to mainstream education, thereby further reducing the need or demand for segregated provision (i.e. in schools for the deaf and in units). Nevertheless, these pupils will almost certainly need high levels of TOD support. From a different perspective there have been expressions of concern that cochlear implants will reduce the population of the Deaf community, thereby decreasing the opportunities of Deaf people to meet together locally and to act effectively as a political force.

6. The total number of full-time equivalent TOD posts in England would seem to be around 2,000 (Eatough 1995). The total number of qualified personnel is somewhat higher than this as there are also many part-time teachers. This figure is considered by BATOD (1994) to be inadequate to meet the needs of the full range of deaf children in all settings. BATOD (1994) has also campaigned for Government guidelines to be drawn up specifying a TOD : pupil ratio for a particular pupil population.

7. There are now fewer TODs undertaking specialist training. The report from the Special Educational Needs Training Consortium (SENTC 1996) shows a reduction in the number of teachers of the deaf qualifying each year in the UK from 153 in 1989 to 83 in 1996. Significantly there is also a marked change in the pattern of training (Powers and Fraser 1995). In 1989 there were 130 home students undertaking full-time courses but only 23 in 1996 and 10 in 1997/98. The majority of teachers now train on a part-time or distance education basis. Unfortunately the reduction in funds and routes to training do not make it easy for aspiring TODs to enter the profession. Indeed many in the profession believe that there has been a failure by the Government and its agencies to fully recognise the status and expertise of TODs. The mandatory qualification, still in force, and for so long seen as a

benchmark of excellence, has come under increasing pressure from those who perceive it as an elitist, unnecessary and expensive form of training. There is anecdotal evidence that inadequate pay and conditions, a lack of entitlement to funds for in-service training and little opportunity to pursue a staged career, is also thought by many service and school head teachers to have an impact on the quantity and perhaps even the quality of those teachers wishing to gain the qualification.

8. It would appear that the number of deaf children without hearing aids who are being supported by hearing-impaired services in mainstream schools is falling (M. Eatough, BATOD Survey Manager, personal communication, 1996). This is more likely to be the result of services having to cut back on whom they support rather than a reduction in need.

Where next?

It is obvious that legislation will continue apace. However, we set out below some optimistic aspirations for the future.

1. There will be a national framework for the education of deaf children incorporating recognised staff : pupil ratios; the setting up of appropriately staffed teams of TODs within particular areas; adequate funding and equipment for specialist teachers and learning support assistants; sufficient funds and breadth of provision to allow ease of placement of pupils into mainstream, unit or special school, and appropriate pay and conditions for all staff.

2. There will be readily accessible funds for teachers in both the maintained and non-maintained sectors to undertake the mandatory training course which will be available in a variety of formats. Special bursaries will also be accessible for recently qualified mainstream teachers to encourage and enable young teachers to enter the profession. All TODs, regardless of place of employment, will receive a specific amount of funding on an annual basis for continuing professional development. Additional specialist training modules will be available for TODs to develop their skills and a re-accreditation system will be in operation whereby after five years they will have to undertake a course of study to update their knowledge, skills and teaching effectiveness. In order to enhance the quality of provision for children with other difficulties or disabilities, mandatory courses will be introduced for teachers working within all areas of SEN.

3. Developments in audiology and information and communications technology (e.g. video-phones, e-mail, improved subtitling), as well as freely available interpreter services, will allow for greater access to information for deaf people. This will, in turn, enable them to increase their options in the job market and allow for greater independence.

4. All maternity hospitals will undertake neonatal screening of hearing to enable early diagnosis of hearing loss and consequent early support for the child and family.

Cochlear implants will be available to all who want them. Hearing aids will become further miniaturised, will virtually eliminate background noise and will have built-in radio hearing aid reception.

5. Government funding will help parents who request it, to have free access to sign language instruction from the age of diagnosis onwards.

6. Research will be undertaken to identify and then inform the teaching profession of successful practice, thereby enhancing the education of deaf children and opening up a wider range of vocational and social opportunities for deaf young people.

There have been many important issues briefly discussed in this chapter, but many new questions continue to be raised and will have to be answered. At the time of writing (autumn 1997) responses to the Green Paper (DfEE 1997a) are being drawn up by many schools and services. When the consultative period is over, legislation is likely to be introduced which will structure the shape of the education of deaf pupils for perhaps the next decade. The current national policy context is an exciting one for professionals working in the SEN field. The opportunities are there to influence policy development in a positive way. All those involved in deaf education must take up the challenge on behalf of deaf and hearing-impaired children and young people to improve their educational achievements.

The international dimension

Lesley Barcham

Introduction

At the World Conference on Education for All (WCEFA) in Jomtein, Thailand, in 1990 the world's leading educational politicians and members of key international organisations declared that:

> The learning needs of the disabled demand special attention. Steps need to be taken to provide equal access to education to every category of disabled persons as an integral part of the education system (WCEFA 1990, p. 5).

Four years later in 1994 at a similar conference in Salamanca in Spain held under the auspices of the United Nations Educational, Scientific and Cultural Organization (UNESCO) delegates agreed that:

> Every child has a fundamental right to education and must be given the opportunity to achieve and maintain an acceptable level of learning ... Those with special educational needs must have access to regular schools which should accommodate them within a child centred pedagogy capable of meeting these needs (UNESCO 1994a, p. viii).

But interestingly, in the same document for the first time in a major international declaration, the specific needs of deaf and deaf/blind people were mentioned as being different from those of other disability groups.

> Educational policies should take account of individual differences and situations. The importance of sign language as the medium of communication among the deaf, for example should be recognised and provision made to ensure that all deaf persons have access to education in their national sign language. Owing to the particular communication needs of deaf and deaf/blind persons, their education may be more suitably provided in special schools or special classes and units in mainstream schools (UNESCO 1994a, p. 18).

Starting this chapter by focusing on two recent international declarations relating to the educational rights and needs of children with disabilities enables us to see deaf education in a much wider international context. Mittler (1995) notes that under the Education for All initiatives and the Salamanca Statement world leaders are now committed to setting targets to increase the proportion of children with disabilities entitled to basic education.

Although the attention of world leaders and politicians are occasionally focused on the educational needs of deaf and disabled children, it would seem that many teachers, administrators and parents of deaf children in the UK know very little about the lives of deaf children in, say, France, or Ireland or the Netherlands, some of our nearest neighbours. There is even less likelihood of us knowing about deaf education, say, in Poland or Bulgaria or even India or Kenya. It is possible to work in the field of special education in this country with no reference to what happens overseas, but an understanding of the development, policies and practices in deaf education in other countries can help us in two main ways, first in identifying international trends and developments and secondly in providing information for comparison, to allow reflection on our own practice. Mazurek and Winzer (1994) in their book on international comparative studies in special education consider that:

> The greatest hope and ultimate utility of comparative studies is to help groups and institutions reflect upon their own practice, policies and theories by bringing to bear relevant information and insights from around the world (p. ix).

As the opening quotes on this chapter indicate, there is a growing international interest in the development of special education around the world. The International Year of Disabled Persons (IYDP) in 1981 and the following international decade of disabled persons 1982–1992 acted as a focus for work by, and on behalf of, disabled adults and children. In the 1980s there was also a growing understanding in the developed countries of North America, Europe and Australasia of the needs of children with disabilities and learning difficulties in the more developing regions of Asia, Africa and South America.

The IYDP also helped to highlight for parents, teachers, policy makers and politicians the human rights issues involved in providing education for deaf and other disabled children. As Hegarty notes (1993) all children have a right to be educated, but one of the 'tragedies of our time is that very many children are not educated – and have no opportunity to go to school' (p. 16). The challenge to provide education to all children has even more force and conviction when the children concerned have a disability or a learning difficulty. The irony is that those children most in need of an education, perhaps because of a sensory or physical impairment, are often excluded from the education system or have less-well-developed schools and services. The United Nations Declaration of Human Rights enshrines the right of all children to an education, although millions are not accorded this right. Adults and children with disabilities also have the rights to equality of opportunity and to full participation in society (Herr 1993).

The majority of the world's deaf children live in developing countries and are unlikely to go to school. Deaf people in developing countries are 'frequently considered a marginal, neglected and socially discriminated (against) group with a limited share of even the very elementary human and civil rights within their community' (Joutselainen 1993, p. 76). This first major survey of the lives of deaf people in developing countries, conducted by the World Federation of the Deaf, revealed that 'education is a privilege of very few deaf children and young people' (p. 28). The percentage of deaf children attending school is very small in developing countries, 'deaf children are among the last in their generation to become literate and numerate' (Joutselainen 1991, p. 32).

Estimates of the number of deaf children in any country are fraught with difficulties. Estimating numbers globally is even more difficult. Latest World Health Organization figures on moderate and severe disabilities estimate that in developing countries between 0.5 and one per cent of the population will have a hearing or speech difficulty. Difficulties in making estimates include variations in definitions of certain disabilities and the method of data collection and analysis. The pattern of disabilities also varies from country to country because of differences in health care and the levels of immunisation against potentially disabling diseases. In developing countries sensory impairments are more common as a result of infectious diseases and the lack of treatment for common infections as well as malnutrition, wars, conflicts and accidents.

In the next section of this chapter three key themes are explored:

*   the growing globalisation of the debates and issues in deaf education;
*   the major shift in emphasis regarding the main conflicts and struggles in deaf education, particularly in relation to the type of provision for deaf children and the methods of communication used in education;
*   the changing role of the Deaf community in the education of deaf children and young people.

Globalisation

The international comparative literature on special education and the education of deaf children has been expanding over the last 20 years. The field is still, however, fragmented and dispersed made up mostly of papers, conference proceedings and project reports. For people researching international issues in deaf education the literature search can be made easier by consulting specialist libraries such as that at the Royal National Institute for the Deaf (RNID) in London.

One international contributor to the literature on deaf education has been UNESCO, the United Nations intergovernmental organisation with a specific responsibility for special education.[1] Other contributions have come from international deaf organisations such as the World Federation of the Deaf, INITIATIVES for Deaf Education in the Third World and the Commonwealth Society for the Deaf.

Walters (1995) writing on globalisation and the development of the global society noted the significance of a global network of intergovernmental and international non-governmental organisations and their significance in international goal setting and decision making. This network of organisations can in certain situations, he argued, outflank the role of the nation state. Since the 1960s, intergovernmental organisations (such as those under the United Nations auspices) have concentrated international concern on issues such as the environment, education, sport and religion. The international non-governmental sector has also built up over the last 20 to 30 years a parallel process of consensus-building that extends beyond the role of national governments. Walters goes on to note 'it is clear that national governments are obliged to take IGOs (intergovernmental organisations) and INGOs (international non-governmental organisations) seriously' (1995, p. 113).

What does this general analysis of globalisation mean for people involved in the education of deaf children? Deaf history has shown us that international exchanges of ideas and practice in the field have been on going for over two hundred years (Lane 1984; McLoughlin 1987), but in recent times this process has expanded to include a larger number of countries and a greater diversity of settings. Brill (1984) has documented various topics from international congresses on deaf education, but unfortunately not all of the more recent proceedings have been fully published.

The World Federation of the Deaf, a federation of national organisations of deaf people, has in recent times expanded from its North American and European origins to include a more truly world-wide membership and it has also begun to champion the rights and needs of deaf people in developing countries (Joutselainen 1991). Other international non-governmental organisations have in various ways sought to advance the cause of deaf education in a number of developing countries, for example, the Commonwealth Society for the Deaf and also INITIATIVES (De Carpentier 1995).

Conflict and struggles

The second key theme is that of conflict and struggle evident internationally in the education of deaf children and young people. Tomlinson (1985) noted that 'the development and expansion of special education are the result of a variety of conflicting interest groups, both inside and outside education' (p. 160). Similarly, Oliver (1988) writing on policy development around disability issues notes that

> notions of conflict and vested interests can also be used to explain the development of special education. The power of certain groups to advance their interests at the expense of others is a crucial part of this explanation (p. 18).

A number of interest groups are usually influential in policy development in the education of deaf children, including central and local government officials, teachers, academics, parents and Deaf people. These various groups often have different agendas and interact in various policy-making arenas and at different levels to bring about change (Fulcher 1989).

Nationally and internationally two key areas of conflict and struggle over policy can be identified, first over the methods of communication used in the education of deaf children, and secondly over the type of educational provision (either in special schools or in integrated or inclusive education settings).

Regarding the development of deaf education in developing countries Miles (1995) in a paper on special education in southern Africa noted the development of what she called a 'Deaf dilemma' and highlighted a number of conflicts not all of which are specific to southern Africa or even developing countries. With regard to placement issues, Miles argued that the special school model of education for deaf children was unsustainable in developing countries, as it was only able in most situations to provide for a minority. However, at the same time many professionals and Deaf people in these countries said 'no' to integration. Miles also noted that in those countries she knew the disability movement had a poor understanding of deaf issues.

The changing role of the Deaf community

Linked in a number of ways to the two previous themes is the third, the changing role of the Deaf community in the education of deaf children, both at the national and international levels. This development should be seen in the wider context of the disability movement in general recently successfully challenging the dominance of professionals in rehabilitation and educational services (Driedger 1988a, 1988b; Coleridge 1993).

With regard to international policies on the education of deaf children the World Federation of the Deaf (WFD) has sought in the last ten years to provide a distinctive view. The WFD is generally in agreement with the wider disability movement regarding human rights, employment and services issues. However, it has a distinctive agenda specific to the needs of Deaf people which includes:

- linguistic rights
- recognition by governments and international organisations of sign language as the first language of the Deaf community
- the use of sign language in the education of deaf children (Lindquist 1995).

These three themes, the globalisation of the debates in deaf education, the changing areas of conflict and struggle and the changing role of the Deaf community will be illustrated in the two short country case studies which follow. These two countries, Finland and Zimbabwe, were chosen to illustrate a number of similarities and differences between a developed and a developing country.

Two case studies

Finland

Finland is a northern European country with a population of approximately five million. Education for deaf children in the country started in the 1840s when a deaf young man educated in Sweden opened a school in Porvoo. The early schools in Sweden and Finland followed the French method of using writing, finger-spelling and some sign language. The country's second school was opened in 1860 in Turku. In the 1870s educators in Scandinavia in general began to demand a more oral method of education for deaf children, and separate classes and schools developed for those using the oral/speech method and those using the written method (Rissanen 1987).

By the end of the 1800s the oral method had begun to gain dominance in Finland. However, by this time deaf people were beginning to form organisations to help themselves, and the emerging Deaf community organised adult education and cultural activities where sign language was used. The Finnish Association of the Deaf was established in 1905 (Kauppinen 1988) and about the same time the first sign language dictionary was published.

Oral methods dominated in Finland from the 1900s to the 1970s. In 1973 the issue of sign language was addressed in the government curriculum document for deaf education, but it was mentioned as an auxiliary method of communication and not as a subject in its own right. The crucial change came in 1987 when the curriculum document mentioned bilingual education and placed an emphasis on educating deaf children in sign language. It also argued that to use sign language and spoken Finnish simultaneously is in fact to use a pidgin language. In 1990 a curriculum for teaching sign language was published which stated that sign language is the first language of deaf pupils, but that the first language of 'hard of hearing' pupils, although it can be sign language, is usually Finnish or Swedish (Takala 1995).

A significant consideration in understanding the change to a bilingual approach in the education of deaf children in Finland is that it is a multi-lingual country, where there are three official languages in recognition of the presence of sizeable Swedish and Lapp communities.

Currently the country has about 8,000 deaf people, 5,000 of whom use sign language as their main means of communication. There are 18 schools for the deaf, which offer a bilingual education to the large majority of pupils who have a severe or profound hearing loss. Those with mild or moderate hearing loss attend mainstream schools and generally use oral methods.

Takala (1995) notes that in the 1990s the major debate in Finland concerning methodology has been about the signing skills of the teachers. Almost all teachers of the deaf now sign, but the issue is what they sign. There are competing interests between the use of Finnish Sign Language (FinnSL) and Signed Finnish (a combination of the syntax of Finnish and the vocabulary of FinnSL).

Most parents of deaf and hard of hearing children accept and use sign language. Parents are offered government paid courses and home instruction in FinnSL. Tillander (1994) notes that there are three important aspects to the bilingual education of deaf children in Finland:

- the parents' acceptance of the child's deafness
- the parents' willingness to learn sign language
- the child being provided with access to both cultures, that of the Deaf community and Finnish culture.

Tillander (1994) notes that parents are still caught in an ideological controversy between the medical view of staff involved in initial diagnosis and the assessment and ideas of using sign language as the main means of communication. Although the government encourages parents to use sign language with their young deaf children by providing 100 hours of home instruction for the family and then access to sign language classes, there are still obstacles to the child learning sign language. These obstacles include concerns from some hearing professionals, finding an appropriate sign language teacher near to the home, parents' concern over the spoken language development of their child, and parental worries that they and their child will become over-reliant on sign language. As a consequence some families use Signed Finnish in preference to FinnSL.

Young deaf children gaining access to both the Finnish and Deaf community are highly dependent on their parents to explain information from the mainstream culture and equally to negotiate access for them to the Deaf community. The Finnish Association of the Deaf provides free monthly videos of news and events and also signed stories for children and young people.

Wider educational policy in relation to deaf education has changed to keep pace with the changes toward bilingual education. Together with the change in the national curriculum setting out bilingual training as one goal of deaf education, the educational programme of teachers of the deaf has been revised. There has also been a change in the legislation regarding the employment of teachers which previously required them to have 'normal' hearing and sight. This has allowed deaf teachers to train as teachers of deaf children. There are also programmes to train deaf people to work as both assistant teachers and classroom assistants.

Zimbabwe

Zimbabwe is a southern African country with a population of approximately nine million. The country was a British colony (Southern Rhodesia and then later Rhodesia) from the 1890s to 1965, when a period of Unilateral Declaration of Independence (UDI) was declared under the leadership of Ian Smith's white minority Rhodesia Front party. Following a 15-year struggle for liberation full independence was achieved in 1980.

The education of deaf children started in the 1940s when the Dutch Reformed Church and the Dominican sisters of the Catholic Church opened schools for African deaf children. Later a school for both deaf and blind children was opened by a national African disability welfare charity, and then in the 1960s, following a polio epidemic, the Red Cross opened two schools for white and coloured children with physical disabilities, and visual and hearing impairments.

The early schools used teachers from countries such as South Africa, England and Germany, and these teachers brought with them overseas policies regarding communication methods and types of provision. The Dutch Reformed Church had experience of teaching deaf children in South Africa, and the Dominican sisters had experience from South Africa, Ireland, and Germany. All staff training took place overseas until the mid 1980s, and as a result of this policy a great variety of ideas was brought into deaf education in Zimbabwe.

The legacy for deaf education from the colonial era meant that education was provided for only a small percentage of deaf children in a number of isolated and autonomous special schools and the schools were racially segregated as was all education prior to independence. At independence there was a lack of national coordination and planning for deaf education, each school was financed and administered independently and there was a strongly charitable ethos to provision. The education provided was generally primary school and then vocational training. In the colonial period and beyond there was a negative attitude to deaf people in the country with feelings of superstition and witchcraft surrounding all disability issues (Csapo 1986).

Since independence the government has assumed responsibility for the development and expansion of special education. Government responsibility has extended to the development of a policy of integrated provision for most children with special needs (including deaf children), teacher training, procurement of equipment, and the monitoring and co-ordination of the special education programmes. In 1980 about 4,000 children with special needs were receiving an education in Zimbabwe and this had risen to over 10,000 in 1994. By the mid 1990s Zimbabwe had five special schools for deaf children and also around 40 resource units attached to primary and secondary schools throughout the country catering for approximately 1,000 deaf children (Peresuh and Barcham, in press).

International influences on the development of education in Zimbabwe have changed over time. In the early colonial period the links were predominantly between individual church or charity schools and organisations overseas that provided funds, equipment or opportunities for training. In the 1990s although the individual links between special schools and overseas organisations still exist they have been superseded by government-to-government links regarding funding, and government-to-intergovernmental-organisation links regarding overall policy direction, moral and political imperatives. Since independence, deaf education has been directly and indirectly influenced by, among other things, the International Year of Disabled People, international statements and declarations, funding from a bilateral aid agency (which provides government-to-government funding) and the use of foreign volunteers. The other major external influence has been from international organisations of Deaf and disabled people.

The early influence of the churches and charities on deaf education were in terms of seconding staff from overseas, developing training for national teachers, and providing funding for capital projects and technical equipment. Since independence intergovernmental organisations such as UNESCO and also the World Health Organization (WHO) have exercised a degree of influence on policy development in both education- and community-based rehabilitation programmes in a number of ways:

- through the dissemination of information through publications, conferences, regional and-sub regional meetings and seminars;
- through organising exchanges of ideas between-non governmental organisations and government officials and ministers;
- through the designation of international years and decades relating to disabled persons;

- more recently in the 1990s through the use of international declarations and statements on education issues.

International non-governmental organisations such as the WFD have similarly increased their international profile and their influence on issues relating to the lives of deaf people including education and have lobbied UNESCO on bilingual approaches to communication and also on their preference for special school provision. WFD has also sought to directly and indirectly influence policies in Zimbabwe through the recognition and support of the Association of the Deaf (ASSOD) founded in 1988 and the recent development of regional cooperation and development in southern and eastern Africa.

The final major international influence on the development of education for deaf children has been through financial support for special education given to the government of Zimbabwe by the Swedish government through the Swedish International Development Agency (SIDA). Since 1982 some of this aid money has been used to develop community-based rehabilitation programmes and special education projects including a national programme for specialist teacher training, equipment for the resource units for deaf children and funding for a sign language research project.

Conflicts and struggle in the policy development of deaf education in Zimbabwe abound. Research has confirmed the view of Fulcher (1989) that conflict happens in a number of arenas between different interest groups such as ministry staff, head teachers, teachers, deaf people's organisations, other disability organisations and rehabilitation staff, but the research has also shown that the main sources of conflict have changed over time (Barcham 1997).

The Deaf community in Zimbabwe has been formally organised as the ASSOD since 1988, but deaf people had met informally since independence especially in activities centred around a deaf football team (ASSOD 1993). In the 1990s ASSOD has lobbied the government and other organisations on issues relating to the education of deaf children specifically concerning their preference for schools for the deaf, also to promote the use of Zimbabwean Sign Language (Zimsign) in schools and also for the use of sign language on television.

Conclusions

Understanding the context of policy development in deaf education in another country is a complex matter. As Phillips (1989) writes:

> It is of course clear ... that comparative research in education should take into account the historical, political, social and cultural settings of particular systems and aspects of them. It is only through analysis and understanding of the roots that feed education systems that we can arrive at a proper understanding of why things are as they are ... Outcomes themselves should not be seen in isolation from the processes that have produced them (Phillips 1989, p. 269).

This chapter has argued that the themes of globalisation, conflict and struggle and the changing role of the Deaf community are three possible processes by which to analyse information on international developments in deaf education.

Note

1. UNESCO documents have included a *Consultation on Alternative Approaches in the Education of the Deaf* (UNESCO 1984), *Education of Deaf Children and Young People* (UNESCO 1987), and *Language and Curriculum Planning for Deaf Children* (UNESCO 1988a). Other more general special education publications have plotted and reported on the development of special education, for example *Review of the Present Situation of Special Education* (UNESCO 1988b), and more recently on good practice, *Making it Happen: Examples of Good Practice in Special Needs Education and Community Based Programmes* (UNESCO 1994b).

Bibliography

Abedi, R. (1988) *From Sound to Silence*. London: Hobo.

Abel, P. J. (1986) 'Hearing-impaired children in mainstream schools in Nottinghamshire', *Journal of the British Association of Teachers of the Deaf* **10** (5), 127–31.

Abrahamsen, A., Cavallo, M. M., McCluer, J. A. (1985) 'Is the sign advantage a robust phenomenon? From gesture to language in two modalities', *Merrill-Palmer Quarterly* **31**, 177–209.

Ackerman, J., Kyle, J. G., Woll, B., Ezra, M. (1990) 'Lexical acquisition in sign and speech: evidence from a longitudinal study of infants in deaf families', in Lucas, C. (ed.) *Sign Language Research: Theoretical Issues*, 337–45. Washington DC: Gallaudet University Press.

Adamson, L. B., Bakeman, R., Smith, C. B. (1990) 'Gestures, words and early object sharing', in Volterra, V. and Erting, C. J. (eds). *From Gesture to Language in Hearing and Deaf Children*. Berlin: Springer-Verlag.

Ahlgren, I. (1990) 'Swedish conditions: sign language in deaf education', in Prillwitz, S. and Vollhaber, T. (eds) *Sign Language Research and Application*, 91–94. Hamburg: Signum Press.

Ahmad, W. I. U. (1993) *'Race' and health in contemporary Britain*. Buckingham: Open University Press.

Ahmad, W. I. U. (1996) 'The trouble with culture', in Kelleher, D. and Hillier, S. (eds) *Researching Cultural Difference in Health*. London: Routledge.

Ahmad, W. I. U., Darr, A., Jones, L. (forthcoming) '"I send my child to school and he comes back an Englishman": minority ethnic deaf people, identity politics and services', *Journal of Ethnic and Migration Studies*.

Ahmad, W. I. U. and Husband, C. (1993) 'Religious identity, citizenship and welfare: the case of Muslims in Britain', *American Journal of Islamic Social Science* **10** (2), 217–233.

Ainscow, M. (1997) 'Towards inclusive schooling', *British Journal of Special Education* **24** (1), 3–6.

Akamatsu, C. T. and Armour, V. A. (1987) 'Developing written literacy in deaf children through analysing Sign Language', *American Annals of the Deaf* **132**, 46–51.

Allen, T. E. (1986) 'Patterns of academic achievement among hearing-impaired students: 1974 and 1983', in Schildroth, A. N. and Karchmer M. A. (eds), *Deaf Children in America*. San Diego: College Hill Press.

Allen, T. E. and Osborn, T. I. (1984) 'Academic integration of hearing-impaired students: demographic, handicapping, achievement factors', *American Annals of the Deaf* **129** (4), 100–113.

Altshuler, K. Z. (1971) 'Studies of the deaf: relevance to psychiatric theory', *American Journal of Psychiatry* **127**, 1521–1526.

American National Institutes of Health (ANIH) (1993) 'Early identification of hearing impairment in infants and young children', NIH *Consensus Statement* March 1–3, **11** (1), 1–24.

American Speech-Language-Hearing Association (ASHA) (1991) 'Amplification as a remediation technique for children with normal peripheral hearing' *ASHA* **33** Suppl. 3.

American Speech-Language-Hearing Association (ASHA) (1994) 'Guidelines for fitting and monitoring FM systems', *ASHA* **36** Suppl. 12, 1–9.

American Speech-Language-Hearing Association (ASHA) (1996) 'Central auditory processing: current status of research and implications for clinical practice', *American Journal of Audiology*, 5 (92), July 1996, 41–54.

Andrews, E. (1988) 'Conversation', *Journal of the British Association of Teachers of the Deaf,* **12** (2) 29–32.

Andrews, J. and Jordan, D. (1993) 'Minority and minority deaf professionals. How many and where are they?' *American Annals of the Deaf* **138**, 388–96.

Anwar, M. (1979) *The Myth of Return: Pakistanis in Britain.* London: Heinemann.

Arehole, S. (1995) 'A preliminary study of the relationship between long latency response and learning disorder', *British Journal of Audiology* **29** (6), 295–8.

Arehole S., Augustine, L. E., Simhadri, R. (1995) 'Middle latency response in children with learning disabilities', *Journal of Communication Disorders* **28**, 21–38.

Arends, N. J. M (1993) *The Visual Speech Apparatus, An Aid for Speech Training.* Sint-Michielsgestel: Instituut voor Doven.

Armitage, I. M., Burke, J. P., Buffin, J. T. (1995) 'Visual impairment in severe and profound sensorineural deafness', *Archives of Disease in Childhood,* **73** 53–56.

Association of the Deaf (ASSOD) (1993) *Know Zimbabwe Deaf and Deafness through the Deaf.* Harare: ASSOD.

Badat, H. and Whall-Roberts, D.(1994) *Bridging the Gap: Creating Services for Deaf People from Ethnic Minorities.* London: Royal National Institute for Deaf People.

Baddeley, A. (1990) *Human Memory: Theory and Practice.* Hove: Lawrence Erlbaum Associates.

Bahan, B. (1997) Keynote paper *'Deaf Nations' Symposium.* University of Central Lancashire, Preston, UK.

Baker, A. E. and van den Bogaerde, B. (1996) 'Language input and attentional behaviour', in Johnson, C. E. and Gilbert, J. H. V. (eds) *Children's Language* Vol. 9. Mahwah, NJ: Lawrence Erlbaum Associates.

Baker, C. (1993) *Foundations of Bilingual Education and Bilingualism.* Clevedon: Multilingual Matters.

Baker, C. (1996) 'Educating for bilingualism – key themes and issues', in Knight, P. and Swanwick, R. (eds) *Bilingualism and the Education of Deaf Children.* Leeds: University Press.

Baker, C. and Cokely, D. (1980) *American Sign Language: A Teacher's Resource Text on Grammar and Culture.* Silverspring, MD: T. J. Publishers.

Baker, R. (1990) 'Developing literacy skills through dialogue journals', *Bilingual Education for Deaf Children: From Policy to Practice. Nottingham: LASER Conference Proceedings,* 23–29.

Baker, R. and Child, D. (1993) 'Communication approaches used in schools for the deaf in the UK: a follow-up study', *Journal of the British Association of Teachers of the Deaf* **17** (2), 36–47.

Baldwin, M. and Watkin, P. (1997). 'Otoacoustic emissions', in McCracken,W. and Laoide-Kemp, S. (eds) *Audiology in Education.* London: Whurr Publishers.

Balkany, J. T. (1980) 'Otological aspects of Downs Syndrome', in J. L. Northern and M. Downs (eds) *Seminars in Speech and Hearing* **1**, 39–48.

Bamford, J. (1995) 'Clinical outcomes', in *Occasional Papers in the Field of Early Identification of Hearing Impairment in Children.* London: NDCS.

Bamford, J. and Saunders, E. (1992) *Hearing Impairment, Auditory Perception and Language Disability,* 2nd edn. London: Whurr Publishers.

Bangs, J. (1993) 'Support services: stability or erosion?' *British Journal of Special Education* 20 (3), 105–7.

Banks, J., Gray, P., Fyfe, R. (1990) 'The written recall of printed stories by severely deaf children', *British Journal of Educational Psychology* 60, 192–206.

Barber, M. (1996) *The Learning Game*. London: Victor Gollancz.

Barcham, L. J. (1997) *The Education of Deaf Children in Zimbabwe: The Changing Roles of Non Governmental Organisations, the Government and International Organisations*. Unpublished PhD thesis. Open University.

Barnes, C. and Mercer, G. (1996) *Exploring the Divide: Illness and Disability*. Leeds: Disability Press.

Barnes, D., Britton, J., Rosen, H. (1969) *Language, the Learner and the School*. Harmondsworth, Middlesex: Penguin Education.

Barton, L. (1986) 'The policies of special educational needs', *Disabilities, Handicap and Society*, 1 (3), 273–290.

Bash, L. and Coulby, D. (1989) *The Education Reform Act: Competition and Control*. London: Cassell.

Basilier, T. (1964) 'The psychic consequences of congenital or early acquired deafness – some theoretical and clinical considerations', *Acta Psychiatric Scandinavica* 10, Suppli 180, 362–372.

Beard, R. (1987) *Developing Reading 3–13*. London: Hodder & Stoughton.

Bebko, J. M. and Metcalfe-Haggert, A. (1997) 'Deafness, language skills and rehearsal: a model for the development of a memory strategy', *Journal of Deaf Studies and Deaf Education* 2 (3), 131–140.

Begum, N. (1996) Quoted in Campbell, J. and Oliver, M. (eds), *Disability Politics: Understanding our Past, Changing our Future*. London: Routledge.

Bellinger, D. (1979) 'Changes in the explicitness of mothers' directiveness as children age', *Journal of Child Language* 6, 443–58.

Bellugi, U., Klima, E. S., Siple, P. (1975) 'Remembering in signs', *Cognition*, 3 93–125.

Bellugi, U., O'Grady, L., Lillo-Martin, M., O'Grady Hynes, M. *et al.* (1994) 'Enhancement of spatial cognition in Deaf children' in Volterra, V. and Erting, C. (eds) *From Gesture to Language in Hearing and Deaf Children*. Washington DC: Gallaudet University Press.

Bench R. J. (1992) *Communication Skills in Hearing-impaired Children*, 23–43. London: Whurr Publishers.

Bennett, K. E. and Haggard, M. P. (1996) 'Duration of behaviour and cognitive outcomes from middle ear disease in the UK. Recent advances in otitis media'. *Proceedings of the Sixth International Symposium*. Fort Lauderdale, Florida.

Bennett, M. and Wade, H. K (1980). 'Automated newborn screening using the ARC', in Taylor, I. G. and Markides, A. (eds) *Disorders of Auditory Function*, III. London: Academic Press.

Berlin, C. I. (1995) *Hair Cells and Hearing Aids*. San Diego, CA: Singular Publishing Group.

Berrick, A. (1984) Auditory Processing Tests. *Journal of Speech and Hearing Disorders* 49, 318–325.

Bess, F. H., Gravel, J. S., Tharpe, A. M. (eds) (1996) *Amplification for Children with Auditory Deficits*. Nashville, Tennessee: Bill Wilkerson Press.

Bess, F. H. and Paradise, J. L. (1994) 'Universal hearing screening for infant hearing impairment: not simple, not risk free, not necessarily beneficial, and not presently justified' *Pediatrics* 93, 330–4.

Bettger, J. G., Emmorey, K., McCullough, S. H., Bellugi, U. (1997). 'Enhanced facial discrimination: effects of experience with American Sign Language', *Journal of Deaf Studies and Deaf Education* 2, 223–233.

Bhattacharya, J., Bennett, M., Tucker, S.M. (1984) 'Long term follow up of newborns tested with the Auditory Response Cradle', *Archives of Diseases in Childhood* 59, 4–11.

Bialystok, E. (1991) 'Metalinguistic dimensions of bilingual language proficiency', Bialystok, E. (ed.) *Language Processing in Bilingual Children*, 113–140. Cambridge: Cambridge University Press.

Biklen, D. and Bogdan, R. (1977) 'Media portrayals of disabled people – a study in stereotypes', *Interracial Books for Children Bulletin* 8 4–9.

Bishop, A. J. (1980) 'Spatial abilities and mathematics education – a review. *Educational Studies in Mathematics* 11 (3), 257–269.

Blair, F. X. (1957) 'A study of the visual memory of deaf and hearing children', *American Annals of the Deaf*, 102, 254–263.

Bodner-Johnson, B. (1986) 'The family environment and the achievement of deaf student', *Exceptional Children* 52, 443–449.

Bodner-Johnson, B. (1991) 'Family conversation style: its effect on the deaf child's participation', *Exceptional Children* 57 (6), 502–509.

Bonvillian, J. D. (1983) 'Effects of signability and imagery on word recall by deaf and hearing students', *Perceptual and Motor Skills* 56, 775–791.

Boothman, R. and Orr, N. (1978) 'The value of screening for deafness in the first year of life', *Archives of Diseases in Childhood* 53 (7), 570–573.

Bouvet, D. (1990) *The Path to Language: Bilingual Education for Deaf Children*. Clevedon: Multilingual Matters.

Bowers, T. (1993) 'Funding special education', in: Visser, J. and Upton, G. (eds), *Special Education in Britain After Warnock*. London: David Fulton Publishers.

Bowers, T. (1995) 'Touched by the invisible hand?' *Support for Learning* 10 (3), 113–118.

Bown, M. (1993) 'The role of non-maintained and independent special schools for hearing impaired children – costs and curriculum', *Journal of the British Association of Teachers of the Deaf*, 17 (3), 70–77.

Braden, J. P. (1994) *Deafness, Deprivation and IQ*. London: Plenum Press.

Bradford, B. C., Baudin, J., Conway, M. J., Hazell, J. W. P., *et al.* (1985) 'Identification of sensory neural hearing loss in very preterm infants by brainstem auditory evoked potentials', *Archives of Disease in Childhood* 60:105–109.

Brauer, B. A, (1992) 'The Signer effect of MMPI performance of deaf respondents', *Journal of Personality Assessment* 58, 380–388.

Bray, P. and Kemp, D. T. (1987) 'An advanced cochlear echo technique suitable for infant screening', British Journal of Audiology 21, 191–204.

Brennan, M. (1984) *Words in Hand: a Structural Analysis of British Sign Language*. Edinburgh: Moray House College of Education.

Brennan, M. (1997) 'See what I mean? Exploiting BSL visual encoding in teaching and learning'. Unpublished paper presented at International Conference *'Empower '97'*. Edinburgh: Moray House College of Education.

Brill, R. G. (1984) *International Congresses on the Education of the Deaf, An Analytical History 1878–1980*. Washington, DC: Gallaudet University Press.

Brisenden, S. (1986) 'Independent living and the medical model of disability', *Disability, Handicap and Society* 1 (2), 173–178.

British Association of Teachers of the Deaf National Executive (BATOD) (1994) 'The organisation and management of LEA educational services for hearing-impaired pupils and young people, England and Wales', *British Association of Teachers of the Deaf Association Magazine*, November 1994, 10–11.

British Association of Teachers of the Deaf (BATOD), GCSE Sub-committee (1995) *The Language of Examinations*. British Association of Teachers of the Deaf Publications

British Association of Teachers of the Deaf National Executive (BATOD) (1996) 'Towards a national policy in the education of deaf children and young people', *British Association of Teachers of the Deaf Association Magazine*, May 1996, 18.

British Deaf Association (BDA) (1983) *The Implementation of Total Communication: a Residential Seminar*. Carlisle: British Deaf Association.

British Deaf Association (BDA) (1996) *The Right to be Equal: the British Deaf Association Education Policy*. London: British Deaf Association.

Broadfoot, P. M. (1996) *Education, Assessment and Society*. Buckingham: Open University Press.

Brofenbrenner, U. (1979) *The Ecology of Human Development: Experiments by Nature and Design*. Cambridge, Mass: Harvard University Press.

Brooks, P. H. (1978) 'Some speculations concerning deafness and learning to read', in Lieben, L. (ed.) *Deaf Children: Developmental Perspectives*. New York: Academic Press.

Brown. J., Watson, E., Alberman. E. (1989) 'Screening infants for hearing loss', *Archives of Disease in Childhood* 64, 1488–1495

Brown, R. (1973) *A First Language*. London: Allen and Unwin.

Brown, R. and Hanlon, C. (1970) 'Derivational complexity and order of acquisition in child speech', in Hayes, J. R. (ed.) *Cognition and the Development of Language*. New York: Wiley.

Brown, R. I. (1994) 'Changing concepts of disability in developed and developing countries', in Mitchell, D. and Brown, R. I. (eds) *Early Intervention Studies for Young Children with Special Needs*. London: Chapman Hall.

Buchanan, L. H. (1990) 'Early onset of presbycusis in Down's Syndrome', *Scandanavian Audiology* 34, 312–320.

Bullinger, M. and Ravens-Sieberer, U. (1995) 'Health related quality of life assessment in children: a review of the literature', *Revue Européenne de Psychologie Appliquée, 4ᵉ trimestre 1995*, 45 (4), 245–254.

Caccamise, F. and Newell, W. (1984) 'A review of current terminology used in deaf education and signing', *Journal of Rehabilitative Audiology* 17, 106–129.

Caissie, R. and Cole, E. B. (1993) 'Mothers and hearing-impaired children: directiveness reconsidered'. *Volta Review* 95, 49–59.

Campbell, J. and Oliver, M. (1996) *Disability Politics: Understanding our Past, Changing our Future*. London: Routledge.

Campbell, R. (1992) 'Speech in the head? Rhyme skill, reading and immediate memory in the deaf', in Reisberg, D. (ed.), *Auditory Imagery*, 73–94, New Jersey: Lawrence Erlbaum Associates.

Campbell, R. and Wright, H. (1990) 'Deafness and immediate memory for pictures: dissociations between "inner speech" and the "inner ear", *Journal of Experimental Child Psychology* 50, 259–286.

Carr, G. (1997) 'The development of listening skills', in: McCracken, W. and Laoide-Kemp, S. (eds) *Audiology in Education*. London: Whurr Publishers.

Cashmore, E. and Troyna, B. (1988) *An Introduction to Race Relations* (2nd edn). East Sussex: Falmer Press.

Cass, V. C. (1979) 'Homosexual identity formation: a theoretical model', *Journal of Homosexuality* 4, 219–35.

Central Statistical Office (1996) *A Social Focus on Ethnic Minorities*. London: Central Statistical Office.

Chalmers, D., Stewart, I., Silva, P., Mulvena, A. (1989) *Otitis Media with Effusion in Children in the Dunedin Study*. Oxford: Blackwell.

Chamba, R., Ahmad, W. I. U., Jones, L. (forthcoming) *Improving Health Care for Asian Deaf Children*. Bradford, Ethnicity and Social Policy Research Unit, University of Bradford.

Chamberlain, C. and Mayberry, R. (1995) 'Do the deaf see better? Effects of deafness on visual spatial skills', *Brain and Cognition* **28** (2), 211.

Cheskin, A. (1982) 'The use of language by deaf mothers of hearing children'. *Journal of Communication Disorders* **15**, 145–53.

Child, D. (1991) 'A survey of communication approaches used in schools for the deaf in the UK', *Journal of the British Association of Teachers of the Deaf* **15** (1), 20–24.

The Children Act (1989) London: HMSO.

Chitty, C. (1989) *Towards a New Education System: The Victory of the New Right?* East Sussex: Falmer Press.

Clark, M. (1989) *Language Through Living.* London: Hodder & Stoughton.

Close, G. (1995) 'Real friends', *Therapy Weekly* **21** (35), 8.

Cochrane, A. L. and Holland, W. W. (1971) 'Validation of screening procedures', *British Medical Bulletin* **27**, 3–8.

Cohen, O. P., Fischgrund, J., Redding, R. (1990) 'Deaf children from ethnic, linguistic, and racial minority backgrounds: an overview'. *American Annals of the Deaf* **135**, 67–73.

Coleridge, P. (1993) *Disability, Liberation and Development.* Oxford: Oxfam Publications.

Collins, J. (1988) 'The importance of deaf and hearing adults working together', in: *Conference Proceedings 'Deaf Adults Working In Education', LASER Conference Report*, 26–29.

Condon, M. (1991) 'Unique challenges: children with multiple handicaps', in: *Pediatric Amplification: Proceedings of the National Conference.* Omaha: Boys Town Center, 183–193.

Coninx, F. (1995) 'Aural rehabilitation issues with multiple handicapped hearing impaired children', *Scandanavian Audiology* **24** (41), 61–65.

Conrad, R. (1979) *The Deaf School Child.* London: Harper Row.

Conrad, R. and Hull, A. J. (1964). 'Information, acoustic confusion and memory span', *British Journal of Psychology* **55**, 75–84.

Cook, J. R., Mausbach, T., Burd, L., Gascon, G., *et al.* (1993) 'A preliminary study of the relationship between CAPD and Attention Deficit Disorder', *Journal of Psychiatry and Neuroscience* **18**, 130–137.

Coopers and Lybrand (1988) *Local Management of Schools.* London: HMSO.

Corker, M. (1994) *Counselling – The Deaf Challenge.* London: Jessica Kingsley.

Cowan, R., Barker, E., Pegg, P., Dettman, S. *et al.* (1997) 'Speech perception in children: effects of speech processing strategy and residual hearing', in Clark, G. M. (ed) *Cochlear Implants. Proceedings of the XVI World Congress of Otorhinolaryngology and Head and Neck Surgery.* Bologna: Monduzzi Editore, 297–303.

Crandell, C. C., Smaldino, J. J., Flexer, C. (eds) (1995) 'Sound-field amplification: practical applications', in Danhauer J . L (ed.) *A Singular Audiology Text.* San Diego, California: Singular Publishing Group.

Crittenden, J. B., Ritterman, S. I., Wilcox, E. W. (1986) 'Communication mode as a factor in the performance of hearing-impaired children on a standardized receptive vocabulary test', *American Annals of the Deaf* **131**, 93–135.

Cross, C. M. T. and Prowse, C. K. (1988) 'A case study of a unit for partially hearing pupils', *Journal of the British Association of Teachers of the Deaf* **12** (4), 84–88.

Csapo, M. (1986) 'Zimbabwe: emerging problems of education and special education', *International Journal of Special Education*, **1** (2), 141–160.

Cumming, C. E., Grove, C. and Rodda, M. (1985) 'A note on reading comprehension in hearing impaired adolescents', *Journal of the British Association of Teachers of the Deaf* **9**, 57–60.

Cummins, J. (1991) 'Interdependence of first and second language proficiency in bilingual children', in E. Bialystok (ed.) *Language Processing in Bilingual Children*, 70–89. Cambridge: Cambridge University Press.

Cummins, J. (1994) 'Knowledge, power and identity in teaching English as a second language', in Genesee, F. (ed.) *Educating Second Language Children*, 33–58. Cambridge: Cambridge University Press.

Cunningham, C. and Davis, H. (1985) *Working with Parents: Frameworks for Collaboration*. Buckingham: Open University Press.

Cunningham, C. and McArthur, K. (1981) 'Hearing loss and treatment in young Down's Syndrome children', *Childcare, Health and Development* 7, 357.

Curnock, D. A. (1993) 'Identifying hearing impairments in infants and young children', *British Medical Journal* 307, 1225–1226.

DAHISS (1996) *English as a Foreign Language Curriculum*. Leeds: Leeds Deaf and Hearing Impaired Support Services.

Dale, N. (1996) *Working with Families with Children with Special Needs*. London: Routledge.

Darr, A., Jones, L., Ahmad, W. I. U., Nisar, G. (in press) *Ethnicity and Deafness: Projects and Initiatives*. Bristol: Policy Press.

Davies, S. (1994) 'Attributes for success. Attitudes and practices that facilitate the transition toward bilingualism in the education of deaf children', in Ahlgren, I. and Hyltenstam, K. (eds) *Bilingualism in Deaf Education*, 103–121. Hamburg: Signum Press.

Davis, A. (1984) 'Detecting hearing impairment in neonates – the statistical decision criterion for the Auditory Response Cradle', *British Journal of Audiology* 18, 163–169.

Davis, A., Wharrad, H. J., Sancho, J., Marshall, D. (1991) 'Early detection of hearing impairment: what role is there for behavioural methods in the neonatal period?' *Acta Otolaryngologica* Suppl. 482, 103–109.

Davis, A. C. and Wood, S. (1992) 'The epidemiology of childhood hearing impairment: factors relevant to the planning of services', *British Journal of Audiology* 26, 1–14.

Davis, K. and Davis, M. (1996) Quoted in Campbell, J. and Oliver, M. *Disability Politics: Understanding our Past, Changing our Future*. London: Routledge.

Deaf Education Through Listening and Talking (DELTA) (1997) *The Right to Hear and be Heard – Raising Standards in the Education of Deaf Children*. Haverhill, Suffolk: DELTA.

Dearing, R. (1993) *The National Curriculum and its Assessment: Final Report*. London: SCAA.

De Carpentier, Br. A. L. (1995) 'Initiatives for deaf education in the third world', in UNESCO (ed.) *Making it Happen: Examples of Good Practice in Special Needs Education and Community Rehabilitation Programmes*. Paris: UNESCO.

de Feu, M. (1997) 'Mental health in children with hearing problems', *Health Visitor* 70 (7), 257.

de Monteflores, C. (1986) 'Notes on the management of difference', in Stein, T. S. and Cohen, C. J. (eds) *Contemporary Perspectives on Psychotherapy with Lesbians and Gay Men*. New York: Plenum.

Denton, D. (1976) 'The philosophy of total communication', *Supplement to British Deaf News*. Carlisle: British Deaf Association.

Department for Education and Employment (DfEE) (1997a) *Excellence for All Children: Meeting Special Educational Needs*. (Green Paper). London: HMSO.

Department for Education and Employment (DfEE) (1997b) *Excellence in Schools*. (White Paper). London: HMSO.

Department for Education and Employment (DfEE) (1997c) *The Implementation of the National Literacy Strategy*. London: HMSO.

Department of Education (DoE) (1992) *Choice and Diversity* (White Paper). London: HMSO.

Department of Education (DoEa) (1994a) *Code of Practice on the Identification and Assessment of Special Educational Needs*. London: HMSO.

Department of Education (DoE) (1994b) *Local Management of Schools*. Circular 7/94. London: HMSO.

Department of Education and Science (DES) (1965) *The Organisation of Secondary Education*.

(Circular 10/65). London: HMSO.

Department of Education and Science (DES) (1970) *Education (Handicapped Children) Act.* London: HMSO.

Department of Education and Science (DES) (1978) *Special Educational Needs: Report of the Committee of Enquiry into the Education of Handicapped Children and Young People*, (the Warnock Report). London: HMSO.

Department of Education and Science (DES) (1983) *Assessments and Statements of Special Educational Needs.* Circular 1/83. London: HMSO.

Department of Education and Science (DES) (1990) *Staffing for Pupils with Special Educational Needs.* Circular 11/90. London: HMSO.

Department of Educational Services (1990) *English in the National Curriculum*, (the Cox Report). London: HMSO.

Department of Health (1991) *Screening Children's Hearing. A Review of the Literature and the Implications of Otitis Media.* MRC Department of Health. London: HMSO.

Department of Health (1995) *Health of the Nation.* London: HMSO.

Destombes, F. (1993) 'The development and application of the IBM Speech Viewer', in Elsendoorn, B. A. G. and Coninx, F. (eds) *Interactive Learning Technology for the Deaf*, 187–196. Berlin: Springer-Verlag.

Devens J. S., Hoyer, E. A. and McCroskey, A. (1978) 'Dynamic auditory localisation in normal and learning disabled children', *Journal of American Acoustics Society* **3** (4), 172–178.

Dodd, B. and Hermelin, B. (1977) 'Phonological coding by the prelingually deaf', *Perception and Psychophysics* **21**, 413–417.

Dodd, B. and Murphy, J. (1992) 'Visual thoughts', in Campbell, R. (ed.) *Mental Lives.* Oxford: Basil Blackwell.

Dowe, S. (1995) The use of signing to access deaf students to classes in mainstream schools', *British Association of Teachers of the Deaf Magazine*, April 1995, 3.

Dowell, R. C., Blamey P. J., Clark, G. M. (1997) 'Factors affecting outcomes in children with cochlear implants', in Clark, G. M. (ed.) *Cochlear implants. Proceedings of the XVI World Congress of Otorhinolaryngology and Head and Neck Surgery.* Bologna: Monduzzi Editore, 297–303.

Downs, M. P. (1985) 'Effects of mild hearing loss on auditory processing', *Otolaryngolic Clinics of North America* **18**, 337–344.

Drake, R. (1994) 'The exclusion of disabled people from positions of power in British voluntary organisations', *Disability and Society* **9** (4), 463–82.

Drake, R. (1996) 'A critique of the role of traditional charities', in Barton, L. (ed.) *Disability and Society: Emerging Issues and Insights.* London: Longman.

Driedger, D. (1988a) 'Disabled people – organising world-wide', *Disability Today*, 28–30.

Driedger, D. (1988b) *The Last Civil Rights Movement Disabled Persons International.* London: Hurst.

Durkin, K., Shire, B., Riem, R., Crowther, R. D., Rutter, D. R. (1986) 'The social and linguistic context of early number use', *British Journal of Developmental Psychology* **4** (3), 268–288.

Dyson, A. (1993) 'Do we need special needs co-ordinators?' in Visser, J. and Upton, G. (eds), *Special Education in Britain after Warnock.* London: David Fulton Publishers.

Eatough, M. (1995) 'BATOD Survey 1994, England', *Journal of the British Association of Teachers of the Deaf*, **19** (5), 142–160.

Education Act (1981) London: HMSO.

Education Act (1989) London: HMSO.

Education Act (1992) London: HMSO.

Education Act (1993) London: HMSO.

Education Act (1994) London: HMSO.

Education Act (1996) London: HMSO.

Education Reform Act (1988) London: HMSO.

Efron, R. (1985) 'The central auditory system and issues related to hemispheric specialisation', in Pinheiro, M. L. and Musiek, C. E. (eds) *Assessment of Central Auditory Dysfunction.* Baltimore, MD: Williams and Wilkins.

Eilers, R. E. and Oller, D. K. (1994) 'Infant vocalisations and the early diagnosis of severe hearing impairment', *Journal of Pediatrics* **124**, 199–203.

Ellis, R. and Wells, C. G. (1980) 'Enabling factors in adult-child discourse', *First Language* **1**, 46–62.

Elphick, R. (1989) 'Editorial comment: some implications of the National Curriculum in the education of hearing-impaired children', *Journal of the British Association of Teachers of the Deaf* **13** (5), 119–125.

Elsendoorn, B. A. G and Coninx, F. (1993) 'Interactive learning technology for the deaf'. Proceedings of the NATO Advanced Research Workshop held in Sint Michielsgestel, The Netherlands, 4–7 June 1991. Berlin: Springer-Verlag.

Elsendoorn, B. S. A. G. and Lampropoulou, V. (1997) 'Improving perceptive communication skills with the DICTUM system: some results', in Anogianakis, G., Bühler, G. and Soede, M. (eds) *Advancement of Assistive Technology*, 5–9. Amsterdam: IOS Press.

Emanuel, J. and Ackroyd, D. (1996) 'Breaking down barriers', in Barnes, C. and Mercer, G. (eds) *Exploring the Divide: Illness and Disability.* Leeds: Disability Press.

Emmorey, K. (in press) 'The impact of sign language use on visuospatial cognition', in Marschark, M. and Clark, D. (eds), *Psychological Perspectives on Deafness*, Vol. 2. Hillsdale, New Jersey: Lawrence Erlbaum Associates.

Emmorey, K., Kosslyn, S. M., Bellugi, U. (1993). 'Visual imagery and visual-spatial language: enhanced imagery abilities in deaf and hearing ASL signers', *Cognition* **46**, 139–181.

Erting, C. (1992) *Partnership for Change: Creating New Possible Worlds for Deaf Children and their Families.* Washington, DC: Gallaudet University Press.

Erting, L. C. and Pfau, J. A. (1994) 'Becoming bilingual: facilitating English literacy development using ASL in preschool', in Snider, B. D. (ed.) *Post Milan, ASL and English Literacy: Issues, Trends and Research.* Conference proceedings. Washington, DC: Gallaudet University Press.

Erting, C. J., Prezio, C. and O'Grady-Hynes, M. (1990) 'The interactional context of deaf-mother communication', in Volterra, V. and Erting, C. J. (eds) *From Gesture to Language in Hearing and Deaf Children.* Berlin: Springer-Verlag.

Erting, L. and Stone, R. (1992) 'Deaf and Hearing Team Teaching', *Conference Proceedings: Bilingual Considerations in the Education of Deaf Students.* Gallaudet University, Washington DC: Gallaudet University Press.

Evans, L. (1982) *Total Communication: Structure and Strategy.* Washington, DC: Gallaudet College Press.

Ewing, I. R. and Ewing, A. W. G. (1944) 'The ascertainment of deafness in infancy and early childhood', *Journal of Laryngology* **59** 309–338.

Ewoldt, C. (1985) 'A descriptive study of the developing literacy of young hearing impaired children', *Volta Review* **87**, 109–126.

Feigin, J. A., Kopun, J. K., Stelmachowicz, P. G., Gorga, M. P. (1989) 'Probe-microphone measurements of ear canal sound pressure levels in infants and children', *Ear and Hearing* **10**, 254–258.

Ferman, L., Vershuure, J., Van Zanten, B. (1993) 'Impaired speech perception in noise in patients with a normal audiogram', *Audiology* **32**, 49–54.

Finkelstein, V. (1996) in Campbell, J. and Oliver, M. (eds) *Disability Politics: Understanding our Past, Changing our Future.* London: Routledge.

Fish, J. and Evans, J. (1996) *Managing Special Education: Codes, Charters and Competition.*

Buckingham: Open University Press.

Fitz-Gibbon, C. T. (1996) *Monitoring Education: Indicators, Quality and Effectiveness*. London: Cassell.

Fjermedal, O. and Laukli, E. (1989) 'Pediatric auditory brainstem response and pure-tone audiometry: threshold comparisons', *Scandinavian Audiology* **18**, 105–111.

Fletcher, L. (1987) *A Language for Ben*. London: Souvenir Press.

Flexer, C. (1994) *Facilitating Hearing and Listening in Young Children*. San Diego, California: Singular Publishing Group.

Fortnum, H., Davis, A., Butler, A., Stevens, J. (1996) *Health Service Implications of Changes in Aetiology and Referral Patterns of Hearing Impaired Children in Trent 1985–93. Report to Trent Health*. Nottingham and Sheffield: MRC Institute of Hearing Research and Trent Health.

Foster, S. (1996) 'Communication experiences of deaf people: an ethnographic account', in Parasnis, I. (ed.) *Cultural and Language Diversity*. Cambridge: Cambridge University Press.

Fraser, B. (1996) *Supporting Children with Hearing Impairment in Mainstream Schools*. Franklin Watts.

Freeman, R., Carbin, C., Boese, R. (1981) *Can't your Child Hear?* London: Croom Helm.

Freeman, R. D., Carbin, C. F., Hastings, J. O. (1975) 'Psychosocial problems of deaf children and their families: a comparative study', *American Annals of the Deaf*, **120**, 275–304.

French, S. (1993) 'Disability, impairment or something in between', in Shakespeare, P., Atkinson, D. and French, S. (eds) *Reflecting on Research Practice: Issues in Health and Social Welfare*. Buckingham : Open University Press.

Frowein, H. W., Smoorenburg, G. F., Pijfers, L., Schinkel, D. (1991) 'Improved speech recognition through video telephony: experiments with the hard of hearing', *IEEE Journal on Selected Areas in Communications* **9**, 611–616.

Fulcher, G. (1989) *Disabling Policies? A Comparative Approach to Education Policy and Disability*. East Sussex: Falmer Press.

Furth, H. G. (1966) *Thinking Without Language: Psychological Implications of Deafness*. New York: Free Press.

Galambos, R., Wilson, M. J., Silva, P. D. (1994) 'Identifying hearing loss in the intensive care nursery: a 20 year summary'. *Journal of the American Academy of Audiology* **5**, 151–162.

Gallaway, C. and Johnston, M. (1996) 'Negative feedback in language addressed to hearing impaired children', in Aldridge, M. (ed.) *Child Language*. Clevedon: Multilingual Matters.

Gallaway, C. and Lewis, S. (1993) 'Talking to children. Part One: Fact and fiction in the research'. *Journal of the British Association of Teachers of the Deaf* **17** (5), 137–42.

Gallaway, C. and Richards, B. J. (eds) (1994) *Input and Interaction in Language Acquisition*. Cambridge: Cambridge University Press.

Gallaway, C. and Woll, B. (1994) 'Interaction and childhood deafness', in Gallaway, C. and Richards, B. J. (eds) *Input and Interaction in Language Acquisition*. Cambridge: Cambridge University Press.

Garcia, O. and Baker, C. (eds) (1995) *Policy and Practice in Bilingual Education: Extending the Foundations*. Clevedon: Multilingual Matters.

Gathercole, S. E. and Baddeley, A. D. (1993). *Working Memory and Language*. Hove: Lawrence Erlbaum Associates.

Gdowski, B. S., Sanzer, D. D., Decker, T. N. (1986) 'Otitis media: effect on a child's learning' *Academic Therapy* **21** (3) 283–291.

Geers, A. E., Moog, J., Schick, B. (1984) 'Acquisition of spoken and signed English by profoundly deaf children', *Journal of Speech and Hearing Disorders* **49**, 378–388.

Geers, A. E. and Moog, J. (1989) 'Factors predictive of the development of literacy in profoundly hearing-impaired adolescents', *Volta Review* **91**, 69–86.

Geers, A. E. and Schick, B. (1988) 'Acquisition of spoken and signed English by hearing-impaired children of hearing-impaired or hearing parents', *Journal of Speech and Hearing Disorders* **53**, 136–143.

Gerber, S. E. (1990) 'Review of high risk register for congenital or early onset deafness', *British Journal of Audiology* **24**, 347–356.

Gibson, W. P .R. (1997) Graham Fraser Memorial Lecture.

Gill, D., Mayor, B., Blair, M. (1992) *Racism and Education: Structures and Strategies*. London: Sage Publications.

Gillham, B. (1986) 'Cerebral palsy', in Gillham, B. (ed.) *Handicapping Conditions in Children*. London: Routledge.

Gleason, J. B. (ed.) (1997) *The Development of Language*, 4th edn. Needham Heights, NJ: Allyn and Bacon.

Goode, D. (1994) *Quality of Life as International Disability Policy: Implications for European Research*. Paper prepared for the first European Conference on Quality of Life, Copenhagen, December 1994.

Gravel, J. S., Chute, P. M. (1996) 'Transposition hearing aids for children', in Bess, F. H., Gravel, J. S. and Tharpe, A. M. (eds) *Amplification for Children with Auditory Deficits*. Nashville, Tennessee: Bill Wilkerson Press.

Gravel, J. S. and Wallace, I. F. (1992) 'Listening and language at four years of age: effects of early OME' *Journal of Speech and Hearing Research* **35**, June 1992, 588–595.

Greenberg, M. T. and Kusche, C. A. (1987) 'Cognitive, personal and social development of deaf children and adolescents', in Wang, M. C., Reynolds M. C., Walberb, H. J. (eds) *Handbook of Special Education: Research and Practice, Vol 3, Low incidence conditions*. New York: Pergamon Press.

Gregory, S. (1976, 1995) *The Deaf Child and His Family*. London: George Allen and Unwin, republished as *Deaf Children and their Families*. Cambridge: Cambridge University Press.

Gregory, S. (1991) 'Challenging motherhood: mothers and their deaf children', in Phoenix, A. and Lloyd, E. (eds) *Motherhood, Meaning, Practices and Ideology*. London: Sage Publications.

Gregory, S. (1992) 'The language and culture of deaf people: educational implications', *Language and Education* **6** (2), 183–197.

Gregory, S. (1996) 'Signs across the curriculum: Maths and Science', *Laserbeam* **27**, 3–8.

Gregory, S. and Barlow, S. (1989) 'Interactions between deaf babies and their deaf and hearing mothers', in Woll, B. (ed.) *Language Development and Sign Language*. Bristol: International Sign Linguistics Association.

Gregory, S., Bishop, J., Sheldon, L. (1995) *Deaf Young People and Their Families*. Cambridge: Cambridge University Press.

Gregory, S. and Mogford, K. (1981) 'Early language development in deaf children', in Woll, B., Kyle, J.G., Deuchar, M. (eds) *Perspectives on BSL and Deafness*. London: Croom Helm.

Gregory, S. and Pickersgill, M. (1997) 'Towards a model of bilingual education for deaf children', *Laserbeam*, Spring **28**, 3–8.

Gregory, S., Smith, S., Wells, A. (1997) 'Language and identity in sign bilingual deaf children', *Deafness and Education* **21** (3), 31–38.

Grievlink, E. H., Peters, S. A. F., van Bon, W. H. J., Schilder, A. G. M. (1993) 'The effects of early bilateral otitis media with effusion on language ability: a prospective cohort study', *Journal of Speech and Hearing Research* **36**, October 1993, 1004–1012.

Griggs, M. (in preparation) *Deafness and Mental Health within the Deaf Community*. PhD thesis to be submitted to the University of Bristol.

Haggard, M. (1990) 'Hearing screening in children – state of the art(s)', *Archives of Disease in Childhood* **65**, 1193–1198.

Haggard, M. P., Birkin, J. A., Pringle, D. P. (1994) 'Consequences of otitis media for speech and language', in McCormick, B. (ed.) *Paediatric Audiology*. London: Whurr Publishers.

Haggard, M. and Hughes, E. (1991) *Screening Children's Hearing: A Review of the Literature and the Implications of Otitis Media.* MRC Department of Health, London: HMSO.

Hall, J. (1992) *Handbook of Auditory Evoked Responses.* Needham Heights, NJ: Allyn and Bacon.

Hamilton, F. M. W. and Richards, I. D. G. (1968) 'The at risk register in Glasgow', *Medical Officer* **119** 201–202.

Hansen, B. (1990) 'Trends in the progress towards bilingual education', in Prillwitz, S. and Volhaber, T. (eds) *Sign Language Research and Application*, 51–62. Hamburg: Signum Press.

Hanson, V. L. (1982a) 'Phonology and reading: evidence from profoundly deaf readers', in Shankweiler, D. and Libermane, P. (eds), *Phonology and Reading Disability.* Michigan: University of Michigan Press.

Hanson, V. L. (1982b) 'Short-term recall by deaf signers of ASL: implications for encoding strategy for ordered recall', *Journal of Experimental Psychology* **8**, 572–583.

Harris, M. (1992) *Language Experience and Early Language Development.* Hove: Psychology Press.

Harris, M., Clibbens, J., Chasin, J., Tibbitts, R. (1989) 'The social context of early sign language development', *First Language* **9**, 81–97.

Harris, M. and Mohay, H. (1997) 'Learning to look in the right place: a comparison of attentional behaviour in deaf children with deaf and hearing mothers', *Journal of Deaf Studies and Deaf Education* **2** (2), 95–103.

Harrison, D. (1980) 'Natural oralism – a description', *Journal of the British Association of Teachers of the Deaf*, Magazine, **4** (4).

Harrison, D. R. (1993) 'Promoting the educational and personal development of deaf children in an integrated setting', *Journal of the British Association of Teachers of the Deaf* **17** (2), 29–35.

Harsten, G., Nettelbladt, U., Schalen, L., Kalm, O., Prellner, K. (1993) 'Language development in children with recurrent acute otitis media during the first three years of life. Follow-up study from birth to seven years of age', *Journal of Laryngology and Otology* **107**, May 1993, 407–412.

Hawkins, D. B. and Schum, D. (1985) 'Some effects of FM system coupling on hearing aid characteristics', *Journal of Speech and Hearing Disorders* **50**, 132–141.

Health Advisory Service (1995) *Thematic Review of Services to Deaf People.* London: Department of Health (unpublished).

Hedley-Williams, A., Tharpe, A. M., Bess, F. M. (1996) 'Fitting hearing aids in the pediatric population: a survey of practice procedures', in Bess, F. H., Gravel, J. S., Tharpe, A. M. (eds) *Amplification for Children with Auditory Deficits.* Nashville, Tennessee: Bill Wilkerson Press.

Hegarty, S. (1993) 'Reviewing the literature on integration', *European Journal of Special Needs Education* **8** (3), 194–200.

Hegarty, S., Pocklington, K., Lucas, D. (1982) *Integration in Action: Case Studies in the Education of Pupils with Special Educational Needs.* Windsor: NFER-Nelson.

Heider, F. and Heider, G. M. (1941) 'Studies in the Psychology of the Deaf' (No 2), in Daskiell, J. F. (ed.) *Psychological Monographs*, **53** (5), 131.

Heineman, R. (1997) *Literacy Development in Deaf Children: the Structure of Interaction between Adults and Deaf Children during Reading.* Unpublished thesis, Graduate School of Education, University of Bristol.

Helander, M. (1988) *Handbook of Human–Computer Interaction.* Amsterdam: North-Holland.

Her Majesty's Inspectors (1987) *The Education of Pupils with Severe Hearing Impairment in Special Schools and Units in Scotland. A Report by Her Majesty's Inspectors of Schools.* Edinburgh: HMSO.

Herman, R. (in press) 'Assessing signing', *Journal of the British Association of Teachers of the Deaf.*

Herman, R., Woll, B., Holmes, S. (in preparation) *An Assessment Tool for British Sign Language.*

Herr, S. (1993) 'Special education as a human and legal right', in Mittler, P., Brouillette, R., Harris, D. (eds) *Special Needs Education World Yearbook of Education 1993.* London: Kegan Paul.

Higgins, P. (1980) *Outsiders in a Hearing World: A Sociology of Deafness.* London: Sage Publications.

Hind, S. E., Haggard, M., Greenwood, D. C., Davis, A. (1996) 'Impact of hearing loss from early infancy', *XXIII International Ccongress of Audiology Abstracts* June, 1996.

Hindley, P. A., Hill, P. D., McGuigan, S., Kitson, N. (1994) 'Psychiatric disorder in deaf and hearing impaired children and young people: a prevalance study', *Journal of Child Psychology and Psychiatry* **35** (5), 917–934.

Hoff-Ginsberg, E. (1997) *Language Development.* California: Brooks/Cole Publishing Company.

Holcomb T. K. (1996) 'Social assimilation of deaf high school students: the role of the school environment', in Parasnis, I. (ed.) *Cultural and Language Diversity and the Deaf Experience.* Cambridge: Cambridge University Press.

Holmes, S. (1997) 'The development of an assessment for British Sign Language – an account of work in progress', *Deafness and Education* **21** (3), 62–63.

Howarth, I. E. (1958) 'Screening tests of hearing in pre-school children with particular reference to selective testing', *Medical Officer* **100**, 307–308.

Hughes, G., Green, C., Silo, J. (1997) 'Deaf teachers of the deaf; experiences of training and employment', *Laserbeam* **29** 4–13.

Humphries, B. (1957) 'The ascertainment and management of defective hearing in the very young', *Public Health* **71** (6), 221–228.

Huntington, A. and Watton, F. (1981) 'Language and interaction in the classroom', *Journal of the British Association of Teachers of the Deaf* **5** (6), 162–173.

Husband, C. (1991) '"Race", conflictual politics and anti-racist social work', in CCETSW (ed.) *Anti-racist Social Work: Setting the Context for Social Change.* London: Central Council for Education and Training in Social Work.

Hyde, M. L., Malizia, K., Riko, K., Alberti, P. W. (1991)'Audiometric estimation error with ABR in high risk infants', *Acta Otolaryngologica* **111** (2), 212–219.

Ingall, B. I. (1980) 'A structured oral programme', *Journal of the British Association of Teachers of the Deaf* **4** (4).

Jacobson, R. (1995) 'Allocating two languages as a key feature of a bilingual methodology', in Garcia, O. and Baker, C. (eds) *Policy and Practice in Bilingual Education: Extending the Foundations.* Clevedon: Multilingual Matters.

Jerger, S., Martin, C., Jerger, J. (1987) 'Specific auditory perceptual dysfunction in learning disabled children' *Ear and Hearing* **3**, 78–86.

Jirsa, R. E. (1992) P3 'AERP's in children', *Journal of Speech and Hearing Research* **35**, 903–912.

Johnson, R., Liddell, S., Erting, C. (1989) 'Unlocking the curriculum: principles for achieving access in deaf education', *Working Paper 89–3* .Washington DC: Gallaudet Research Institute.

Jones, L. and Pullen, G. (1989) 'Inside we are all equal: A European social policy survey of people who are deaf', in Barton, L. (ed.), *Disability and Dependency.* East Sussex: Falmer Press.

Jones, T. and Johnson, J. (1985) 'Characteristics of programs for multiply handicapped hearing impaired students'. *Paper presented at Convention of American Instructors of the Deaf.* Florida: St Augustine.

Jordan, King I. (1986) 'The growth of Total Communication in the United Kingdom', in Montgomery, G. *Beyond Hobsons Choice: The Appraisal of Methods of Teaching Language to Deaf Children.* Edinburgh: Scottish Workshop Publications.

Joutselainen, M. (1991) *WFD Survey of Deaf People in Developing Countries.* Helsinki: World Federation of the Deaf.

Joutselainen, M. (1993) 'Deaf people in the developing world', in Mittler, P,. Brouillette, R., Harris, D. (eds), *Special Needs Education World Year Book 1993.* London: Kegan Paul.

Karchmer, M. (1985) 'A demographic perspective', in Cherow, E., Matkin, N., Trybus, R. (eds) *Hearing Impaired Youths with Developmental Disabilities.* Washington, DC: Gallaudet College Press.

Kauppinen, L. (1988) 'The deaf in Finland: status and services', *WFD Proceedings Xth World Congress*, 185–187. Helsinki: World Federation of the Deaf.

Keith, R. W. (1977) *Central Auditory Dysfunction*. New York: Grune and Stratton.

Keith R. W. (1981) *Central Auditory and Language Disorders in Children*. San Diego: College Hill Press.

Keith R. W. (1994) ACPT: *Auditory Continuous Performance Test*. San Antonio, The Psychological Corporation: Harcourt Brace and Co.

Keith R. W. (1995) *SCAN: A Screening Test for Auditory Processing Disorder*. San Antonio. The Psychological Corporation: Harcourt Brace and Co.

Kemp, D. T. (1978) 'Stimulated acoustic emissions from within the human auditory system', *Journal of the Acoustical Society of America* **64**, 1386–1391.

Kidd, D. H. (1991) 'A language analysis of mathematical word problems: no wonder they are so difficult', *Teaching English to Deaf Second Language Students* **9** (1), 14–18.

Kirk, B., Kyle, J. G., Ackerman, J. (1990) 'Measuring Sign Language development in deaf school children', in Kyle, J. G. (ed.) *Deafness and Sign Language Into the 1990s*. Bristol: Deaf Studies Trust.

Kitson, N. and Fry, R. (1990) 'Prelingual deafness and psychiatry', *British Journal of Hospital Medicine* **44**, 353–356.

Klima, E. S. and Bellugi, U. (1979) *The Signs of Language*. London: Harvard University Press.

Klopping, H. (1972) 'Language understanding of deaf students under three auditory-visual stimulus conditions', *American Annals of the Deaf* **117** (3), 389–396.

Kluwin, T. N. (1993) 'Cumulative effects of mainstreaming on the achievement of deaf adolescents', *Exceptional Children* **60** (1), 73–81.

Kluwin T. N. and Gaustad, M. G. (1992) 'How family factors influence school achievement', in Kluwin, T. N., Moores, D. F., Gaustad, M. G. (eds), *Toward Defining Effective Public School Programs for Deaf Students*. New York: Teachers College Press.

Kluwin, T. N. and Moores, D. F. (1985) 'The effects of integration on the mathematics achievement of hearing-impaired adolescents', *Exceptional Children* **52** (2), 153–160.

Kluwin, T. N. and Moores, D. F. (1989) 'Mathematics achievement of hearing impaired adolescents in different placements', *Exceptional Children* **55** (4), 327–335.

Kluwin, T. N., Moores, D. F., Gaustad, M. G. (eds) (1992) *Toward Defining Effective Public School Programs for Deaf Students*. New York: Teachers College Press.

Knight, P. (1996) 'Deaf children in a BSL nursery – who is doing what?' in Knight, P. and Swanwick, R. (eds) *Bilingualism and the Education of Deaf Children*. Leeds: University Press.

Knox, E. G. and Mahon, D. F. (1970) 'Evaluation of "Infant at Risk" registers', *Archives of Disease in Childhood* **45**, 634–639.

Konstantares, N., Webster, C., Oxman, J. (1977) 'Manual language acquisition and its influence on other areas of functioning in four autistic and autistic like children', *Journal of Child Psychology and Psychiatry* **20**, 337–350.

Krakow, R. A. and Hanson, V. L. (1985) 'Deaf signers and serial recall in the visual modality: memory for signs, fingerspelling and print', *Memory and Cognition* **13** (3), 265–272.

Kruger, B. and Ruben, J. A. (1987) 'The acoustic properties of the infant ear', *Actaotolaryngologica*. (Stockholm) **103**, 577–585.

Kumsang, M. (1987) 'The 1981 Education Act: a survey of effects on policy and provision for hearing-impaired pupils in the ordinary school', *Journal of the British Association of Teachers of the Deaf* **11** (4), 109–117.

Kyle, J. (1990) *From Gesture to Sign and Speech*. Final Report to the Economic and Social Research Council. University of Bristol.

Kyle, J. G., Ackerman, J., Woll, B. (1987) 'Early mother–infant interaction: language and pre-language in deaf families', in Griffiths, P., Mills, A., Local, J. (eds) *Proceedings of the Child Language Seminar*, 163–178. Clevedon: Multilingual Matters.

Kyle, J. and Woll, B. (1985) *Sign Language: the Study of Deaf People and their Language*. Cambridge: Cambridge University Press.

Ladd, P. (1991) 'Making plans for Nigel: The erosion of identity by mainstreaming', in Taylor, G. and Bishop, J. (eds) *Being Deaf: The Experience of Deafness*. Buckingham: Open University.

Lane, H. (1984) *When the Mind Hears: A History of the Deaf*. New York: Random House.

Lane, H. (1988) *Paternalism and Deaf People – An Open Letter to Madam UMUVYEYI*. London: Royal National Institute for the Deaf, Occasional Papers.

Lane, H. (1992) *The Mask of Benevolence: Displaying the Deaf Community*. New York: Alfred Knopf.

Lane, H., Hoffmeister, R., Bahan, B. (1996) *A Journey into the Deaf-World*. San Diego, CA: Dawn Sign Press.

Laurie, H. (1966) 'An investigation into the links between linguistic ability, impulsivity, rigid and concrete thinking and childhood deprivation in a life population'. *British Psychological Society Proceedings*. London: BPS.

Lawlor, S. (1988) *Away with LEAs: ILEA Abolition as a Pilot*. London: Centre for Policy Studies.

Lawton, D. (1994) *The Tory Mind on Education 1979–94*. East Sussex: Falmer Press.

Lederberg, A. R. (1991) 'Social interaction among deaf pre-schoolers', *American Annals of the Deaf* 1 (36), 53–59.

Lederberg, A. R. (1993) 'The impact of child deafness on social relationships', in Marschark, M. and Clark, D. (eds), *Psychological Perspectives on Deafness*. Hillsdale, NJ: Lawrence Erlbaum.

Lederberg, A. R. and Mobley, C. E. (1990) 'The effect of hearing impairment on the quality of attachment and mother–toddler interaction', *Child Development* 61, 1596–1604.

Lederberg, A. R., Rosenblatt, V., Vandell, D. L., Chapin, S. L. (1987) 'Temporary and long term friendships in hearing and deaf pre-schoolers', *Merrill-Palmer Quarterly* 33 (4), 515–533.

Leeds Local Education Authority (1995) *Deaf and Hearing-Impaired Service (DAHISS) Policy Statement*. Leeds LEA Publications.

Leigh, I., Robbins, S. J., Welkowitz, J., Bond, R. N. (1989) 'Towards greater understanding of depression in deaf individuals', *American Annals of the Deaf*, October, 249–54.

Lenneberg, E. H. (1967) *Biological Foundations of Language*. New York: Wiley.

Lewis, D., Feigin, J. A., Karasek, A., Stelmachowicz, P. G (1991) 'Evaluation and assessment of FM systems', *Ear and Hearing* 12 (4), 268–280.

Lewis, S. (1996) 'The reading achievements of a group of severely and profoundly hearing-impaired school leavers educated within a natural aural approach', *Journal of the British Association of Teachers of the Deaf* 20 (1), 1–7.

Lewis, S. and Lyon, D. (1997) 'Listening/learning devices: management', in McCracken, W. and Laoide-Kemp, S. (eds) *Audiology in Education*. London: Whurr Publishers.

Lewis, S. and Richards, S. (1988) 'The early stages of language development: a natural aural approach', *Journal of the British Association of Teachers of the Deaf* 12 (2) 33–38.

Lieven, E. V. M. (1994) 'Crosslinguistic and crosscultural aspects of language addressed to children', in Gallaway, C. and Richards, B. J. (eds) *Input and Interaction in Language Acquisition*. Cambridge: Cambridge University Press.

Lindquist, B. (1995) 'Standard rules – a new instrument for participation', *World Federation of the Deaf News* 1 (4).

Lister, C., Leach, C., Wesencraft, K. (1988) 'Sequence in hearing impaired children's development of concepts', *British Journal of Educational Psychology* 58, 127–133.

Logan, K., Mayberry, M., Fletcher, J. (1996) 'The short-term memory of profoundly deaf people for words, signs, and abstract spatial stimuli', *Applied Cognitive Psychology* 10, 105–119.

Loncke, F., Quertinmont, S., Ferreyra, P. (1990) 'Deaf children in schools: more or less native signers?', in Prillwitx, S. and Vollhaber, T. (eds) *Current trends in European Sign Language Research. Proceedings of the 3rd European Congress on Sign Language Research*, 163–178.

London Borough of Bromley (1994) *Marathon Dictionary of Science Signs*. Bromley: London Borough of Bromley.

London Borough of Bromley (1997) *Marathon Sign Language Dictionary*, 3rd edn. Bromley: London Borough of Bromley.

Lous, J. (1995) 'Otitis media and reading achievement: a review', *International Journal of Pediatric Otorhinolaryngology* 32, 105–121.

Lunt, I. and Evans, J. (1994) 'Dilemmas in special educational needs: some effects of local management of schools', in Riddell, S. and Brown, S. (eds) *Special Educational Needs Policy in the 1990s: Warnock in the Marketplace*. London: Routledge.

Lunzer, E. and Gardner, K. (1984) *Learning from the Written Word*. Edinburgh: Oliver and Boyd for the Schools Council.

Lustig, L. R., Leake, P. A., Snyder, R. L., Rebscher, S. J. (1994) 'Changes in the cat cochlear nucleus following neonatal deafening and chronic intracochlear electrical stimulation', *Hearing Research* 74, 29–37.

Luterman, D. (1984) *Counselling the Communicatively Disordered and their Families*. Boston, Mass: Little, Brown.

Luterman, D. (1987) *Deafness in the Family*. Boston, Mass: College Hill Publication.

Luterman, D. M. and Ross, M. (1991) *When your Child is Deaf – a Guide for Parents*. Maryland: York Press.

Lynas, W. (1986) *Integrating the Handicapped into Ordinary Schools: A Study of Hearing-Impaired Pupils*. London: Croom Helm.

Lynas, W. (1994) *Communication Options in the Education of Deaf Children*. London: Whurr Publishers.

Lynas, W., Lewis, S., Hopwood, V. (1997) 'Supporting the education of deaf children in mainstream schools', *Deafness and Education* 21 (2), 41–45.

Lynas, W. and Turner, S. (1995) *Young Children with Sensori-neural Hearing Loss from Ethnic Minority Families*. Manchester: Centre for Audiology, Education of the Deaf and Speech Pathology.

Lynn, G. and Gilroy, J. (1972) 'Neuroaudiological correlates in cerebral hemisphere lesions', *Audiology* 7, 66–75.

Maclure, S. (1988) *Education Reformed*. Sevenoaks: Hodder & Stoughton.

MacSweeney, M., Campbell, R., Donlan, C. (1996) 'Varieties of short-term memory coding in deaf teenagers', *Journal of Deaf Studies and Deaf Education* 1(4), 249–262.

Maestas y Moores, J. (1980) 'Early language environment: interactions of deaf parents and their infants', *Sign Language Studies* 26, 1–13.

Mahon, M. (1997) *Conversational Interaction Between Young Deaf Children and their Families in Homes Where English is not the First Language*. Unpublished PhD thesis, University of London.

Mahshie, S. M. (1995) *Educating Deaf Children Bilingually*. Washington, DC: Gallaudet University Press.

Marcotte, A. C. and Morere, D. A. (1990) 'Speech lateralization in deaf populations: evidence for a developmental critical period', *Journal of Brain and Language* 39, 134–152.

Markides, A. (1986) 'Age of fitting of hearing aids and speech intelligibility', *British Journal of Audiology* 20, 165–168.

Markides, A. (1989) 'Integration: the speech intelligibility, friendship and associations of hearing-impaired children in secondary schools', *Journal of the British Association of Teachers of the Deaf* 13, 63–72.

Marschark, M. (1993) *Psychological Development of Deaf Children*. New York: Oxford University Press.

Marschark, M. (1997) *Raising and Educating a Deaf Child*. Oxford: Oxford University Press.

Marschark, M. and Clark, D. (in press) *Psychological Perspectives on Deafness*, Vol. 2. Hillsdale, New Jersey: Lawrence Erlbaum Associates.

Marschark, M. and Everhart, V. S. (1997), 'Relations of language and cognition: what do deaf children tell us?' in Marschark, M., Siple, P., Lillo-Martin, D., Campbell, R., *et al.* (eds) *Relations of Language and Thought: The View from Sign Language and Deaf Children*. New York: Oxford University Press.

Marx, G. and McAdam, D. (1994) *Collective Behaviour and Social Movements*. New Jersey: Prentice Hall.

Mason, M. (1996) Quoted in Campbell, J. and Oliver, M. (eds) *Disability Politics: Understanding our Past, Changing our Future*. London: Routledge.

Mason, S. (1988) 'Automated system for screening hearing using the auditory brainstem response', *British Journal of Audiology* 22, 211–213

Mason, S., Davis, A., Wood, S., Farnsworth, A. (1997) 'Field sensitivity of targeted neonatal hearing screening using the Nottingham ABR screener'. *Abstracts from the 10th Annual Workshop on Hearing Screening in Children*. Nottingham: MRC Institute of Hearing Research.

Matkin, N. (1994) 'Strategies for enhancing multidisciplinary working', in Rousch, J. and Matkin, D. (eds) *Infants and Toddlers with Hearing Loss*. Baltimore: York Press.

Maxwell, M. (1992) 'Simultaneous communication: the state of the art and proposals for change', in Stokoe, W. (ed.) *Simultaneous Communication, ASL, and Other Classroom Communication Modes*, 67–160. Burtonsville, MD: Linstok Press.

Mayberry, R. I. (1993). 'First-language acquisition after childhood differs from second-language acquisition: the case of American Sign Language', *Journal of Speech and Hearing Research* 36, 1258–1270.

Mayberry, R. I. and Eichen, E. B. (1991) 'The long-lasting advantage of learning sign language in childhood: another look at the critical period for language acquisition', *Journal of Memory and Language* 30, 486–512.

Mayer, C. (1996) 'Can the linguistic interdependence theory support a bilingual–bicultural model of literacy education for deaf students?' *Journal of Deaf Studies and Deaf Education* 1 (2), 93–107.

Mazurek, K. and Winzer, M. (1994) *Comparative Studies in Special Education*. Washington, DC: Gallaudet University Press.

McConkey, A. (1986) 'Facilitating language comprehension in young hearing-impaired children', *Topics in Language Disorders* 6, 12–24.

McCormick, B. (1983) 'Hearing screening by health visitors; a critical appraisal of the distraction test', *Health Visitor* 56, 449–451.

McCormick, B. (1990) Commentary on: Scanlon, P. and Bamford, J. (1990) 'Early identification of hearing loss: screening and surveillance methods', *Archives of Disease in Childhood* 65, 484–485.

McCormick, B. (1997) 'Thirty years of the British Journal of Audiology: Guest Editorial: Paediatric audiology and cochlear implantation in the UK taking off in the fast lane', *British Journal of Audiology* 31 (5), 303–308.

McCracken, W. (1997) 'Interdisciplinary working across multiple agencies, the case of multiply handicapped deaf children as an example of need'. *Paper presented at the 3rd European Conference on Audiology*. Prague.

McCracken, W. and Laoide-Kemp, S. (1997) *Audiology in Education*. London: Whurr Publishers.

McCracken, W. and Sutherland, H. (1991) *Deaf Ability Not Disability*. Clevedon: Multilingual Matters.

McCroskey, R. L. and Keith, R. W. (1996) *AFT-R Auditory Fusion Test – Revised*. Distributed by Auditec, St. Louis.

McGee, T. and Kraus, N. (1996) 'Auditory development as reflected by the middle latency response', *Ear and Hearing* 17, 419–429.

McLoughlin, M. G. (1987) *A History of Deaf Education in England*. Liverpool: G. M. McLoughlin.

McNeill, D. (1966) 'Developmental psycholinguistics', in Smith, F. and Miller, G. (eds) *The Genesis of Language*. Cambridge, Mass.: MIT Press.

Mead, M. (1964) 'Vicissitudes of the study of the Total Communication process', in Sebeok, T. (ed.) *Approaches to Semiotics*. The Hague: Mouton.

Meadow, K. (1980) *Deafness and Child Development*. Berkeley: California Press.

Meadow, K. P. (1976) 'Personality and social development of deaf people', *Journal of Rehabilitation of the Deaf* 9, 1–12.

Meadow-Orlans, K. P. (1990) 'Research on developmental aspects of deafness', in Moores, D. F. and Meadow-Orlans, K. P. (eds) *Educational and Developmental Aspects of Deafness*. Washington, DC: Gallaudet University Press.

Meadow-Orlans, K. P. (1997) 'Effects of mother and infant hearing status on interactions at twelve and eighteen months', *Journal of Deaf Studies and Deaf Education* 2 (1), 26–36.

Meherali, R. (1985) 'The deaf Asian child and his family'. Unpublished MA thesis, University of Nottingham, cited in *Issues in Deafness, Unit 5*. (1991). Buckingham: Open University Press.

Meherali, R. (1994) 'Being black and deaf', in Laurenzi, C. and Hindley, P. (eds) *Keep Deaf Children in Mind: Current Issues in Mental Health*. London: NDCS.

Messer, D. J. (1994) *The Development of Communication: From Social Interaction to Language*. New York: Wiley.

Meyer, M. F. (1921) *The Psychology of the Other One*. Columbia, MO: The Missouri Book Co.

Miles, S. (1995) *Partnership with Disabled People, Parents and Community Lessons from Southern Africa*. Paper given at the International Special Education Congress, Birmingham, UK.

Mittler, P. (1993) 'Special needs at the crossroads', in Visser, J. and Upton, G. (eds) *Special Education in Britain After Warnock*. London: David Fulton Publishers.

Mittler, P. (1995) 'Special need education: an international perspective', *British Journal of Special Education* 22 (3), 105–9.

Mobley, M. (1987) *Making Ourselves Clearer: Readability in the GCSE*. London: Secondary Examinations Council.

Modood, T. (1994) *Changing Ethnic Identities*. London: Policy Studies Institute.

Mogford, K. and Gregory, S. (1982) *The Development of Communication Skills in Young Deaf Children: Picture-Book Reading with Mother*. Paper given to the Psycholinguistics and Language Pathology Colloquium, University of Newcastle.

Montanini-Manfredi, M. (1993) 'The emotional development of deaf children', in Marschark, M. and Clark, M. D. (eds) *Psychological Perspectives on Deafness*. New Jersey: Lawrence Erlbaum Associates.

Montgomery, J. (1986) 'The normalisation of language development and emotional behaviour through Total Communication', in Montgomery, G. (ed.) *Beyond Hobson's Choice: The Appraisal of Methods of Teaching Language to Deaf Children*. Edinburgh: Scottish Workshop Publications.

Moores, D. F. (1996) *Educating the Deaf: Psychology, Principles and Practices*. Boston, Mass.: Houghton Mifflin.

Moores, D. and Meadow-Orlans, K. (1990) *Educational and Developmental Aspects of Deafness*. Washington, DC: Gallaudet University Press.

Moorhead, D. (1995) 'Knowing who I am', in *Issues in Deafness, Unit 10*. Buckingham: Open University Press.

Morgan, G. (1996) 'Spatial anaphoric mechanisms in British Sign Language', in Botely, S., Grass,

J., McEnery, T., Wilson, A. (eds) *Approaches to Discourse Anaphora 8*. University of Lancaster Press.

Morgan, J. L. and Demuth, K. (eds) (1996) *Signal to Syntax: Bootstrapping from Speech to Grammar in Early Acquisition*. Mahwah, NJ: Lawrence Erlbaum Associates.

Morgan-Redshaw, M., Wilgosh, L., Bibby, M. A. (1990) 'The parental experience of mothers of adolescence with hearing impairment', *American Annals of the Deaf* 135, 293–298.

Morris, T. (1986) 'The effect of education/communication mode on aspects of the deaf child's development', in Montgomery, G. (ed.) *Beyond Hobson's Choice: the Appraisal of Methods of Teaching Language to Deaf Children*. Edinburgh: Scottish Workshop Publications.

Morrison, G. and Zetlin, A. (1988) 'Perceptions of communication, cohesion and adaptability in families of adolescents with and without learning handicaps', *Journal of Abnormal and Child Psychology* 16, 675–685.

Mortimore, P., Sammons, P., Stoll, L., Lewis, D., *et al.* (1988) *School Matters: The Junior Years*. Wells: Open Books.

Musselman, C. and Churchill, A. (1993) 'Maternal conversational control and the development of deaf children: a test of the stage hypothesis', *First Language* 13, 271–90.

Myklebust, H. R. and Bruton, A. (1953) 'Towards a new understanding of the deaf child', *American Annals of the Deaf* 98, 496–99.

Nabalek, A. and Nabalek, I. (1985) 'Room acoustics and speech perception', in Katz, J. (ed.) *Handbook of Clinical Audiology*. Baltimore: Williams and Wilkins.

Naeem, Z. and Newton, V. (1996) 'The prevalence of sensori-neural hearing loss in Asian children', *British Journal of Audiology* 30 (5), 332–340.

Narula A. A. and Mason S. M. (1988) 'Selective dysacusis – a preliminary report', *Journal of the Royal Society of Medicine* 81, 338–339.

National Children's Bureau (1987) *Investing in the future*. London: National Children's Bureau.

National Council of Teachers of the Deaf (1957) 'The teaching of mathematics in schools for the deaf', *Teacher of the Deaf* 15 (2), 165–172.

National Curriculum Assessment (1993) *Core Subjects Standard Assessment Tasks for 1993, Reference Notes, A Supplement for the Hearing Impaired*. London: School Examination and Assessment Council.

National Deaf Children's Society (NDCS) (1983) *Discovering Deafness*. London: NDCS.

National Deaf Children's Society (NDCS) (1989) *Report on the Initial Process of Diagnosis of Deafness and also Follow-Up Audiology Service*. London: NDCS.

National Deaf Children's Society (NDCS) (1994) *Quality Standards in Paediatric Audiology. Volume I: Guidelines for the Early Identification of Hearing Impairment*. London: NDCS.

National Deaf Children's Society (NDCS) (1996a) *NDCS Directory 1996–7*. London: NDCS.

National Deaf Children's Society (NDCS) (1996b) *Report on the Initial Process of Diagnosis of Deafness and Also Follow-Up Audiology Service*. London: NDCS.

National Deaf Children's Society (NDCS) (1996c) *Quality Standards in Paediatric Audiology. Volume II: The Audiological Management of the Child with a Permanent Hearing Loss*. London: NDCS.

Neilson, R. and Armour, V. A. (1983) 'The effects of concurrent and complementary instruction in reading, writing and simultaneous communication on receptive and expressive language skills of hearing impaired youth adults'. *Paper Presented at CAID*, Winnipeg, Canada.

Nelson, K., Loncke, F., Camarata, S. (1993) 'Implications of research on deaf and hearing children's language learning', in Marschark, M. and Clark, M. D. (eds) *Psychological Perspectives on Deafness*. New Jersey: Lawrence Erlbaum Associates.

Neuroth-Gimbrone, C. and Logiodice, C. M. (1990) 'A Cooperative Language Program for the Deaf Adolescent Utilizing Bilingual Principles', in Cebe, J. (ed.) *Bilingual Considerations in the*

Education of Deaf Students: ASL and English. Washington, DC: Gallaudet University Press.

Neville, H. J., Coffey, S. A., Lawson, D. S., Fischer, A., *et al.* (1997) 'Neural systems mediating American Sign Language: effects of sensory experience and age of acquisition', *Brain and Language* 57, 285–308.

Neville, H. J. and Lawson, D. (1987) 'Attention to central and peripheral visual space in a movement detection task: an event-related potential and behavioural study. II. Congenitally deaf adults', *Brain Research* 40 (5), 268–283.

Nevins, M. E. and Chute, P. M. (1996) *Children with Cochlear Implants in Educational Settings.* London: Singular Publishing Group.

Newell, W., Stinson, M., Castle, D., Mallery-Ruganis, D., Holcomb, B. (1990) 'Simultaneous Communication: a description by deaf professionals working in an educational setting', *Sign Language Studies* 69, 391–414.

Newton, L. (1985) 'Linguistic environment of the deaf child', *Journal of Speech and Hearing Research* 28, 336–344.

Nicholls, J., Bauers, A., Pettitt, D., Redgwell, V., Seaman, E., Watson, G. (1989) *Beginning Writing.* Boston, Mass.: Little, Brown.

Nittrouer, S. (1996) 'The relation between speech perception and phonemic awareness: evidence from low-SES children and children with chronic OM', *Journal of Speech and Hearing Research* 39, 1059–1070.

Noback, C. R. (1985) 'Neuroanatomical correlates of central auditory dysfunction', in Pinheiro, M. L. and Musiek, F. E. (eds) *Assessment of Central Auditory Dysfunction: Foundations and Clinical Correlates.* Baltimore: Williams and Wilkins.

Nolte, P., Printzen, R., Esser, G. (1993) 'Sprach-Farbbild-Transformation (SFT): The conversion of sound to coloured light as a visual aid in speech therapy', in Elsendoorn, B. A. G. and Coninx, F. (eds) *Interactive Learning Technology for the Deaf*, 175–186. Berlin: Springer-Verlag.

Norwich, B. (1996) 'Special needs education or education for all: connective specialisation and ideological impurity', *British Journal of Special Education* 23 (3), 100–103.

Nottingham Paediatric Cochlear Implant Programme (1997) *Progress Report.* Nottingham: NPCIP.

Nunes, T. and Moreno, C. (1997a) 'Is hearing impairment a cause of difficulty in learning mathematics?' *Report to Nuffield Foundation.*

Nunes, T. and Moreno, C. (1997b) 'Solving problems with different ways of representing the task: how do deaf children perform?' *Equals* 3 (2), 15–17.

Nunes, T. and Moreno, C. (1998) 'The signed algorithm and its bugs', *Educational Studies in Mathematics* 5, 85–92.

O'Donnell, A., Moores, D. F., Kluwin, T. N. (1992) 'Identifying the contributions of school factors to the success of deaf students', in Kluwin, T. N., Moores, D. F., Gaustad, M. G. (eds) *Toward Defining the Effective Public School Programs for Deaf Students.* New York: Teachers College Press.

OFSTED (1996) *LEA Support for School Improvement.* Consultation Paper. London: Crown Copyright.

Oliver, M. (1988) 'The social and political context of educational policy: the case of special needs', in Barton, L. (ed.) *The Politics of Special Educational Needs.* East Sussex: Falmer Press.

Oliver, M. (1996) 'Defining impairment and disability: issues at stake', in Barnes, C. and Mercer, G. (eds) *Exploring the Divide: Illness and Disability.* Leeds: Disability Press.

Oppe, T. (1967) 'Risk registers for babies', *Developmental Medicine and Child Neurology* 9, 13.

Osberger, M. J., Robbins, A. M., Todd, S. L., Riley, A., *et al.* (1996) 'Cochlear implants and tactile aids for children with profound hearing impairment', in Bess, F. H., Gravel, J. S., Tharpe, A. M. (eds) *Amplification for Children with Auditory Deficits.* Nashville, Tennessee: Bill Wilkerson Press.

Owers, R. (1996) 'Hearing children's attitudes to deaf children', *Journal of the British Association of Teachers of the Deaf* 20 (3), 83–89.

Padden, C. and Humphries, T. (1988) *Deaf in America – Voices from a Culture*. London: Harvard University Press.

Parasnis, I., Samar, V. J., Bettger, J. G., Sathe, K. (1996), 'Does deafness lead to enhancement of visual spatial cognition in children? Negative evidence from deaf non-signers', *Journal of Deaf Studies and Deaf Education* 1 (2), 145–152.

Partridge, S. (1996) 'Video stories for 7–11s', in Gallaway, C. (ed.) *Using Videos with Deaf Children*, 41–45. Manchester: Centre for Audiology, Education of the Deaf and Speech Pathology, University of Manchester.

Passman, J. (1994) 'The modern foreign language teaching methods and their relevance to teaching English to deaf children', *Laserbeam* 23, 15–21.

Pau, C. S. (1995) 'The deaf child and solving the problems of arithmetic', *American Annals of the Deaf* 140 (3), 287–290.

Paul, P. V. and Quigley, S. P. (1994) *Language and Deafness*, 2nd edn. San Diego, California: Singular Publishing Group.

Peach, C. (1996) *Ethnicity in the 1991 Statistics: Vol 2. The Ethnic Minority Populations of Great Britain*. London: HMSO.

Peresuh, M. and Barcham, L. (in press) 'Special education provision in Zimbabwe', *British Journal of Special Education*.

Peter, M. (1997) 'The keys to understanding', *Special!* Spring 1997, 11–13.

Peters, S. A. F., Grievink, E. H., van Bon, W. H. J., *et al.* (1997) 'The contribution of risk factors to the effect of early otitis media with effusion on later language, reading and spelling'. *Developmental Medicine and Child Neurology* 39, 31–39.

Petitto, L. A. and Marentette, P. F. (1991) 'Babbling in the manual mode: evidence for the ontegeny of language', *Science* 251, 1493–1496.

Phillips, D. (1989) 'Neither a borrower nor a lender be? The problem of cross-national attraction in education', *Comparative Education* 25 (3), 267–274.

Phoenix, S. (1988) *An Interim Report on a Pilot Survey of Deaf Adults in Northern Ireland*. Belfast: Northern Ireland Workshop with Deaf.

Pickersgill, M. (1997) 'Towards a model of bilingual education for deaf children', *Deafness and Education* 21 (3), 10–20.

Pine, J. M. (1994) 'The language of primary caregivers', in Gallaway, C. and Richards, B. J. (eds) *Input and Interaction in Language Acquisition*. Cambridge: Cambridge University Press.

Pintner, R., Eisenson, J., Stanton, M. (1941) *The Psychology of the Physically Handicapped*. New York: Crofts.

Pintner, R. and Paterson, D. G., (1916) 'The ability of deaf and hearing children to follow printed directions', *Paediatric Seminary* 23, 477–497.

Plowden Report (1967) *Children and their Primary Schools*. London: HMSO.

Poizner, H., Battison, R., and Lane, H. (1979) 'Cerebral asymmetry for American Sign Language: the effects of moving stimuli', *Brain and Language* 7, 351–362.

Poizner, H., Klima, E. S., Bellugi, U. (1987) *What the Hands Reveal about the Brain*. Cambridge, Mass.: MIT Press.

Poizner, H., Tallal, P. (1987), 'Temporal processing in deaf signers', *Brain and Language* 30, 52–62.

Ponton, C., Don, M., Eggermont, J., Waring, M., Masuda, A. (1996) 'Maturation of auditorycortical function: differences between normal hearing children and children with cochlear implants', *Ear and Hearing* 17 (5), 430–537.

Powell, C. (1995) 'GCSE Examination Results 1994', *British Association of Teachers of the Deaf Magazine*, March 1995, 10–11.

Powers, S. (1990) 'A survey of secondary units for hearing impaired children', *Journal of the British Association of Teachers of the Deaf* 14 (3), 69–79.

Powers, S. (1996a) 'Deaf pupils' achievements in ordinary schools', *The Journal of the British Association of Teachers of the Deaf* 20, 111–123.

Powers, S. (1996b) 'Inclusion is an attitude not a place, Part I', *Journal of the British Association of Teachers of the Deaf* 20 (2), 35–41.

Powers, S. (1996c) 'Inclusion is an attitude not a place, Part II', *Journal of the British Association of Teachers of the Deaf* 20 (3), 65–69.

Powers, S. (in press) 'An analysis of deaf pupils' exam results in ordinary schools in 1996', *Deafness and Education.*

Powers, S. and Fraser, B. (1995) 'The move towards part-time training: should we decry it?' *Journal of the British Association of Teachers of the Deaf* 19 (4), 97–110.

Prinz, P. M. and Prinz, E. A. (1979) 'Simultaneous acquisition of ASL and spoken English', *Sign Language Studies* 25, 283–296.

Quigley, S. P. and Paul, P. V. (1984) *Language and Deafness.* London: Croom Helm.

Ramkalawan, T. and Davis, A. C. (1992) 'The effects of hearing loss and age of intervention on some language metrics in a population of young hearing impaired children', *British Journal of Audiology* 26, 97–107.

Ranson, S. (1990) 'From 1944 to 1988: education, citizenship and democracy', in Flude, M. and Hammer, M. (eds), *The Education Reform Act 1988, Its Origins and Implications.* East Sussex: Falmer Press.

Ranson, S. (1992) *The Role of Local Government in Education: Assuring Quality and Accountability.* London: Longman.

Rattansi, A. (1992) 'Changing the subject? Racism, culture and education', in Donald, J. and Rattansi, A. (eds) *'Race', Culture and Difference.* London: Sage Publications.

Reagan, T. (1985) 'The deaf as a linguistic minority: educational considerations', *Harvard Educational Review* 55, 265–277.

Reagan, T. (1990) 'Cultural considerations in the education of deaf children', in Moores, D. and Meadow-Orlans, K. (eds), *Educational and Developmental Aspects of Deafness.* Washington, DC: Gallaudet University Press.

Reynell, J. (1977) *The Reynell Developmental Language Scales.* Windsor: NFER-Nelson.

Reynolds, D. (1992) 'School effectiveness and school improvement: an updated review of the British literature', in Reynolds, D. and Cuttance, P. (eds) *School Effectiveness: Research, Policy and Practice.* London: Cassell.

Richards, B. J. (1994) 'Child-directed speech and influences on language acquisition: methodology and interpretation', in Gallaway, C. and Richards, B. J. (eds) *Input and Interaction in Language Acquisition.* Cambridge: Cambridge University Press.

Richards, B. J. and Gallaway, C. (1994) 'Input and interaction in child language acquisition', in Asher, R. E. and Simpson, J. M. Y. (eds) *Encyclopaedia of Language and Linguistics,* Vol. 4, 1907–1912. Edinburgh: Pergamon Press.

Richards, I. D. G. and Roberts, C. J. (1967) 'The at risk infant', *The Lancet* 2, 711–714.

Riddell, S. (1996) 'Theorising Special Educational Needs', in Barton, L. (ed.) *Disability and Society – Emerging Issues and Insights.* London: Longman.

Ridgeway, S. (1997) *Psychological Health and Well being in a Deaf Population* (unpublished). Manchester: Manchester University.

Rissanen, T. (1987) 'Finnish Sign Language', in Van Cleve, J. V. (ed.) *Gallaudet Encyclopaedia of Deaf People and Deafness,* Vol. 3, 71–74. New York: McGraw-Hill.

Rittenhouse, R. K. and Spiro, R. J. (1979) 'Conservation performance in day and residential school children', *Volta Review* 81, 501–509.

Ritter-Brinton, K. (1993) 'Families in evaluation: a review of the American literature in deaf education', *Association of Canadian Educators of the Hearing Impaired* 19, 3–13.

Roberts, J. E., Burchinal, M. R., Campbell, F. (1994) 'Otitis media in early childhood and patterns of intellectual development and later academic performance', *Journal of Pediatric Psychology* **19** (3), 374–367.

Robertson, C., Aldreidge, S., Jarman, F., Saunders, K., *et al.* (1995) 'Late diagnosis of congenital sensorineural hearing impairment: why are detection methods failing?' *Archives of Disease in Childhood* **72**, 11–15.

Robinshaw, H. M. (1995) 'Early intervention for hearing impairment: differences in the timing of communicative and linguistic development', *British Journal of Audiology* **29**, 315–34.

Robinshaw, H. and Evans, R. (1995) 'Caregivers' sensitivity to the communicative and linguistic needs of their deaf infants', *Early Child Development and Care* **109**, 23–41.

Robinson, K. (1991) *Children of Silence*. London: Gollancz.

Rodda, M. and Grove, C. (1987) *Language, Cognition and Deafness*. Hillsdale, NJ: Lawrence Erlbaum.

Rosenstein, J. (1961) 'Perception, cognition and language in deaf children', *Exceptional Children* **27** (3) 276–284.

Ross, M. and Seewald, R. (1988) 'Hearing aid selection and evaluation with young children', in Pollack, M. C. (ed.) *Amplification for the Hearing Impaired*. Orlando, Florida: Grune and Stratton.

Rowe, S. J. (1991) 'An evaluation of ABR audiometry for the screening and detection of hearing loss in ex-SCBU infants', *British Journal of Audiology* **25**, 259–274.

Royal National Institute for Deaf People (RNID) (1984) *Schools Using a Form of Total Communication* (Unpublished).

Ruben, R. J. (1986) 'Unsolved issues around critical periods with emphasis on clinical application', *Acta Otolaryngologica (Stockholm)* Suppl. 429: 61–64.

Ruben, R. J., Wallace, I. F., Gravel, J. (1997) 'Long-term communication deficiencies in children with otitis media during their first year of life', *Acta Otolaryngologica (Stockholm)* **117**, 206–7.

Sachs, J. (1997) 'Communication development in infancy', in Gleason, J. B. (ed.) *The Development of Language*. Needham Heights, NJ: Allyn and Bacon.

Sancho, J., Hughes, E., Davis, A., Haggard, M., Ruben, R. J. (1987) 'Epidemiological basis for screening hearing', in McCormick, B. (ed.) *Paediatric audiology, 0–5 years*. London: Taylor & Francis.

Saunders, G. H., Field, D. L. Haggard, M. P. (1992) 'A clinical test battery for obscure auditory dysfunction: development, selection and use of tests', *British Journal of Audiology* **26**, 33–42.

Saxton, M. (1997) 'The contrast theory of negative input', *Journal of Child Language* **24** (1), 139–162.

Scanlon, P. and Bamford, J. (1990) 'Early identification of hearing loss : screening and surveillance methods', *Archives of Disease in Childhood* **65**, 479–485.

Schilder, A. G. M., van Manen, J. G., Zielhuis, G. A., *et al.* (1993) 'Long-term effects of otitis media with effusion on language, reading and spelling', *Clinical Otolaryngology* **18**, 234–241.

Schildroth, A. and Motto, S. (1994) 'Inclusion or exclusion?' *American Annals of the Deaf* **139** (2), 163–171.

Schildroth, A. and Motto, S. (1995) 'Race and ethnic background in the annual survey of deaf and hard of hearing children and youth', *American Annals of the Deaf* **140**, 96–99.

Schirmer, B. S. (1989) 'Relationship between imaginative play and language development in hearing impaired children', *American Annals of the Deaf* **134**, 219–222.

Schlesinger, H. and Meadow, K. (1972) *Sound and Sign*. Berkeley: University of California Press.

Schneiderman, E. (1986) 'Using the known to teach the unknown', *American Annals of the Deaf* **131**, 51–52.

School Curriculum and Assessment Authority (SCAA) (1996a) 'Assessment, recording and accreditation of achievement for pupils with learning difficulties', *SCAA Discussion Papers: No. 7.* SCAA Publications. Ref: COM/96/551.

School Curriculum and Assessment Authority (SCAA) (1996b) *Baseline Assessment: Draft Proposals.* SCAA publications. Ref: COM/96/556.

School Curriculum and Assessment Authority (SCAA) (1996c) *Inform.* July 1996.

School Curriculum and Assessment Authority (SCAA) (1997a) *Corporate Plan 1997–2000.* SCAA Internal Publications.

School Curriculum and Assessment Authority (SCAA) (1997b) *Key Stage 3: Assessment Arrangements.* DfEE Ref: KS3/96/563.

School Curriculum and Assessment Authority (SCAA) (1997c) *SCAA Consultation on Baseline Assessment.* SCAA Internal Publications.

Secada, W. G. (1984) *Counting in Sign: The Number String, Accuracy and Use.* Unpublished doctoral dissertation, Evanston, Chicago: Northwestern University, quoted in Nunes and Moreno (1997a).

Seewald, R. C. (1992) 'The desired sensation level method of fitting children: Version 3.0', *Hearing Journal* 45 (4), 36–41.

Seewald, R. C. and Moodie, K. S. (1992) 'Electroacoustic considerations', in Ross, M. (ed.) *FM Auditory Training Systems: Characteristics, Selection and Use.* Timonium, MD: York Press.

Shakespeare, T. (1996) 'Disability, identity, difference',. in Barnes, C. and Mercer, G. (eds) *Exploring the Divide: Illness and Disability.* Leeds: Disability Press.

Shand, M. A. (1982) 'Sign-based short-term coding of ASL signs and printed English words by congenitally deaf signers', *Cognitive Psychology* 14, 1–12.

Sharma, A. and Love, D. (1991) *A Change in Approach: A Report on the Experience of Deaf People from Black and Ethnic Minority Communities.* London: Royal Association in Aid of Deaf People.

Shaw, P. (1989) 'Segregation for integration', *Deafness* 5 (3).

Shroyer, E. (1982) 'Introduction', in Tweedie, D. and Shroyer, E. (eds) *The Multi Handicapped Hearing Impaired.* Washington, DC: Gallaudet College Press.

Simmons, F. B. and Russ, F. N. (1974) 'Automated newborn hearing screening: the Crib-O-Gram', *Archives of Otolaryngology* 100, 1–7.

Simpson, P. A., Stuart, A., Harrison, D. R. (1989) 'Integration of severely and profoundly hearing-impaired children into ordinary schools', *Journal of the British Association of Teachers of the Deaf* 13 (4), 114–115.

Skutnabb-Kangas, T. (1994) 'Linguistic human rights – a prerequisite for bilingualism', in Ahlgren, I. and Hyltenstam, N. (eds) *Bilingualism and Deaf Education.* Hamburg: Signum Press.

Smith, M. (1997) 'Hearing aids', in McCracken, W. and Laoide-Kemp, S. (eds) *Audiology in Education.* London: Whurr Publishers.

Smith, S. (1996) 'Adult–child interaction in a BSL nursery – getting their attention!' in Knight, P. and Swanwick, R. (eds) *Bilingualism and the Education of Deaf Children: Advances in Practice.* Conference Proceedings, University of Leeds.

Smythe, R. L. and Bamford, J. M. (1997) 'Speech perception of hearing impaired children in mainstream acoustic environments: an exploratory study', *Deafness and Education* 21 (2), 26–31.

Snider, B. D. (1994) *Post Milan, ASL and English Literacy: Issues, Trends and Research.* Washington, DC: Gallaudet University Press.

Snow, C. E. (1994) 'Beginning from baby talk: twenty years of research on input in interaction', in Gallaway, C. and Richards, B. J. (eds) *Input and Interaction in Language Acquisition.* Cambridge: Cambridge University Press.

Snow, C. E. (1995) 'Issues in the study of input: finetuning, universality, individual and developmental differences and necessary causes', in Fletcher, P. and MacWhinney, B. (eds) *The Handbook of Child Language.* Oxford: Blackwell.

Soderfeldt, B., Ronnberg, J., Risberg, J. (1994a) 'Regional cerebral blood flow in sign language users', *Brain and Language* 46, 59–68.

Soderfeldt, B., Ronnberg, J., Risberg, J. (1994b) 'Regional cerebral blood flow during sign language perception: deaf and hearing subjects with deaf parents compared', *Sign Language Studies* 84, 199–208.

Sokolov, J. L. and Snow, C. E. (1994) 'The changing role of negative evidence in theories of language development', in Gallaway, C. and Richards, B. J. (eds) *Input and Interaction in Language Acquisition.* Cambridge: Cambridge University Press.

Somers, M. N. (1991) 'Speech perception abilities in children with cochlear implants or hearing aids', *American Journal of Otology* 12, Suppl. 174–178.

Special Educational Needs Training Consortium (SENTC) (1996) *Professional Development to Meet Special Educational Needs: Report to the Department for Education and Employment.* Stafford: Staffordshire County Council.

Speedy, J. (1987) 'Breaking down barriers', *TALK* 125, 12–14.

Spencer, P. E. (1993) 'Communication behaviors of infants with hearing loss and their mothers'. *Journal of Speech and Hearing Research* 36, 311–21.

Spradley, T. S. and Spradley, J. P. (1971) *Deaf Like Me.* New York: Random House.

Stach, B., Loiselle, L., Jerger, J. (1991) 'Special hearing aid considerations for elderly patients with auditory processing disorders', *Ear and Hearing* 12 Suppl, 131s–138s.

Stelmachowicz, P. G. (1996) 'Situational Hearing Aid Response Profile (SHARP)', in Bess, F. H., Gravel, J. S., Tharpe, A. M. (eds) *Amplification for Children with Auditory Deficits.* Nashville, Tennessee: Bill Wilkerson Press.

Stelmachowicz, P., Mace, A., Kopun, J., Carney, E. (1993) 'Long-term and short-term characteristics of speech: implications for hearing aid selection for young children', *Journal of Speech and Hearing Research* 36, 609–620.

Sterne, A. (1996) *Phonological Awareness, Memory and Reading in Deaf Children.* Unpublished PhD thesis, University of London.

Stevens, J. C., Hall, D. M. B., Davis, A., Davies, C. M., Dixon, S. (1997) 'The costs of early hearing screening in England and Wales', *Archives of Disease in Childhood.*

Stevens, J. C., Webb, H. D., Smith, M. F., Buffin, J. T., Ruddy, H. (1987) 'A comparison of otoacoustic emissions and brainstem electric response audiometry', *Clinical Physiology and Physiology Measurement and Research* 8, 95–104.

Stevens, J. C., Webb, H. D., Hutchinson, J., Connell, J., *et al.* (1989) 'Click-evoked otoacoustic emissions compared with brain stem electric response', *Archives of Disease in Childhood* 64, 1105–1111.

Stevens, J. C., Webb, H. D., Hutchinson, J., Connell, J., Smith, M. F., Buffin, J. T. (1991) 'Evaluation of click-evoked otoacoustic emissions in the newborn', *British Journal of Audiology* 25, 11–14.

Stokoe, W. (1978) *Sign Language Structure*, revised edn. Silverspring, MD: Linstok Press.

Stokoe, W. and Battison, R. (1981) 'Sign language, mental health, and satisfactory interaction', in Stein, L. Mendel, E., Jabaley, T. (eds) *Deafness and Mental Health.* New York: Grune and Statton.

Stredler-Brown, A. and Yoshiago-Itano, C. (1994) 'Family, a multidisciplinary evaluation tool', in Rousch, J. and Matkin, N. D. (eds) *Infants and Toddlers with Hearing Loss.* Baltimore: York Press.

Strong, M. (1988) *Language, Learning and Deafness.* Cambridge: Cambridge University Press.

Strong, M. and Prinz, P. M. (1997) 'A study of the relationship between American Sign Language and English literacy', *Journal of Deaf Studies and Deaf Education* 2 (1), 37–46.

Sue, D. W. and Sue, D. (1990) *Counselling the Culturally Different.* New York: Wiley.

Sugden, J. (1997) 'Success for gang', *British Deaf News*, 9 June.

Sutherland, H. (1991) 'Family reactions', in McCracken, W. and Sutherland, H. (eds) *Deaf Ability*

Not Disability. Clevedon: Multilingual Matters.

Sutherland, H. (1993) *A Deaf Child at Home Project (1990–93).* Bristol: Centre for Deaf Studies.

Sutton, G. J. and Scanlon, P. (1997) *Health visitor screening versus vigilance in West Berkshire – a 10 year review.* Unpublished.

Sutton-Spence, R. L. and Woll, B. (in press) *The Linguistics of British Sign Language: An Introduction.* Cambridge: Cambridge University Press.

Svartholm K. (1994) 'Second language learning in the deaf', in Ahlgren, I. and Hytlenstam, N. (eds) *Bilingualism in Deaf Education.* Hamburg: Signum Press.

Swanns-Joha, D., Mol, I., Ian, P. (1988) *On Terminology.* European Society of Mental Health and Deafness.

Swanwick, R. (1993) 'The use of DARTs to develop deaf children's literacy skills within a bilingual context', *Deafness and Development* 3 (2), 4–9.

Swanwick, R. (1994) 'English as a foreign language for deaf children. From MFL to EFL'. *Laserbeam* 23, 4–15.

Swanwick R. (1996) 'Deaf children's strategies for learning English; how do they do it?' in Knight, P. and Swanwick, R. (eds) *Bilingualism and the Education of Deaf Children.* Leeds: University Press.

Swisher, V. (1989) 'The language learning situation of deaf students', *Tesol Quarterly* 23 (2), 239–257.

Swisher, V. (1992) 'Conversational interaction between deaf children and their hearing mothers: the role of visual attention', in Siple, P. and Fischer, S. D. (eds) *Theoretical Issues in Sign Language Research*, Vol 2. University of Chicago Press.

Tait, M. (1994) 'Using video analysis to monitor progress in young cochlear implant users', in McCormick, B. Archibold, S., Sheppard, S. (eds) *Cochlear Implants for Young Children.* London: Whurr Publishers.

Takala, M. (1995) *They Say I'm Stupid But I Just Don't HEAR: Hearing Impaired Adults' View of Finnish Society.* Research Report 142: University of Helsinki.

Tallal, P., Miller, S., Sitch, R. (1993) quoted in 'Central Auditory Processing Current Status of Research', *American Journal of Audiology* 5 (2), 46.

Taylor, I. G. (1988) (ed.) *The Education of Deaf Children: Current Perspectives Vol. I–IV.* London: Croom Helm.

Teele, D. W., Klein, J. O., Chase, C., 'Menyuk, P., Rasner, B. A., and the Greater Boston Otitis Media Study Group (1990) 'Otitis media in infancy and intellectual ability, school achievement, speech and language at age 7 years', *Journal of Infectious Diseases* 162, 685–694.

Thibodeau, L. M., McCaffrey, H., Abrahamson, J. (1988) 'The effects of coupling hearing aids to FM systems via neckloops', *Journal of the Academy of Rehabilitative Audiology* 21, 49–56.

Thomas, G. (1997) 'Inclusive schools for an inclusive society', *British Journal of Special Education* 24 (3), 103–107.

Thomas, H. (1990) *Education Costs and Performance.* London: Cassell.

Thompson, M. and Weber, B. A. (1974) 'Responses of infants and young children to behaviour observation audiometry'. *Journal of Speech and Hearing Disorder* 39, 140–147.

Tillander, M. (1994) 'Bring up a child to be bilingual and bicultural: a three part presentation [second part]', in Erting, C. J., Johnson, R., Smith, D. L., Snider, B. D. (eds) *The Deaf Way: Perspectives from the International Conference on Deaf Culture*, 556–559. Washington, DC: Gallaudet University Press.

Tomlinson S. (1985) 'The expansion of special education', *Oxford Review of Education* 11 (2), 157–164.

Trybus, R. J. and Karchmer, M. A. (1977) 'School achievement scores of hearing impaired children: national data on achievement status and growth patterns', *American Annals of the Deaf* 122, 62–69.

Tucker, S. M. and Bhattacharya, J. (1992) 'Screening hearing impairment in the newborn using the auditory response cradle', *Archives of Disease in Childhood* **67**, 911–919.

Turner, S. (1994) 'Collaboration in support for the under fives', *Journal of the British Association of Teachers of the Deaf* **18**, 154–162.

Tye-Murray, N., Spencer, L., Woodworth, G. G. (1995) 'Acquisition of speech by children who have prolonged cochlear implant experience', *Journal of Speech and Hearing Research* **38**, 327–337.

Tymms, P. (1996) 'Theories, models and simulations: school effectiveness at an impasse', in Gray, J., Reynolds, D., Fitz-Gibbon, C., Jesson, D. (eds) *Merging Traditions: The Future of Research on School Effectiveness and School Improvement*. London: Cassell.

UNESCO (1984) *Consultation on Alternative Approaches in the Education of the Deaf*. Paris: UNESCO.

UNESCO (1987) *Education of Deaf Children and Young People*. Paris: UNESCO.

UNESCO (1988a) *Language and Curriculum Planning for Deaf Children*. Paris: UNESCO.

UNESCO (1988b) *Review of the Present Situation of Special Education*. Paris: UNESCO.

UNESCO (1994a) *The Salamanca Statement and the Framework for Action on Special Needs Education*. Paris: UNESCO.

UNESCO (1994b) *Making it Happen: Examples of Good Practice in Special Needs Education and Community Based Programmes*. Paris: UNESCO.

Updike, C. and Thornburg, J. D. (1992) 'Reading skills and auditory processing ability in children with chronic otitis media in early childhood', *Ann Otol Rhinol Laryngol*. **101**, 530–537.

Valente, M., Fabry, D. A., Potts, L. G. (1995) 'Recognition of speech in noise with hearing aids using dual-microphones', *Journal of the American Academy of Audiology* **6** (4), 214–327.

van Uden, A. (1977) *A World of Language for Deaf Children*. Lisse, Netherlands: Swets and Zeitlinger.

Vanniasegaram, I., Tungland, O. P., Bellman, S. (1993) 'A five year review of children with deafness in a multiethnic community', *Journal of Audiological Medicine* **2**, 9–19.

Vernon, M. and Andrews, J. (1990) *The Psychology of Deafness: Understanding Deaf and Hard of Hearing People*. White Plains, NY: Longman.

Vernon-Feagans, L., Manlove, E. E., Volling, B. L. (1996) 'Otitis media and the social behavior of day-care-attending children', *Child Development* **67**, 1528–1539

Visser, J. (1993) 'A broad, balanced, relevant and differentiated curriculum', in Visser, J. and Upton, G. (eds) *Special Education in Britain After Warnock*. London: David Fulton Publishers.

Visser, J. and Upton, G. (eds) (1993) *Special Education in Britain After Warnock*. London: David Fulton Publishers.

Volterra, V. (1983) 'Gestures, signs and words at two years', in Kyle, J. G. and Woll, B. (eds) *Language in Sign*. London: Croom Helm.

Volterra, V. and Caselli, C. (1985) 'From gestures and vocalisations to signs and words', in Stokoe W. C. and Volterra, V. (eds) *The Third International Symposium on Sign Language Research*. Silverspring, MD: Linstok Press.

Volterra, V. and Erting, C. (1994) *From Gesture to Language in Hearing and Deaf Children*. Washington, DC: Gallaudet University Press.

Von Tetzchner, S. and Martinsen, M. (1992) *Introduction to Sign Teaching and the Use of Communication Aids*. London: Whurr Publishers.

Wakefield, T. (1998) 'National Curriculum questionnaire results', *British Association of Teachers of the Deaf Association* Magazine, January 1998.

Walters, M. (1995) *Globalisation*. London: Routledge.

Ward, H. (1989) 'Amplification for hearing impaired children attending mainstream schools', *British Association of Teachers of the Deaf Association Magazine*, May, 4–6.

Watkin, P. M. (1996a) 'Neonatal otoacoustic emission screening and the identification of deafness', *Archives of Disease in Childhood* 74, F16–F25.

Watkin, P. M. (1996b) 'Outcomes of neonatal screening for hearing loss by otoacoustic emission', *Archives of Disease in Childhood* 75, F158–F168.

Watkin, P. M. (1997) 'The implications for educational services of neonatal hearing screening', *Deafness and Education* 21 (1), 19–33.

Watkin, P. M., Baldwin, M., Laoide, S. (1990) 'Parental suspicion and the identification of hearing impairment', *Archives of Disease in Childhood* 65, 846–850.

Watkin, P. M., Baldwin, M., McEnery, G. (1991) 'Neonatal at risk screening and the identification of deafness'. *Archives of Disease in Childhood* 66, 1130–1135.

Watkin, P. M. and Nanor, J. (1997) 'The implications for educational services of universal neonatal hearing screening', *Deafness and Education* 21 (1), 19–34.

Watson, L. M. (1996) *Spotlight on Special Educational Needs: Hearing Impairment.* Tamworth: NASEN Publications.

Waxman, R. P. and Spencer, P. E. (1997) 'What mothers do to support infant visual attention: sensitivities to age and hearing status', *Journal of Deaf Studies and Deaf Education* 2 (2), 104–114.

Weber, E. (1984) *Ideas Influencing Early Childhood Education.* New York: Teachers College Press.

Webster, A. (1986) *Deafness, Development and Literacy.* London: Methuen.

Wells A. (1994) 'On writing'. Paper presented at Seminar on Bilingual Education, Sheffield, December 1993, a summary of which was published in *British Deaf News* 25 (3), 9.

Wells, G. (1985) *Language, Learning and Education.* Windsor: NFER-Nelson.

Wells, G. (1986a) *The Meaning Makers.* London: Hodder & Stoughton.

Wells, G. (1986b) *Language Development in the Pre School Years.* Cambridge: Cambridge University Press.

Wheeler C. N. (1997) *Auditory Disability With Normal Hearing Sensitivity in Children 2–15 Years: Current UK Practice.* MSc Thesis, University of Manchester.

White, A. and Stevenson, V. (1975) 'The effects of Total Communication, manual communication, oral communication and reading on the learning of factual information in residential school deaf children', *American Annals of the Deaf* 120, 48–57.

White, K. R. and Behrens, T. R. (1993) 'The Rhode Island Hearing Assessment Project: implications for universal newborn hearing screening', *Seminars in Hearing* 14 (1), 1–120.

White, K. R. and Maxon, A. B. (1995) 'Universal screening for infant hearing impairment: simple, beneficial, and presently justified', *International Journal of Pediatric Otorhinolaryngology* 32, 201–211.

Wilson, A. and Wakefield, T. (1990) 'Key Stage 1 Standard Assessment Tasks – implications for the hearing impaired', *British Association of Teachers of the Deaf Association Magazine*, November 1990, 9–12.

Wilson, M. and Emmorey, K. (1997) 'Working memory for sign language: a window into the architecture of the working memory system', *Journal of Deaf Studies and Deaf Education* 2 (3), 121–130.

Woelders, W. W., Frowein, H. F., Nielson, J., Questa, P., Sandini, G. (1997) 'New developments in low-bit rate videotelephony for people who are deaf', *Journal of Speech, Language and Hearing Research* 40, 1425–1433.

Wolfendale, S. (1992) *Primary Schools and Special Needs: Policy Planning and Provision.* London: Cassell.

Woll, B. (1994) 'Bilingualism and deaf education: the need for definitions', in Kyle, J. G. (ed.) *Growing up in Sign and Word.* Bristol: Centre for Deaf Studies.

Woll, B. and Kyle, J. (1989) 'Communication and language development in children of deaf parents', in Von-Tetzcher, S., Siegel, L. S., Smith, L. (eds) *Social and Cognitive Aspects of Normal and Atypical Language Development.* New York: Springer-Verlag.

Wollman, D. C. (1965) 'The attainments in English and arithmetic of secondary school pupils with impaired hearing', *Teacher of the Deaf* **159**, 121–129.

Wolverhampton Metropolitan Borough Council (1996) *Access Signing Materials – an Aid for the Hearing Impaired.*

Wood, D. (1982) 'The linguistic experiences of the prelingually hearing-impaired child', *Journal of the British Association of Teachers of the Deaf* **6**, 86–93.

Wood, D. J., Wood, H. A., Griffiths, A. J., Howarth, S. P., Howarth, C. I. (1982) 'The structure of conversations with 6–10 year-old deaf children', *Journal of Child Psychology and Psychiatry* **23**, 295–308.

Wood, D., Wood, H., Griffiths, A., Howarth, I. (1986) *Teaching and Talking with Deaf Children.* Chichester: Wiley.

Wood, D., Wood, H., Howarth, P. (1983) 'Mathematical abilities of deaf school leavers', *British Journal of Developmental Psychology* **1**, 67–73.

Wood, R. (1996) Quoted in Campbell, J. and Oliver, M. (eds) *Disability Politics: Understanding our Past, Changing our Future.* London: Routledge.

Woodward, J. (1976) 'Beliefs about and attitudes towards deaf people and sign language on Providence Island', in Woodward, J. (ed.) *How You Get to Heaven If You Can't Talk to Jesus: On Depathologising Deafness.* Maryland: T. J. Publishers.

World Conference On Education For All (WCEFA) (1990) *World Declaration on Education for All.* New York: WCEFA.

Wray, D. and Medwell, J. (1991) *Literacy and Language in the Primary Years.* London: Routledge.

Yeates, S. (1995) 'The incidence and importance of hearing loss in people with severe learning disability: the evolution of a service', *British Journal of Learning Disabilities* **23**, 79–84.

Young, A. (1995/96) 'Working towards a bilingual bicultural approach at home', *Laserbeam*, Winter **25**, 1–7.

Young, M. L. (1983) 'Neuroscience, pragmatic competence and auditory processing', in Laskey, E. and Katx, J. (eds) *Central Auditory Processing Disorder: Problems of Speech, Language and Learning.* Baltimore: University Park Press.

Zielhuis, G. A., Rach, G. H., van den Bosch, A., van den Broeck, P. (1990) 'The prevalence of otitis media with effusion: a critical review of the literature', *Clinical Otolaryngology* **15**, 283–288.

Zweibel, A. and Allen, T. (1988) 'Mathematics achievement of hearing impaired students in different educational settings: a cross cultural perspective', *Volta Review* **90** (6), 287–293.

Index